The 8 Layers of the OSI Cake
A Forensic Taste of Each Layer

By
Information Warfare Center
And Cyber Secrets

The 8 Layers of the OSI Cake: A Forensic Taste of Each Layer
Cyber Secrets: 203
Copyright © 2020 by Information Warfare Center

All rights reserved. No part of this book may be reproduced in any form or by any electronic or mechanical means including information storage and retrieval systems without permission in writing from the publisher

First Edition First Published: July 1, 2020

Authors: Jeremy Martin, Richard Medlin, Nitin Sharma, LaShanda Edwards, Mossaraf Zaman Khan, Ambadi MP
Editors: Jeremy Martin, Daniel Traci, Brady Genz

The information in this book is distributed on an "As IS" basis, without warranty. The author and publisher have taken great care in preparation of this book but assumes no responsibility for errors or omissions. No liability is assumed for incidental or consequential damages in connection with or arising out of the use of the information or programs contained herein.

Rather than use a trademark symbol with every occurrence of a trademarked name, this book uses the names only in an editorial fashion and to the benefit of the trademark owner, with no intention of infringement of the trademark. All trademarks presented in the magazine were used only for informative purposes. All rights to trademarks presented in the magazine are reserved by the companies which own them.

The writer and publisher of this article do not condone the misuse of Tor for illegal activity. This is purely instructional for the purposes of anonymous surfing on the internet for legal usage and for testing Tor traffic monitoring in a subsequent article. **To access .onion sites, you must have access to the Tor network. To access i2p sites, you must have access to the I2P network. To access any Surface Web site, you must have access to the Internet.**

Cataloging-in-Publication Data:
ISBN: 9798652368944

Disclaimer: Do NOT break the law!

Table of Contents

- About the Authors ..... A
- What is inside? 1
- Evidence 1
  - IOT Cyber Investigation Challenges 3
- Dark Web Corner 4
  - Dark Markets 5
  - Dark Market Busts 6
- Tech Giants help Law Enforcement: 7
  - Exploit Those That Exploit Children 7
- #BlueLeak 9
- Article Title Hacker Groups 10
  - Something cools about hacker groups 10
- CSI Linux 13
- CSI Linux Forensic Challenge 204 15
- CSI Linux Forensic Challenge 201 17
  - Winner: Apostolos Gkletos 17
  - The Challenge 17
  - CTF 201 Chain of Custody 18
  - Case Challenge - Apostolos Gkletos 21
  - Lessons Learned 37
  - Finding the Evidence - Keith Swagler 38
- Layers of the OSI Model: 50
  - Where the hardware and data fits 50
  - OSI Model Layers 51
  - Application layer 51
  - Presentation Layer 52
  - Session Layer 53
  - Transport Layer 54
  - Network Layer 56
  - Data Link Layer 57
  - Physical layer 58

- Forensic Data Recovery 61
  - Capturing Evidence in a Forensically sound manner 61
  - What is Recoverable? 63
  - Chain of Custody 65
  - Write Blocking Labs 66
  - Data Destruction / Wiping 69
  - Forensic Imaging Labs 71
  - Data Carving Labs 78
  - EVIDENCE CHAIN OF CUSTODY TRACKING FORM 84
- Introduction to Network Forensics 86
- Prepping Wireshark 95
  - Wireshark Basics 97
- Wireshark Data Taster for ARP Poisoning 107
  - Detection of ARP Poisoning 108
  - Detection of ARP Poisoning through Wireshark: 110
- The Delicious Network Layer 114
  - Layer 3 – The Network Layer Explained 115
- Taking a Bigger Bite With Wireshark 131
  - Windows Analysis 133
  - Analyzing Conversations 143
  - Analyzing traffic graphs 144
- Analysing the Application Layer 151
  - Analyzing malware traffic through Wireshark 152
  - Analyzing a MODBUS DoS attack on SCADA 168
- Analyzing the Trickbot Malware 175
  - Trickbot: The Beginning 177
  - Trickbot: Capabilities 177
  - Trickbot: Infection Vectors 178
  - Trickbot: Symptoms of Infection 179
  - How Trickbot works 179
  - Trickbot Targeting 182
  - Walkthrough: Trickbot PCAP Analysis 185
  - Trickbot PCAP Analysis – Scenario 190
  - References 200

Email Forensic Analysis 202
    Email: OSI Perspective 203
  Email Headers 204
    MIME Encoding 206
    Advantages of MIME 207
    Email Authentication 207
    Walkthrough: Email Header Analysis 211
    Best Practices for Email Security 218
    References 219
  Kibana, ElasticSearch, and Logstash 220
    Visualizing your Data 220
    Creating Visualizations for the SIEM Dashboard 222
    Saving Visualizations 227
    View the Newly Created Visualization 228
    GeoIP Unique Count 229
    Top Network Traffic Generation 233
    Top Network Traffic Destination 237
    Sum of Bytes 242
    Building the Dashboard 247
    Saving the Dashboard 248
AWS Phishing - Layer 8 249
  The Individual 250
    Introduction 250
    Extended OSI Model 251
    Layer 8: Perspective and Use Cases 252
    Layer 8: The OSINT Connection 253
    Analysis: AWS Phishing Campaign 254
  CIR Contributors 257
  Information Warfare Center Publications 258

About the Authors

Jeremy Martin, CISSP-ISSAP/ISSMP
LinkedIn.com/in/infosecwriter

A Security Researcher that has focused his work on Red Team penetration testing, Computer Forensics, and Cyber Warfare. Starting his career in 1995 Mr. Martin has worked with fortune 200 companies and Federal Government agencies, receiving a number of awards for service. He is also a qualified expert witness with cyber/digital forensics. He has been teaching classes such as the Advanced Ethical Hacking, Computer Forensics, Data Recovery, SCADA/ICS security, and Security Management since 2003. Most of his certification bootcamps follow DoD 8570.1m/8140 mandates.

As a security evangelist, his current research projects include OSINT, threat profiling, exploitation automation, anti-forensics, digital surveillance, and reverse engineering. This included the CSI Linux project, an investigation system originally built for Law Enforcement online /social media/dark web investigations.

Richard Medlin
LinkedIn.com/in/richard-medlin1

An Information Security researcher with 20 years of information security experience. I have written several articles and walkthroughs in the Cyber Intelligence Report and other publications. I enjoy teaching industry experts from many regions around the world how to investigate and minimize risks on their networks using Risk Management Framework. I am currently focused on writing about bug hunting, vulnerability research, exploitation, and digital forensic investigations. I am an author and one of the original developers on the first all-inclusive digital forensic investigations operating systems, CSI Linux. I primarily focus on red and blue team operations, and digital forensics.

I enjoy playing GUItar, bowling, working out, shooting pool, and spending time with my family. My dogs are like people to me, and I enjoy having them both nearby! I have had an extraordinarily strong interest in computing since I was 5 years old and taught myself how to use computers using MS-DOS and messing around with an original Macintosh machine. Computing has always been a part of my life, and I highly enjoy working with technology. Info Sec is the perfect field for me because it is what I genuinely love.

Nitin Sharma
LinkedIn.com/in/nitinsharma87

A cyber and cloud enthusiast who can help you in starting your Infosec journey and automating your manual security burden with his tech skillset and articles related to IT world. He found his first love, Linux while working on Embedded Systems during college projects. And met his second love, Python while programming for web automation tools and security.

As a Security Analyst, he has completed a couple of projects related to vulnerability remediation and management. Fascinated by emerging cloud providers like AWS, he has started his cloud journey and became a core member of AWS User Group Delhi NCR. He is still working around the AWS buzz and currently holding 4 AWS certifications including DevOps Professional and Security Specialty.

He has been writing articles and blogs since 2014. He specializes in writing content related to AWS Cloud, Linux, Python, Databases, Ansible, Cybersecurity, etc. He is also managing a GOOGLE-Adsense approved blog titled as "4hathacker.in". Apart from being a tech freak, Nitin enjoys staying fit and going to gym daily. He is a veg foodie and sing-a-lot crooner. Having an ice-calm persona and love for nature, he is looking for new challenges to uncover.

Justin Casey
LinkedIn.com/in/justin-casey-80517415b

young but dedicated security professional who has spent the past number of years seizing each and every opportunity that has crossed his path in order to learn and progress within the industry, including extensive training in Physical, Cyber and Intelligence sectors. As an instructor & official representative of the European Security Academy (ESA) over the years Justin has been involved in the delivery of specialist training solutions for various international Law Enforcement, Military, and government units. He has led both covert surveillance and close protection operations as well as previously putting in the groundwork here in Ireland as a security operative for Celtic Security Solutions and working in Dublin as a trainer for the International Center for Security Excellence (ICSE).

LaShanda Edwards CECS-A, MSN, BS
LinkedIn.com/in/lashanda-edwards-cecs-a-msn-bs-221282140
facebook.com/AbstractionsPrintingandDesigns

As a Cyber Defense Infrastructure Support Specialist and a Freelance Graphic Artist, her background is not traditional but extensive. Capable of facing challenges head on, offering diverse experiences, and I am an agile learner. 11+ years of military service, as well as, healthcare experience. Also, freelance graphic artist for over 20 years. Recently graduated with a master's of Cybersecurity Technology degree, 3.8 GPA, offering a strong academic background in Cybersecurity. Swiftly to study and master new technologies; equally successful in both teams and self-directed setting; and skillful in a variety of computer systems, tools, and testing methodologies. Seeking to leverage my experience and passion towards cybersecurity. My goal is to obtain a challenging career within the cybersecurity career field with a leading company, healthcare facility, or the federal government as a Security Architect Cybersecurity and Technology Architecture, Information Systems Security Developer, Cybersecurity Analysis and Engineering, Board Advising, Security Control Assessor, Cybersecurity Consultant or Threat/Warning Analyst.

Mossaraf Zaman Khan
LinkedIn.com/in/mossaraf

Mossaraf is a Cyber Forensic Enthusiast. His areas of interest are Digital Forensics, Malware Analysis & Cyber Security. He is passionate and works hard to put his knowledge practically into the field of Cyber.

Ambadi MP
LinkedIn: LinkedIn.com/in/ambadi-m-p-16a95217b

A Cyber Security Researcher and a non-IT Graduate primarily focused on Red Teaming and Penetration Testing. Experience within web application and network penetration testing and Vulnerability Assessment. Passion towards IT Industry led to choose career in IT Sector. Within one year of experience in Cyber Security got several achievements and Acknowledged by Top Reputed Companies and Governmental Organizations for reporting vulnerabilities.

What is inside?

The Cyber Intelligence Report (CIR) is an Open Source Intelligence (**AKA OSINT**) resource centering around an array of subjects ranging from Exploits, Advanced Persistent Threats, National Infrastructure, Dark Web, Digital Forensics & Incident Response (DIFR), and the gambit of digital dangers.

The CIR rotates between odd issues focusing on Blue Team / Defense and the even issues on Red Team / Offense.

Weekly Awareness Report

We have another publication called the Cyber WAR. It contains information pulled from many different sources to keep you up to date with what is going on in the Cyber Security Realm. You can read past Cyber WAR editions at:

InformationWarfareCenter.com/CIR

Evidence Everywhere

Post 2000, almost everyone has some sort of digital footprint. If you have a cellphone and use Social Media, your footprint is a unique signature that identifies you as a person in many different databases. Most of the services you use are probably running analytics on your data for marketing, troubleshooting, or maybe even more nefarious reasons. The government is watching you because they can. If you are using smart devices, you are probably bleeding far more data than you realize. Your data (your digital self) is now a commodity that is now considered the new gold. Data is everywhere... This means trace evidence is also everywhere.

What does this mean for you personally?

Big companies and governments are getting hacked daily. Facebook data gets leaked. Insert name here gets leaked... It is interesting to see how much sensitive data is being leaked. For about $8 USD, you can download billions of username/email password combinations at Raidforums.com. Here is a link to their archived data: raidforums.com/Announcement-Database-Index-CLICK-ME. Please look at those databases. There is an exceptionally good chance YOU are in there. Not just your passwords, it also contains voter registration databases and more.

These are big organizations that spend a lot of money on IT and Security solutions to protect their data and they are still leaking data. Many of the hacking groups, especially state sponsored Advanced Persistent Threats, will go over the top and seem paranoid when communicating or accessing their data. However, it just takes one mistake to take down the entire security house of cards. There is a saying that goes: "the bad guy has to be lucky every single time and the investigator only has to be lucky once". Most people do not put forth the same due care and diligence into protecting their own systems and data at home. Some bad guys do not either and that is a very good thing for an investigation.

Now... To turn the tables, a lot of the tools and tactics the attackers employ are ESPECIALLY useful during cyber investigations. Think of it as two sides of the same coin. This goes without saying, DO NOT break the law... However, using the same methods the bad actors do can drastically increase your capability during the "anti-hack". As for using leaked data, it can help your investigation if you have access to it.

Open Source Intelligence (OSINT) can sometimes give you a ton of good information. Your network is a goldmine of transactional evidence and if you can get access to a device, there is more data than most people realize. Just remember to always make sure you are within your jurisdictional limitations and you have legal access to the data you are seeking.

Using tools like packet sniffers and protocol analyzers have always been a staple in network forensics. It is amazing how much data your systems are hemorrhaging. When investigating either a hacking incident or inappropriate use, there is trace evidence in many different areas that can help you *break the case*.

Network traffic analysis can also help you identify devices that were previously unknown or accounted for. It is amazing how many times an organization just adds "things" to the environment without proper documentation. This makes managing security a daunting task and preventing risk near impossible at times.

IOT Cyber Investigation Challenges

Cyber forensic investigations in the IoT space have come across a few speedbumps or challenges that have made the process more difficult than your average cases. These include but are not limited to:

- The increasing number of objects with evidence on them.
- Relevance of the devices for the investigation.
- Network boundaries that cross jurisdictions and ownership.
- Edgeless networks.
- Lack of properly documented devices.
- Small OS or Storage capability with limited access.
- Lack of firmware validation.

Now you must plan on what kind of evidence you can get from the suspect devices. Can you get a physical (bitstream) copy of the storage on the device? Can you only get a logical copy of the data? Do you have the tools and access to even get the data? Do you know where the devices are physically located? Do you even know of all the devices on the network? Who owns them? If the firmware is what you need to analyze, now you are going into the realm of Reverse Engineering.

Here are some smaller scoped IoT devices that are easier to identify, but also have their own challenges. Especially if they have an Internet connection.

- Smart car navigation systems (Hacked for full control)
- Drone or antonymous vehicles (Hacked video feeds and hijack control)
- RFID access control systems (Easy to Duplicate)
- CCTV Cameras (Hacked using IR and over networks)

Sometimes these hacks are only identified when they trip security sensors like the traditional IDS/IPS or when the organization does full traffic analysis through a SIEM.

With so many different devices and implementations of the devices, there is not a canned or off the shelf solution to cover every situation. Even mobile device forensics has this challenge, but not nearly at this scale. Sometimes you will need to contact the vendor to get the right tools or access for the job. The first step though is being able to identify all the devices that are relevant to the investigation. Only then can you move to the next step, acquisition.

This publication will describe cyber forensics and investigation methods that cross through the multiple layers of the OSI model ("*OSI Cake*").

Dark Web Corner

Dark Web Search Engines

Ahmia: searches hidden services on the Tor network. To access these hidden services, you need the Tor browser bundle. Abuse material is not allowed on Ahmia. See our service blacklist and report abuse material if you find it in the index. It will be removed as soon as possible.
Be careful with the RAW link!

Link: msydqstlz2kzerdg.onion
Raw: msydqstlz2kzerdg.onion/address

Candle: Tor Search is a "Google" like search engine that crawls Tor sites.

Link: gjobqjj7wyczbqie.onion

TORCH: "Tor Search is a very efficient crawler and search engine which is 24 hour indexing new contents from the TOR network. It serves over 80,000 search requests every day from TOR users looking for content in TOR network and it is referred by hundreds of sites within TOR and on the clear web."

Link: xmh57jrzrnw6insl.onion

Below is a list of secure communications methods using Tor Onion network. Just remember, you can only access these if you are going through the Tor network

ProtonMail is a Swiss encrypted email service. They use end-to-end encryption and don't keep any logs. Moreover, you do not need personal information to create an account.

protonirockerxow.onion

"SecureDrop is an open source whistleblower submission system that media organizations and NGOs can install to securely accept documents from anonymous sources. It was originally created by the late Aaron Swartz and is now managed by Freedom of the Press Foundation. SecureDrop is available in 20 languages."

Notable SecureDrop links

2600: lxa4rh3xy2s7cvfy.onion
Reuters: smb7p276iht3i2fj.onion

secrdrop5wyphb5x.onion

SecMail has become one of the most used dark web email providers. "We won't ask you for your name, address or any personal data. We are using the safest security protocols, so you don't have to worry about nothing."

secmailw453j7piv.onion

Dark Markets

A Dark Market or *"cryptomarket is a commercial website on the web that operates via darknets such as Tor or I2P. They function primarily as black markets, selling or brokering transactions involving drugs, cyber-arms, weapons, counterfeit currency, stolen credit card details, forged documents, unlicensed pharmaceuticals, steroids, and other illicit goods as well as the sale of legal products."* - wikipedia.org

White House Market is a market with a high level of security and anonymity while maintaining a simple user interface.

I2P Address: eeej5nynwa5pe4slg6ny66l2rck37m2rtaglair53cff56xmssaq.b32.i2p
Tor Address: auzbdiguv5qtp37xoma3n4xfch62duxtdiu4cfrrwbxgckipd4aktxid.onion

Monopoly Market: a direct deal, walletless, userless, XMR exclusive, drug-focused, marketplace aimed to provide a portfolio of well-vetted vendors for reliable, safe trading. Over the course of the past few months, we have built Monopoly from the ground up while taking keynotes from comments made on Dread, especially within /d/DarkNetMarkets.

Tor Address:
- monopolyberbucxu.onion
- 2lbcyr5kftntuvfbd22h3ayxtrvzymk5vzcc54oj3qc62xuvcefqtlid.onion

Recon is the largest Dark Net Market vendor archive service and multi marketplace search engine, providing up to date content from the majority of established markets all in one place. We strive to serve a fast and easy to use platform allowing you to cross reference vendor details, listings, statistics and marketplace addresses.

Tor Address: reconponydonugup.onion

Fun Facts

65%

"Bitcoin Activity on the Dark Web Grew by 65% first Quarter" - Crystal Blockchain Analytics

Dark Market Busts

This section showcases recent busts made on the Dark Web within the Dark Market Communities. This ranges from buyers to sellers to admins of these websites.

The information is taken from several online resources including, but not limited to

reddit.com/r/DNMBusts

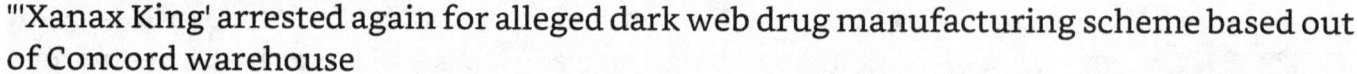

Law enforcement got access to all customer info of anyone who dealt with:

"'Xanax King' arrested again for alleged dark web drug manufacturing scheme based out of Concord warehouse

Jeremy Donagal had previously been charged with selling pills designed to look like Xanax" - mercurynews.com

"Pharmacist Arrested in Plot to Firebomb a Rival to Sell More Drugs on the Dark Web. Hyrum T. Wilson of Auburn, Neb., conspired with a drug dealer to rob, then destroy a competitor's pharmacy, according to federal prosecutors." - nytimes.com
"Empire Vendor NeverPressedRX Arrested by the FBI

A Maryland man accused of running the "NeverPressedRX" vendor account on Empire market was arrested for unlawful distribution of medications and money laundering. NeverPressedRX sold a variety of prescription medications on marketplaces as well as through Wickr." - darknetlive.com

"An 18-year-old man from Lindisfarne has been arrested and charged with trafficking in a controlled drug following an operation focused on the mail corridor into Tasmania.

The work of dedicated detectives resulted in the seizure of approximately $100,000 worth of controlled drugs" - police.tas.gov.au

Tech Giants help Law Enforcement:
Exploit Those That Exploit Children

Facebook recently hit the news when they paid a security research firm to exploit the popular Tor live bootable workstation called The Amnesic Incognito Live System or Tails (htttails.boum.org). *"The FBI and Facebook used a so-called zero-day exploit in the privacy-focused operating system Tails, which automatically routes all of a user's internet traffic through the Tor anonymity network, to unmask Hernandez's real IP address, which ultimately led to his arrest."* -vice.com

"Tails is a complete operating system designed to be used from a DVD, USB stick, or SD card independently of the computer's original operating system. It is free software and based on Debian GNU/Linux. Tails comes with several built-in applications pre-configured with security in mind: a web browser, an instant messaging client, an email client, an office suite, an image and sound editor, etc." - torproject.org

This is not the first time that big tech has helped Law Enforcement track down pedophiles and it will not be the last. Companies like Google, Microsoft, and others use algorithms to monitor uploads and downloads of material that contain possible child pornography. When detected, they review the data and contact The National Center for Missing and Exploited Children, known as NCMEC and send the sample image along with information about the digital fingerprints of the traffic source and destination.

This is also not the first time that exploits have been used to deanonymize people on Dark Web networks. On August 4, 2013: "all the sites hosted by Freedom Hosting – some with no connection to child porn – began serving an error message with hidden code embedded in the page. Security researchers dissected the code and found it exploited a security hole in Firefox to identify users of the Tor Browser Bundle, reporting back to a mysterious server in Northern Virginia." – wired.com

The FBI also used a project codenamed called Torpedo that targeted Pedophiles on the Tor network. *"Operation Torpedo was a 2011 operation in which the FBI compromised three different hidden services hosting child pornography, which would then target anyone who happened to access them using a network investigative technique (NIT)."* -wikipedia The use of the project was said by a judge to be "crossing the line". However, in the case of Gabriel Werdene, 53, of Bucks County, Philadelphia serving two years in a federal prison for rummaging through the Playpen dark-web filth souk for images and footage of child sexual abuse, the judge said that the line was crossed in "good faith".

Not all people that use Tor, I2P, Freenet, and all the other Dark Web networks are criminals, terrorists, and evil people. With that said, there are a lot of bad guys that do. Always be careful where you go and what you do. So, who use it for legitimate purposes? Well, let's list a few:

- Activists
- Businesses
- Intelligence Officers
- Journalists and News Agencies
- Law Enforcement
- Political Dissidents
- Security Researchers

"Keep in mind that only activities you do inside of Tor Browser itself will be anonymized. Having Tor Browser installed on your computer does not make things you do on the same computer using other software (such as your regular web browser) anonymous." – ssd.eff.org

This comes down to a level of effort issue. How anonymous do you want? If you are investigating a small-time drug dealer on a dark market, your name is probably going to be added to the public court records. If you are a political dissident and are afraid your family may be executed for your crimes, you need to take a few more steps.

Keep this in mind when investigating a suspect or target websites. This is all about Operational Security or OPSEC. The running joke with Law Enforcement is that the bad guy must be lucky EVERY SINGLE TIME and you only must be lucky once. Now, from the darkest of places, I do know of officers investigating some wretched guys (Cartels and Terrorists) getting murdered because they did not follow basic OPSEC procedures. Know the risk and protect yourself accordingly.

You also need to be on the same network as the suspect if you plan to access their open resources. This is where the technical knowledge kicks in. You need to understand the mechanics of how network traffic works.

Tor Resources:

Tor must be installed…
"Just like Tor users, the developers, researchers, and founders who've made Tor possible are a diverse group of people. But all of the people who have been involved in Tor are united by a common belief: internet users should have private access to an uncensored web."

- Tor Project

Local proxies

- Corridor
- Privoxy
- Proxychains
- Torsocks

Tor Network Gateway

These are systems that you can run to send traffic through.

- CSI Linux
- Whonix Gateway

Tor Workstations

- CSI Linux
- Tails
- Whonix Workstation *

Multi-layer Environment

- CSI Linux
- Qubes OS

#BlueLeak

In June 19, 2020, the user @DDoSecrets posted on Twitter that they released a 269 Gb leak of 10 years' worth of Law Enforcement data. When you follow their link, it does take some time to load the page. After a few minutes, it comes up with what you see in the graphic below. Further investigation shows that a large bulk of this data is already public information. This seems to be more of a political statement for a news clip than an actual leak of sensitive investigation and other sensitive data. However, when everything is on one easy to search database, useful data may still be parsed from it. Intelligence is all about seeing patterns and trying to predict future behavior.

With this said, here is another tweet from @DDoSecrets: "#BlueLeaks provides unique insights into law enforcement and a wide array of government activities, including thousands of documents mentioning #COVID19". This was taken down by both Twitter and Archive.org, but can be found on BitTorrent sites.

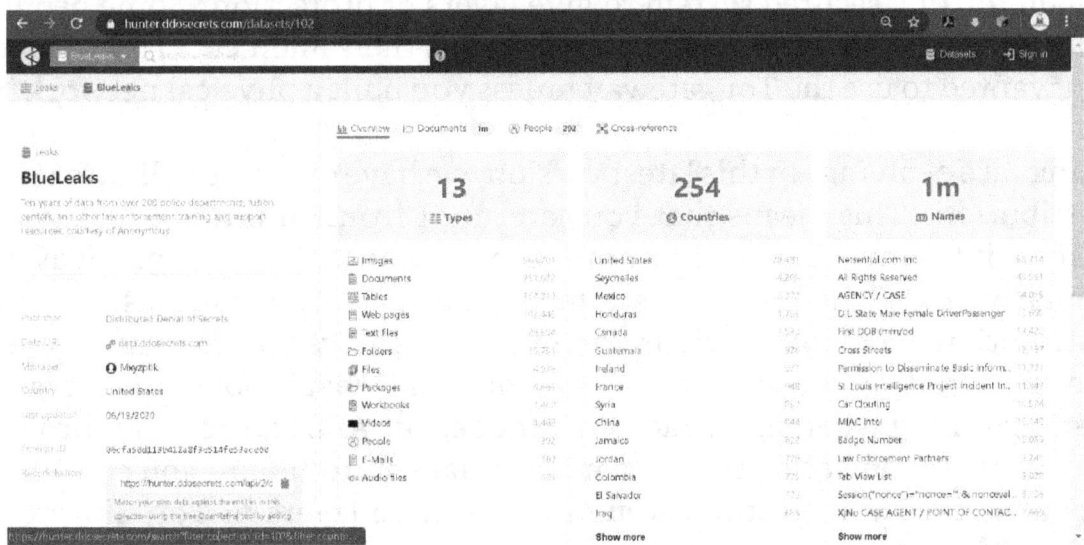

Here is the original link: hunter.ddosecrets.com/datasets/102

The user Emma Best/@the_mike_best also uploaded the leak to Archive.org: archive.org/details/BlueLeaks The torrent file has a lot of individual files and doesn't work with all BitTorrent programs like uTorrent. It does however work with Transmission on Linux.

CSI Linux
The Evolving Forensic Investigation Environment

This project started about a year ago when several of the environments we commonly used were either going in different directions than we were wanting, or support stopped when the project hit its end of life. The original purpose was to have a Linux environment that could be used for Online, Social Media, and Dark Web investigations. We took a lot of the base inspiration from the amazing work from Michael Bazzell's Buscador at Intel Techniques. We switched out some tools, added some more, and thought, why not make this an all in one environment? Then, the project exploded.

The first revisions of the environment became 3 separate operating systems that would work together or work separately. It was designed this way to make it as simple as possible to run right out of the box with little Linux and networking experience. We used the same idea some had with using Buscador with Whonix and by version 2020.2, created our own Tor gateway to replace Whonix. Our SIEM was a stand-alone system that was set to replace the Security Onion. Everything was built for virtual machines to run on top of a secured system to give layers of protection. Some people wanted to be able to run the Analyst on a single system as their main OS. This was not an option if you wanted to use the Tor gateway unless you built a physical network infrastructure.

Things are evolving. In this latest version, we have combined all three into one bootable distribution. This means that you can run it from an internal/external hard drive or push it into any Virtual Environment you want. The Tor gateway no longer runs similarly to Whonix but uses similar methods to tunnel as the Tails Tor based distribution. Like the previous versions, this allows you to turn on a level of security and anonymity if needed but can be turned off if that is not your primary goal. The Tor is still running when in Surface Web mode, but ALL traffic is not protected, just what you want. If you decide to run in in a virtual environment, you can add Whonix to the mix and force your traffic through up to three layers of Tor, akin to how some use Qubes-OS. It is now up to you how far you want to go.

whonix.org
tails.boum.org
qubes-os.org

The SIEM is now in a Docker, still stand alone, and can be integrated into the Analyst. This allows us to rename the Analyst to just CSI Linux, as was originally indented. The SIEM has been given some steroids... Amazon ics protocols, ClamAV, Cyber chef, Elastalert, geolite2, Mitre cyber analytics, Moloch, Nginx for https reverse proxying, and more... With the extra power, it means that it will need more resources. A minimum of 6 GB Ram is needed for CSI Linux or 12 GB Ram for CSI Linux to run the SEIM on top to run comfortably.

With the Gateway being merged with Analyst, the "sub" distros will be SIEM and Acquisition. Acquisition will be a bootable distro built for imaging and evidence capture. Acquisition is planned for release in the next month.

So, what does all of this mean?

Well, CSI Linux can be booted off an internal/external drive or within a Virtual MAchine since it no longer requires the use of an external Tor gateway. If you would like to run it the traditional way, you absolutely can run CSI Linux through Whonix. You can Even Tor gateway through the Whonix Tor Gateway for an added layer of security. You can decide not to install the SIEM on CSI Linux, run it on a completely different system, or not at all. There are many configuration options now availible. You can make it as simple or as complicate as you want.

We have also added a Bug Tracker website http://tracker.csilinux.com to help for future development. We are also in the process of creating a training site as well.

Now to highlight some of the additions to the base CSI Linux system.

* CSI Linux updater
* Tools updated
* More GUI options for the CSI Tools
* Updated CSI Tools
* SIGINT Tools added
* More OSINT resources
* More computer forensics tools added

This is update is a major update with many of the mechanics fundamentally changed. Thank you to all of those that have helped build the distribution with the countless hours spent and all of the suggestions from the users. This has been a great project and the ever evolving product of the labor is amazing to watch.

If you have any suggestions on making CSI Linux better, whether it be tools, methods, resources, or engineering ideas, pleas let us know.

CSI Linux
Forensic Challenge 204

This Capture the Flag (CTF) can be done anywhere since it is a downloadable image. We are using one of the prebuilt cases from CFREDS.NIST.GOV.

Download: cfreds.nist.gov/dfrws/Rhino_Hunt.html

The Challenge... Using whatever tool of your choice. Identify the flags, write a report, and write a walk through on how you found each item. The findings and final report will then be graded, with the best combo being the winner. Make sure that the report and the walkthrough are two separate documents.

Winner will have their report and walkthrough showcased in a future issue of the Cyber Intelligence Report (CIR) and win a commemorative Bitcoin challenge coin (Not a real Bitcoin). Submit reports to CTF@informationwarfarecenter.com.

Scenario:

The city of New Orleans passed a law in 2004 making possession of nine or more unique rhino images a serious crime. The network administrator at the University of New Orleans recently alerted police when his instance of RHINOVORE flagged illegal rhino traffic. Evidence in the case includes a computer and USB key seized from one of the University's labs. Unfortunately, the computer had no hard drive. The USB key was imaged and a copy of the dd image is on the CD-ROM you have been given. In addition to the USB key drive image, three network traces are also available—these were provided by the network administrator and involve the machine with the missing hard drive. The suspect is the primary user of this machine, who has been pursuing his Ph.D. at the University since 1972.

CTF TARGET DETAILS

rhino.log
c0d0093eb1664cd7b73f3a5225ae3f30
rhino2.log
cd21eaf4acfb50f71ffff857d7968341
rhino3.log
7e29f9d67346df25faaf18efcd95fc30
RHINOUSB.dd
80348c58eec4c328ef1f7709adc56a54

CSI Linux:

- CSILinux.com

Additional Resources:

- Wireshark
- Autopsy

The Rhino Hunt data set requires examination of a small image file and three network traces.

Deadline: December 15th

The task:

Recover at least nine rhino pictures from the available evidence and include them in a brief report. In your report, provide answers to as many of the following questions as possible:

- Who gave the accused a telnet/ftp account?
- What is the username/password for the account?
- What relevant file transfers appear in the network traces?
- What happened to the hard drive in the computer? Where is it now?
- What happened to the USB key?
- What is recoverable from the dd image of the USB key?
- Is there any evidence that connects the USB key and the network traces? If so, what?

Remember: Score is based off the quality of the report and walkthrough.

To receive full credit, use CSI Linux as your base investigation system. You can add more tools on top, but make sure to document what you have added in your walkthrough and step by step actions for gathering the evidence.

CSI Linux Forensic Challenge 201

* Winner: Apostolos Gkletos
* Honorable Mention Keith Swagler

The Challenge

Using CSI Linux and the tools included, go through this forensic project, and identify all the flags you can. Use Autopsy as your main application. Write a walk through on how you found each item within Autopsy and any other tools within your final report. The findings and final report will then be graded, with the best combo being the winner.

You can try the challenge yourself: www.cfreds.nist.gov/Hacking_Case.html

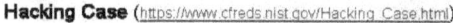

CSI Linux Forensic Challenge

Using CSI Linux and the tools included, go through this forensic project and identify all the flags you can. Use Autopsy as your main application. Write a walk through on how you found each item within Autopsy and any other tools within your final report. The findings and final report will then be graded, with the best combo being the winner.

Winner will have their report and walkthrough showcased in a future issue of the Cyber Intelligence Report (CIR) and win a commemorative Bitcoin challenge coin (Not a real Bitcoin). Submit reports to csilinux@informationwarfarecenter.com. Deadline is June 15th, 2020!

Here is the Autopsy user manual: https://sleuthkit.org/autopsy/docs/user-docs/4.0/
Sign up here: https://comms.informationwarfarecenter.com/?p=subscribe&id=4

Hacking Case (https://www.cfreds.nist.gov/Hacking_Case.html)

This test image requires a variety of skills to answer the given questions.

Scenario

On 09/20/04, a Dell CPi notebook computer, serial # VLQLW, was found abandoned along with a wireless PCMCIA card and an external homemade 802.11b antennae. It is suspected that this computer was used for hacking purposes, although cannot be tied to a hacking suspect, G=r=e=g S=c=h=a=r=d=t. (The equal signs are just to prevent web crawlers from indexing this name; there are no equal signs in the image files.) Schardt also goes by the online nickname of "Mr. Evil" and some of his associates have said that he would park his vehicle within range of Wireless Access Points (like Starbucks and other T-Mobile Hotspots) where he would then intercept internet traffic, attempting to get credit card numbers, usernames & passwords.

Find any hacking software, evidence of their use, and any data that might have been generated. Attempt to tie the computer to the suspect, G=r=e=g S=c=h=a=r=d=t.

A DD image (in seven parts: 1, 2, 3, 4, 5, 6, 7, 8, and notes) and a EnCase image (second part) of the abandoned computer have already been made.

1. What is the image hash? Does the acquisition and verification hash match?
2. What operating system was used on the computer?
3. When was the install date?
4. What is the timezone settings?
5. Who is the registered owner?
6. What is the computer account name?
7. What is the primary domain name?
8. When was the last recorded computer shutdown date/time?
9. How many accounts are recorded (total number)?
10. What is the account name of the user who mostly uses the computer?
11. Who was the last user to logon to the computer?
12. A search for the name of "G=r=e=g S=c=h=a=r=d=t" reveals multiple hits. One of these proves that G=r=e=g S=c=h=a=r=d=t is Mr. Evil and is also the administrator of this computer. What file is it? What software program does this file relate to?
13. List the network cards used by this computer
14. This same file reports the IP address and MAC address of the computer. What are they?
15. An internet search for vendor name/model of NIC cards by MAC address can be used to find out which network interface was used. In the above answer, the first 3 hex characters of the MAC address report the vendor of the card. Which NIC card was used during the installation and set-up for LOOK@LAN?
16. Find 6 installed programs that may be used for hacking.
17. What is the SMTP email address for Mr. Evil?
18. What is the NNTP (news server) settings for Mr. Evil?
19. What two installed programs show this information?
20. List 5 newsgroups that Mr. Evil has subscribed to.
21. A popular IRC (Internet Relay Chat) program called MIRC was installed. What are the user settings that was shown when the user was online and in a chat channel?
22. This IRC program has the capability to log chat sessions. List 3 IRC channels that the user of this computer accessed.
23. Ethereal, a popular "sniffing" program that can be used to intercept wired and wireless internet packets was also found to be installed. When TCP packets are collected and re-assembled, the default save directory is that users \My Documents directory. What is the name of the file that contains the intercepted data?
24. Viewing the file in a text format reveals much information about who and what was intercepted. What type of wireless computer was the victim (person who had his internet surfing recorded) using?
25. What websites was the victim accessing?
26. Search for the main user's web-based email address. What is it?
27. Yahoo mail, a popular web-based email service, saves copies of the email under what file name?
28. How many executable files are in the recycle bin?
29. Are these files really deleted?
30. How many files are reported to be deleted by the file system?
31. Perform an Anti-Virus check. Are there any viruses on the computer?

Steps

- Download the DD/Raw images
- Start a case within Autopsy
- Use other tools within CSI Linux as needed.
- Document everything.
- Walk through with screenshots including the third-party modules you've added
- Complete a Chain of Custody (Use the attached form below).
- Complete a final report
- Profit!

Information Warfare Center
CSI Linux Forensic Challenge

CTF 201 Chain of Custody

SUBMITTER: PLEASE COMPLETE SECTIONS 1 AND 2 AND SIGN/DATE ON SUBMITTER LINE OF SECTION 4. DOCUMENT ALL SUBSEQUENT EVIDENCE TRANSFERS IN SECTION 4.

SECTION 1

INVESTIGATOR NAME: Apostolos Gkletos	DATE SUBMITTED: 01/01/2020
AGENCY: INFORMATION WARFARE CENTER	AGENCY CASE NO.: 01072020-SHARDT
ADDRESS: *********	
CITY/COUNTY: Athens Greece	STATE: Attiki	ZIP CODE: ******
PHONE NO.: ******************** FAX NO.:	E-MAIL: gklapostolos@gmail.com
EMERGENCY CONTACT:	PHONE NO.:

SECTION 2

Sampling Site: CSI Linux Forensics Challenge	Site Address: csilinux.com
Collected By: NIST	Date Collected: 01/01/2020	Agency: Information warfare center

SUBMITTER DESCRIPTION: INCLUDE THE NUMBER OF CONTAINERS, IDENTIFICATION NUMBER(S) AND A PHYSICAL DESCRIPTION OF EACH SAMPLE SUBMITTED FOR TESTING.

The image of a laptop was taken by NIST.gov.

They have submitted via the website www.cfreds.nist.gov/Hacking Case.html for review. We do not have access to the original hardware. There are two different image formats including a split DD image and an EnCase .E01 format. Both images contain a forensic copy of the same drive.

SUBMITTER COMMENTS:

When trying to download the images initially I have the option to save them as txt which is solved by cancelling the action and resuming the downloading action which saves them to their original type.

Laboratory Description of Sample: Include the number of containers, identification number(s) and a physical description of each item submitted for testing.

SIGNATURE:	DATE:

SECTION 4

Chain of Custody: Persons relinquishing and receiving evidence must provide their signature, organization and date/time to document evidence transfers.

Submitter Signature: IWC Signature			Agency: INFORMATION WARFARE CENTER	Date: 01/01/2020	
Received by	Organization	Date/Time	Relinquished by	Organization	Date/Time
1. Apostolos Gkletos	IWC	14/06/2020	2.		
Received by	Organization	Date/Time	Relinquished by	Organization	Date/Time
3.			4.		
Received by	Organization	Date/Time	Relinquished by	Organization	Date/Time
5.			6.		
Received by	Organization	Date/Time	Relinquished by	Organization	Date/Time
7.			8.		
Received by	Organization	Date/Time	Relinquished by	Organization	Date/Time
9.			10.		

SECTION 5 – EVIDENCE DISPOSAL (TO BE COMPLETED BY LABORATORY EVIDENCE CUSTODIAN)

Disposition Site:	Destruction No.:	Method of Destruction/Date:
Performed by:		Date:
Witnessed by:		Date:

SECTION 6

Supplemental Information (i.e. sample description, comments, other)

Case Challenge - Apostolos Gkletos

On 09/20/04, a Dell CPi notebook computer, serial # VLQLW, was found abandoned along with a wireless PCMCIA card and an external homemade 802.11b antennae. It is suspected that this computer was used for hacking purposes, although cannot be tied to a hacking suspect, G=r=e=g S=c=h=a=r=d=t. Schardt also goes by the online nickname of "Mr. Evil" and some of his associates have said that he would park his vehicle within range of Wireless Access Points (like Starbucks and other T-Mobile Hotspots) where he would then intercept internet traffic, attempting to get credit card numbers, usernames & passwords.

Solution

For investigation purposes a DD image and an EnCase image were acquired from the laptop found and CSI Linux tools were used to analyze these images. The procedure that was followed is described below supported by screenshots where needed.

Requirements Section

Section #1
- Requirement 1
    - A laptop with at least 8 Gb of Ram, 16Gb recommended
- Requirement 2
    - Latest edition of Virtual Box installed along with its additions
- Requirement 3
    - Hard disk with at least 80 Gb of free space, recommended 100 Gb at least
- Requirement 4
    - CSI Linux .ova file

Section #2:
- Requirement 1
    - Autopsy NSRL hash sets
- Requirement 2
    - Case DD, EnCase images

CSI Linux Challenge Answers

1. What is the image hash? Does the acquisition and verification hash match? The image hash is:

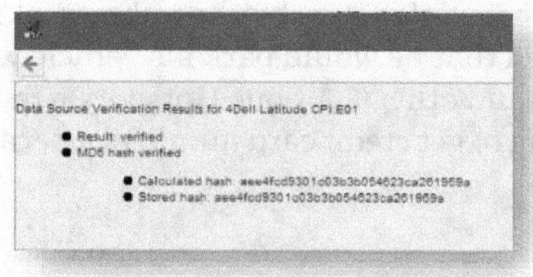
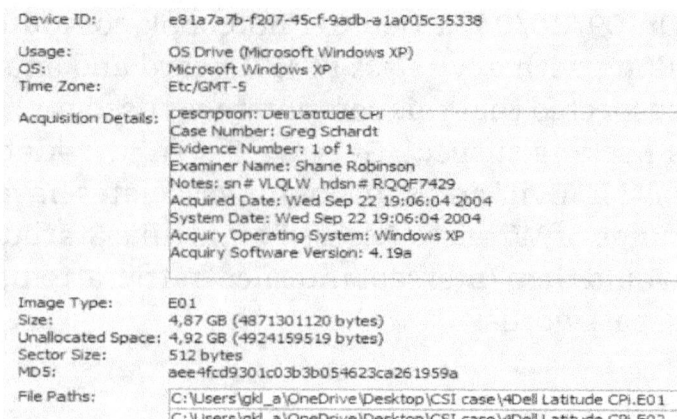

aee4fcd9301c03b3b054623ca261959a. Yes, they are the same.

Picture 1:Acquisition and verification hash match *Picture 2:Image MD5*

2. What operating system was used on the computer? On the system the software that was used is **Microsoft Windows XP**.

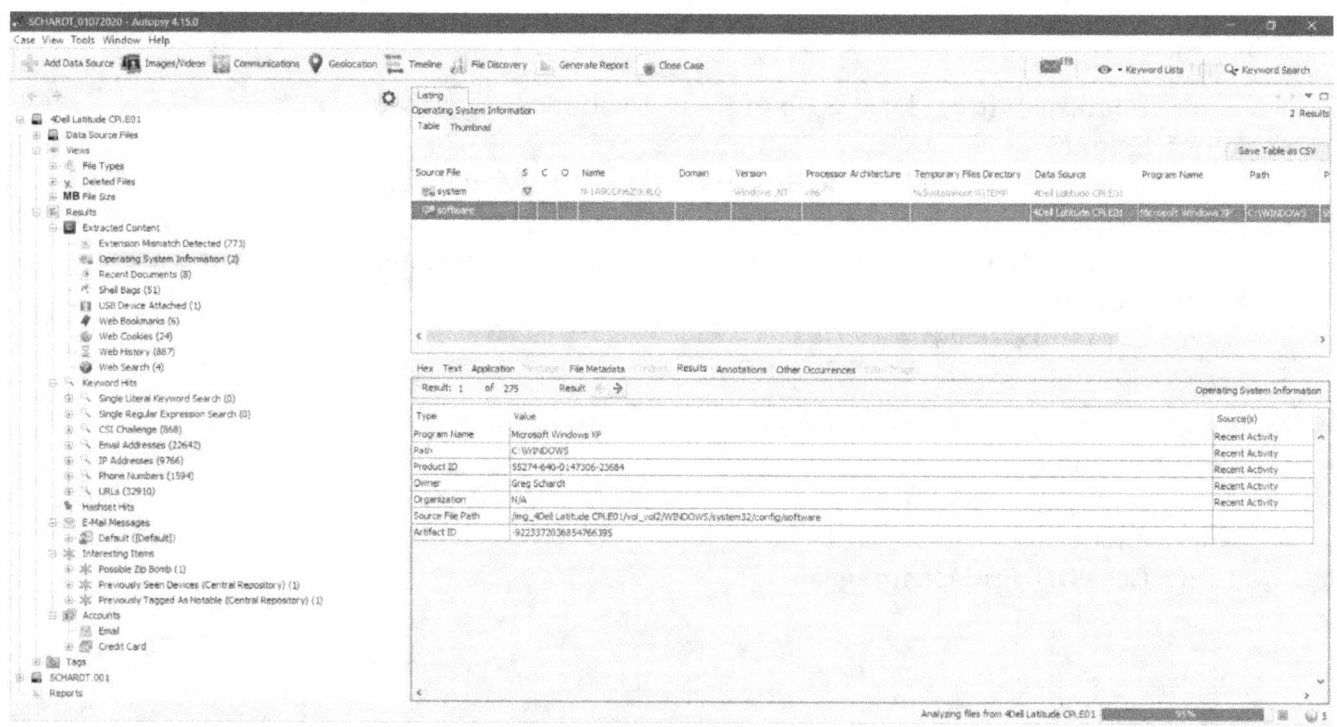

Picture 3:Software used

3. When was the install date? 0x41252e3b (1092955707)
   a. GMT: **Thursday, August 19, 2004 10:48:27 PM**

4. What is the timezone settings? Etc/**GMT-5** as it is shown in picture 1
5. Who is the registered owner? The registered owner is **Greg Schardt**.

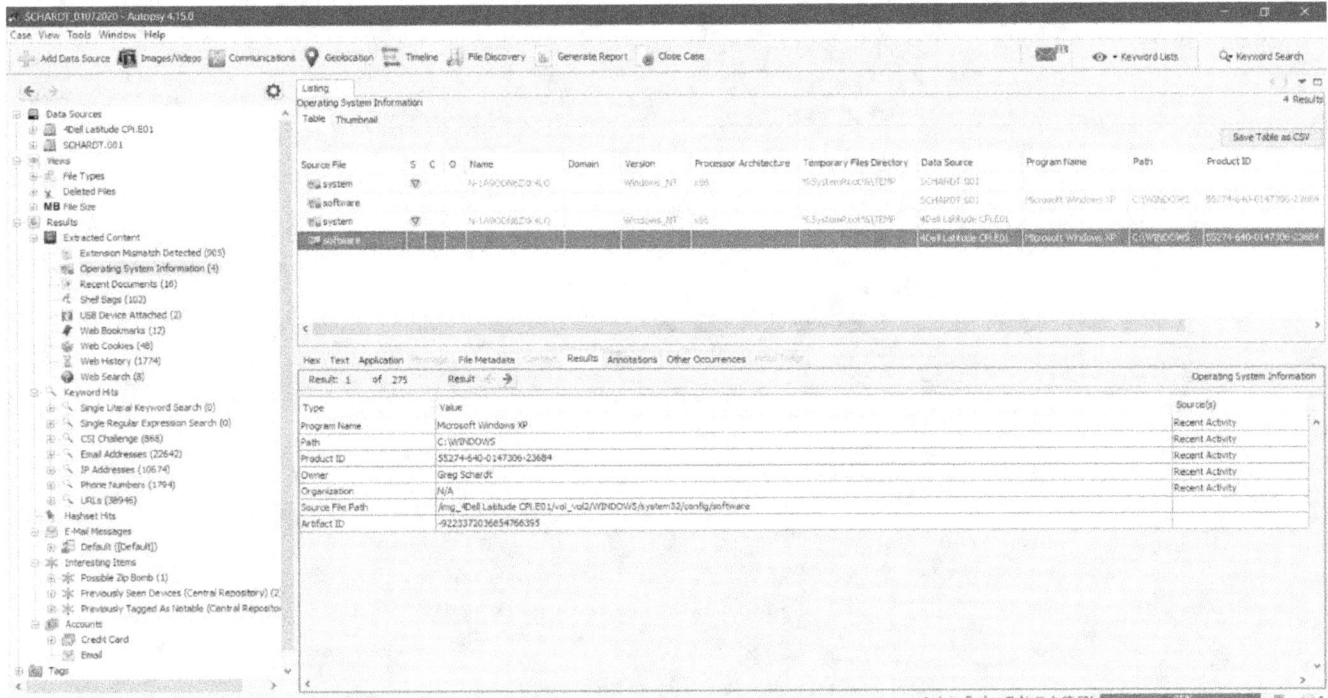

Picture 4: Registered owner

6. What is the computer account name? The computer name is **N-1A9ODN6ZXK4LQ**

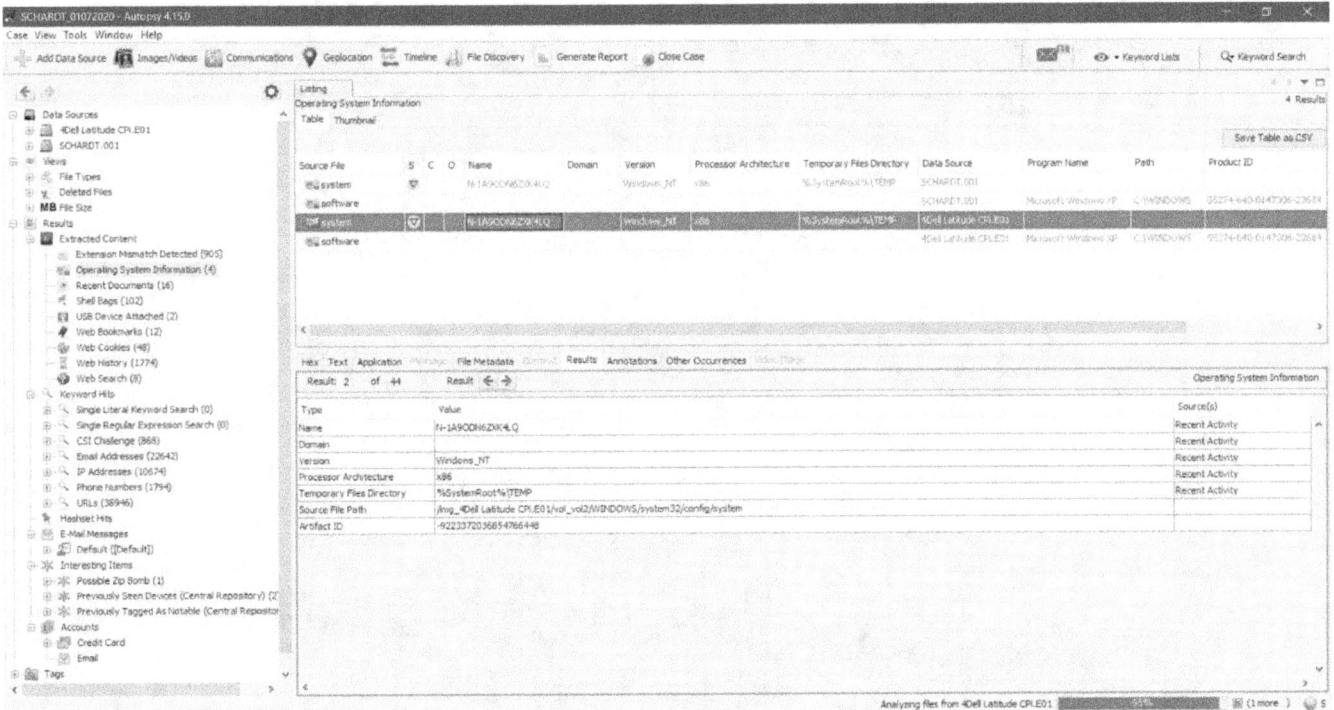

Picture 5: Computer name

7. What is the primary domain name? The Domain Name is **N-1A9ODN6ZXK4LQ**

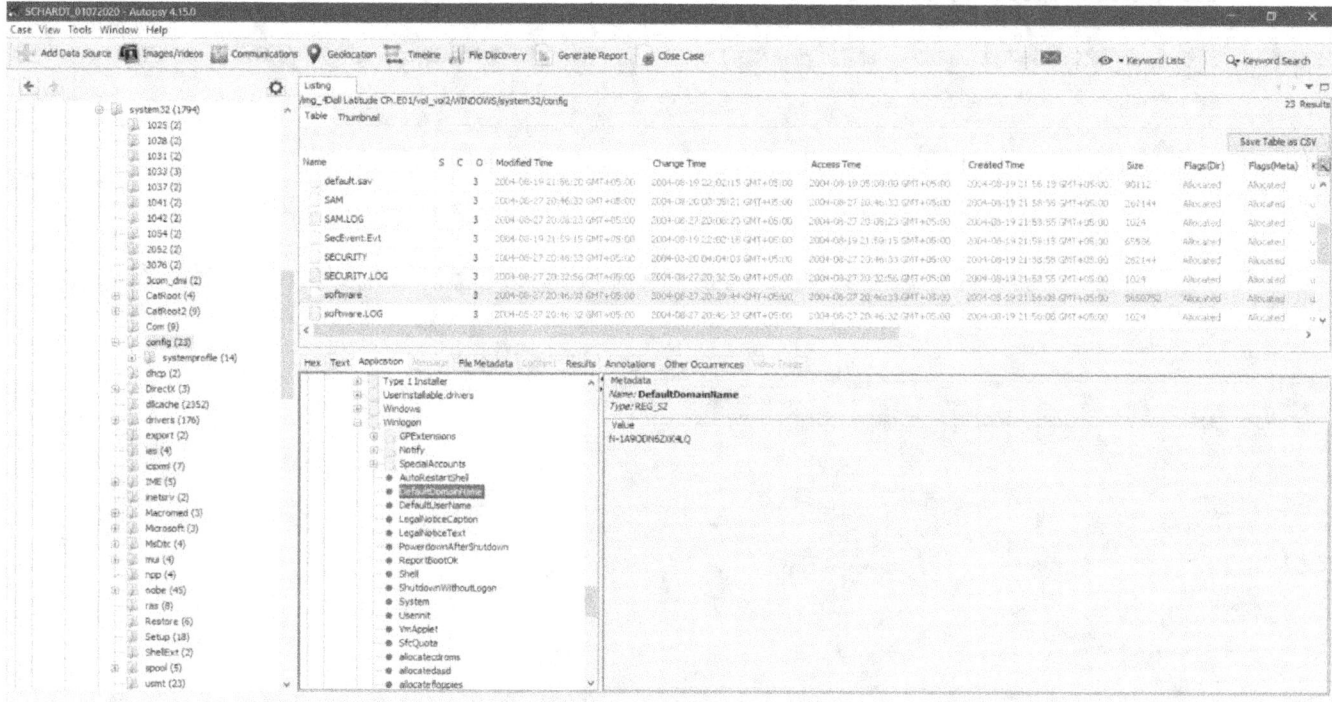

Picture 6: Primary Domain name

8. When was the last recorded computer shutdown date/time? The last recorded shutdown time at **27-08-2004 10:46:27**.

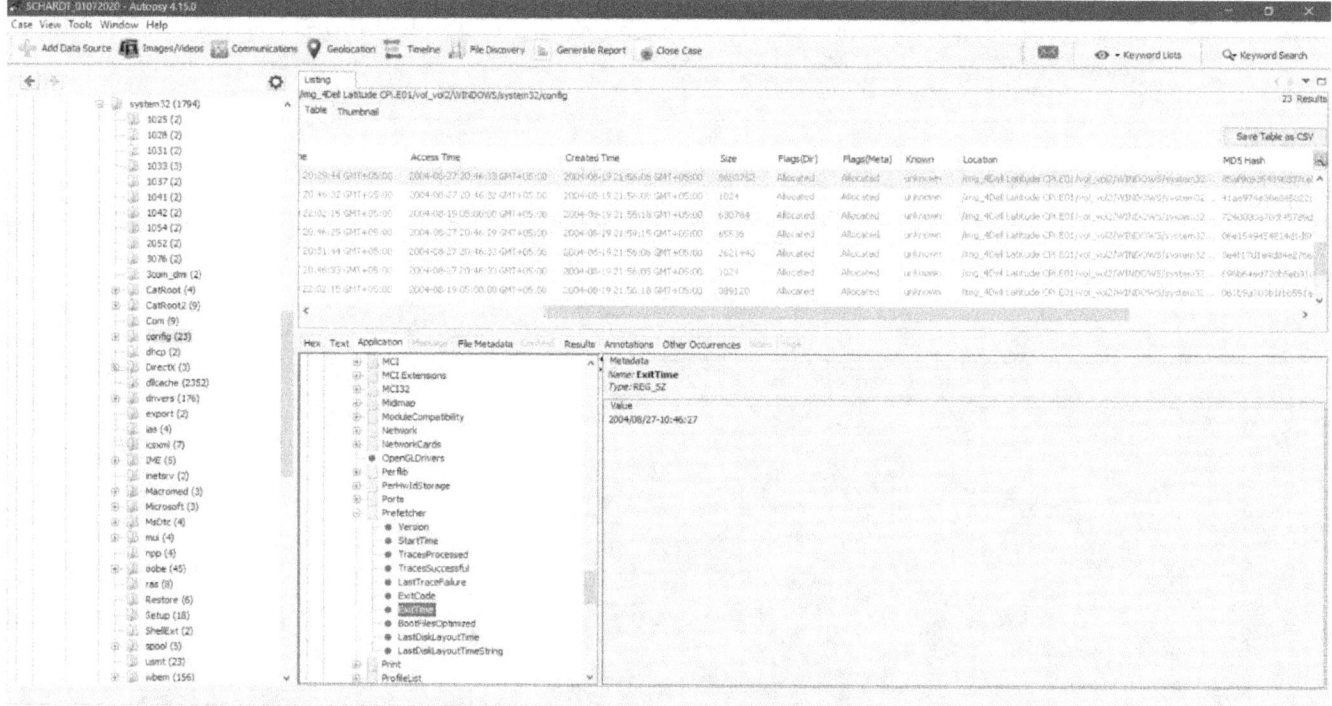

Picture 7: Last recorded Shutdown Time

9. How many accounts are recorded (total number)? There are 5 accounts: **Administrator, Guest, Help Assistant, Mr.Evil, Support 388945a0**.

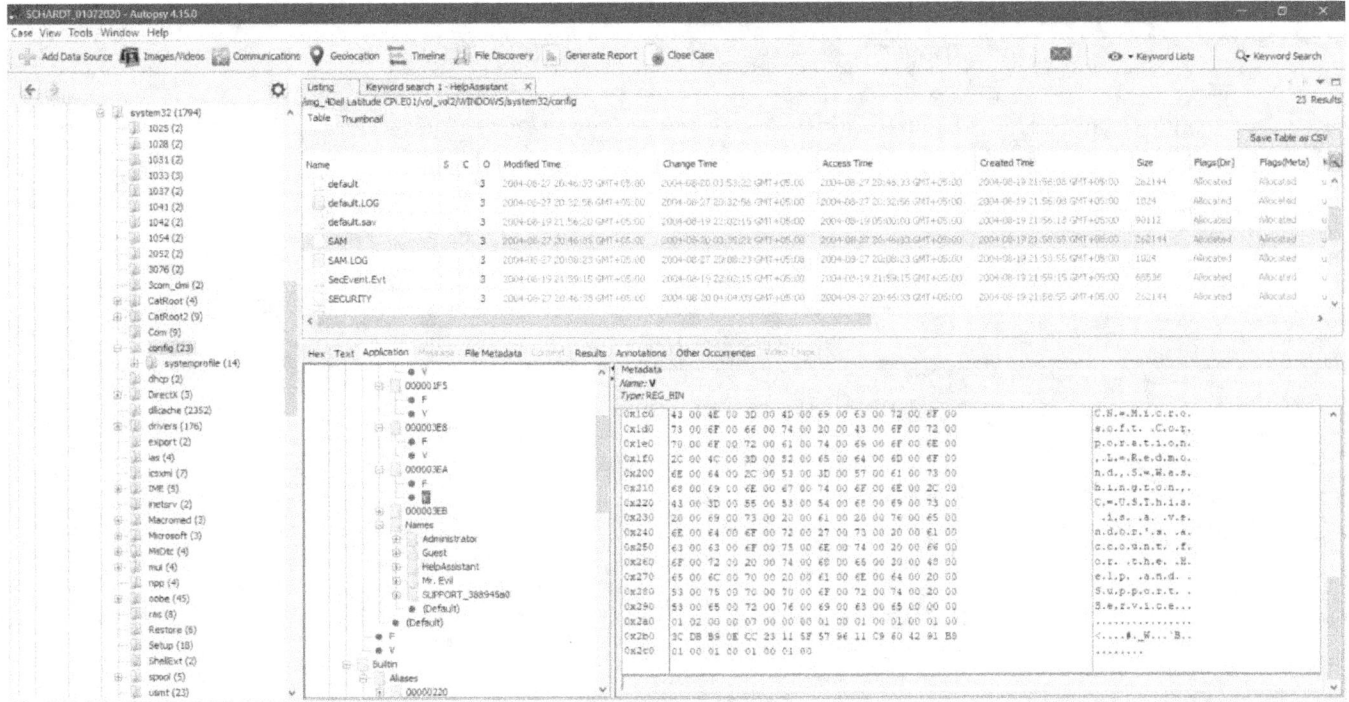

Picture 8: Existing accounts

10. What is the account name of the user who mostly uses the computer? The user that mostly uses the computer is **Mr.Evil**.

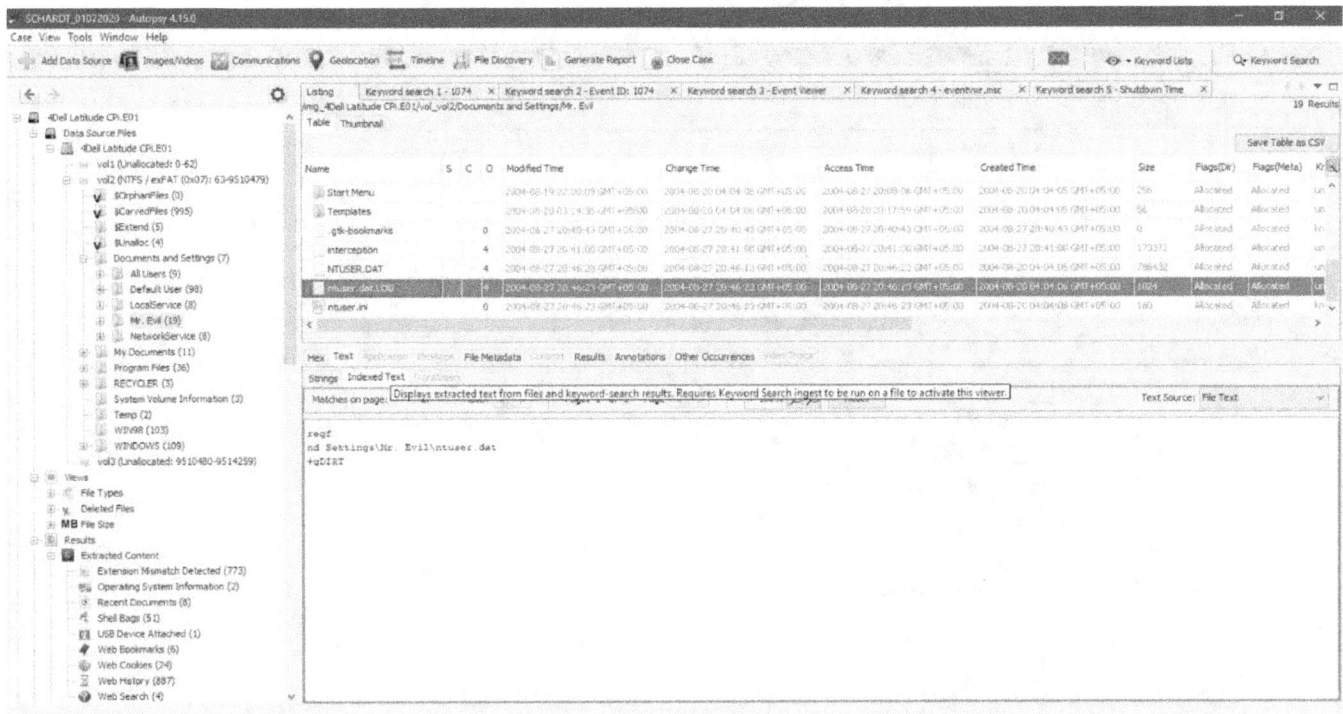

Picture 9: User mostly used the computer

11. Who was the last user to logon to the computer? Last user was **Mr.Evil**

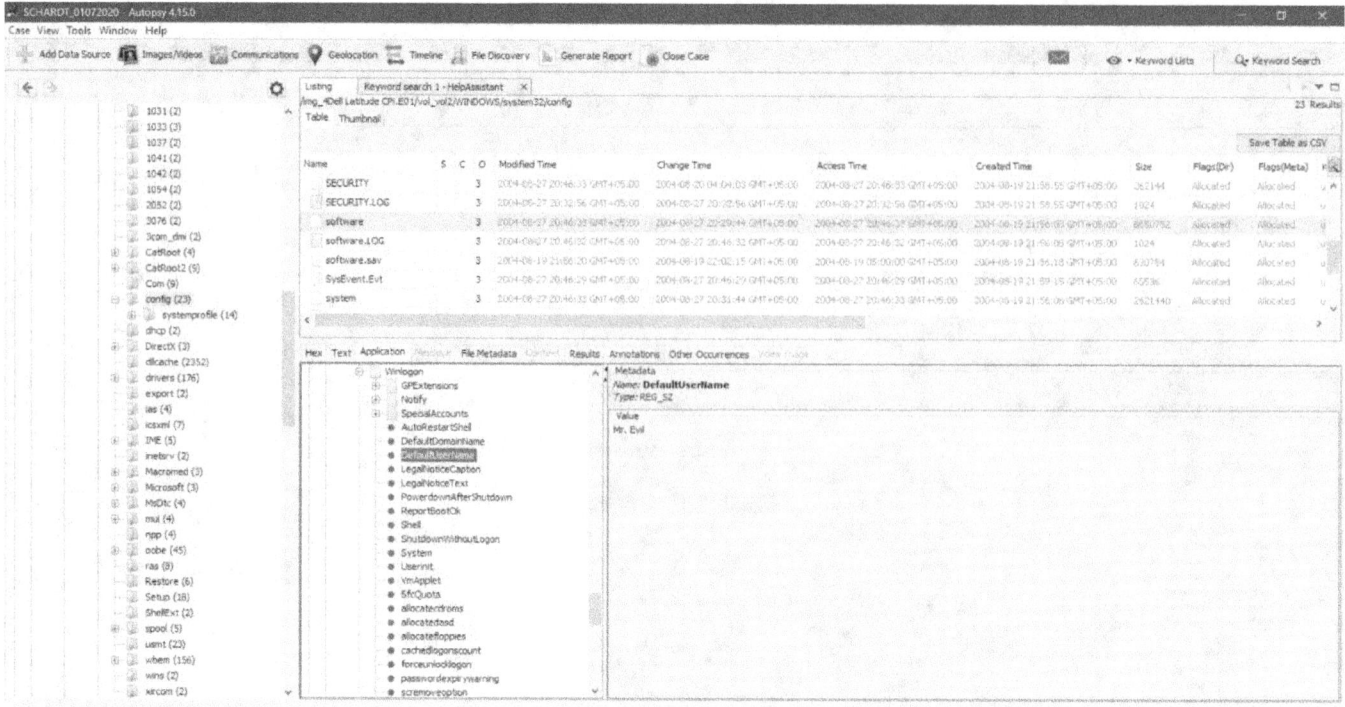

Picture 10:Last user

12. A search for the name of "G=r=e=g S=c=h=a=r=d=t" reveals multiple hits. One of these proves that G=r=e=g S=c=h=a=r=d=t is Mr. Evil and is also the administrator of this computer. What file is it? What software program does this file relate to? The file is the **irunin.ini** and is related to **Look@LAN**

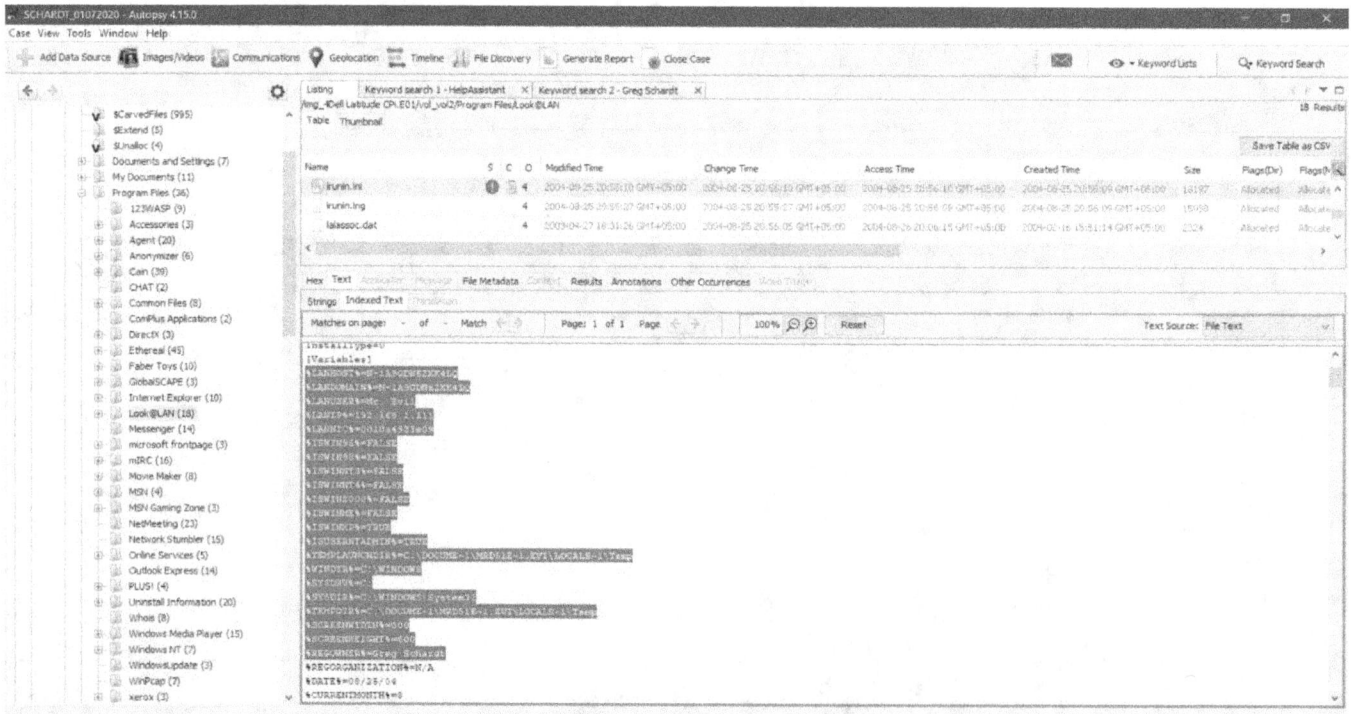

Picture 11:Mr.Evil is the Administrator

25

13. List the network cards used by this computer. There are two cards.

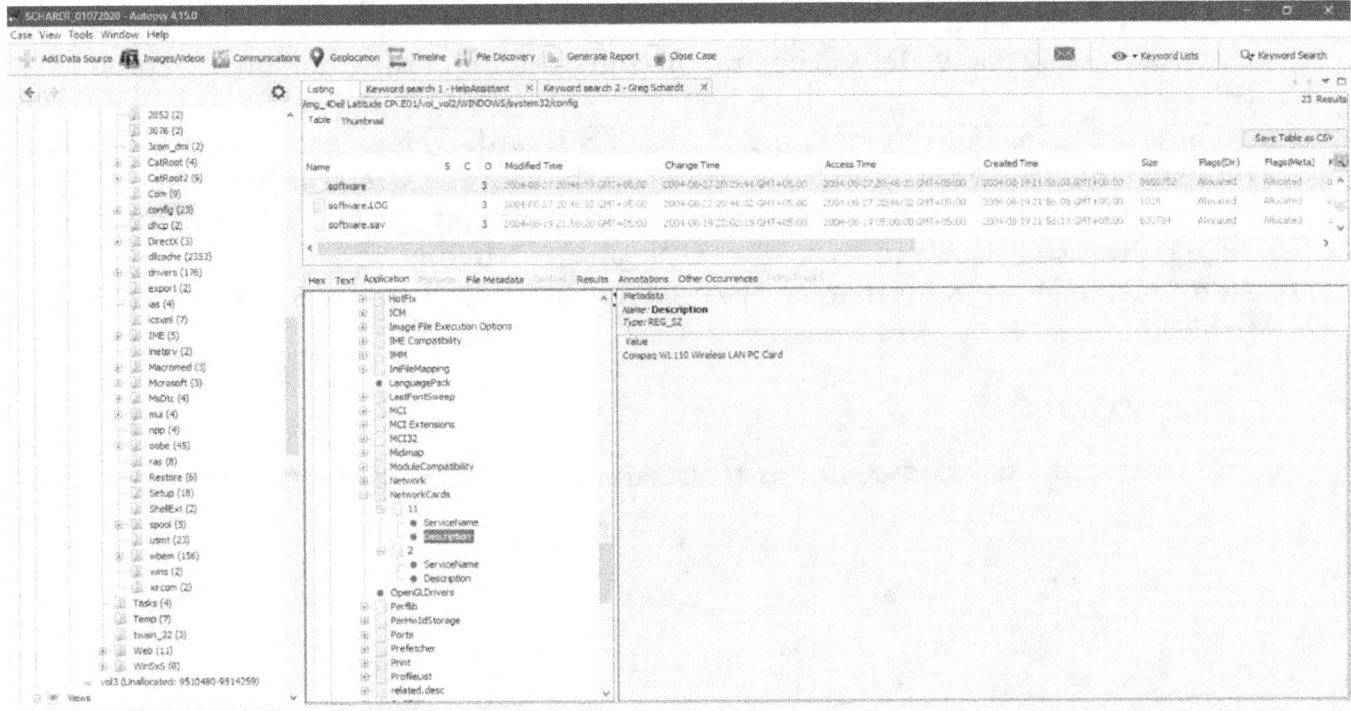

Picture 12: Wireless card

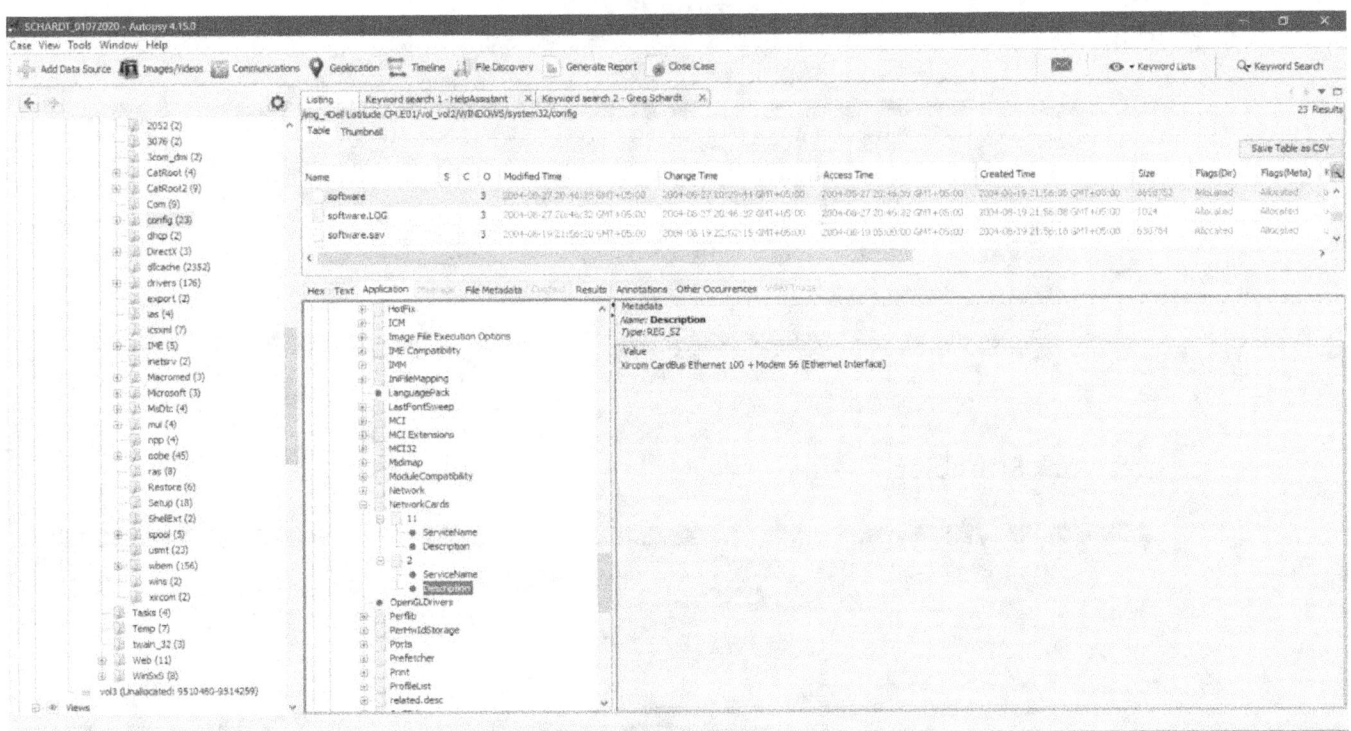

Picture 13: Ethernet interface card

14. This same file reports the IP address and MAC address of the computer. What are they? The information can be found in picture 11 and is the following:
    IP Address:**192.168.1.1**
    MAC Address:**0010a4933e09** (The first three digits refer to the company that produce this card)
15. An internet search for vendor name/model of NIC cards by MAC address can be used to find out which network interface was used. In the above answer, the first 3 hex characters of the MAC address report the vendor of the card. Which NIC card was used during the installation and set-up for LOOK@LAN? **Xircom**
16. Find 6 installed programs that may be used for hacking. There are 6 programs related to hacking.

    a. 123Wasp

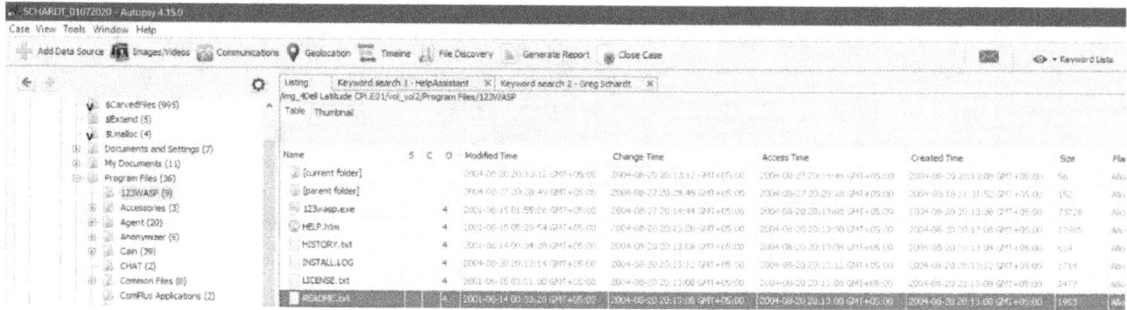

Picture 14:123Wasp

    b. Cain

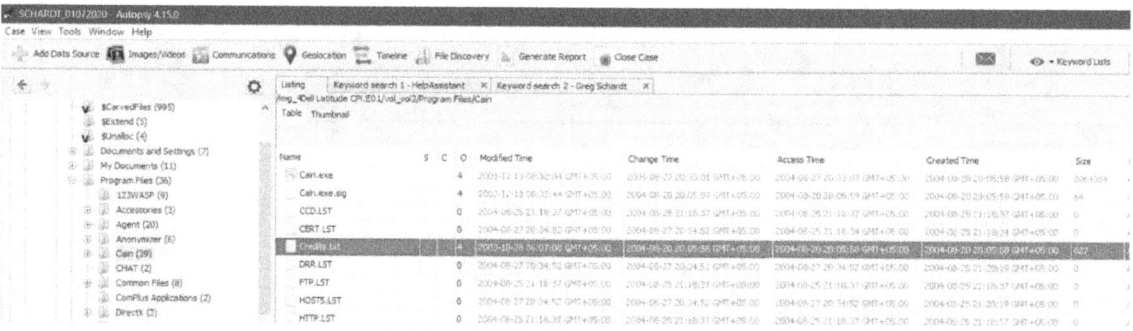

Picture 15:Cain

    c. Network Stumbler

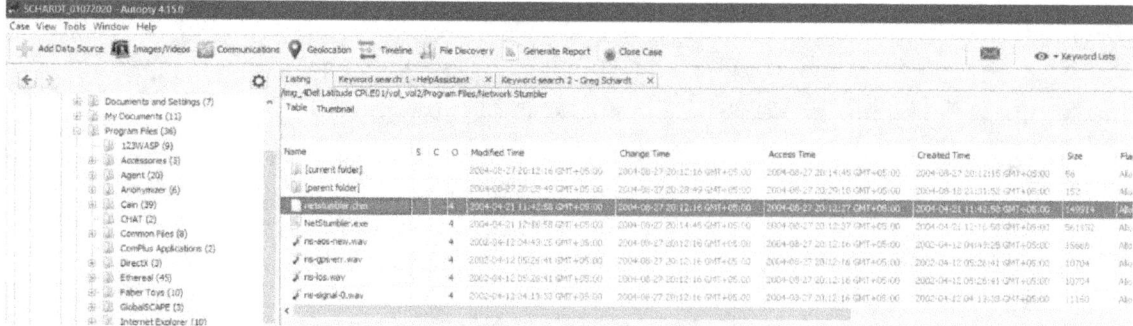

Picture 16:Network Stumbler

d. Look@LAN

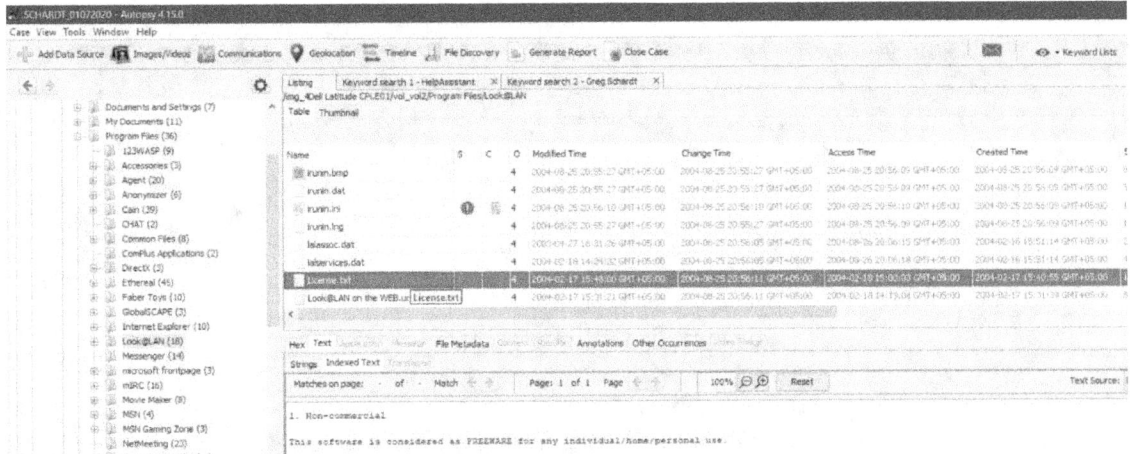

Picture 17:Look@LAN

e. mIRC

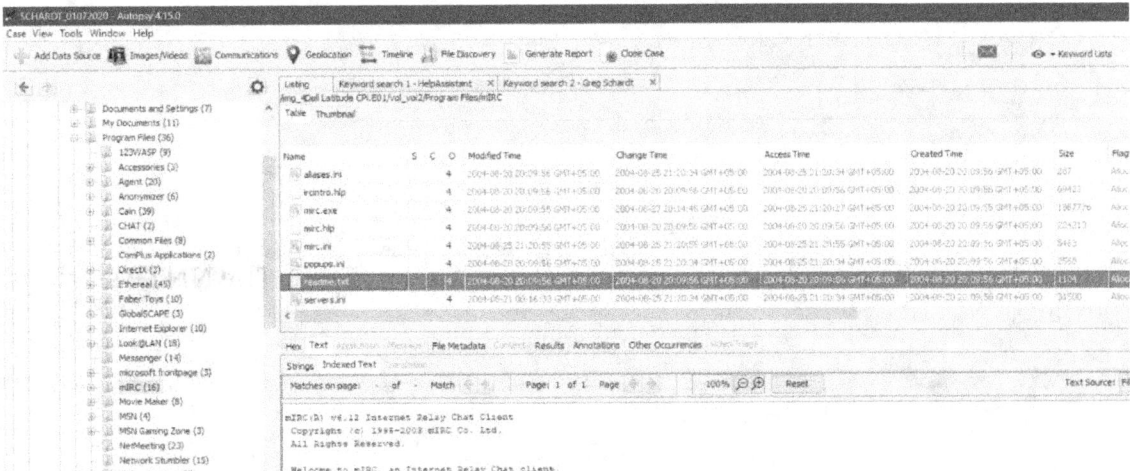

Picture 18:mIRC

f. Ethereal

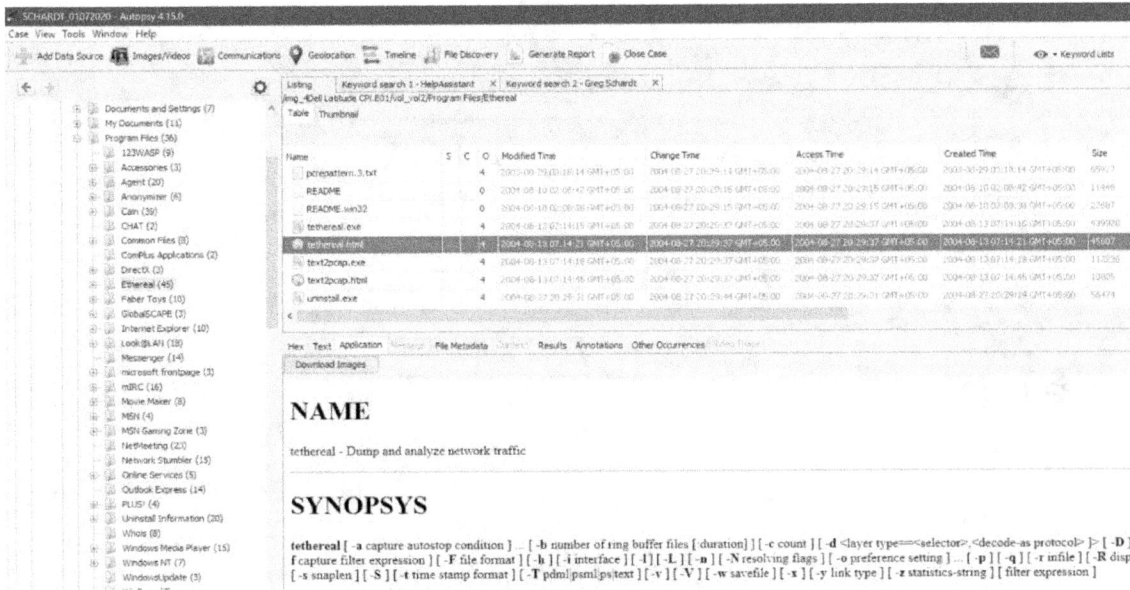

Picture 19:Ethereal

17. What is the SMTP email address for Mr. Evil? The SMTP email address for Mr.Evil is: **iswhoknowsme@sbcglobal.net**

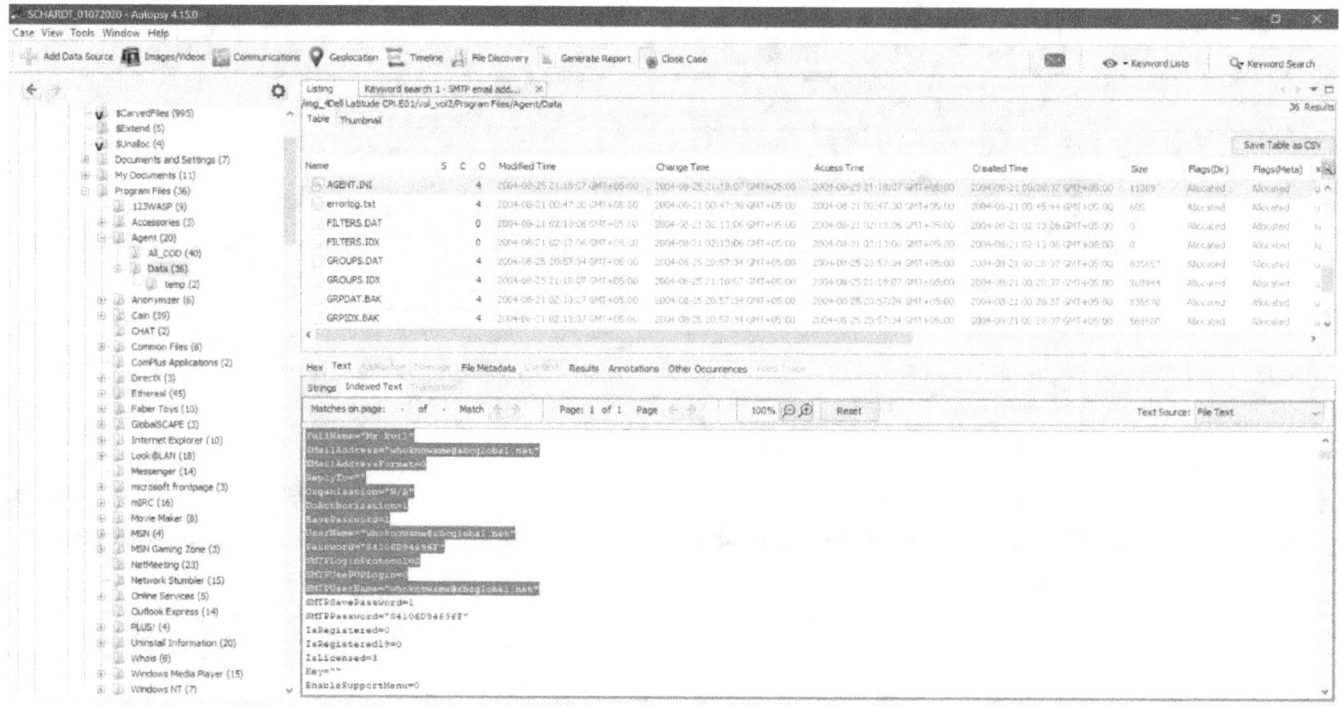

Picture 20:SMTP email address

18. What are the NNTP (news server) settings for Mr. Evil? The NNTP settings for Mr.Evil are:

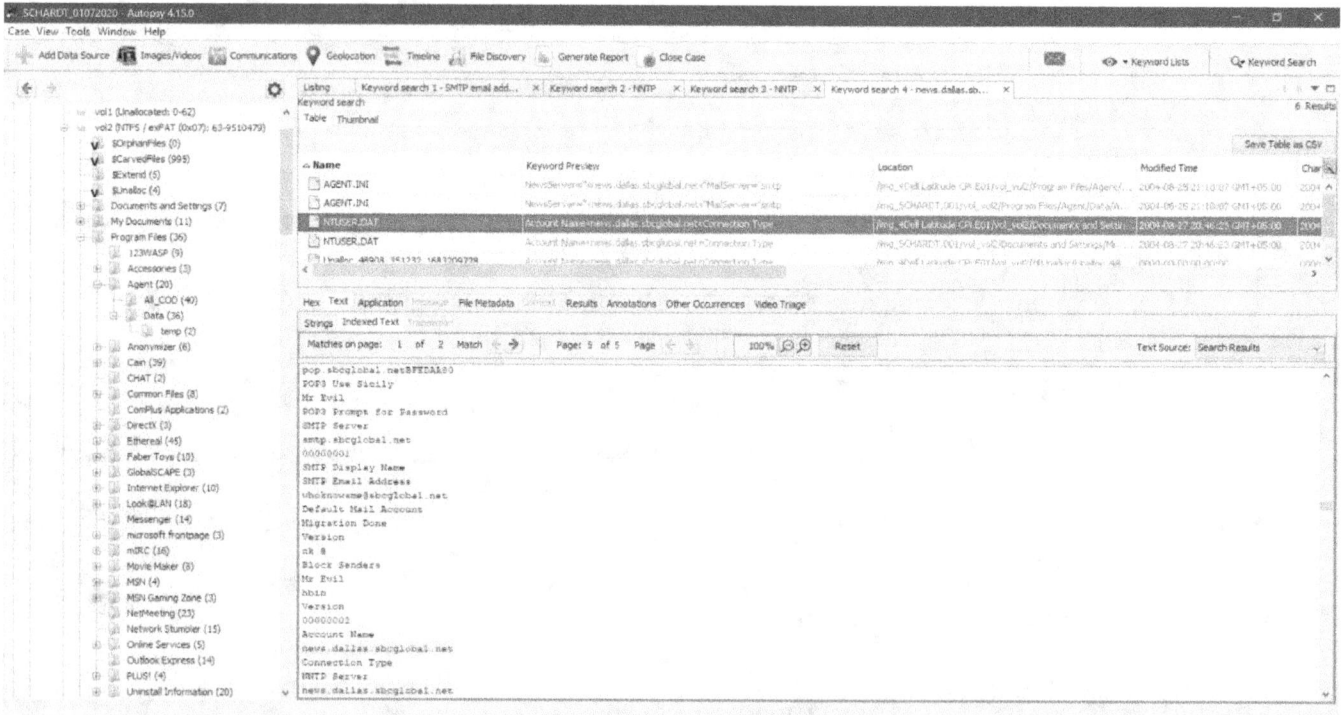

Picture 21:NNTP news server settings

19. What two installed programs show this information? MS Outlook Express and Forte Agent

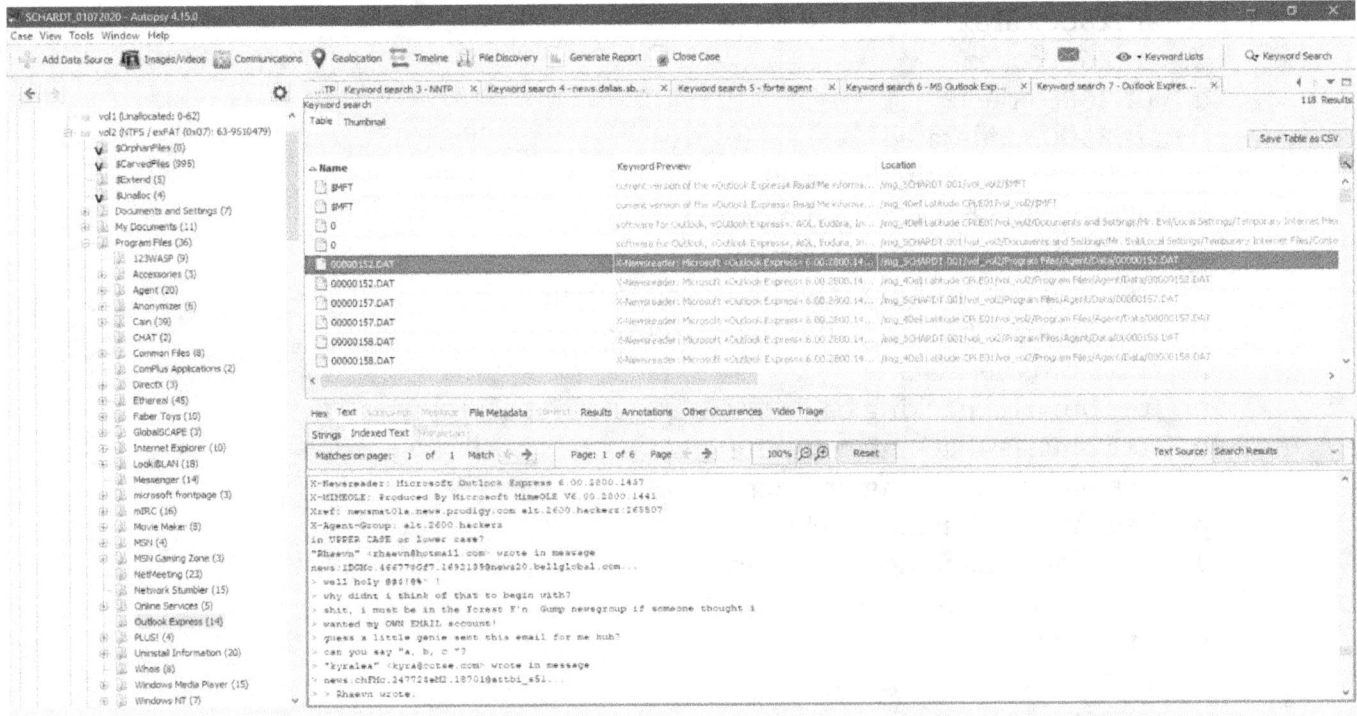

Picture 22: MS Outlook Express

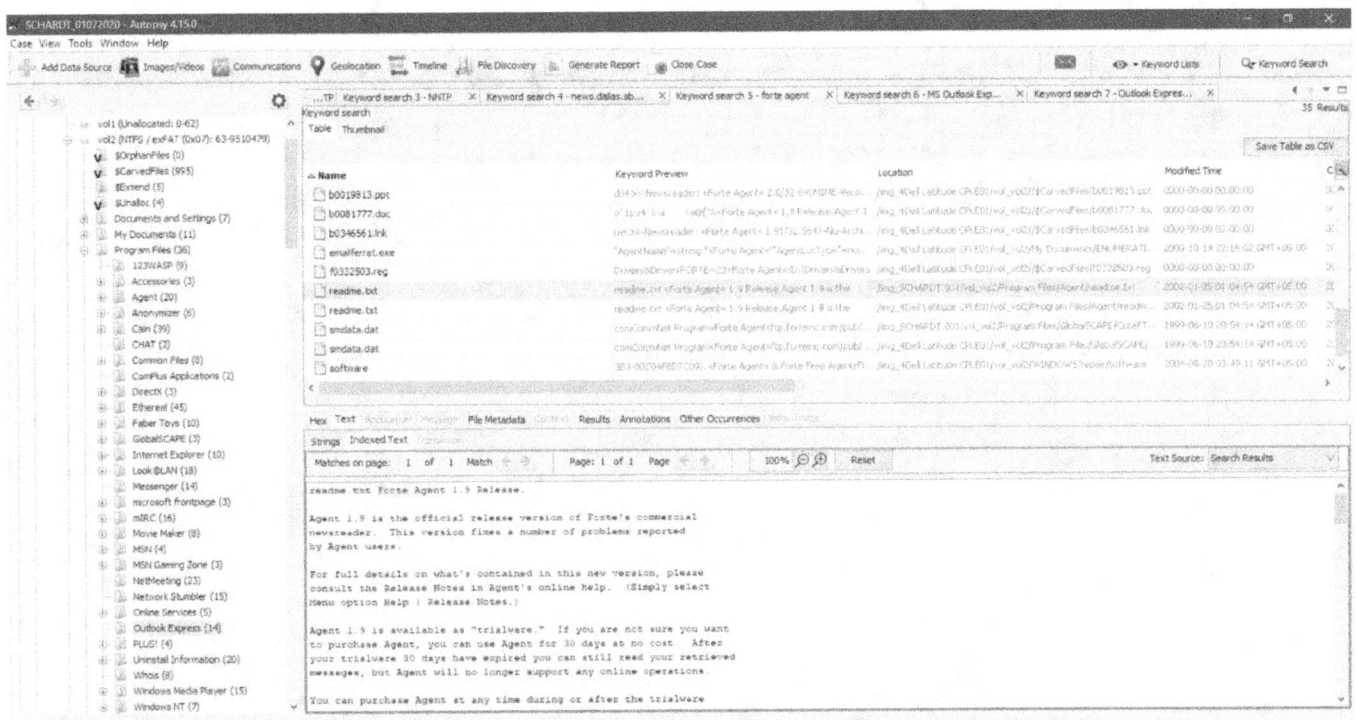

Picture 23: Forte Agent

20. List 5 newsgroups that Mr. Evil has subscribed to. News Groups found:
    a. alt.2600.phreakz
    b. alt.2600
    c. alt.2600.cardz
    d. alt.2600codez
    e. alt.2600.crackz
    f. alt.2600.moderated
    g. alt.binaries.hacking.utilities
    h. alt.stupidity.hackers.malicious
    i. free.binaries.hackers.malicious
    j. free.binaries.hacking.talentless.troll_haven
    k. free.binaries.hacking.talentless.troll-haven
    l. alt.nl.binaries.hack
    m. free.binaries.hacking.beginner
    n. free.binaries.hacking.computers
    o. free.binaries.hacking.utilities
    p. free.binaries.hacking.websites
    q. alt.binaries.hacking.computers
    r. alt.binaries.hacking.websites
    s. alt.dss.hack
    t. alt.binaries.hacking.beginner
    u. alt.hacking
    v. alt.2600.programz
    w. alt.2600.hackerz

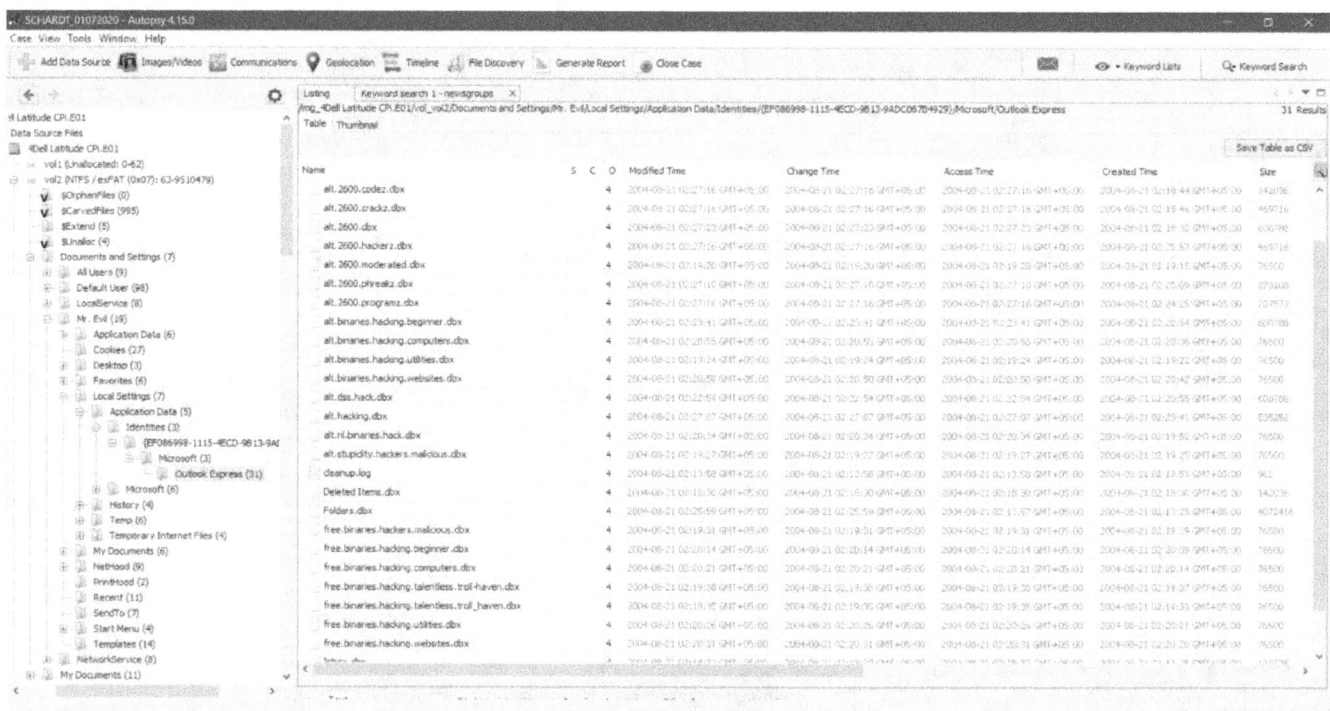

Picture 24:Newsgroups

21. A popular IRC (Internet Relay Chat) program called MIRC was installed. What are the user settings that was shown when the user was online and in a chat channel?
    a. user=**Mini Me**
    b. email=**none@of.ya**
    c. nick=**Mr**
    d. anick=**mrevilrulez**

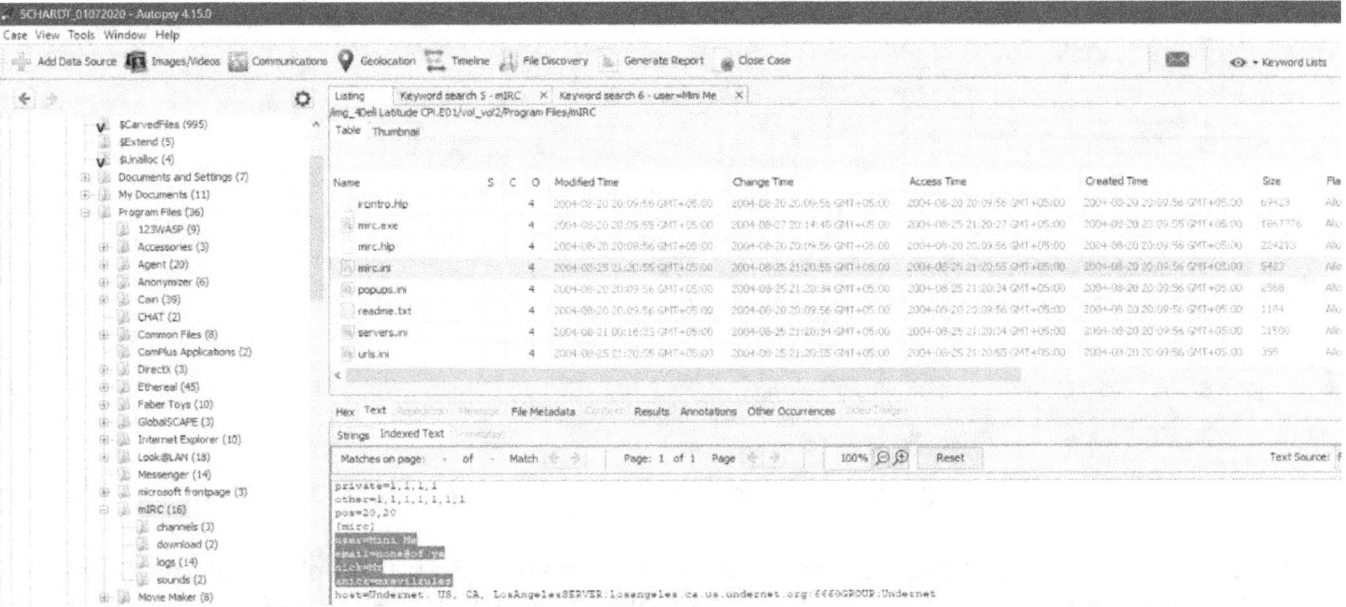

Picture 25:mIRC user settings

22. This IRC program has the capability to log chat sessions. List 3 IRC channels that the user of this computer accessed. IRC Channels found are:
    a. Chataholics.undernet.log
    b. Chataholics.undernet.log
    c. Cybercafé.undernet.log
    d. Elite.hackers.undernet.log
    e. evilfork.efnet.log
    f. funny.undernet.log
    g. houston.undernet.log
    h. Iso-warez.efnet.log
    i. Luxshell.undernet.log
    j. mp3xserv.undernet.log
    k. thedarktower.afternet.log
    l. ushells.undernet.log
    m. m5tar.undernet.log

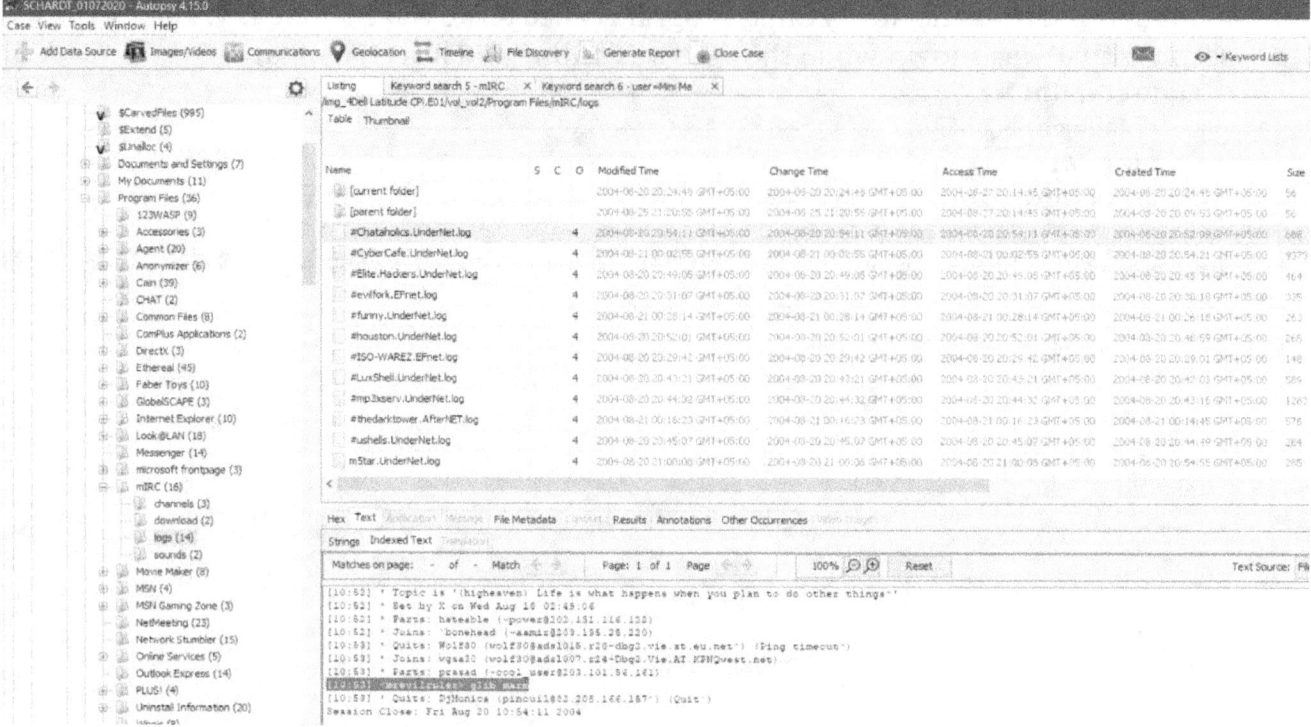

Picture 26: IRC channels that the user of this computer accessed

23. Ethereal, a popular "sniffing" program that can be used to intercept wired and wireless internet packets was also found to be installed. When TCP packets are collected and re-assembled, the default save directory is that users \My Documents directory. What is the name of the file that contains the intercepted data? The file is **Interception**

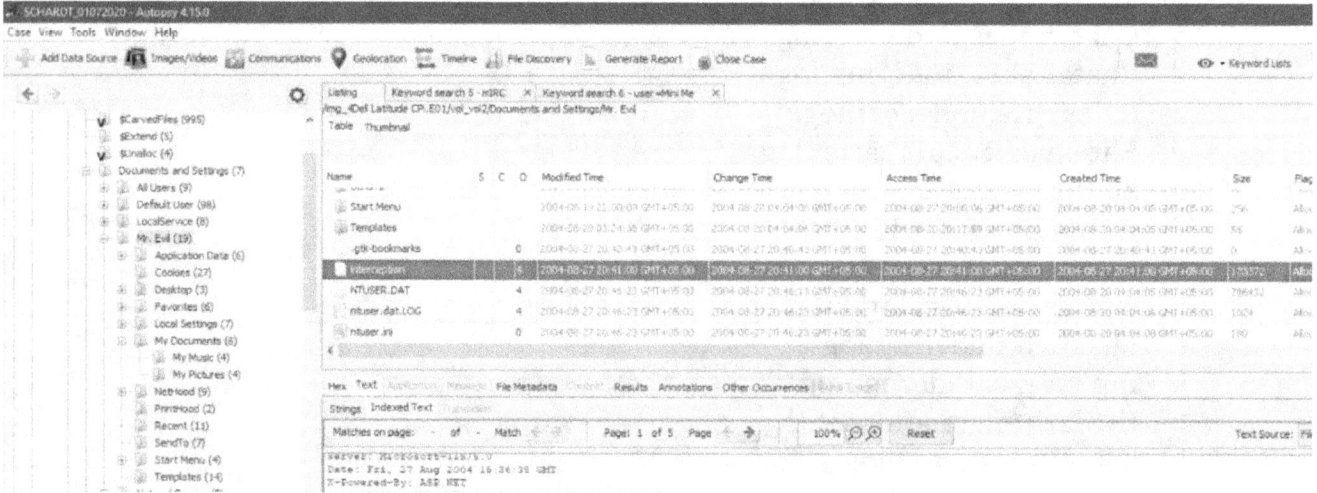

Picture 27: Re-assembled packets file

24. Viewing the file in a text format reveals much information about who and what was intercepted. What type of wireless computer was the victim (person who had his internet surfing recorded) using? **Windows CE (Pocket PC)**

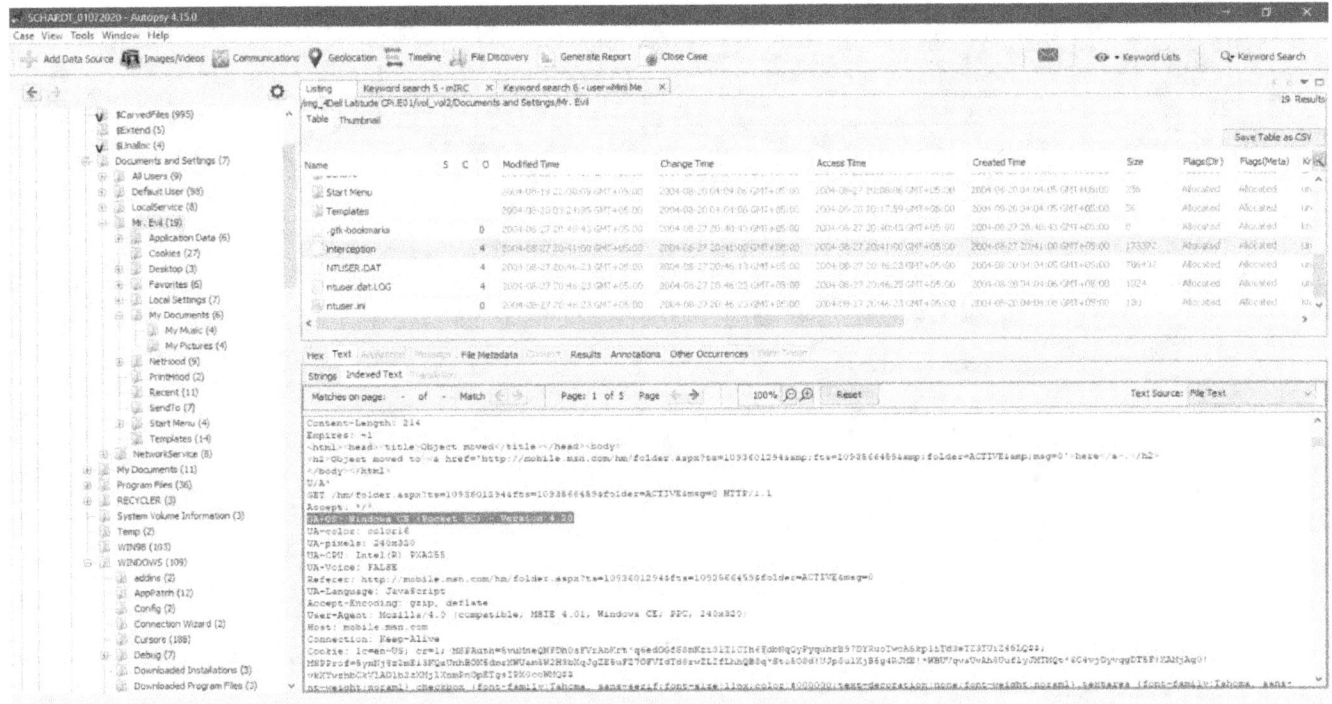

Picture 28: Victim's wireless computer

25. What websites was the victim accessing?
    a. Mobile.msn.com
    b. msn(hotmail) email

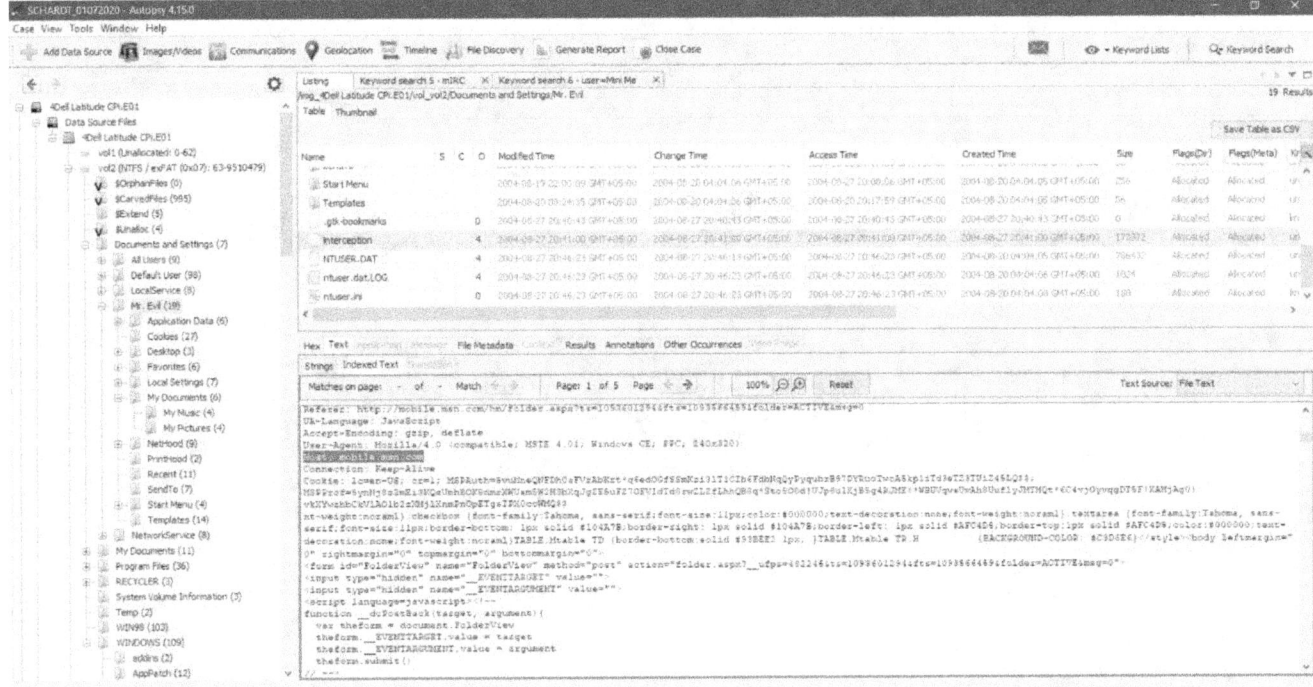

Picture 29: mobile.msn.com

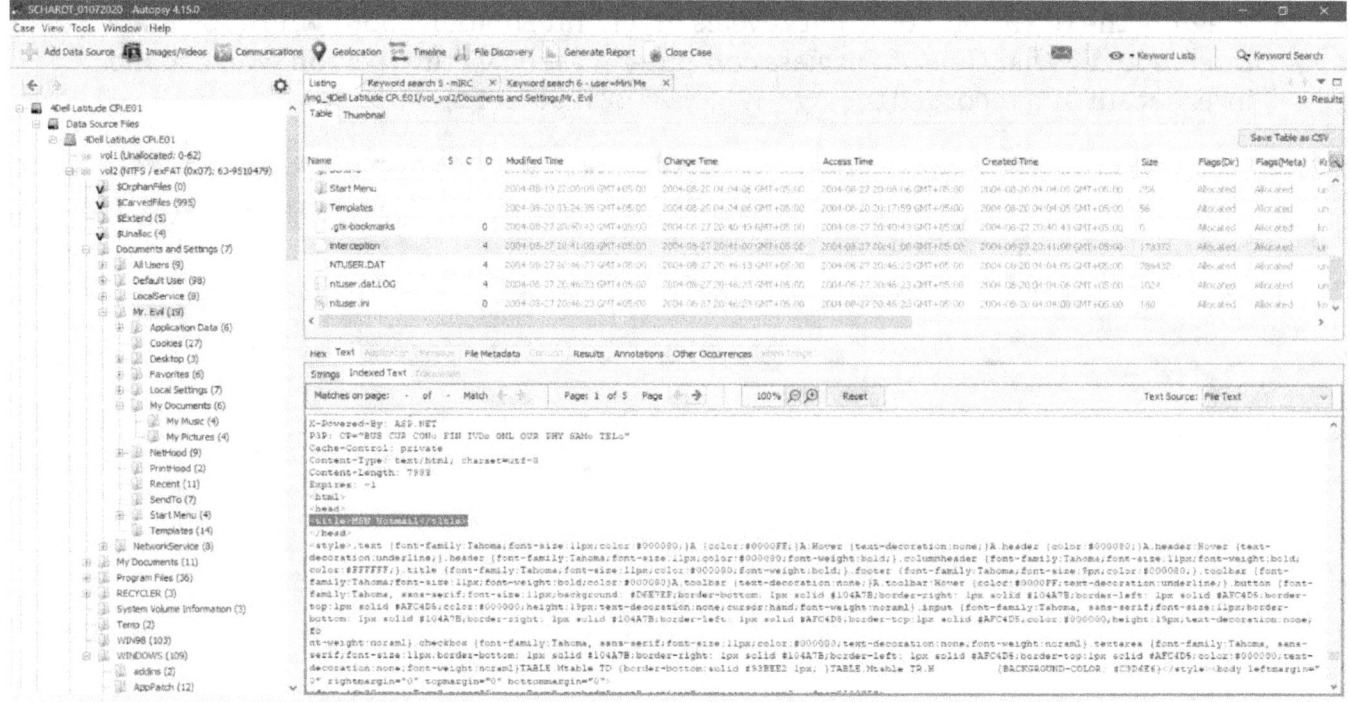

Picture 30: MSN Hotmail

26. Search for the main users web-based email address. What is it? **mrevilrulez@yahoo.com**

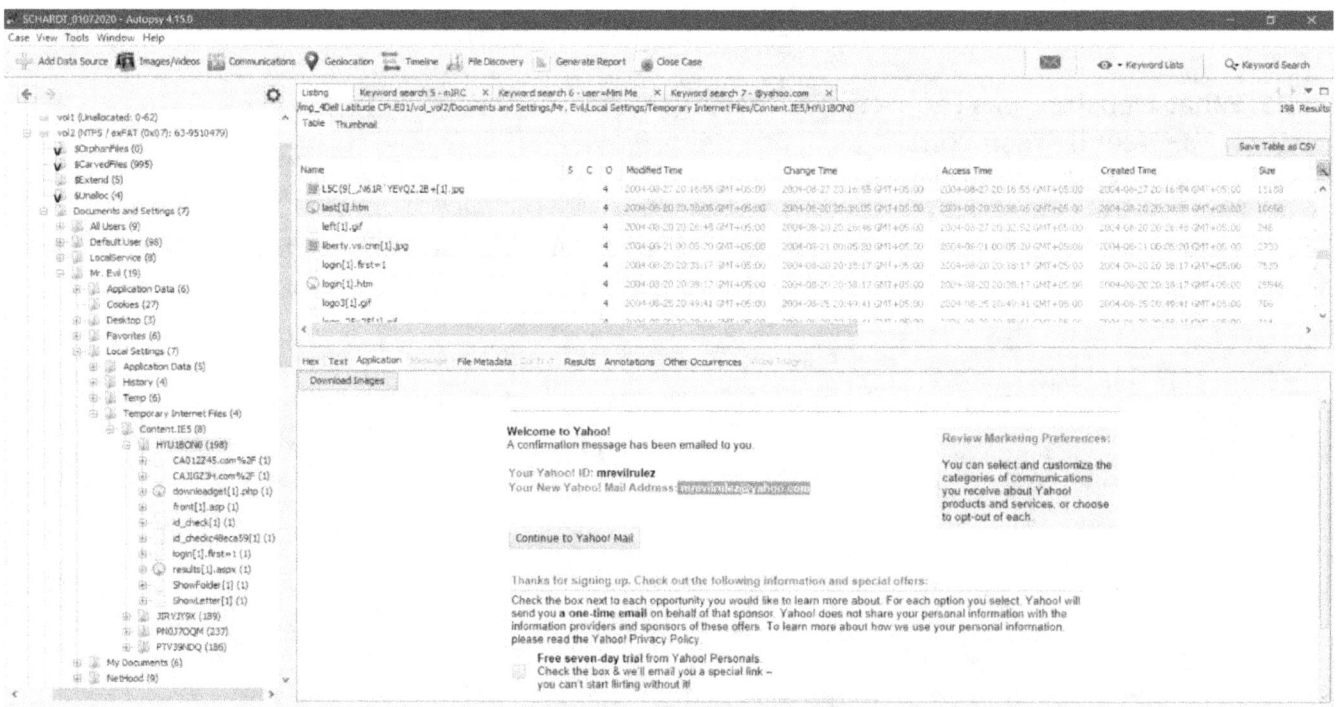

Picture 31: Main user's web-based email address

27. Yahoo mail, a popular web based email service, saves copies of the email under what file name? **Showletter[1].htm**

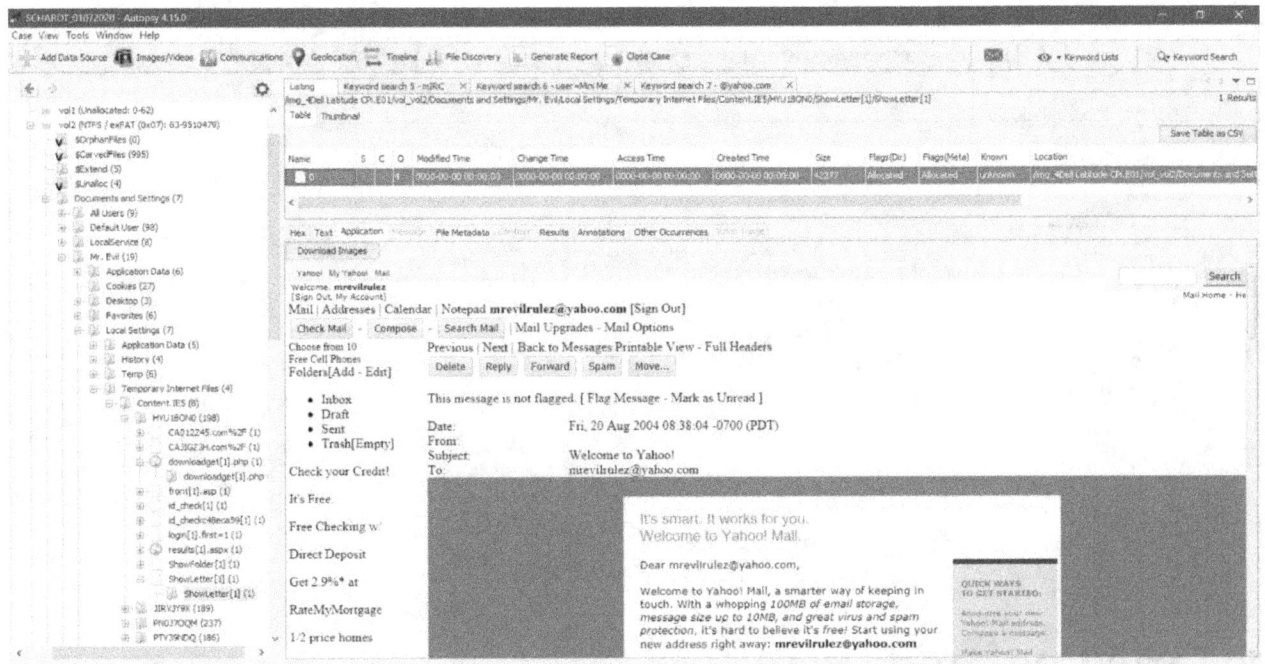

Picture 32:Showletter[1].htm

28. How many executable files are in the recycle bin? **4 executables**

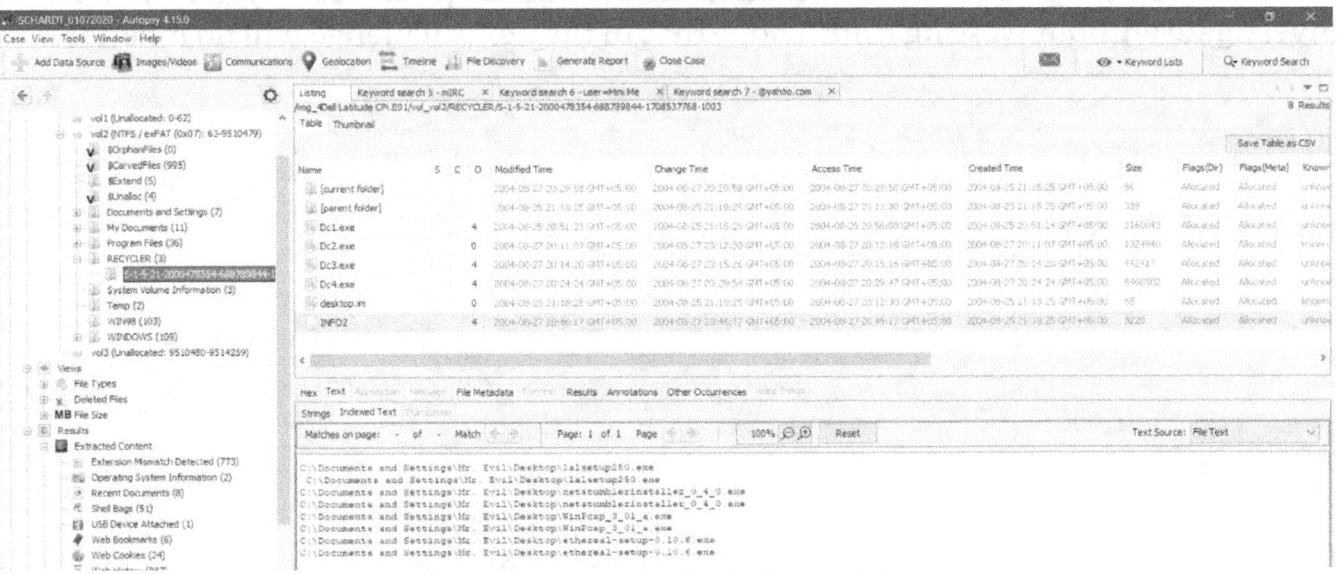

Picture 33:Executable files in the Recycle Bin

29. Are these files really deleted? **No**
30. How many files are actually reported to be deleted by the file system? **3**
31. Perform a Anti-Virus check. Are there any viruses on the computer? **Yes, there is one interesting file, possible malware.**

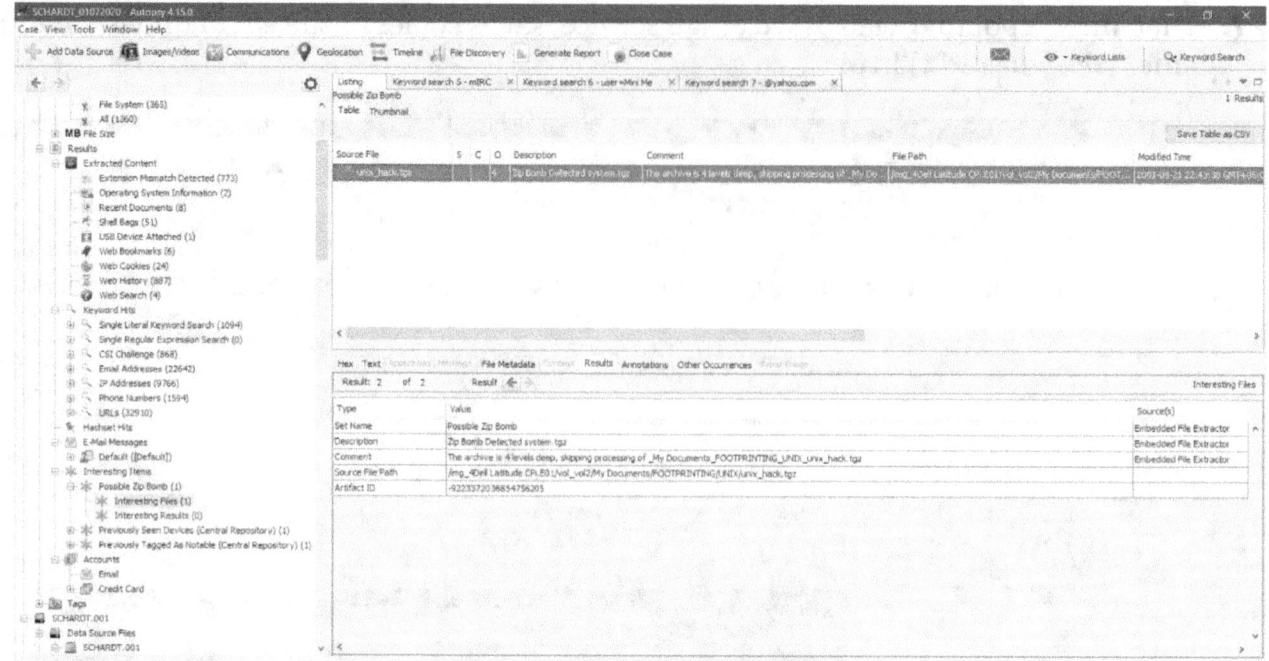

Picture 34:Possible malware

Lessons Learned

During the investigation I had the chance to search and learn for the location of many windows files, registry entries location and build a guide for myself on how to investigate without wasting time. I hope that in the next challenge will do it better.

Finding the Evidence - Keith Swagler

CSI Linux Forensic Challenge Installation and setup:

Due to CSI Linux being a virtual appliance, it was relatively easy to install. Being a KVM/QEMU user and not a VirtualBox or VMWare user it was a little bit more difficult but doable. I wrote on my blog on how to do this and even wrote a script for this situation. Unfortunately, the script only works with one disk image, not multiple per file, so I had to do it the manual way. It was not more than to be expected from being a KVM user, but still I usually prefer ISO images to already built appliances.

Especially considering that many DFIR distros do double duty to run live and serve as evidence collection distros. Overall, just again a minor inconvenience.

Extra tools installed:

- Sleuthkit
- RegRipper Fred

Sleuthkit is in the default repos, so installation is as easy as running:

> $ sudo apt install sleuthkit

I do find it odd that Autopsy is installed and even recommended when sleuthkit was not installed. Due to its small size but huge impact, and since they are from the same author as Autopsy.

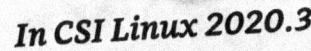

In CSI Linux 2020.3 Sleuthkit and FRED have been added and the RegRipper has been resolved

RegRipper is a Registry parser and something I find hugely valuable when performing Windows Forensics. I was disappointed to find that it was installed but not working correctly for me. I ended up redownloading and following the instructions on DFIR blog to get it working again. I ended up writing a set of scripts to automate it in the future. Apparently I am behind the times and Version 3 is out, so maybe it will work easier in that version.

FRED is a Linux compatible Windows Registry viewer similar to the one found on Windows computers. When RegRipper does not have a plugin for a certain registry key, Fred is incredibly valuable.

Installation is as simple as adding the authors repo to your machine as per the instructions, and running apt install. Full commands are

```
$ sudo wget -P /etc/apt/sources.list.d/ deb.pinGUIn.lu/pinGUIn.lu.list
$ wget -q deb.pinGUIn.lu/debsign_public.key -O- | sudo apt-key add -
$ sudo apt-get update
$ sudo apt install fred
```

After the second boot of my CSI Linux VM Autopsy would not run for me. It was mildly frustrating as I am sure there were many answers, I missed because of it, but by the time I noticed it was too late to do much troubleshooting and meet the deadline.

When adding the image to Autopsy I disabled Plaso parser.

There are some answers in which the files are mentioned. I mounted the image to examine the filesystem directly using the following steps.

Create directories "/mnt/schardt/" "/mnt/schardtraw"

```
$ mkdir "/mnt/schardt" "/mnt/schardtraw"
```

Find the offset of the main partition by running: mmls on SCHARDT.001

```
$ mmls "/home/csi/Documents/Cases/SCHARDT.001"
```

```
csi@csi-analyst:~/Documents/Cases/CSIlinux$ mmls SCHARDT.001
DOS Partition Table
Offset Sector: 0
Units are in 512-byte sectors

      Slot       Start        End          Length       Description
000:  Meta       0000000000   0000000000   0000000001   Primary Table (#0)
001:  -------    0000000000   0000000062   0000000063   Unallocated
002:  000:000    0000000063   0009510479   0009510417   NTFS / exFAT (0x07)
003:  -------    0009510480   0009514259   0000003780   Unallocated
csi@csi-analyst:~/Documents/Cases/CSIlinux$
```

Mount the image using affuse, which groups all of the disk images together into one "device" for other commands like mount to more easily understand.

```
$ sudo affuse SCHARDT.001 "/mnt/schardt"
```

Using the offset we found in mmls 32256 = (the offset * the sector size (512))

```
$ sudo mount -o loop,ro,offset=32256 "/mnt/schardt/SCHARDT.001.raw" "/mnt/schardtraw"
```

A quick note, could also be written in bash as $((63 * 512)) ie

> $ sudo mount -o loop,ro,offset=$((63 * 512))"/mnt/schardt/SCHARDT.001.raw" "/mnt/schardtraw"

What is the image hash? Does the acquisition and verification hash match?

The images hashes were only available for the SCHARDT images. The hash files from the acquisition log (SCHARDT.LOG) and the computed hashes do match. Also, of note images 006 and 007 are the same, leading us to believe that those images are in fact completely empty.

28a9b613d6eefe8a0515ef0a675bdebd	SCHARDT.001
c7227e7eea82d2186632573797679a7c4	SCHARDT.002
ebba35acd7b8aa85a5a7c13f3dd733d2	SCHARDT.003
669b6636dcb4783fd5509c4710856c59	SCHARDT.004
c46e5760e3821522ee81e675422025bb	SCHARDT.005
99511901da2dea772005b5d0d764e750	SCHARDT.006
99511901da2dea772005b5d0d764e750	SCHARDT.007
8194a79a5356df79883ae2dc7415929f	SCHARDT.008

What operating system was used on the computer?

Running mmls from Sleuthkit to see the partitions on the raw disk.

```
csi@csi-analyst:~/Documents/Cases/CSIlinux$ mmls SCHARDT.001
DOS Partition Table
Offset Sector: 0
Units are in 512-byte sectors

      Slot       Start        End          Length       Description
000:  Meta       0000000000   0000000000   0000000001   Primary Table (#0)
001:  -------    0000000000   0000000062   0000000063   Unallocated
002:  000:000    0000000063   0009510479   0009510417   NTFS / exFAT (0x07)
003:  -------    0009510480   0009514259   0000003780   Unallocated
csi@csi-analyst:~/Documents/Cases/CSIlinux$
```

As we can see the File system format is either NTFS or exFAT so it is likely a Windows OS, but we don't know what version.

Using the fsstat command using the offset that was determined by the mmls output we can see the version is reported as Windows XP.

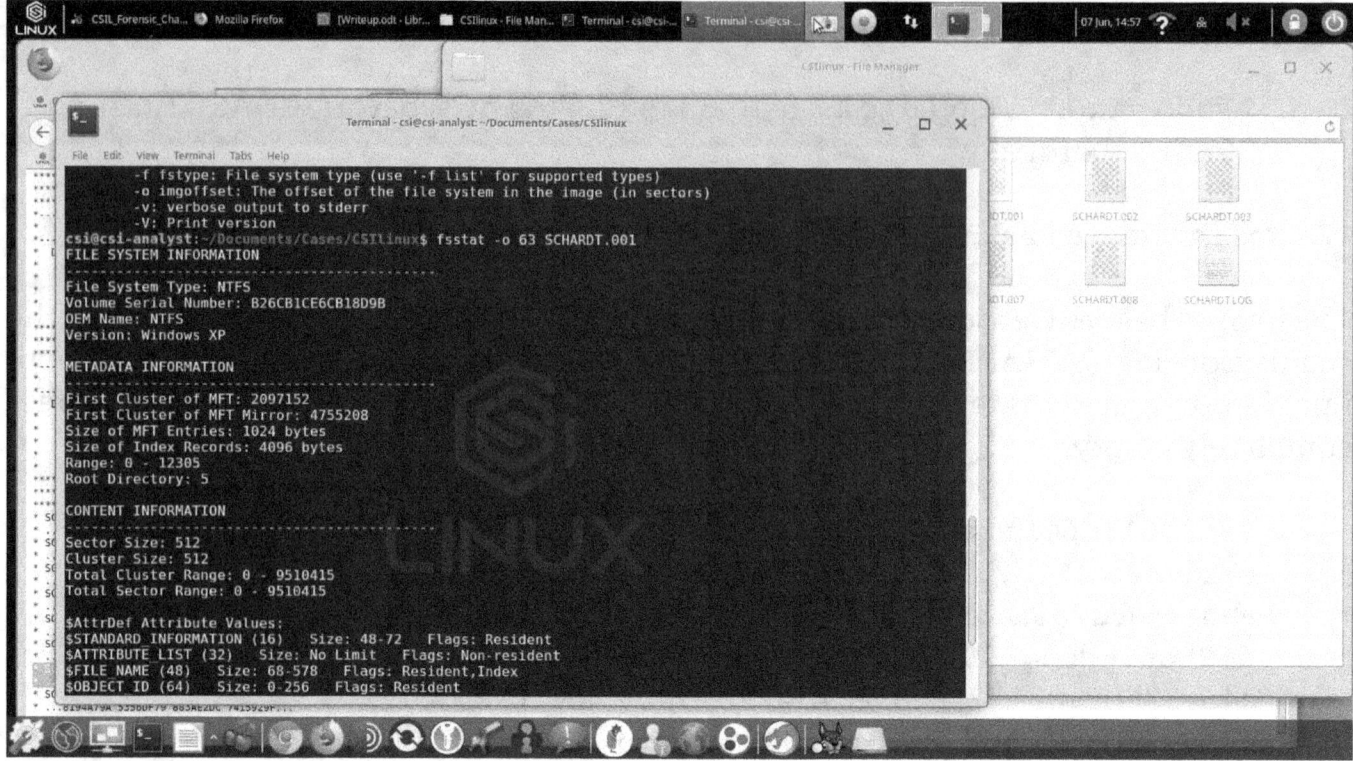

When was the install date?

Reference: forensics-matters.com/2018/09/15/find-out-windows-installation-date/

The install date should be under Windows NT. I instead accidentally clicked Windows and explored around a bit and found the key

> SOFTWARE\Microsoft\Windows\CurrentVersion\Installer\User Data\S-1-5-18\Products\ 0B79C053C7D38EE4AB9A00CB3B5D2472\InstallProperties

The value of key **InstallDate** is 20040819, which would indicate **August 19th, 2004.**

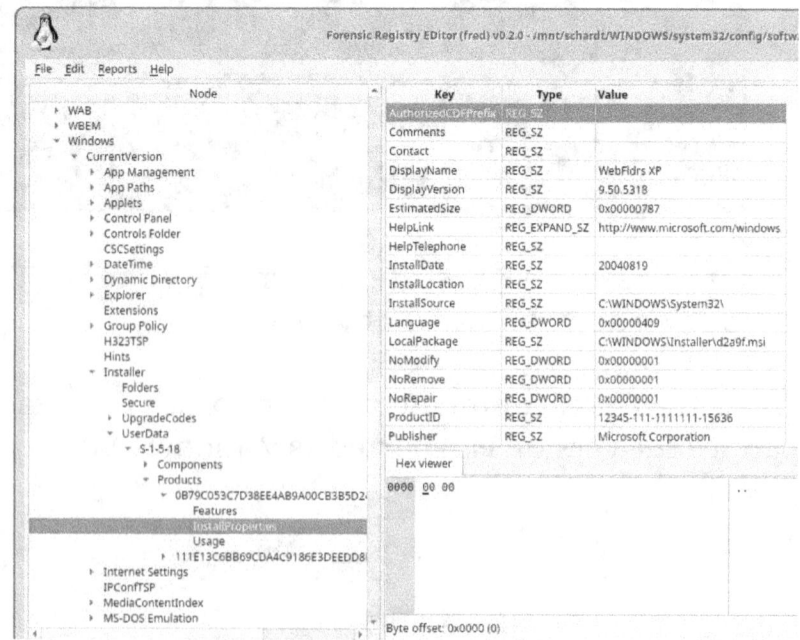

What is the timezone settings?

Central Time, currently in Daylight savings.

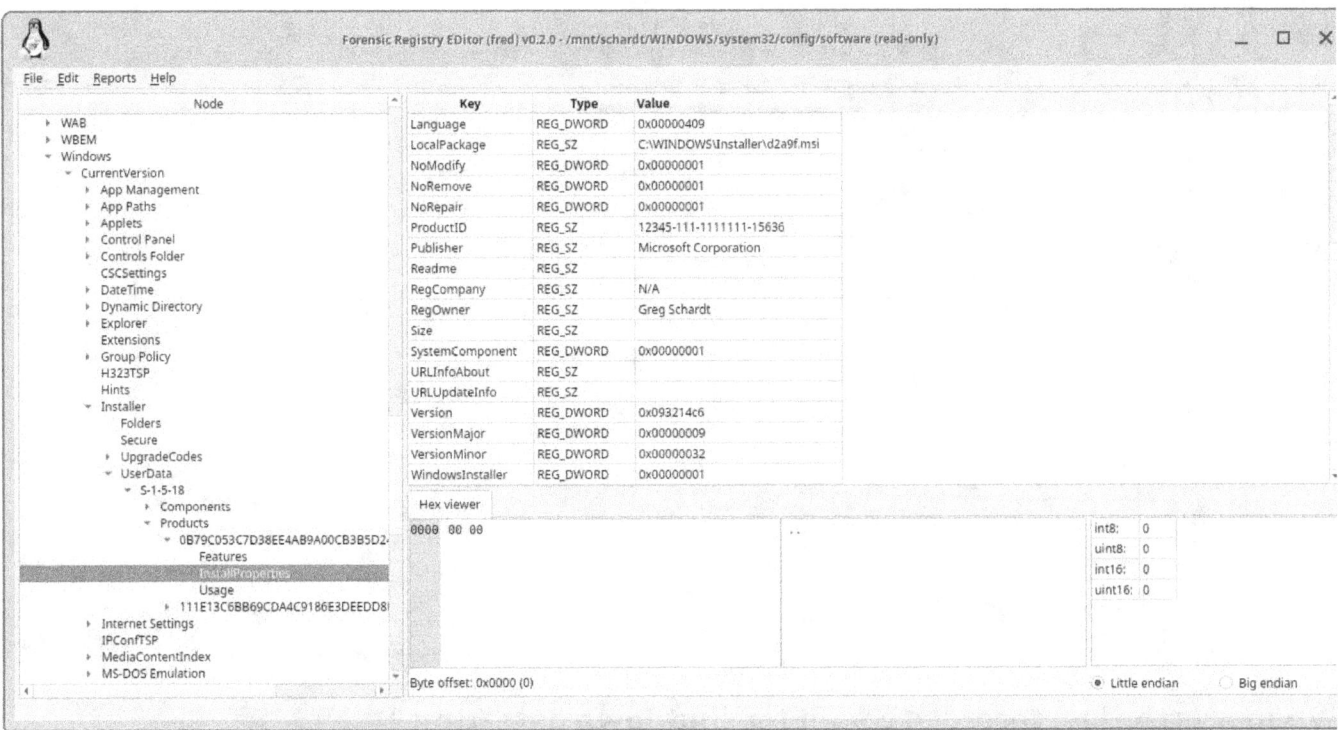

Who is the registered owner?

Using the same parent key as the install date the registered owner is **Greg Schardt**

What is the computer account name?

Using **compname** plugin for **RegRipper** we can see it is **N-1A9ODN6ZXK4LQ**

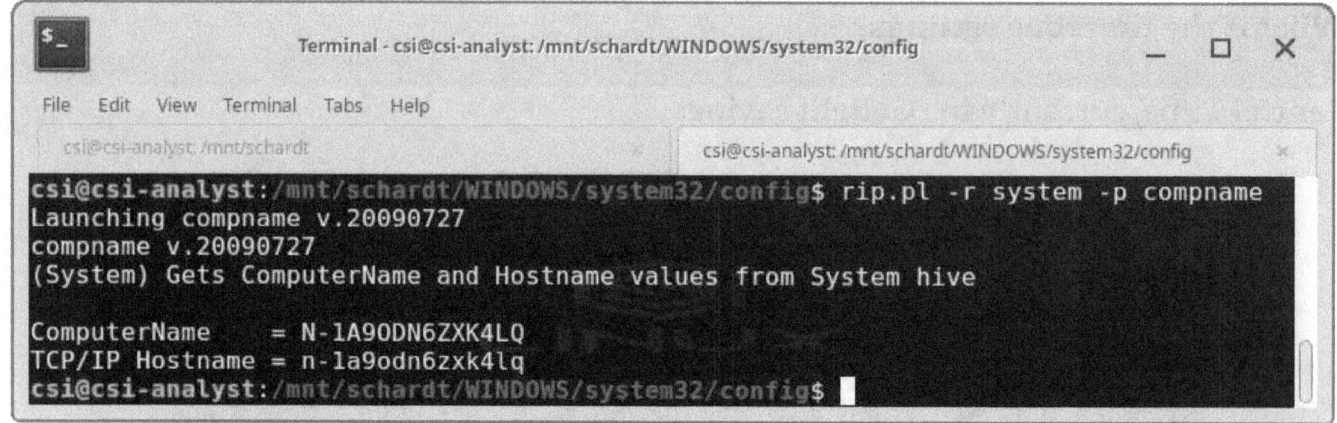

What is the primary domain name?

In the *SOFTWARE\Microsoft\Windows NT\CurrentVersion\Winlogon* key we can find the *DefaultDomainName* is "**N-1A9ODN6ZXK4LQ**" the same as the computer name, which is common in individual installations.

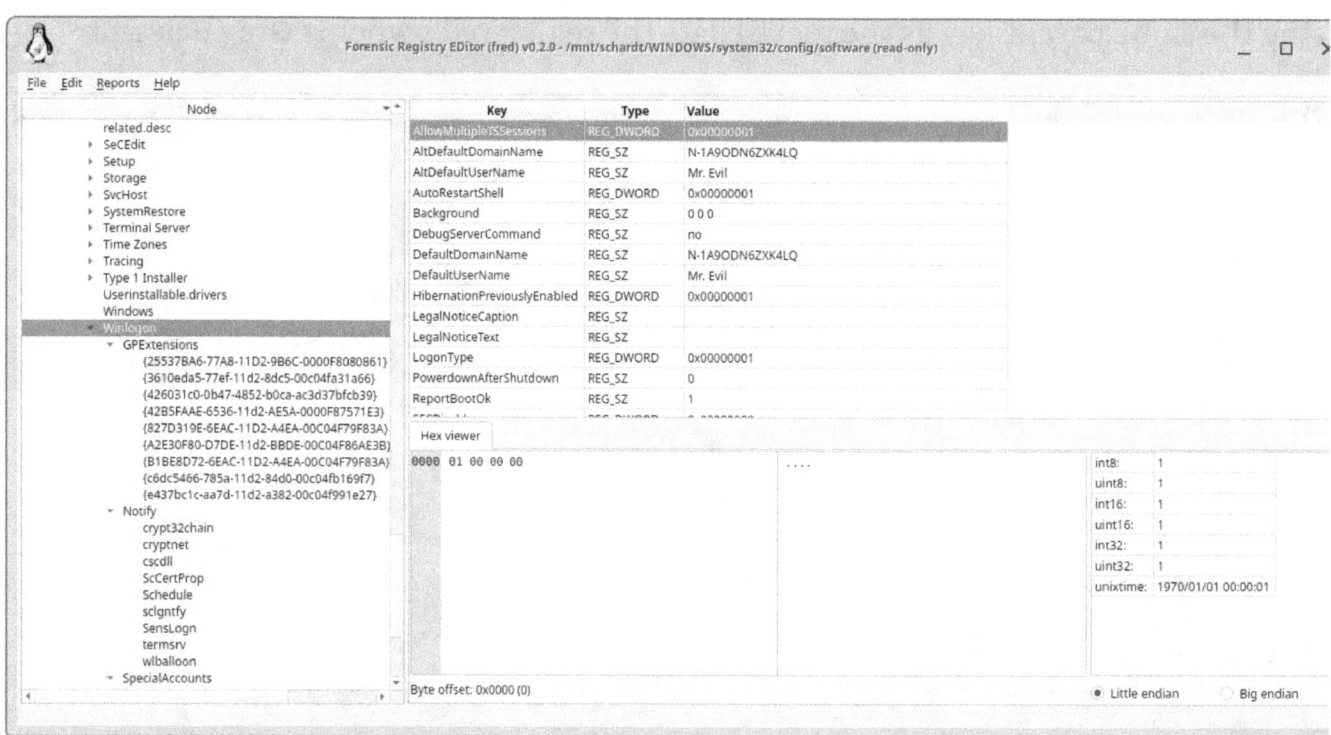

When was the last recorded computer shutdown date/time?

According to the registry the last shutdown time was. **Fri Aug 27 15:46:33 2004 (UTC)**

![terminal screenshot]

How many accounts are recorded (total number)?

By counting the number of accounts in samparse (see screenshot below) the computer has **5** accounts.

What is the account name of the user who mostly uses the computer?

RegRipper samparse plugin we can see that **Mr. Evil** has logged into the computer 15 times, while the other users have login counts of zero.

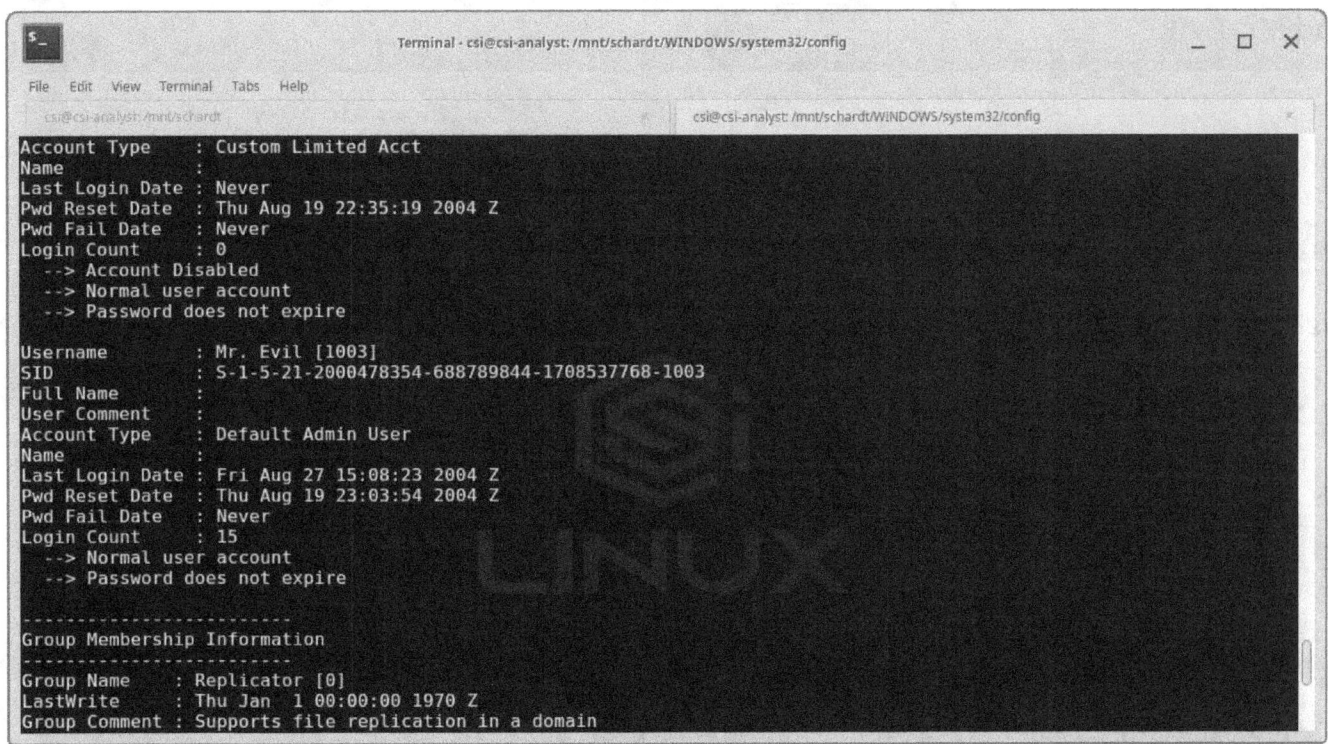

Who was the last user to logon to the computer?

According to **samparse** in the answer above **Mr. Evil** is the only user to have logged in.

A search for the name of Greg Schardt reveals multiple hits. One of these proves that Greg is Mr. Evil and is also the administrator of this computer. What file is it? What software program does this file relate to?

While I'm not certain what the first part of the questions relates to, we can see that Greg Schardt is the registered owner of the laptop and has the local account named "Mr. Evil". Given that there is only one user account on the computer as seen previously we can say that Greg Schardt is the administrator and Mr. Evil.

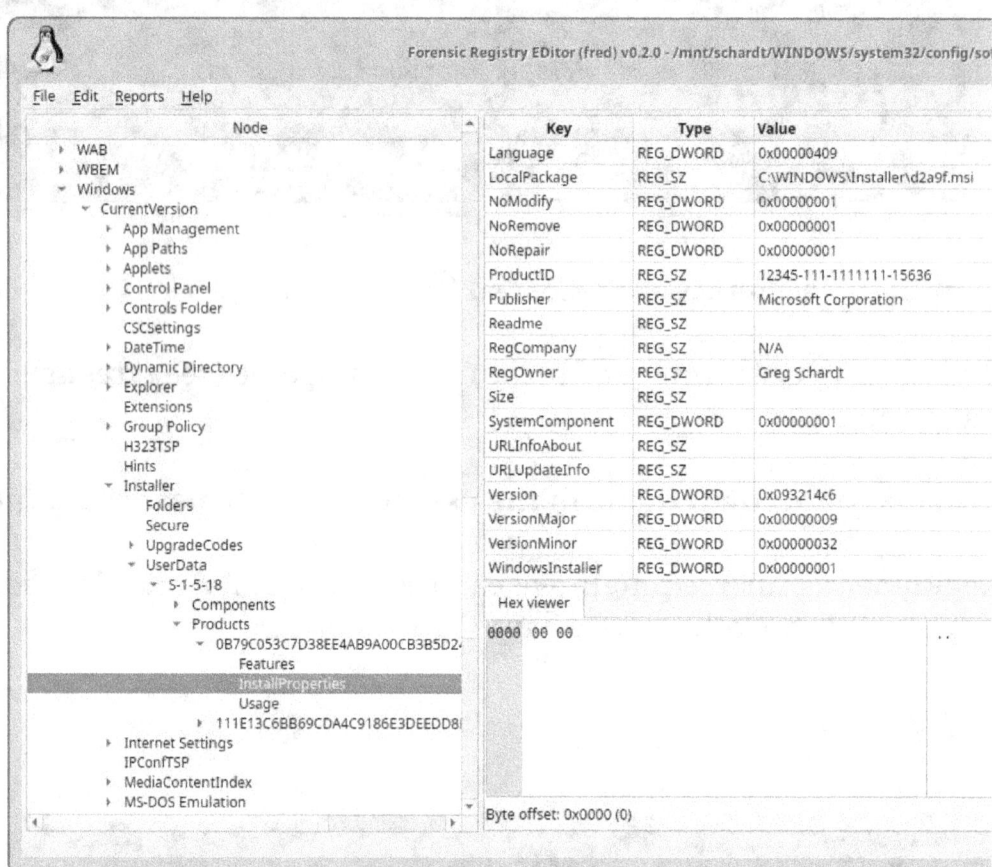

List the network cards

- Xircom CardBus Ethernet 100 + modem 56
- Compaq WL110 Wireless LAN

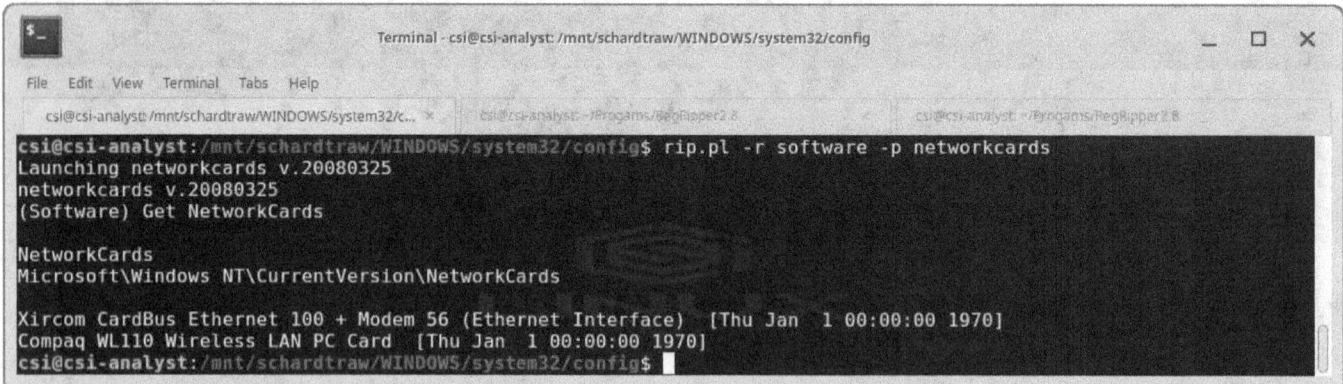

Find 6 installed programs that may be used for hacking.

Thought they are not "installed" as such there are a number of programs located under the "My Documents" folder. For a small sample this is a screenshot under the "EXPLOITATION" and "NT" folder

- Brutus
- Get Admin
- l0pht301
- lsadump2
- SMBGrind Crack
- John

There are a number of "hacking" applications installed that can be found under the Program Files directory, including 123WASP, Cain, and Anonymizer.

A popular IRC (Internet Relay Chat) program called MIRC was installed. What are the user settings that was shown when the user was online and in a chat channel?

From the logs directory under "C:\Program Files\mIRC" the enter and exit times are

This IRC program has the capability to log chat sessions. List 3 IRC channels that the user of this computer accessed.

From the logs directory under "**C:\Program Files\mIRC**" there are a number of channels including #LuxShell, #CyberCafe, #Chatacholics, #Elite.Hackers, and #houston. It appears that mrevilrulez only appears to have posted in #Chataholics, #CyberCafe, and #LuxShell

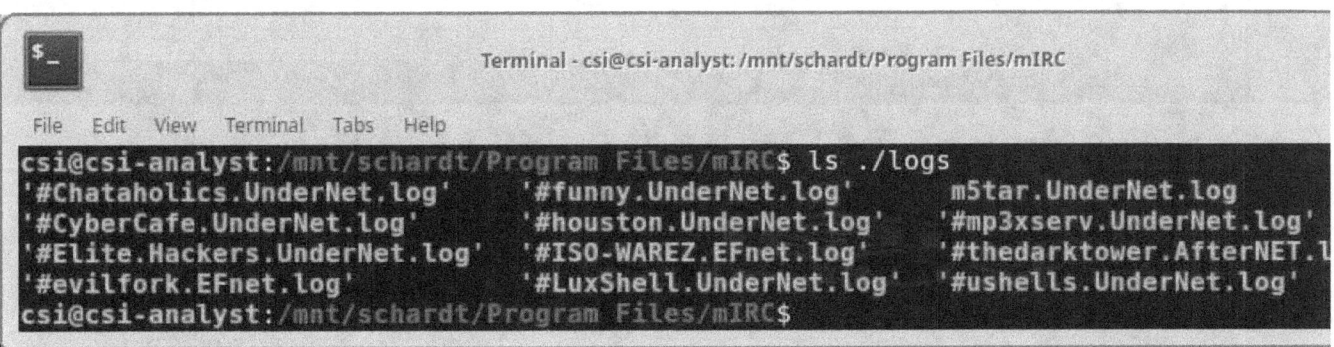

Ethereal, a popular "sniffing" program that can be used to intercept wired and wireless internet packets was also found to be installed. When TCP packets are collected and re-assembled, the default save directory is that users \My Documents directory. What is the name of the file that contains the intercepted data?

The file is as stated in the question in the My Documents directory, the file is named interception.

Viewing the file in a text format reveals much information about who and what was intercepted.

What type of wireless computer was the victim (person who had his internet surfing recorded) using?

User agent in the packet capture says that the intercepted machine is a Windows CE (Pocket PC) - Version 4.20

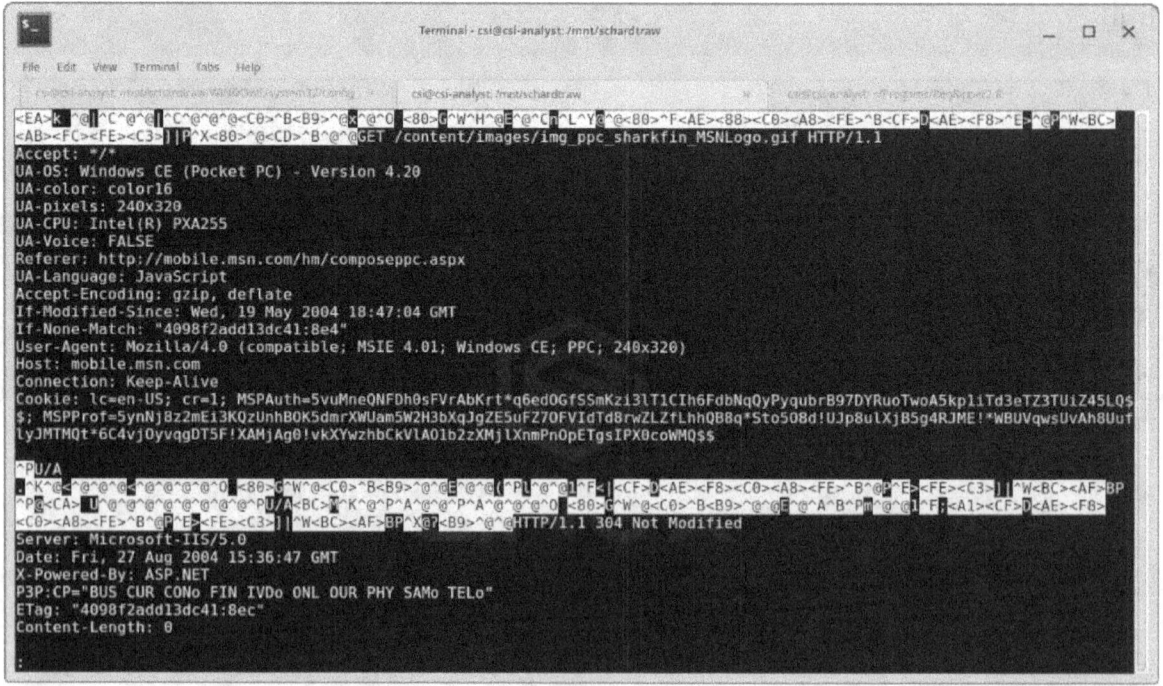

What websites was the victim accessing?

After doing a grep of the file it appears most of the sites visited were mobile.msn.com and login.passport.net

Search for the main user's web-based email address. What is it?

From the *Local Settings/History/History.IE5/index.dat* file we can see a few visits to Yahoo mail with the email address of **mrevilrulez@yahoo.com**

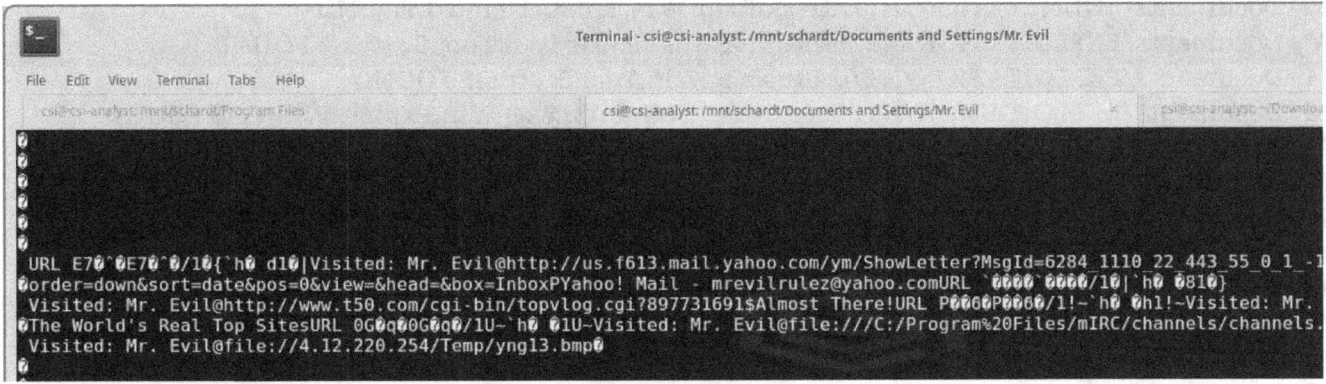

How many executables are in the recycle bin?

4 (named Dc1.exe, Dc2.exe, Dc3.exe, and Dc4.exe)

Are these files really deleted?

No, they are fully functional in the Recycle Bin.

Perform an Anti-Virus check. Are there any viruses on the computer?

Running clamscan with the database versions in footnotes returned 25 infected files. The majority of which are located under directories titled ENUMERATION, EXPLOITATION, COMMANDS, and FOOTPRINTING, in the My Documents directory. Given the suspects purported level of technical skills and the file location, it is unlikely that these files were used to infect this machine. There are a number of other infected files under the System32 directory that could actually be viruses that the user of the machine installed or another malicious user.

- daily.cld: 25836
- main.cvd: 59
- bytecode.cLinux 3 vd: 331

Appendix

Anti-Virus scan

```
csi@csi-analyst:/mnt/schardtraw$ clamscan -ri ./
./My Documents/COMMANDS/enum.exe: Win.Tool.EnumPlus-1 FOUND
./My Documents/COMMANDS/SAMDUMP.EXE: Win.Trojan.Pwdump-2 FOUND
./My Documents/COMMANDS/snitch.exe: Win.Trojan.Snitch-1 FOUND
./My Documents/ENUMERATION/NT/enum/enum.tar.gz: Win.Tool.EnumPlus-1 FOUND
./My Documents/ENUMERATION/NT/enum/files/enum.exe: Win.Tool.EnumPlus-1 FOUND
./My Documents/ENUMERATION/NT/Legion/Chrono.dl_: Win.Trojan.Bruteforce-3 FOUND
./My Documents/ENUMERATION/NT/Legion/NetTools.ex_: Win.Trojan.Spion-4 FOUND
./My Documents/ENUMERATION/NT/ntreskit.zip: Win.Trojan.Nemo-1 FOUND
./My Documents/EXPLOITATION/NT/Brutus/BrutusA2.exe: Win.Tool.Brutus-3 FOUND
./My Documents/EXPLOITATION/NT/brutus.zip: Win.Tool.Brutus-3 FOUND
./My Documents/EXPLOITATION/NT/Get Admin/GetAdmin.exe: Win.Exploit.WinNT-3 FOUND
./My Documents/EXPLOITATION/NT/lsadump2/lsadump2.exe: Win.Trojan.Lsadump-1 FOUND
./My Documents/EXPLOITATION/NT/lsadump2/lsadump2.zip: Win.Trojan.Lsadump-1 FOUND
./My Documents/EXPLOITATION/NT/netbus/NetBus170.zip: Win.Trojan.Netbus-2 FOUND
./My Documents/EXPLOITATION/NT/sechole/SECHOLE.EXE: Win.Trojan.Sehole-1 FOUND
./My Documents/EXPLOITATION/NT/sechole/sechole3.zip: Win.Trojan.Sehole-1 FOUND
./My Documents/EXPLOITATION/NT/WinVNC/Windows/vnc-3.3.3r7_x86_win32.zip: Win.Tool.Winvnc-10 FOUND
./My Documents/FOOTPRINTING/NT/superscan/superscan.exe: Win.Trojan.Agent-6240252-0 FOUND
./Program Files/Cain/Abel.dll: Win.Trojan.Cain-9 FOUND
./Program Files/Online Services/MSN50/MSN50.CAB: Txt.Malware.CMSTPEvasion-6664831-0 FOUND
./WIN98/WIN98_OL.CAB: Txt.Malware.CMSTPEvasion-6664831-0 FOUND
./WINDOWS/system32/ahui.exe: Win.Virus.Virut-6804272-0 FOUND
./WINDOWS/system32/dllcache/ahui.exe: Win.Virus.Virut-6804272-0 FOUND
./WINDOWS/system32/dllcache/mmc.exe: Win.Virus.Virut-6804520-0 FOUND
./WINDOWS/system32/mmc.exe: Win.Virus.Virut-6804520-0 FOUND

----------- SCAN SUMMARY -----------
Known viruses: 7162840
Engine version: 0.102.1
Scanned directories: 766
Scanned files: 11305
Infected files: 25
Data scanned: 1806.71 MB
Data read: 1768.03 MB (ratio 1.02:1)
Time: 2432.815 sec (40 m 32 s)
```

Layers of the OSI Model:
Where the hardware and data fits
LaShanda Edwards

The use of networks is everywhere. Examples of network use include the following: using social media, browsing the web, as well as accessing your email. When the "SEND" button is hit after writing an email, the email then goes only to the specified destination. The OSI model contains a lot of information that could be overwhelming to understand and remember; although, understanding the model will help you in everyday networking activities and will make troubleshooting problems within the network much faster and easier. The OSI model is comprised of 7 layers that help information technology professionals figure out what is going on in a networking system. The OSI model was birthed in the 70s by the International Organization of Standards (ISO) as Open System Interconnection (OSI) to make this form of communication standard over different systems and unique across the world.

In accordance with Shaw, during the time when computer networking was expanding, two separate models were merged in 1983 and published in 1984 to create the OSI model that most people are familiar with today (2018). This seven-layer model is greatly used by all organizations to continuously improve the network today. The model consists of the following layers as shown in figure 1 from top to bottom: Layer 7 – Application, Layer 6 – Presentation, Layer 5 – Session, Layer 4 – Transport, Layer 3 – Network, Layer 2 – Datalink, and Layer 1 – Physical.

The OSI model is simply a theory or structured way to ensure the performance, security, and integrity of data delivery. The model essentially divides the responsibility of communication in each independent layer.

Editor's Note: According to the Industry, there is an unofficial 8th layer. The Layer 8 is referred to as the human factor. From an attack perspective, social engineering fits here. From the investigation side, this is where Open Source Intelligence OSINT resides.

"Open-source intelligence is data collected from publicly available sources to be used in an intelligence context. In the intelligence community, the term "open" refers to overt, publicly available sources. It is not related to open-source software or collective intelligence." - Wikipedia

---

OSI Model Layers

The International Organization for Standardization (ISO) conceived the OSI model which is a hypothetical model created to aid various communication systems to communicate to interchange data using standard protocols. According to Cloudflare, the modern Internet doesn't strictly follow the OSI model, although the model is still very useful for troubleshooting network problems. Whether it's a person

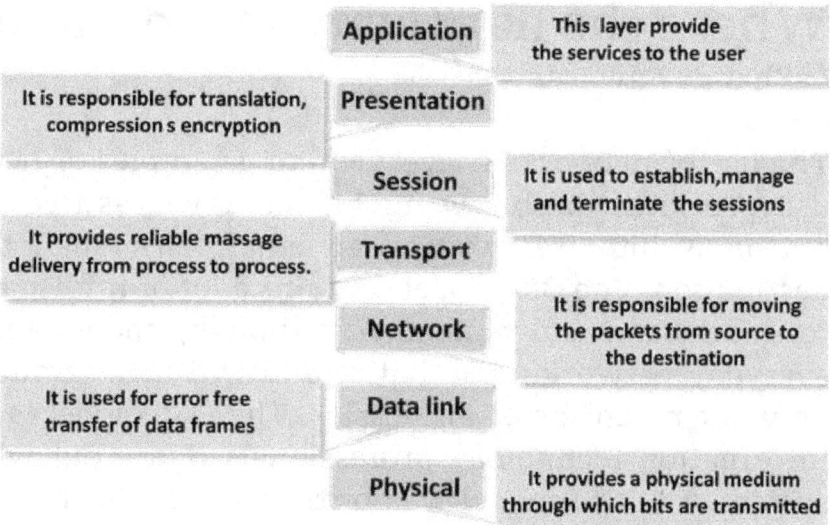

Figure 2: OSI Model credit - static.javatpoint.com

who is unable to get their laptop on the Internet, the OSI model can help to break down the problem and separate the source of the trouble. If the problem can be attached to one specific layer of the model, a lot of useless work can be avoided. Each layer of the OSI model is responsible for certain roles and responsibilities as shown in figure 2.

Application layer

Layer 7 is called the Application Layer. The responsibility of this layer is to integrate the services on the network with the operating system in order for users to gain access to the network (Codecamp, 2019). This layer would probably be the most familiar to consumers due to it being the closest to the end-user. The end-user interacts with this layer of the OSI model generally every day by simply

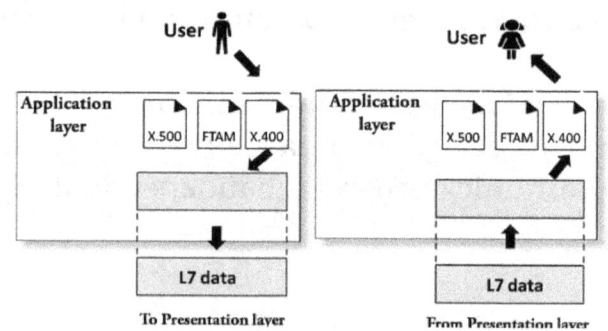

Figure 3: Layer 7 credit - static.javatpoint.com

using applications such as web browsers (Microsoft Edge, Firefox, Internet Explorer, Chrome, Safari) and Social Media Platforms (Instagram, Facebook, Twitter, Hangouts).

As shown in figure 3, the Application Layer's basic job is to provide an interface between the user and the network. This layer does not refer to the application itself, but it provides all the needed services to support applications to run properly. Some protocols contained within in the Application Layer include the following: File Transfer Protocol (FTP), Simple Mail Transfer Protocol (SMTP), Internet Message Access Protocol (IMAP), Hypertext Transfer Protocol (HTTP), Post Office Protocol (POP), Trivial File Transfer Protocol (TFTP), Simple Network Management Protocol (SNMP), and Network News Transfer Protocol (NNTP) (Codecamp, 2019). Most protocols will extend down to the Session Layer, although protocols flow down multiple layers.

Application Layer Roles and Responsibility

The Application Layer is the request sender or File transfer, access, and management (FTAM). It uses multiple applications to allow the user the ability to perform or access different operations such as uploading pictures, sending emails, blogging, etc. The Application Layer also represents the response. It acts as a mail service; it can view the response or destination of the user's data seen by another user from an alternate system. Lastly, it involves directory services, which is when the application provides the distributed database source.

Presentation Layer

Layer 6 is called the Presentation Layer. The responsibility of this layer is to provide a format. This layer is consumed by encryption, compression, and syntax in which the communication will occur. Since it is attached with the Application Layer, the layer is also responsible for configuring the message into the Application Layer usable format. In other words, the Presentation Layer makes information presentable for the application or network as shown in figure 4.

An example of this is when a website is using the HTTP protocol. If the data is encrypted then the HTTP protocol would not do this: as an alternative, the SSL would encrypt the data in the Presentation Layer. The following are main the function of the Presentation Layer: Translation, Encryption, and Compression.

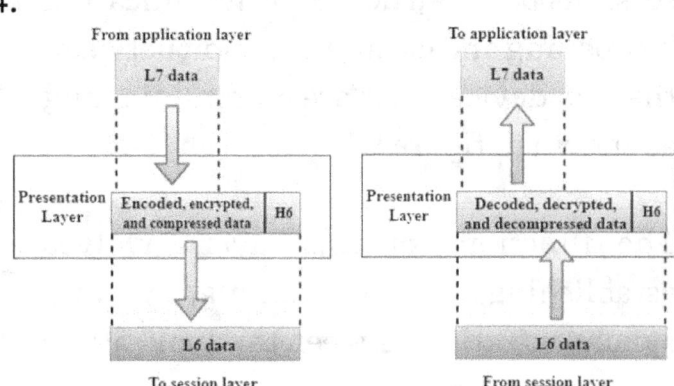

Figure 4: Layer 7 credit -static.javatpoint.com

Presentation Layer Roles and Responsibility

Javatpoint states, translation is the process of duel systems exchanging information in character string form, numbers, etc. The data received from the sender's device is not consumable by any given application directly. Because different encoding methods are used for different computers, interoperability is handled by the Presentation Layer between various encoding methods (Javatpoint, 2018). It transforms the data from sender- dependent format to a common format and transforms the common format into a receiver-dependent format at the receiving end. To maintain privacy encryption is a necessity. The encryption method is a process of transforming the sender-transmitted information in a different form and transmits the resulting message over the network (Javatpoint, 2018).

The last function of the Presentation Layer is compression. Compression is the process of compressing the data. It is responsible for compressing the date received from the Application Layer. The number of bits is reduced to be transmitted. Compression is important in multimedia such as the following: video, text messaging, and audio. The protocols used in the Presentation Layer of the OSI model are SSL and TLS (Codecamp, 2019).

Session Layer

Layer 5 is called the Session Layer. The responsibility of this layer is to create sessions between device communication by opening and closing a session between the two devices that are communicating as shown in figure 5.

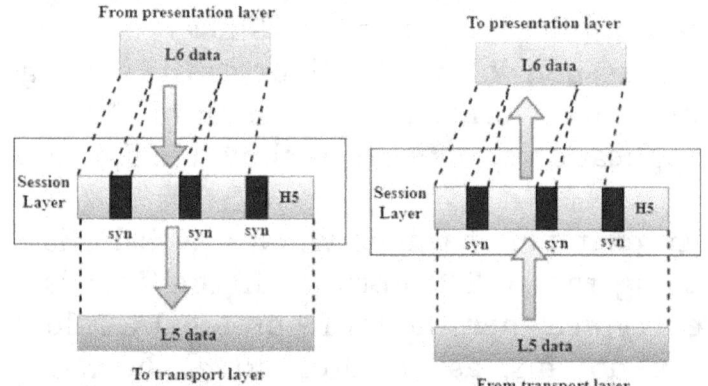

Figure 5: Layer 6 credit -static.javatpoint.com

The functions of this layer involves establishing, maintaining, and synchronization between the applications at each end of the sessions (Javatpoint, 2018).

Protocols at this layer

> ADSP, ASP, H.245, ISO-SP, OSI session-layer protocol (X.225, ISO 8327), iSNS, L2F, L2TP, NetBIOS, PAP, PPTP, RPC, RTCP, SMPP, SCP, SOCKS, ZIP, and SDP

Session Layer Roles and Responsibility

Dialog control and synchronization are important in the Session Layer. Within the dialog control the Session Layer is the dialog controller that develops dialog between duel processes. It determines whose turn to speak in a session, very useful for video conferencing (Codecamp, 2019). Synchronization occurs when the Session Layer adds barriers to be met when transmitting data in sequential order. If an error occurs during the data transmission process, then the transmission will restart again from the barrier set. The protocols used in the Session Layer is NetBIOS (Codecamp, 2019).

Transport Layer

Layer 4 is called the Transport Layer. The responsibility of this layer is to deliver data on the network as shown in figure 6. In accordance with Javatpoint, the Transport Layer ensures that the transmission of messages in the order in which they are sent without duplicating the data (2018).

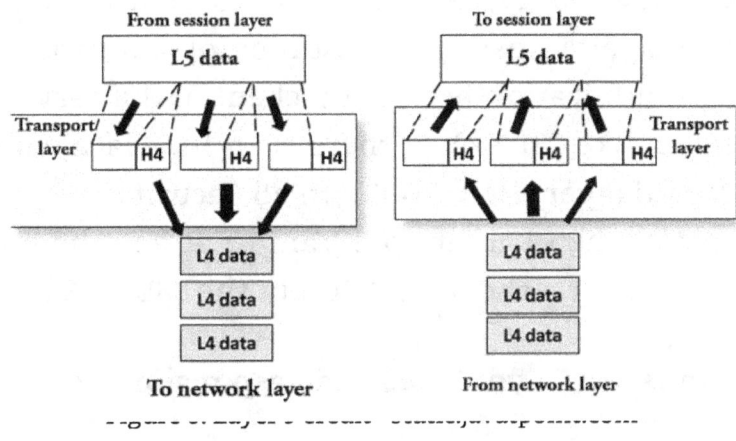

The Transport layer generates a circuit that is used by the Session Layer to communicate with session. This layer can be thought of as the end-to-end layer because it offers a point-to-point connection amongst the source and destination to reliably deliver data.

Protocols Used

Transmission Control Protocol (TCP) and User Datagram Protocol (UDP) are two protocols used in this layer. Shaw states, the best-known example of the Transport Layer is the TCP, this protocol is built at the top of the Internet Protocol (IP). The IP is known as TCP/IP (2018). TCP is the standard protocol that allows systems to communicate over the internet. It maintains and establishes host connections.

Segments are formed when data is transported over the TCP connection and the TCP protocol distributes the data into smaller units. UDP is an original protocol in the Transport Layer. Due to the internet being unsecured the TCP/IP provides no security. The UDP protocol is considered unreliable due to the receiver not receiving an acknowledgment when the packet is received and the sender not waiting for an acknowledgment. Netscape created the Secure Socket Layer (SSL) protocol that was later adopted as a standard for Transport Layer Security (TLS) and it is now known as SSL/TLS (Holl, 2003). Countless financial institutions use these protocols to encrypt data crossing the Internet. SSL/TLS is not TCP/IP reliant and can layer on top of any transport protocol. They can even run under application protocols such as HTTP, FTP, and TELNET. SSL/TLS offers all three of the critical "CIA" security components: Confidentiality, Authentication, and Integrity. These protocols give protection against message tampering, eavesdropping, and spoofing. SSL counteracts eavesdropping of communication between a client and a server by encrypting passwords. TLS is very much like SSL except there is an interface between the handshaking portion and the record layer (Holl, 2003). In all Security efforts, there are going to be weaknesses and that's when hackers program to attack the vulnerabilities. TLS seems to have fewer security breaches than SSL, but the SSL/TLS combination improves them both.

Transport Layer Roles and Responsibility

Data transfer, dividing and reassembling, flow control, and error handling are the essential role and responsibility of the Transport Layer. Data transfer is simply transferring data between the sender and receiver accumulated from the Session Layer. To make communication quicker the data received from the Session Layer gets packaged into smaller segments on the sender device by dividing and reassembling.

Once the receiver receives the segments it collects, all segments reassembles back to the original data to be presented to the Session Layer. Flow control is the responsibility of the Transport Layer, although it is performed end-to-end rather than across a single link. Lastly, error handling is also the responsibility of this Layer. The error control is useful to ensure full data delivery, as the data are divided into segments.

Network Layer

Layer 3 is called the Network Layer. The responsibility of this layer is moving data between systems throughout the network as shown in figure 7.

Routers are strongly used in the Network Layer; its job is very crucial within this layer to help determine the route for the fastest data delivery. Furthermore, the Network layer is responsible for determining the

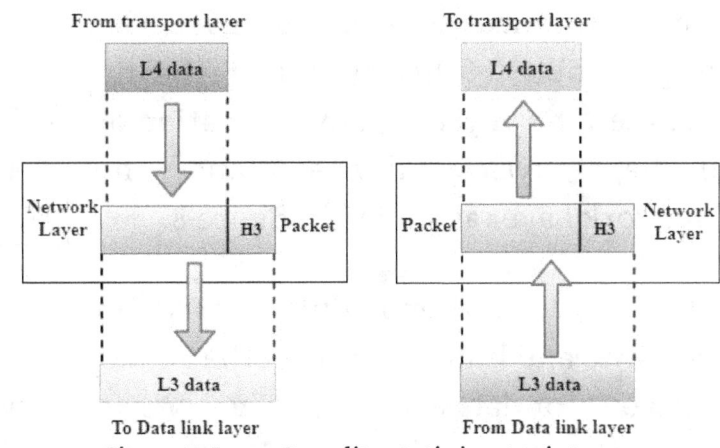

Figure 7: Layer 5 credit - static.javatpoint.com

effective path for the data. The routing protocols specify how the router identifies destination networks and the path data should travel to the destination network. Routers are the third layer devices and their main job is to provide the routing services within an internetwork. The Network Layer is also responsible for further breaking down the segments into small units called packets. The receiver side renovates packets back to segment. The Data Link Layer is responsible for routing and forwarding packets. Assignment of internet protocol (IP) addresses is another important thing that happens on the Network Layer. The IP address is often referred to as the Network Layer address or third level address.

Network Layer Roles and Responsibility

The primary functions of the Network Layer are Routing, Internetworking, Addressing, and Packetizing. Internetworking is the main responsibility of the Network Layer. It delivers a logical connection between multiple devices (Javatpoint, 2018). Routing is intelligently designed to find the shortest and fastest route available from the multiple routes using a routing table, which is used by the Network Layer to perform routing. Addressing identifies each network distinctively in the network-connection and determines what device is on the internet, the Network Layer uses the IP address. A Network Layer collects the packets from the upper layer and converts them into packets, this process is known as packetizing achieved by IP. The protocols used in the Network Layer are the following: IP, Internet Protocol version 4 (IPv4), Internet Protocol version 6 (IPv6), Internet Protocol Security (IPSec), Internet Control Message Protocol (ICMP), and Internet Group Management Protocol (IGMP) (Codecamp, 2019).

Data Link Layer

Layer 2 is called the Data Link Layer. The responsibility of this layer is interfacing between the physical communication of media, physical devices, and the Network Layer as shown in figure 8.

The Data link layer mainly consists of switches and hubs to connect the actual network for data exchange. The layer is split into two sub layers called Logical

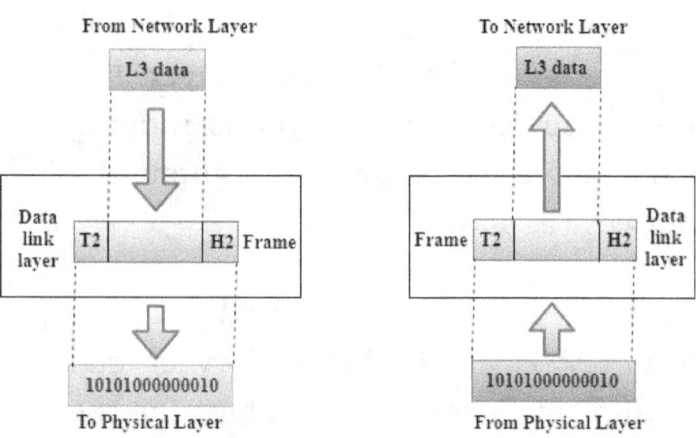

Figure 8: Data Link Layer – Layer 2 static.javatpoint.com

Link Control (LLC) and Media Access Control (MAC). The LLC is the top sublayer and provides the interfacing between the lower layers and upper layers. It's liable for transporting the packets to the Network Layer of the receiver collecting, identifies the Network Layer protocol address from the header, and provides flow control.

The bottom layer is the MAC sublayer and it is responsible for identifying how devices can access the physical medium and it is used for transferring the packets over the network (Javatpoint, 2018). The Data Link layer is responsible for data exchange between two interconnected switches or hubs via the Network Layer. In other words, this OSI layer ensures the data moves node to node. Once the packets are received in the Data Link Layer from the Network Layer it further distributes packets into frames to transmit data using MAC address.

Data Link Layer Roles and Responsibility:

Framing, Acknowledgement, Retransmission, Error Control, Flow Control, Physical Addressing, and Access Control all play a major role in the Data Link Layer. The Data Link Layer transforms physical raw bit stream into packets that are called frames. Framing enable a way of transmitting a set of frames in bits that are useable by the receiver. When notice is sent by the accepting end to inform the source that the frame was received without any mistakes is the Acknowledgment (Codecamp, 2019). If the source fails to receive an acknowledgement, then the packet goes through a process called Retransmission and will be retransmitted.

Error and Flow Control provides error control by identifying an error in the Physical Layer and rectifying it. Flow control can also be achieved by regulating the data rate on both sides to prevent data corruption. This layer adds header and trailer to the frame. The header added to the frame contains the hardware destination and source addresses. Physical Addressing of the Data Link Layer adds headers to the frames that includes the destination address. Access Control is when more than one device is connected to the same communication channel. The protocols used within the Data Link Layer are PPP, ATM, Ethernet (Codecamp, 2019).

Physical layer

Layer 1 of the OSI model is called the Physical Layer as it provides the actual connection between two devices using cables as shown in figure 9. It consists of the information in the form of bits. This is also the layer where the data gets converted into a bit stream from the Data Link layer (Layer 2) into electrical signals. Codecamp, refers to the Physical Layer as a way to help transmit data between duel machines communicating in a physical manner, which can be optical fibers, copper wire, wireless, etc. (2019).

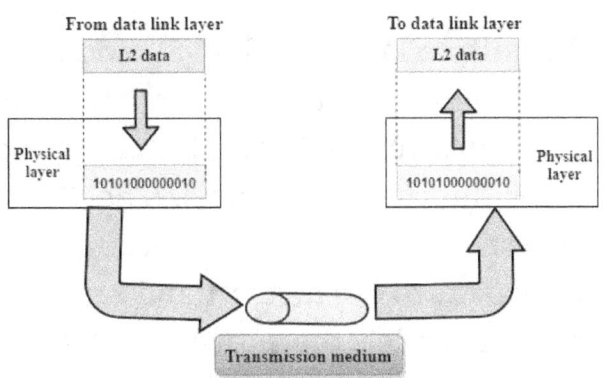

Figure 9: Layer 1 static.javatpoint.com

Physical Layer Roles and Responsibility

The following are the roles and responsibility of the Physical Layer: Line Configuration, Signals, Physical Topology, and Data Transmission Mode. The Line configuration defines the way multiple devices physically connects. Signals used within the Physical Layer determines the type of signal used for the transmission of information (Javatpoint, 2018). When using cables and switches within the Physical Layer, the layer is enabled to connect multiple devices into a Physical Topology. This can also be done with mesh topology, bus topology, star topology, and hybrid topology ideas. The Physical Layer also defines the way the transmission will be done between two devices by a process called Transmission Mode. Transmission Modes in the Physical Layer can be categorized into three modes: simplex, half-duplex, or full duplex. Protocols used by this layer are USB, Bluetooth, etc. (Codecamp, 2019).

The OSI model describes how devices communicate with each other. The model divides network communication between two hosts. The OSI model is divided into seven different layers, and has data being transformed at each layer to prepare it to be sent through the network. It is important to memorize the 7 Layers of the OSI model: Application Layer, Presentation Layer, Session Layer, Transport Layer, Network Layer, Data Link Layer, and Physical Layer. Added to the data at the upper layers are encrypted, formatting, and session numbers. Data is broken down into bit segments with accordance to a port number, then given an IP address at the middle layers. At the lower levels, packets are changed into frames that include the source and destination MAC address; frames are changed into bits for communication through the network.

The bottom layers of the OSI model are heavily related to the hardware. The top layers of the OSI model are related to the protocols. The Transmission Control Protocol/Internet Protocol (TCP/IP) protocol has 4 layers. This is the main protocol used in all Internet operations. The Open System Interconnection (OSI) model divides network communication between 2 hosts into layers. The network access layer is equivalent to OSI layers 1 and 2, the Internet Protocol layer is comparable to layer 3 in the OSI model, the host-to-host layer is equivalent to OSI layer 4, and finally, the application layer is similar to OSI layers 5, 6, and 7 combined (Frenzel, 2013). TCP/IP is the older of the two methods of data communications and is well recognized throughout the world. The OSI model, however, is a proven concept that is used in all other data communications protocols. It will continue to be used as a GUIdeline for all other communications applications.

Let us walk through an example that will explain how the process takes place to convey the data. If I wanted to send an email to my mom, I will compose the email on yahoo and click send. Yahoo will pass my email message to the Application Layer, which will select a protocol and pass the data to the presentation layer. The Presentation Layer will encrypt depending upon the security level and condense the data. It will move to the Session Layer next, which will initialize the communication session by opening the session to ensure the quality delivery of the data. The data then goes to the sender's Transportation Layer. Here is where the data will be divided into small segments. Those segments will then hit the network layer and will be broken up into packets. These packets will break down into frames at the Data Link Layer. The Data Link Layer will then send those frames to the Physical Layer. Here, the data will be converted into a bit stream of 1s and 0s and sent through the network.

On the other end, on my mom's computer, it will first capture the bit stream at the Physical Layer and wait until every bit stream transforms into frames to go to the Data Link Layer. If there are any errors in the Physical Layer, they will be trapped in the Data Link Layer, which is now liable to take all frames and reunite them into packets. From the Data Link Layer, it will go to the Network Layer, to generate segments from the given packets. It will then flow into the Transport Layer where the original data will be formed from segments through the reassembly function. After the initial data are formed, it will move to the Session Layer. Here in this layer, the session will terminate once the data is received completely and move into the next layer called the Presentation Layer. The Presentation Layer will now decrypt the data that is consumed for the application. Finally comes the Application Layer from where the application will be able to function and display the email sent to my mom's computer screen using the Application Layer's services.

Citation

Codecamp. (2019, October 29). 7 layer of OSI Model | 7 Layer OSI model in Computer Network. Retrieved February 12, 2020, from mycodecamp.blogspot.com/2019/10/7-layer-of-osi-model.html

Cloudflare. (n.d.). Retrieved January 19, 2020, from cloudflare.com/learning/ddos/glossary/open-systems- interconnection-model-osi/

Frenzel, L. (2013, October 02). What's The Difference Between The OSI Seven-Layer Network Model And TCP/IP? Retrieved February 21, 2010. electronicdesign.com/what-s-difference-between/what-s-difference- between-osi-seven-layer-network-model-and-tcpip

Holl, K. (2003). OSI Defense in Depth to Increase Application Security. Retrieved March 8, 2020. giac.org/paper/gsec/2868/osi-defense-in-depth-increase- application-security/104841

Javatpoint. (2018). Retrieved February 20, 2020, from javatpoint.com/osi- model

Shaw, K. (2018, October 22). The OSI model explained: How to understand (and remember) the 7-layer network model. Retrieved February 8, 2020, from networkworld.com/article/3239677/the-osi-model-explained-how-to-understand-and-remember-the-7-layer-network-model.html

Forensic Data Recovery
Capturing Evidence in a Forensically sound manner
Layer 1

By
Jeremy Martin

Data Destruction

We will cover the different levels of data destruction from full files to completely obliterated hardware. Some stages are recoverable while some others are not. There are several labs ready for you to follow along with. We will cover the potential of data recovery of five of those phases, and only a handful of methods and software at each phase. To follow along, create your own "evidence disk" by copying known graphics, documents, and other files to create a known base line. Once you are comfortable with basic recovery, move on to more advanced content.

An easy way to think about data recovery is that if data is written to a data container (RAM, file, database, partition, drive, etc.), it is always there until it is overwritten or in the case of RAM, released. You can format a drive a thousand times, and it does not overwrite the entire drive. This is why there have been many cases over the years that digital evidence was still found even after the suspect took great lengths to hide or destroy it.

Un-deleting vs. Data carving

Un-deleting is recovering data from a file system after it has been deleted. This means that the record in the file system's index (FAT, MFT, Catalog, etc...) still points to the location of the data on the drive. With the FAT file systems, the first character of the file name is overwritten with the hex characters "E5". When you recover the data, you may have the original file name with the file. This method of recovery is a far faster than data carving.

Data carving does not look for a file system index. Instead, this method starts at the beginning of the data set and searches for the header (first few bytes) and/or footer (last few bytes) of a file. For example, a common header of a .JPG file is the hex combination "**FF D8 FF E0**" with a footer of "**FF D9**". When a data carving utility finds the header, it copies the data until it finds the footer and that becomes a recovered data set or file. Some of the programs will even allow you to ignore the footer to recover "partially recoverable files". The challenge with not looking for the footer of a file type means that you will get a lot more "false positives".

What is Recoverable?

What can you carve? Well, any data container that may contain files. What I mean by that is you can carve an entire disk, a partition, a raw copy of a drive, a swap file (pagefile.sys in windows), and even memory. You can even recover data from a drive that had an operating system reinstalled over a previous system. During this section of training, we will make a forensically sound bit-stream image of a "suspect" USB thumb drive. After the raw image is complete, we will use several tools to recover "evidence" including mounting the raw DD image to data carving both deleted and undeleted files. Some of the open source Linux tools we will look at are RecoverJPEG, Foremost, and Scalpel.

The Different Phases of Data Destruction

Full files: Files have not been deleted. The index (FAT, MFT, Catalog, etc.) for the file system is 100% intact. Data can easily be recovered.

Deleted files: Files have been deleted. The index for the file system is 100% intact. These files can be "Undeleted" or recovered as long as the data on the disk has not been overwritten.

Formatted: The Operating System index (FAT, MFT, Catalog, etc.) has been rebuilt or the records in that index have been overwritten. If the data on the disk has not been overwritten, they can be recovered with data carving. Names cannot be recovered unless located in the MATA information of the file & file signatures/headers need to be known.

Partially overwritten: Some data is recoverable, but usually in bits and pieces. This is where forensic tools become handy.

Physical Failure: The data is still there in most cases and the devices need to be repaired before an attempt to recover it can be made.

Wiped: All data has been overwritten or "nuked" and is unrecoverable within reasonable means.

Physical Annihilation: Drive or media is destroyed and unrecoverable.

Volatile Data: This is the data that you will lose when the system is turned off. This includes RAM, System Processes, and Network connections. Capturing this data can be extremely important in many cases.

Semi-Volatile Data: Swap space (pagefile.sys for Windows for example), temp files, slack space, and free space on the drive are examples of data that can still be recovered if the acquisition of the evidence is done properly. Simply turning on the system or computer can overwrite and make data unrecoverable.

Chain of Custody

Now you understand that data can be recovered, even from a formatted drive, what next? Before you touch anything, you need to start a Chain of Custody. Even though you may not be dealing with forensic investigations, getting in the habit of documenting everything. This helps with logistics to make sure you know what you received and what needs to go back. If you do find illegal content and it goes to court, if you treat it like a "forensic" recovery, you will not have tampered with or destroyed the evidence. *An example of a Chain of Custody will be added to the end of this section.*

Scope

Before you do anything, you need to determine the intent and scope of the investigation or recovery. You need to know what to find BEFORE you can find it. This only helps you. If they want to recover family pictures, this will be your first target to recover. If the client wants everything, you can hand the drive back and request payment for services rendered. If you are recovering data for a forensic investigation, if there is no scope, there is no case. In the United States, the 4th Amendment is clear *"The right of the people to be secure in their persons, houses, papers, and effects, against unreasonable searches and seizures, shall not be violated, and no Warrants shall issue, but upon probable cause, supported by Oath or affirmation, and particularly describing the place to be searched, and the persons or things to be seized"*. It is always better to err on the side of caution.

Capturing Volatile Memory

If you need to pull the volatile memory, there are many tools that you can accomplish this with. In the spirit of being free, I will mention two that are currently free. You can use FTK Imager from Access Data. This is a phenomenal forensic imaging tool and is currently free. DumpIt is another good free tool out there that will capture memory and works great with the memory analysis tool Volatility. We will not cover these in this section.

There are many tools out there you can use, just remember, minimize interaction with the system to minimize the destruction of evidence, know what your tool is/is not doing, and document EVERYTHING. If you did not document it, it did not happen. This can bite you in the butt if it ever gets to court.

Now you need to image the drive. We are specifically covering physical acquisition of evidence, so the system needs to be off so you can pull the drive and move forward.

Write Blocking Labs

First, print off a copy of the Chain of Custody included in this lab manual. Fill in everything related to the "case". Now you have your Scope and Chain of Custody, you can start to acquire the physical evidence.

For a lab-based environment, download a group of files to create a known baseline. When you know what files you have copied, you know what content should be recoverable. For example:

- (20) .JPG images,
- (10) .PDF documents
- (10) .DOCX documents
- (5)   .TXT files

Now you can test the differences between the different tools and see the levels of recoverability with each tool and method. You can also use the recovery.001 image that is used in the IWC Cyber Secrets episodes dealing with data recovery. If you use that downloaded image, skip to "File Recovery Labs".

Now, imagine you have a suspect drive and a hardware write blocker (aka: forensic bridge). Make sure you read the different ports that the drive connects into, versus the output that plugs into the computer.

Lab: Hardware

1. Buy a hardware write blocker & connect it to the drive to be protected.
    a. Skip if you don't have a hardware forensic bridge/write blocker.
    b. Follow the instructions provided by the vendor.
    c. Forensic Bridges or Write Blockers from vendors like: Firefly, Tableau, etc...

Imagine that you need to write block and do NOT have a hardware write blocker. Your workstation is a Linux system and you still want to make sure you connect the evidence drive in a forensically sound manner. The first thing you are going to have to do is log in and make sure you have root privileges in Linux. You will also need access to a terminal or a Command Line Interface "CLI" prompt.

Lab: Windows Registry Hack for External USB Devices

1. Open Windows Run dialog by pressing Win + R keys together.
2. Type in **regedit**
3. Press **Enter** to open Windows Registry Editor.

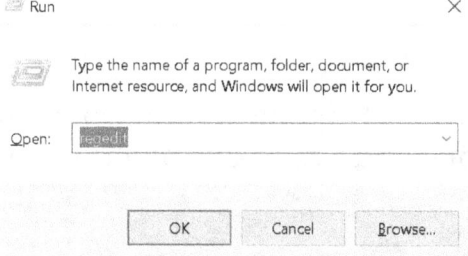

4. Navigate to: HKLM\SYSTEM\CurrentControlSet\Control\StorageDevicePolicies.
5. If StorageDevicePolicies key does not exist, you will have to create.
    a. Right click on '**Control**' key.
    b. Click **New**.
    c. Click **Key**.
    d. Name the new key StorageDevicePolicies
6. Select StorageDevicePolicies.
7. Right-click in the right window.
    a. Select New
    b. Dword (32-bit) Value.
8. Name the new entry **WriteProtect**.
9. Double-click on **WriteProtect**
10. Change the value from 0 to 1. (1 tuns on write blocking and 0 turns it off).

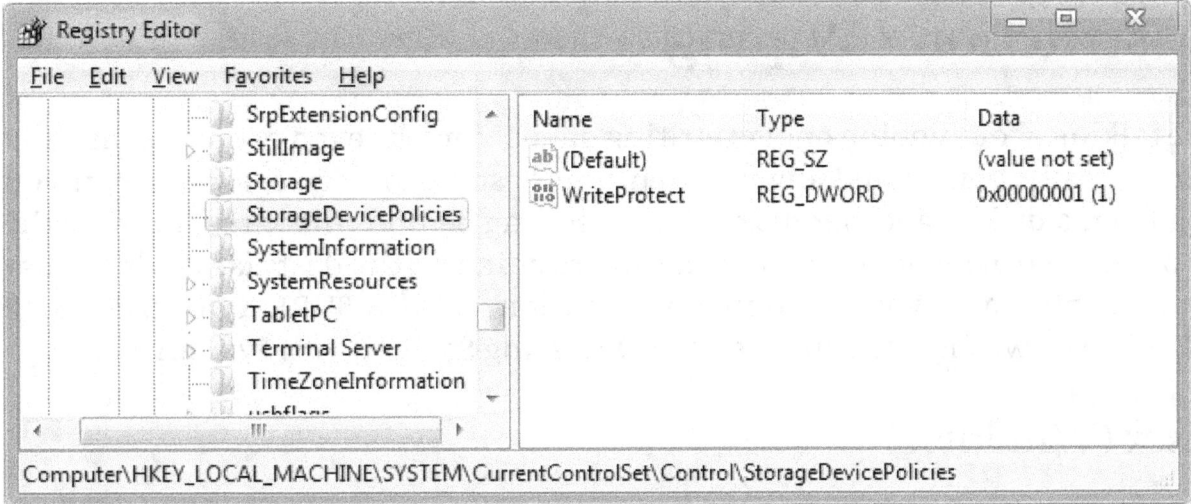

11. Insert the USB

The USB should now be write protected.

Lab: Linux Mount as Read-Only

12. Insert the USB (below are multiple options in Linux to identify the right drive).
    a. Verify your USB device by typing "lsblk" and look for the sd(?) drive
    b. Verify your USB device by typing "df" and look for the sd(?) drive
    c. Verify your USB device by typing "dmesg | grep sd" and look for the sd(?) drive
    d. Verify your USB device by typing "ls /dev/sd*" and look for the sd(?) drive

Assume the drive is sdb for the rest of the lab.

1. sudo mkdir /media/usbdrive
2. sudo mount /dev/sdb1 /media/usbdrive -o ro

This will mount the drive or make the drive usable as read-only to the folder "**/media/usbdrive**"

If the drive is already mounted, type:

sudo mount -o remount,ro /media/usbdrive

Data Destruction / Wiping

Why are we talking about wiping or overwriting data before we even get to the imaging portion? Logistically, you should always wipe your destination drive, especially if you are copying from a disk to another disk. The reasoning behind this is to eliminate the possibility of residual evidence or contamination residing on the destination drive that could get misidentified in your current investigation. MAKE SURE YOU WIPE THE RIGHT DRIVE!!! The wrong one could be your Operating System! Always verify!

Lab: Eraser (Windows)

1. Instal Eraser from sourceforge.net/projects/eraser/files/latest/download
2. Use the default settings.
3. Once installed, run Eraser

4. Click on the down arrow between Erase Schedule and Settings

5. Click **New Task** or use the keys **ctrl+N**.
6. Name the task

We are using "Wipe" for our name.

7. Chose Run immediately.
8. Click Add Data.

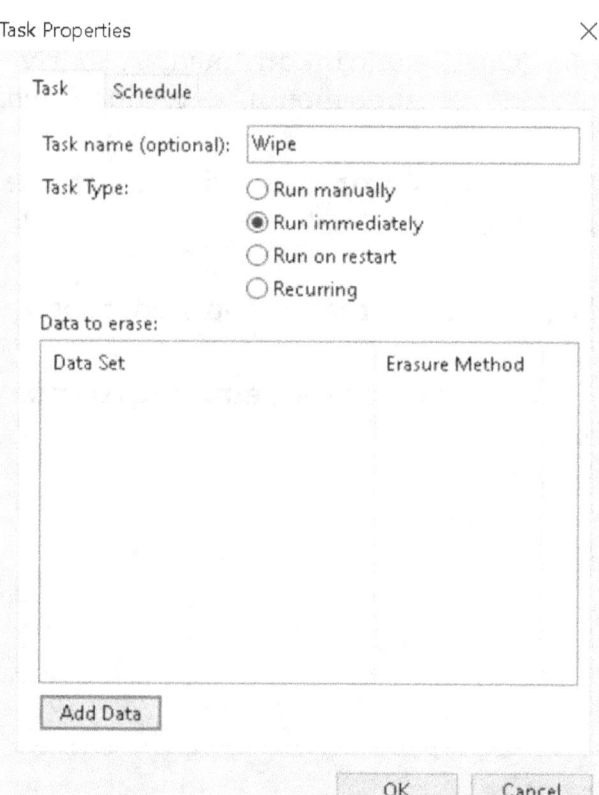

9. Click on the **Target type**: dropdown box and choose **Drive/Partition**.
10. Click on the **Erasure method**: dropdown box and choose **US DoD 5220.22-M**.
11. Click on the Settings dropdown box and choose the drive to wipe

This will be the external USB drive that you are going to use in your lab

12. Click **OK**.

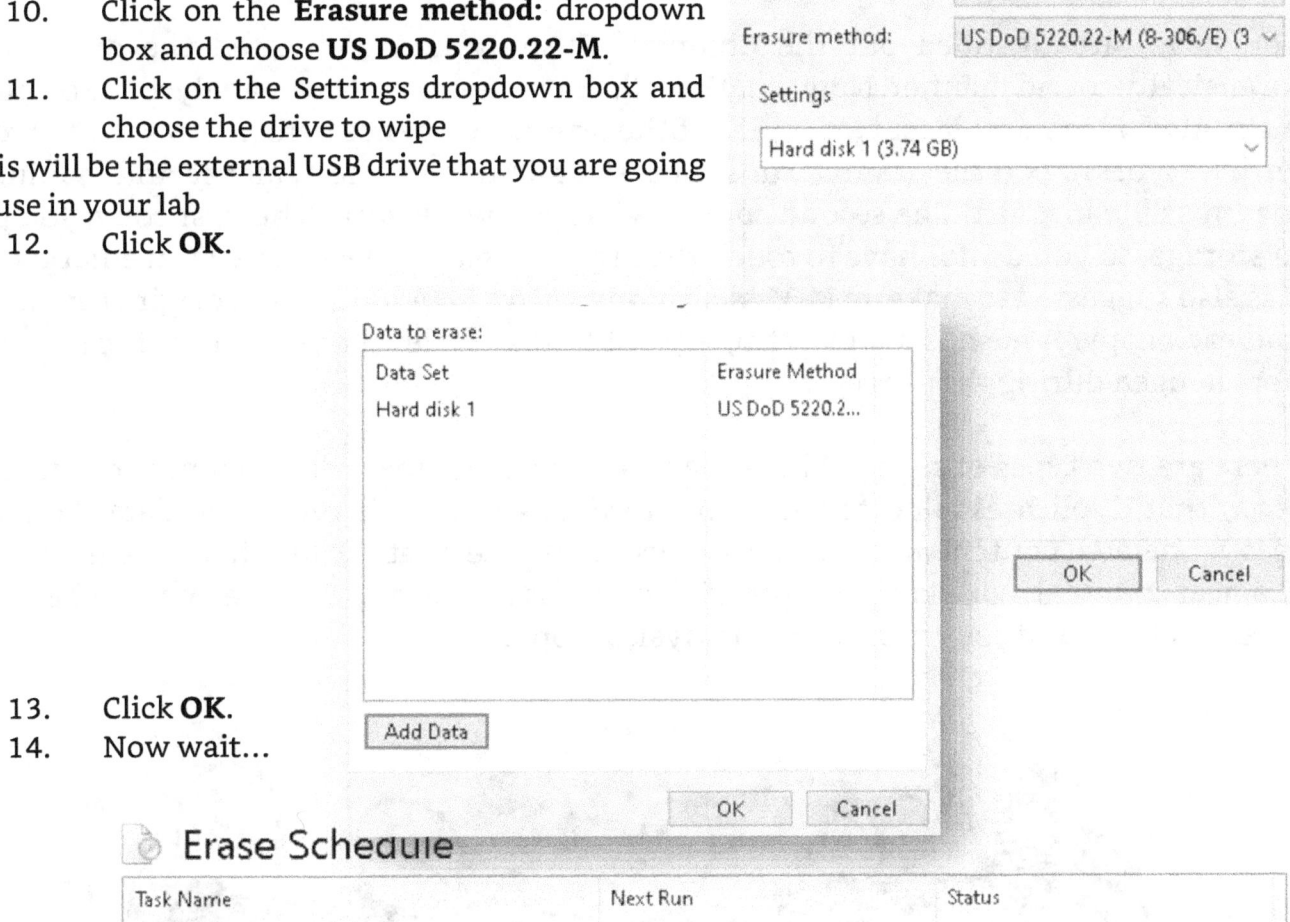

13. Click **OK**.
14. Now wait...

Lab: dcfldd/dd (CLI) (Linux)

1. Once the OS is loaded, open a terminal window with root access.
2. Verify your drive letter
   a. Type **lsblk**
   b. Type fdisk -l
3. Assuming the drive is sdb
4. Type dcfldd if=/dev/zero of=/dev/sdb

Forensic Imaging Labs

You have already filled out the Chain of Custody and connected the drive in a forensically sound manner. Now what? Well, Copy the data… Never analyze the original disk. Always make at least two copies of the original evidence before you start to work with it. Working on the original runs the risk of damaging the evidence and making it inadmissible in court. The second copy is what you work with. The first copy, you put in storage, so you do not have to touch the original again unless there is an emergency. It is also suggested to make an MD5 hash along with a SHA hash of the original evidence and each copy. A hash is a digital fingerprint that ads a level of trust that the data has not changed during the usage.

There are two types of copies. There is a "Physical copy" (aka: bit stream, clone, image, etc…) that duplicates allocated and un-allocated space. This means all data. You can recover deleted content and even partially over written data. The other copy is called a "Logical copy" (aka: backup, archive, file copy, dos copy, copy & paste, etc…). The most forensically sound copy is of course a physical copy.

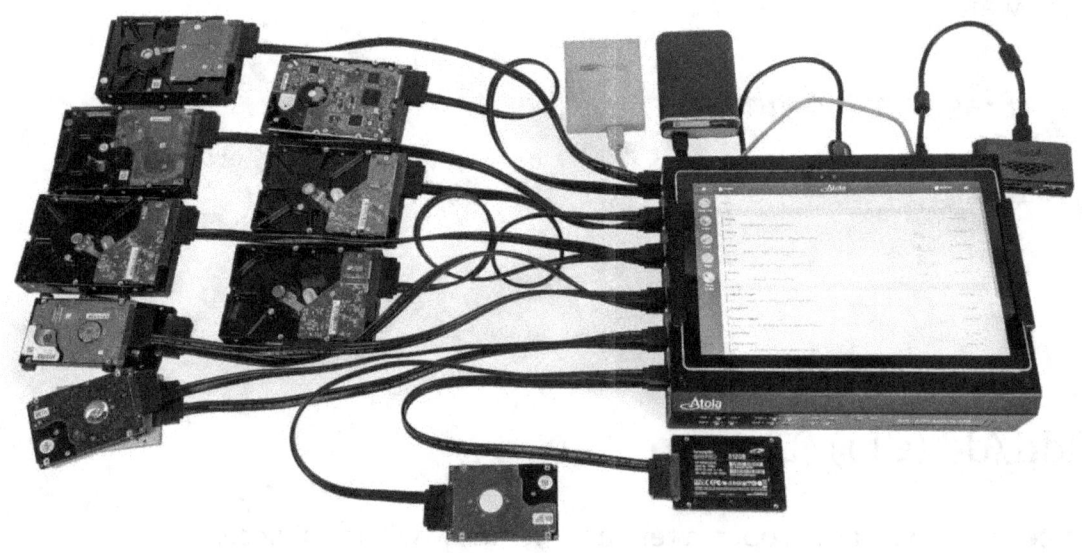

Image credit: Atola TaskForce atola.com

Most physical forensic imagers have write blockers built into them and it takes some of the risk out of the equation. Just make sure to put the evidence drive as the source and if you are imaging to another disk, that will be your destination. Too many people destroy the evidence by attaching the wrong drive to the destination…

What we want to do in these labs: create a known baseline. As mentioned previously, copy files in groups so we have a consistent set to play with. Since computer forensics IS a science, everything you do needs to be done is a consistent and reproducible manner. Once you are comfortable with the tools and methods, you can use what you have learned with real evidence and have confidence in your scientific results or analysis.

If you want to do your Imaging from a Windows computer, use FTK Imager. FTK Imager has software write blocking built in, so you will not destroy the evidence, but your next issue is the Operating System. Microsoft has had a history of trying to "help" the user when a new drive is added by adding data to the drive. If this happens, the evidence is destroyed due to contamination. To prevent this, use a physical write blocker. With that said, FTK Imager can be downloaded from accessdata.com. You may have to register to download the tool here: accessdata.com/product-download

FTK Imager Walkthrough

1. Do Write Blocking Lab first
2. Run FTK Imager

DO NOT pick your boot drive and copy to your boot drive. You will run out of space and no fun will be had.

3. Left click the **File** menu

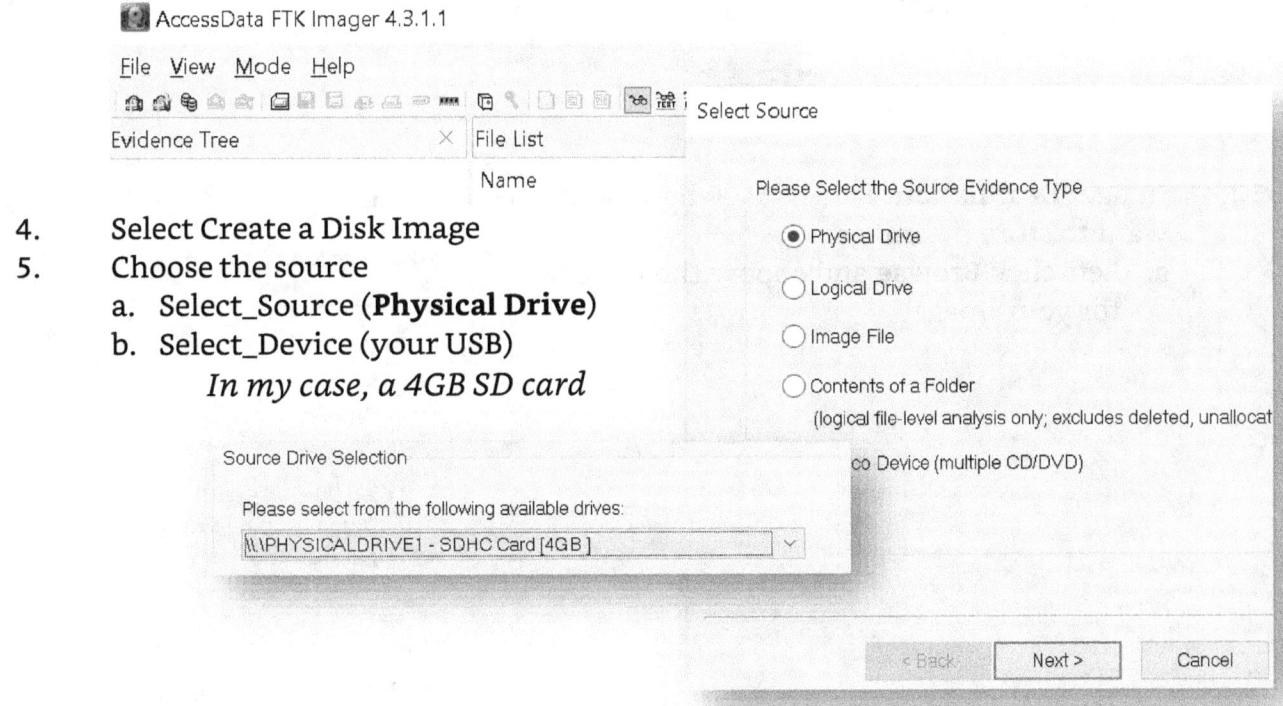

4. Select Create a Disk Image
5. Choose the source
   a. Select_Source (**Physical Drive**)
   b. Select_Device (your USB)
      In my case, a 4GB SD card

6. Click **Finish**:

7. Click **Add**

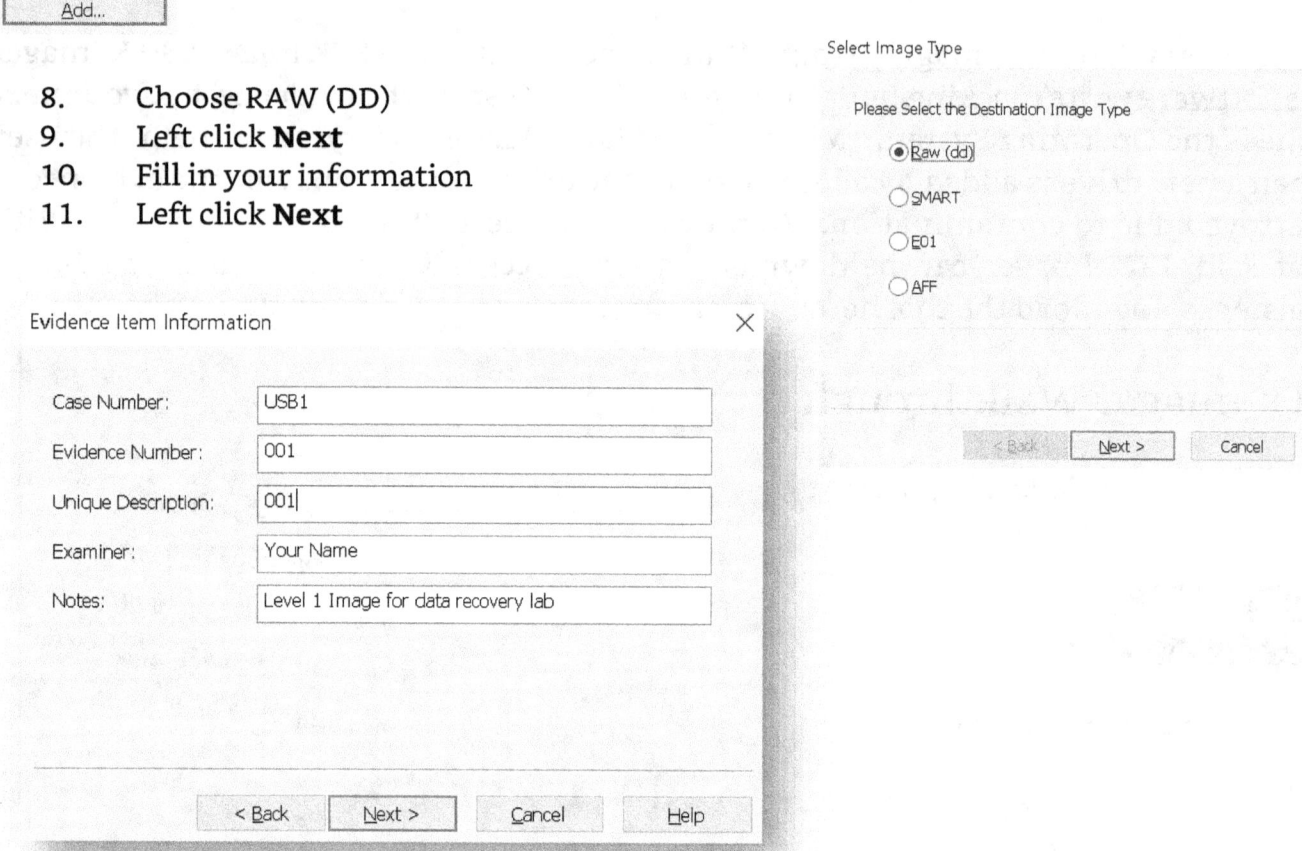

8. Choose RAW (DD)
9. Left click **Next**
10. Fill in your information
11. Left click **Next**

12. Image Destination Folder is where you want to store the image
    a. Left click **Browse** and choose the folder for your image

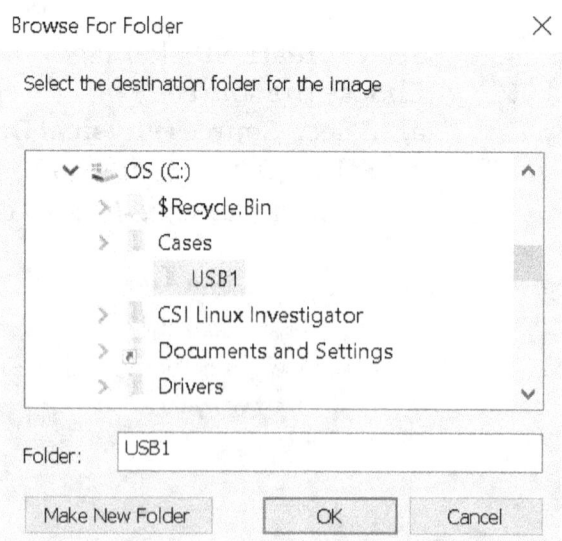

13. Name the image
14. Image segment size
    a. Type in "**0**" or zero
15. Click **Finish**

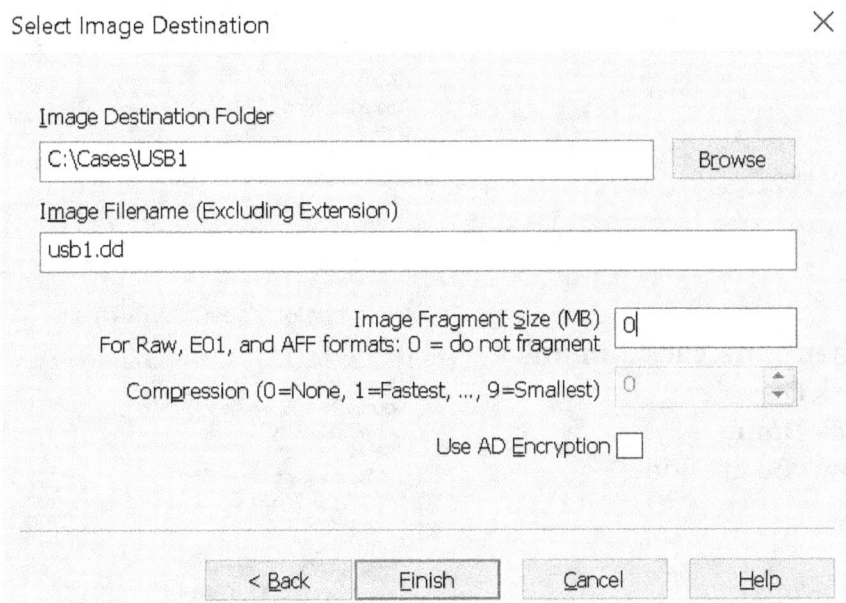

16. Check "Verify images after they are created"
17. Left click **Start**...

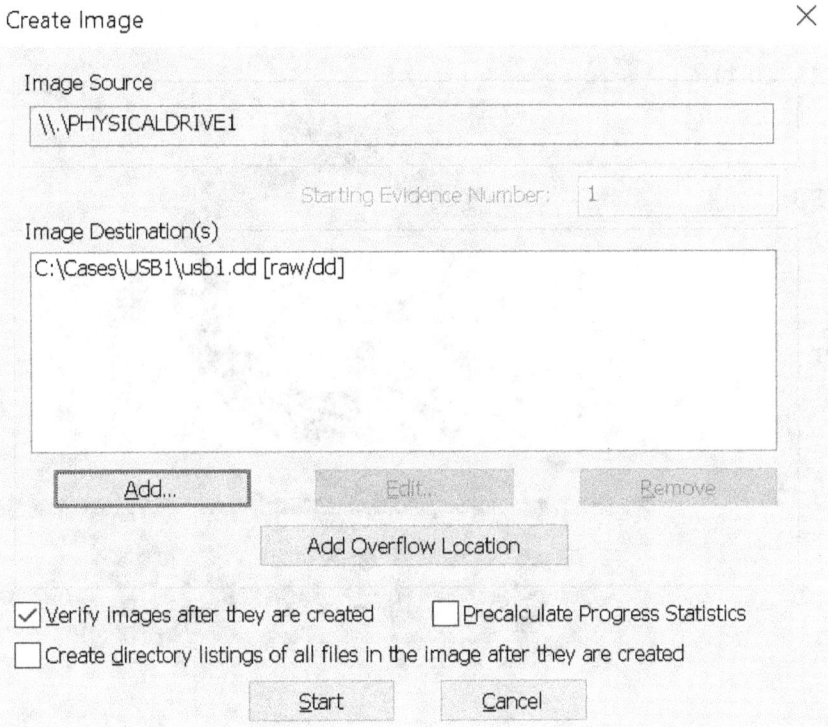

18. Now wait...

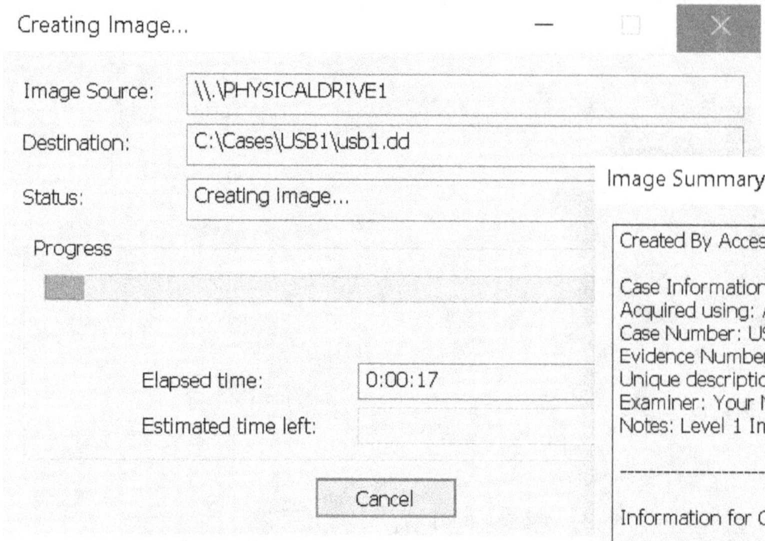

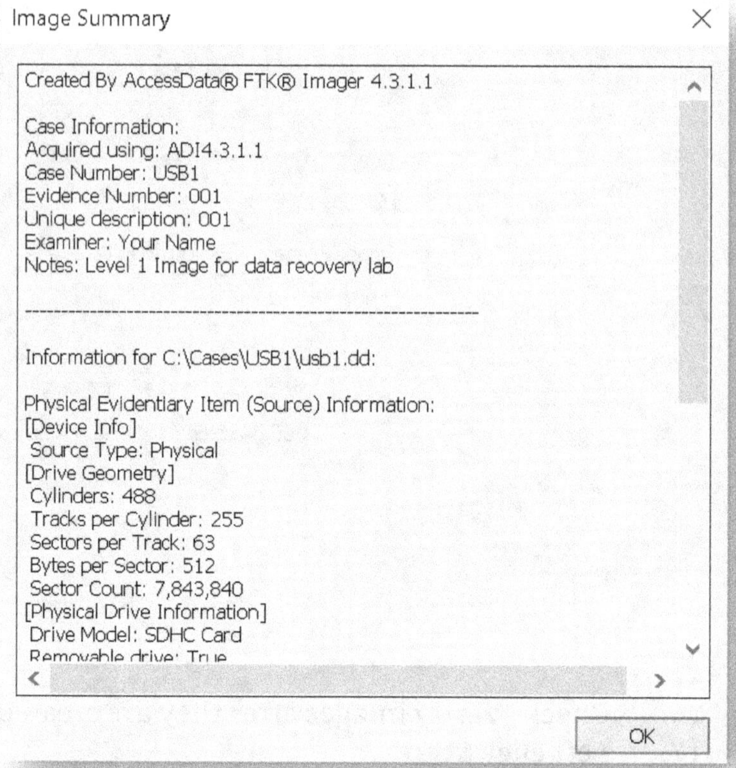

19. When done, click **Summary**
20. Click **OK**
21. Click **Done**
22. Now you are done!

You have successfully created a forensic image using FTK Imager. Now to create your different images for the data carving labs.

1. Delete all the files on the USB.
2. Repeat the FTK Imager steps.
3. Quick Format the USB.
4. Repeat the FTK Imager steps.
5. Wipe the drive using Eraser
6. Repeat the FTK Imager steps.

Now, if you are using a Linux or Unix computer, dcfldd is a command line imager that creates a physical copy. DCFLDD is based off dd with some upgrades. It gives a progress of the data copied and it allows you to create a hash. Best of all is it is free. If you do not have dcfldd installed, you can substitute "dcfldd" with "dd" in the commands.

Note: Unless you are logged in as root (NOT suggested for security reasons), you must use the "sudo" command any time you touch hardware or run a system level utility.

"sudo is a program for Unix-like computer operating systems that allows users to run programs with the security privileges of another user, by default the superuser. It originally stood for "superuser do" as the older versions of sudo were designed to run commands only as the superuser." - wikipedia.org

---

Lab: dcfldd (Linux)

1. Do Write Blocking Lab first
2. Burn a live Linux .iso to a bootable CD, DVD, or USB.
3. Boot off the CD, DVD. or bootable USB.

We use CSI Linux Acquisition for imaging, but any Linux distribution will do.

4. Once the OS is loaded, open a terminal window with root access.
5. Type "mkdir /recovery"
6. Type "cd /recovery"
7. Type "mkdir usb1"
8. Repeat for usb2-4
9. Wipe the drive by typing "sudo dcfldd if=/dev/zero of=/dev/sdb"
10. Format the USB with FAT by typing "**sudo mkfs.vfat /dev/sdb1**"
11. Download a theme of files (.jpg, .pdf, .txt). This will create a controlled environment.
12. Copy the files onto the USB.
13. Image the drive typing "sudo dcfldd if=/dev/sdb of=/recovery/usb1.dd".
14. Delete all the files on the USB.
15. Image the drive typing "sudo dcfldd if=/dev/sdb of=/recovery/usb2.dd".
16. Format the USB with FAT by typing **"sudo mkfs.vfat /dev/sdb1"**
17. Image the drive typing "sudo dcfldd if=/dev/sdb of=/recovery/usb3.dd".
18. Wipe the drive by typing "sudo dcfldd if=/dev/zero of=/dev/sdb"
19. Image the drive typing "sudo dcfldd if=/dev/sdb of=/recovery/usb4.dd".

To benefit of DCFLDD, is that it can create a hash instead of being forced to use a third-party tool. This makes scripting things or automation that much easier.

Example:

> **sudo dcfldd if=/dev/sdb1 of=usb(?).dd hashwindow=0 hashlog=hash.txt**
> **cat hash.txt**

If you have the hardware, use it. Doing this will minimize the risk of destroying evidence...

Lab: Hardware Imaging

1. Skip if you do not have a hardware imager or buy one & connect it to the drive to be duplicated.

Make sure you connect it to the right port. You do not want to wipe or overwrite the evidence drive. Then follow the instructions provided by the forensic imager vendor

Here is a list of vendors for forensic Imagers
  a. Forensics: SuperChief, Tableau, Forensic Duplicator...

  Here is a list of vendors for Data Recovery Imagers
  b. Data Recovery: DeepSpar, Atola, Data Copy King, etc...

If you image the logical drive/volume/partition, you can mount the volume directly.

Lab: Volume Image Mount in Linux

> **mkdir /mnt/evidence**
> **sudo mount usb(?).dd /mnt/evidence**
> **cd /mnt/evidence**
> **ls**

If you image the physical drive, all partitions, you can use **losetup** (losetup is used to associate loop devices with regular files or block devices).

Lab: Drive Image Mount for All Partitions in Linux

> **sudo losetup --show -f -P usb(?).dd**

Data Carving Labs

Now for recovering the data from the images. During your investigation, you are given an image (the ones created in the imaging lab) and it is your job to recover any data that you can. In this lab, we will cover several possible tools to use.

Lab: Using Autopsy

"Autopsy® is a digital forensics platform and graphical interface to The Sleuth Kit® and other digital forensics tools. It is used by law enforcement, military, and corporate examiners to investigate what happened on a computer. You can even use it to recover photos from your camera's memory card." - *sleuthkit.org/autopsy*

1. Download and install Autopsy GUI
   a. You can also use CSI Linux. Autopsy is already installed
2. Run Autopsy

3. Click on **New Case**.
4. Enter your **Case Name**.
5. Click on **Browse** to pick the folder you want your case content.

This will be the temp files and exported data. We traditionally use a "Cases" folder with the subfolder being named after the **Case Name**.

6. Keep the Case Type: as **Single-user**.
7. You will see the case folder at the bottom of the window.

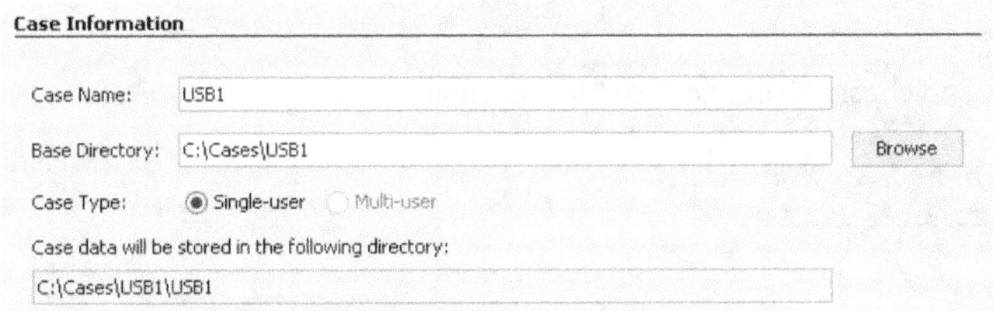

8. Under Case **Number:**, enter your case number.

This would be assigned by your organization, but in this lab, use 001.

9. Under Examiner **Name:** enter your name.
10. Under Examiner **Phone:** enter your phone number.
11. Under Examiner **Email:** enter your email.

12. Under Examiner **Notes**, enter the description or notes for the case.
13. Click on **Finish**.

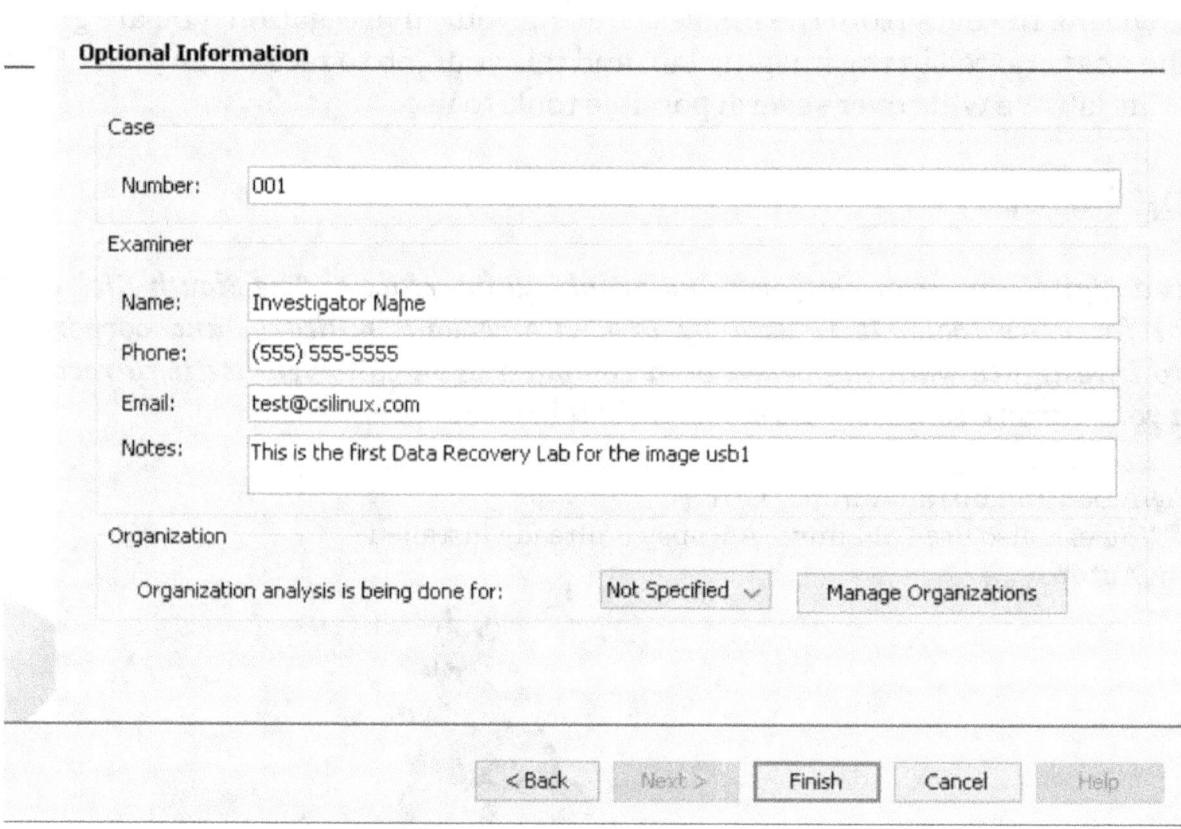

14. Select the Disk Image or VM File option.
15. Click **Next**.

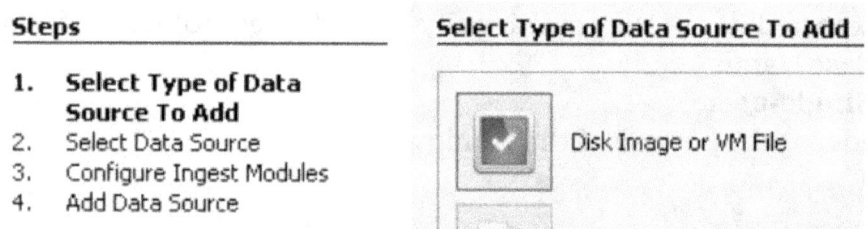

16. Click on Browse and chose the image (DD) file you created.
17. Click on **Next**.

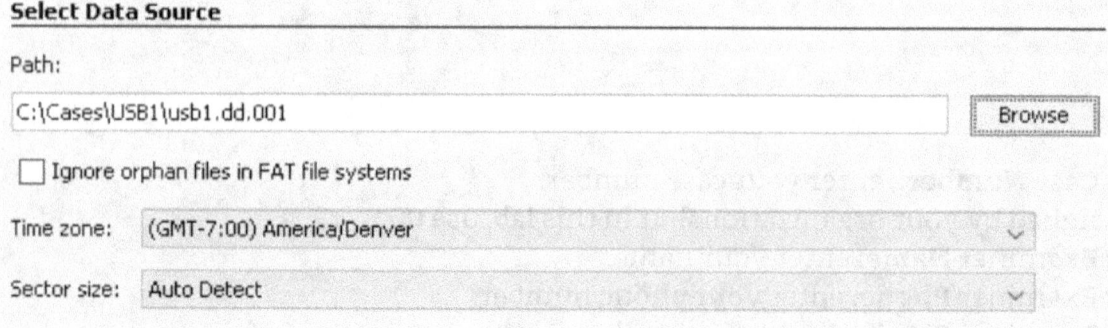

18. Click on **Select All**.

This is a small lab and should not be an issue. For larger cases, pick only the options you want to use

19. Click on **Next**.

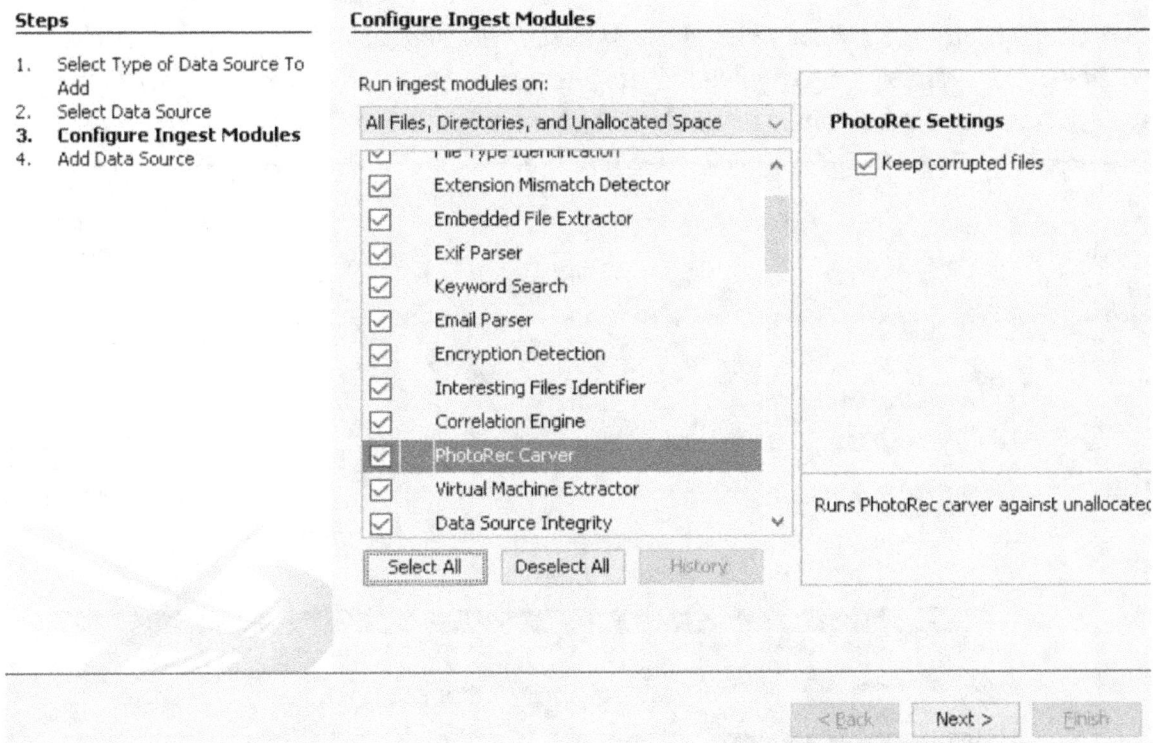

20. Click on **Finish**.

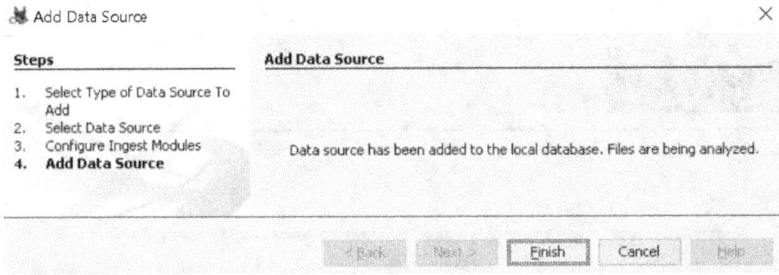

21. Now Wait...

You should see a progress bar on the bottom right of the Autopsy window.

80

Once Autopsy has completed the Ingest Modules, you should see data on the left-hand side, assuming that data was recoverable. Autopsy is more than just a recovery tool like some of the other tools we are going to cover, it is a very powerful forensics tool, especially for it being free.

Notice in the screenshot below that Autopsy also parsed out deleted files and even EXIF data from the JPG files it recovered. This means even location data if GPS or location services were enabled when the picture was taken.

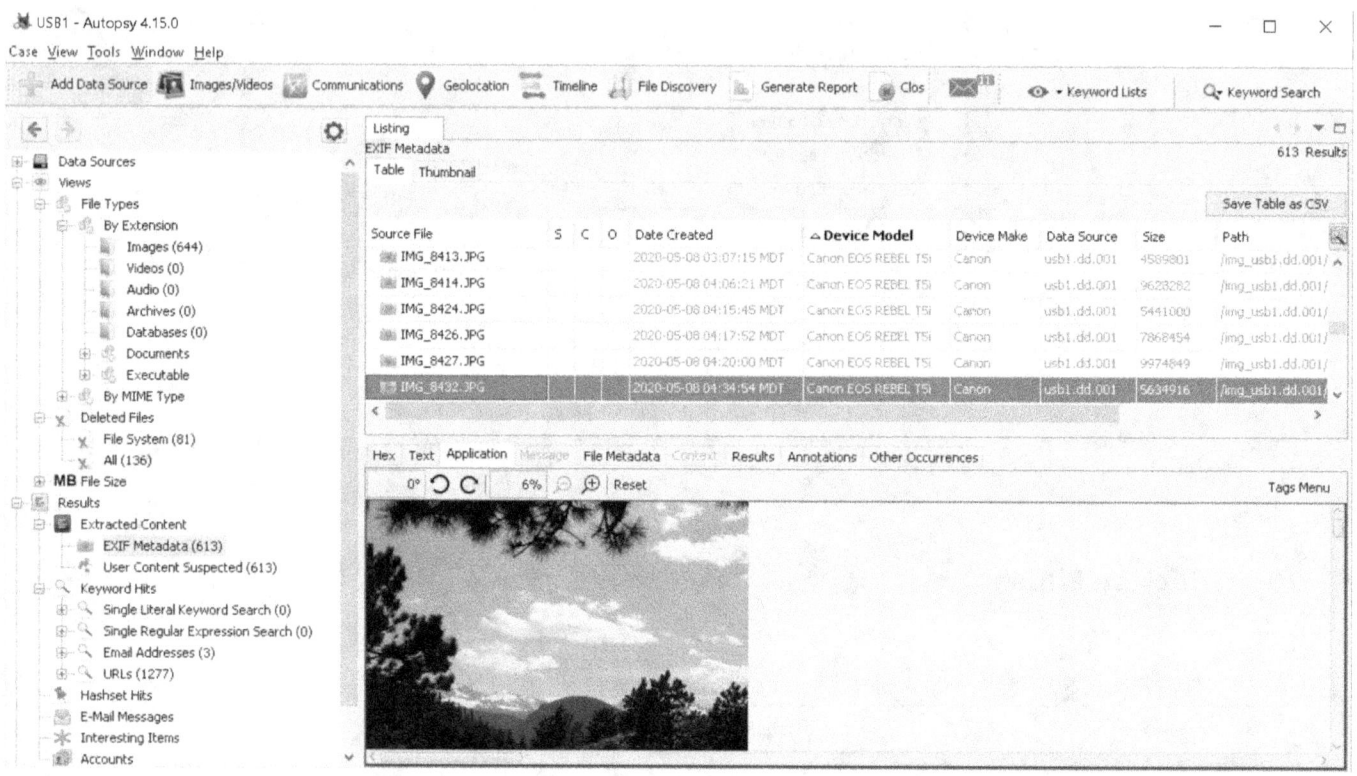

NOTE: The Autopsy application works in Windows, MAC, and Linux. Some of the third party ingest modules however may only work in Windows since they tie into .EXE files.

Lab: Using RecoverJPEG

"A tool to recover lost files on damaged memory cards or USB drives. recoverjpeg tries to recover JFIF (JPEG) pictures and MOV movies (using recovermov) from a peripheral."
- rfc1149.net/devel/recoverjpeg.html

1. Do Imaging Lab 1 first
2. recoverjpeg usb(?).dd

Lab: Using Foremost

"Foremost is a console program to recover files based on their headers, footers, and internal data structures. This process is commonly referred to as data carving. Foremost can work on image files, such as those generated by dd, Safeback, Encase, etc, or directly on a drive. The headers and footers can be specified by a configuration file or you can use command line switches to specify built-in file types. These built-in types look at the data structures of a given file format allowing for a more reliable and faster recovery.

Originally developed by the United States Air Force Office of Special Investigations and The Center for Information Systems Security Studies and Research, foremost has been opened to the general public. We welcome any comments, suggestions, patches, or feedback you have on this program. Please direct all correspondence to namikus@users.sf.net." - foremost.sourceforge.net

23. Do Imaging Lab 1 first
24. Type "foremost –i usb1.dd –o usb1 -v". Wait until complete.
25. Repeat step 2 for each other usb?.dd image
26. Use a file explorer or manager to view results
27. View and compare the results.

Optional: Only generate an audit file and print to the screen (verbose mode).

foremost -av usb(?).dd

Search all defined types

foremost -t all -i usb(?).dd Search for gif and pdf
foremost -t jpg,pdf -i usb(?).dd Run the default case
foremost usb(?).dd

Lab: Scalpel (Linux)

"Scalpel is a file carving and indexing application that runs on Linux and Windows. The first version of Scalpel, released in 2005, was based on Foremost 0.69". - github.com/machn1k/Scalpel-2.0

Scalpel takes a little more configuring out of the box. We are going to look at the configuration file that will allow us to data carve. This is what the /etc/scalpel/conf/scalpel.conf file will look like:

```
# Extension Case  size       header                      footer #
#
#         GIF and JPG files (very common)
#         gif    y    5000000    \x47\x49\x46\x38\x37\x61    \x00\x3b
#         gif    y    5000000    \x47\x49\x46\x38\x39\x61    \x00\x00\x3b
#         jpg    y    200000000  \xff\xd8\xff\xe0\x00\x10    \xff\xd9
#         jpg    y    200000000  \xff\xd8\xff\xe1            \xff\xd9
```

Once we edit the scalpel.conf file to look for what we want to find, save it and now we can use Scalpel to start carving data.

Using Scalpel

1. Do Imaging Lab 1 first
2. Type "scalpel /dev/sdb –o usb1 -v". Wait until complete.
3. Type "cat /usb1/audit.txt"
4. Repeat steps 2-3 for each other usb?.dd images we created earlier
5. Use a file explorer or manager to view results
6. View and compare the results.

Optional: **scalpel usb(?).dd -o Directory-you-want-the-output-to**

Note: The trick is to use all the tools in your disposal and compare. The easiest way to do this is to create the "evidence" drive yourself and documenting every file on the drive. Then delete several of the files or folders. At this point, you have a known baseline to start from. Create the dd raw image to analyze with the various methods.

EVIDENCE CHAIN OF CUSTODY TRACKING FORM

Event Number: Reason:
Submitting Individual: (Name/ID#)
Client:
Date/Time Seized: Location of Acquisition:

	Description of Evidence	
Item #	**Quantity**	**Description of Item** (Model, Serial #, Condition, Marks, Scratches)

Chain of Custody

Item #	Date/Time	Released by (Signature & ID#)	Received by (Signature & ID#)

APD_Form_#PE003_v.1 (12/2012)   Page 1 of 2 pages (See back)

Technical Working Group on Biological Evidence Preservation. The Biological Evidence Preservation Handbook: Best Practices for Evidence Handlers. U.S. Department of Commerce, National Institute of Standards and Technology. 2013.

(Continued)

Final Disposal Authority
Authorization for Disposal
Item(s) #: on this document pertaining to (suspect): is(are) no longer needed as evidence and is/are authorized for disposal by (check appropriate disposal method) ☐ Return to Owner ☐ Auction/Destroy/Divert Name & ID# of Authorizing Officer: Signature: Date:
Witness to Destruction of Evidence
Item(s) #: on this document were destroyed by Evidence Custodian ID#: in my presence on (date) .   Name & ID# of Witness to destruction: Signature: Date:
Release to Lawful Owner
Item(s) #: on this document was/were released by Evidence Custodian ID#:   Address: City: State: Zip Code: Telephone Number: ( )   Under penalty of law, I certify that I am the lawful owner of the above item(s).   Signature: Date: Copy of Government-issued photo identification is attached. ☐ Yes ☐ No
This Evidence Chain-of-Custody form is to be retained as a permanent record by all parties involved.

APD_Form_#PE003_v.1 (12/2012)

Technical Working Group on Biological Evidence Preservation. The Biological Evidence Preservation Handbook: Best Practices for Evidence Handlers. U.S. Department of Commerce, National Institute of Standards and Technology.

Introduction to Network Forensics

By
Nitin Sharma

Cyber-crime and digital forensics have evolved a lot in last few decades. The History of Computing Project [1] defines 1947 as the beginning of the Industrial Era of Computing and we are still in the midst of this era. So much has happened in the computing since 1947 that it is helpful to break it down into manageable chunks. Digital forensics - or forensic computing as some like to call it – has a shorter history. Mark has emphasized upon some critical elements that combined to create the discipline – people, targets, tools, organizations, and the community as a whole [2].

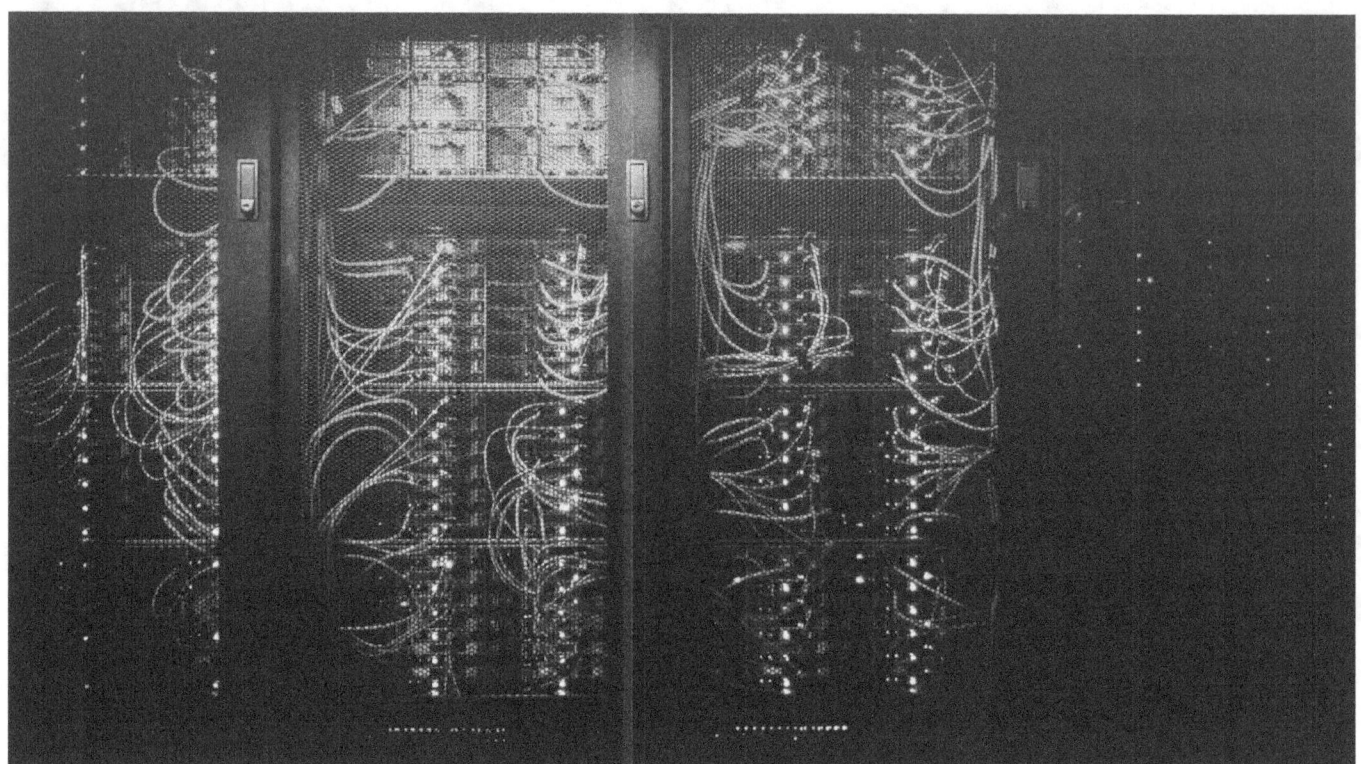

University of Washington, Seattle, United States [3]

With advancement of interconnecting devices in every field whether it be educational universities, large manufacturing industries, information technology companies or legal firms, the traditional computing has evolved into computing networks. This has forced the digital forensics to unfold even more specialized cross-disciplinary domains like Network Forensics.

Network Forensics

"Digital forensics, also known as computer and network forensics, has many definitions. Generally, it is considered the application of science to the identification, collection, examination, and analysis of data while preserving the integrity of the information and maintaining a strict chain of custody for the data." [4]

Network Forensics can be generally defined as science of discovering and retrieving evidential information in a networked environment about a crime in such a way as to make it admissible in court.

Network forensics follow the same basic principle of digital forensics which include data integrity, audit trail, specialist support, appropriate training, and legality. Most of the Network forensics analysis tasks are based on a rigid framework. One such popular framework for performing Network forensics analysis is OSCAR methodology [5].

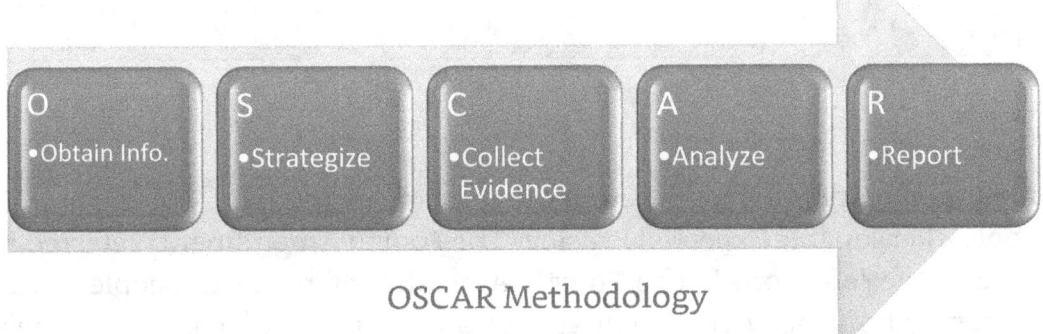

OSCAR Methodology

1. Obtain Information: The gathering of general information about the incident itself and the environment where it took place in, such as the date and time when an incident was discovered, persons and systems involved, what has initially happened, what actions have been taken since then, who is in charge, etc. The goals of investigation should be defined, written down and prioritized, as there will always be resource constraints on the investigation.
2. Strategize: This deals with the planning of the investigation. Acquisition should be prioritized according to the volatility of the sources, their potential value to the investigation and the effort needed to get them. This priority list should be starting point for allocating resources and personnel to conduct the present tasks such as acquiring information and evidence.
3. Collect evidence: Based on the plan from the previous phase, evidence is collected from each identified source. Three points must be considered,
   - Documentation
   - Capture of evidence
   - Store/Transport maintaining Chain of Custody, i.e., "showing the seizure, custody, control, transfer, analysis, and disposition of evidence, physical or electronic."
4. Analyze: During the analysis, an investigator recovers evidence material using a number of different methodologies and tools. The method depends on the case and what leads are already present.
5. Report: This will deal with conveying the results of the investigations to the client(s). It must be understandable by non-technical persons like managers, jury, etc. It must be factual and defensible in detail.

From the perspective of law enforcement officers, investigations will be conducted in response to cyber-crime incidents with appropriate incident timing [6]. This is important to understand as forensic laws differ with investigation timing.

Network Forensics with Laws

1. **Pro-Active Investigations**: Occurs before cyber-crime incidents.
   a. People's Reasonable Expected Privacy (The Fourth Amendment) referred to as the "right to be left alone". The Fourth Amendment protects people's reasonable privacy by limiting government agent's authority to search and seize without a warrant. Govt. Investigators cannot gather digital evidence and identify a suspect based on hunch; they must have probable cause [7].
2. **Real-Time Investigations**: Occurs during cyber-crime incidents.
   a. Title III or Wiretap Act [8] is an important statutory privacy law which prohibits unauthorized government access to private electronic communications in real time.
   b. Pen Register Act [8] also known as the Pen Registers and Trap and Trace Devices statute (Pen/Trap statute) regulates the collection of addressing and other non-content information such as packet size for wire and electronic communications.
3. **Retro-Active Investigation**: Occurs during cyber-crime incidents.
   a. Stored Communications Act (SCA) [9] is a part of Electronic Communications Privacy Act (ECPA) which protects the privacy rights of customers and subscribers of ISPs and regulates the government access to stored content and non-content records held by ISPs.

The single most significant piece of legislation relating to privacy protection in the EU is the **General Data Protection Regulation (GDPR) (EU) 2016/679**. It supersedes the older Data Protection Directive 95/46/EC and affects all organizations that collect or process PII data if they are based in the EU or if the data belongs to a person based in the EU and limited to professional or commercial activity. This hugely impacts commercial investigation processes.

Different Types of Network Based Evidences

There are different types of network-based evidence, all of which have pros and cons w.r.t. network forensics analysis.

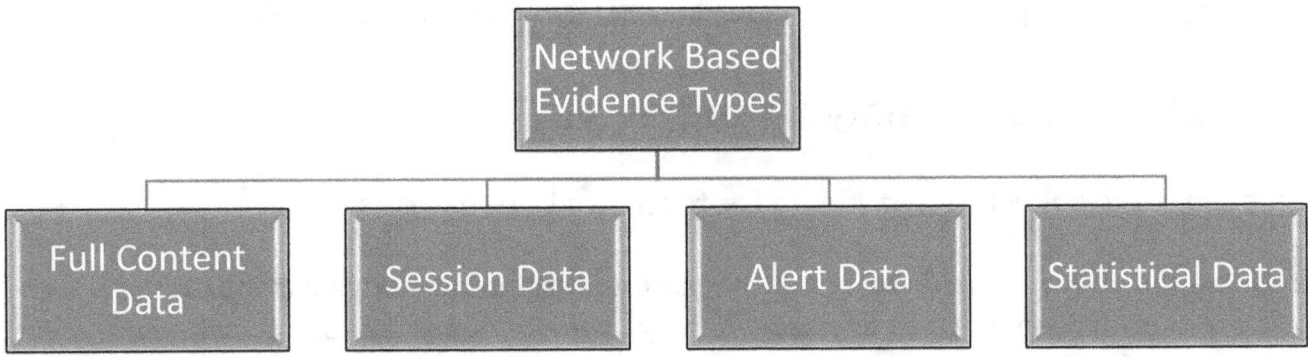

1. **Full Content Data**: This consists of every possible single piece of information that passes across a network (or networks). This is known as "packet capture" (PCAP).
2. **Session Data**: This consists of aggregated metadata and usually refers to the conversation between two network entities, grouped together into "flows" and/or groups of network packets related to one another.
3. **Alert Data**: Whenever network traffic triggers a pre-defined item of interest (such as a particular pattern of bytes, or counts of activity, or other characteristics), the analyst will be dealing with alert data. Typically generated by Network Intrusion Detection Systems (NIDS) such as Suricata or Snort.
4. **Statistical Data**: This consists of different types of metadata which provide the analyst with network related aspects such as the number of bytes contained in a packet trace, start and end times of network conversations, number of services and protocols being used, average packet size, etc.

All of the above information can be used to do a definite network baselining and the deviation from such baseline will provide the definition for an incident, which further lead to network forensics. Here, we can say that incident response analyst/security analyst need to incorporate forensics while mitigating the incident. This is true from corporate perspective. However, there is quite significant thing one can notice,

Security Analyst and Incident Responders have responsibilities such as identifying affected assets, returning those assets to normal operations, preventing similar incident and so on. Network Forensics Analysts, have similar mindset while also taking care of collection of court admissible evidence for a possible legal proceeding. Maintaining proper chain-of-custody is not the only concern here to satisfy all the applicable laws and regulations.

To ascertain the legal value of evidence, some considerations are mentioned as "Guidelines for Evidence Collection and Archiving" [10] which includes,

- **Admissible**: It must conform to certain legal rules before it can be put before a court.
- **Authentic**: It must be possible to positively tie evidentiary material to the incident.
- **Complete**: It must tell the whole story and not just a particular perspective.
- **Reliable**: There must be nothing about how the evidence was collected and subsequently handled that casts doubt about its authenticity and veracity.
- **Believable**: It must be readily believable and understandable by a court.

Network Forensics Analysis and Tools

Systems used to collect network data for forensics in two forms [11]:

1. **Catch-it-as-you-can systems**: All the packets passing through a particular traffic point are captured and written to storage. Analysis is subsequently done in batch mode. This approach requires large amount of storage. Example of such system is tcpdump.
2. **Stop-look and listen systems**: Each packet is analyzed in a rudimentary way in memory and only certain information is saved for future analysis. This requires a faster processor to match the pace of incoming traffic. Example of such system is NetFlow.

Before moving towards different tools, let us look at packet capture and network flow analysis [12].

1. **Network Flow Analysis**: A flow is a traffic stream with a common set of identifiers. It can be defined by a traffic that has the same source IP, destination IP, protocol, source port and destination port. If any of these variables change, then a new flow is defined. For example, when a client is connecting to a server, several flows might be created because the client might establish several connections to the server, involving new source ports. Each one of these connections would be a separate flow. NetFlow, sFlow, IPFIX are all ways to collect information about traffic that is traversing a network. Most NetFlow collection applications use NetFlow v5, which tracks,
    a. Source Interface
    b. Source and Destination IP address
    c. Layer 4 Protocol (for example ICMP, TCP, UDP, OSPF, etc.)
    d. Source and Destination port number (if protocol is TCP/UDP)
    e. Type of service value
2. **Packet Analysis:** Packet analysis is normally associated with SPAN or mirror ports, which are available on most managed network switches. Port mirroring is used on a network switch to send a copy of network packets seen on one switch port (or on an entire VLAN) to a network monitoring connection on another switch port. Port mirroring on a Cisco System switch is generally referred to as Switched Port Analyzer (SPAN); some other vendors have other names for it, such as Roving Analysis Port (RAP) on 3Com switches. Deep Packet Inspection is possible here to extract metadata such as application/website names. This is ideal for monitoring important applications, servers or internet connections where low-level information is critical.

Some popular general-purpose network forensics analysis tools include,

1. Packet Sniffers – dumpcap, pcapdump and netsniff-ng
2. Protocol Analyzer – tcpdump, wireshark/tshark and tstat.
3. Network Forensic Analysis Tools – Xplico and NetworkMiner

Specific Task Tools include,

1. Intrusion Detection – Snort, Suricata, Bro.
2. Match regular expressions – ngrep
3. Extract files or pictures – infex and driftnet
4. Sniff passwords or HTTP sessions – dsniff, firesheep, Ettercap, creds
5. Extract emails – mailsnarf, smtpcat
6. Print network/packet statistics – ntop, tcpstat.
7. Extract SSL information – ssldump
8. Reconstruct TCP flows – tcpflow, tcpick
9. Fingerprinting – p0f, prads

Importance of Network Forensics

Network forensics is an important component of a successful security operations program. It is a significant capability that provides a data of record for the incident responders and security analysts which plays a key role in in their daily workflow. However, network forensics is not limited to security professionals and cyber-crime investigators. Their lies a definite business value in it.

1. Breach Response – Most of the questions that organizations will have during a breach like the rapid identification of extent of damage, containment timelines, affected assets, etc., will only be answered with the help of network forensics analysis results.
2. Threat Hunting – Detecting unusual or suspect activities like APT compromise of endpoints, etc. are very challenging scenarios that could only be handled by skilled threat hunters and network forensic analysts.
3. Intelligence Alerting – In today's modern era, attackers are highly intelligent and sophisticated. The alerting mechanism requires the fundamental of network activity gathering as well as mature, scalable, powerful network forensics solution with a robust query language. Such an implementation can help in alerting the business execs to identify suspicious and malicious activity under the radar.

References

[1] The History of Computing Project, Timeline: Chronology of the history of computing, The History of Computing Foundation, Maurik, The Netherlands, 2010. Last Accessed on June 18, 2020. - thocp.net/timeline/timeline.htm

[2] Mark Pollitt. A History of Digital Forensics. 6th IFIP WG 11.9 International Conference on Digital Forensics (DF), Jan 2010, Hong Kong, China. pp.3-15, ff10.1007/978-3-642-15506-2_1ff. ffhal-01060606f. Last Accessed on June 18, 2020. - hal.inria.fr/hal-01060606/document

[3] University of Washington [Photo], Seattle, United States, Taylor Vick, Unsplash. Last Accessed on June 18, 2020. - unsplash.com/photos/M5tzZtFCOfs

[4] Guide to Integrating Forensic Techniques into Incident Response, Timothy Grance, Suzanne Chevalier, Karen Kent Scarfone, Hung Dang, Special Publication (NIST SP) – 800-86, Published on September 1, 2006. Last Accessed on June 18, 2020. - nist.gov/publications/guide-integrating-forensic-techniques-incident-response

[5] Introduction to Network Forensics Handbook Final V1.1, Cybersecurity ENISA Training, Published August 2019. Last Accessed on June 18, 2020. - enisa.europa.eu/topics/trainings-for-cybersecurity-specialists/online-training-material/documents/introduction-to-network-forensics-handbook.pdf

[6] A Framework of Network Forensics and its Application of Locating Suspects in Wireless Crime Scene Investigation, Junwei Huang, Yinjie Chen, Zhen Ling, Kyungseok Choo, Xinwen Fu University of Massachusetts Lowell, USA + Southeast University, China. Last Accessed on June 18, 2020. - pdfs.semanticscholar.org/10b8/8debc818ca1da825fb9848cfaf8dccf2aa9f.pdf

[7] Privacy and Search, Expectation of Privacy, Wikipedia. Last Accessed on June 18, 2020. Link: en.wikipedia.org/wiki/Expectation_of_privacy#Privacy_and_search

[8] H. Marshall Jarrett and Michael W. Bailie, Searching and Seizing Computers and Obtaining Electronic Evidence in Criminal Investigations (Washington, DC: Office of Legal Education Executive Office, 2009). Last Accessed on June 18, 2020. - justice.gov/sites/default/files/criminal-ccips/legacy/2015/01/14/ssmanual2009.pdf

[9] Stored Communications Act (SCA, codified at 18 U.S.C. Chapter 121 2701-2712), Wikipedia. Last Accessed on June 18, 2020. - en.wikipedia.org/wiki/Stored_Communications_Act

[10] Legal Considerations, Guidelines for Evidence Collection and Archiving, RFC3227. Last Accessed on June 18, 2020. - tools.ietf.org/html/rfc3227

[11] Network Forensics, Wikipedia. Last accessed on June 19, 2020. – en.wikipedia.org/wiki/Network_forensics#Overview

[12] Flow Analysis Versus Packet Analysis, What should you Choose, Netfort.com. Last Accessed on June 19, 2020. - netfort-prod.k8s.corpwebsite.gcp.rapid7.com/content/uploads/PDF/WhitePapers/NetFlow-Vs-Packet-Analysis-What-Should-You-Choose.pdf

NETWORK FORENSICS WITH WIRESHARK

Prepping Wireshark

By
Ambadi MP / Mossaraf Zaman Khan

What is Network Forensic?

Network forensics is concerned with capturing, tracking, and evaluating network activities to detect the source of threats, malware, intrusions, or breaches of security that occur on a network or in network transit. Network forensic research is also considered to be under the umbrella of digital forensics, alongside smartphone forensics or digital image forensics. It includes a detailed knowledge of specific programs and network protocols to identify attack trends. The investigator needs to consider the usual type and actions of certain protocols to distinguish the irregularities associated with an attack.

Web protocols including:

- HTTP
- HTTPS
- FTP
- SMB
- NFS

Network Protocols including:

- Ethernet protocol
- WLAN Protocol
- TCP/IP Protocol

There are two primary sources network forensics experts focused on they are :

- Packet Full capture
- Logging of files

Packet Full Capture

Packet Full capture's main advantage is that it is possible to determine the content and therefore the meaning and value of the transmitted data. Packet capture is normally not implemented in full-time networks due to the large amount of storage required for even one hour of data on a typical business network. While most companies today allow all workers to sign an agreement that they do not have the right to privacy on business-owned systems and networks, privacy issues may exist.

Usually, data collection is applied when suspicious behavior has been observed and may still be in progress. The tap point for the packet-capture-network must be carefully selected so that it can capture traffic flowing between all affected devices, or multiple taps must be implemented.

Logging of files

NetFlow (or equivalent) data can be stored in full-time log files by most modern network devices, such as routers. Web, Proxy servers, firewalls, DS, DNS, DHCP, and server log files from Active Directory also provides valuable information. These log files can be analyzed to detect suspicious source and destination pairs and suspicious client behavior. One main advantage of using log files is that the size of the file is much smaller than the capture of a full packet. Another advantage is that collection points are already in place at key places, so collecting and storing data from various devices into one master log is not difficult to analyze.

Enhance the skills

A lot of free tools are available for the forensic network software. Although some have a GUI, most free tools only have a command-line GUI, and others only run on Linux. Particularly for full packet captures, data needs to be reduced before a thorough filtering analysis is carried out.

Wireshark is an open-source application which captures and displays data on and off a network. It is widely used to troubleshoot network problems and check applications as it has the ability to drill and read each packet's, and is a multi-platform, open source network analyzer running Linux, OS X, BSD, MAC, and Windows. It is particularly useful to know what is happening within your network, which accounts for its widespread use in government, business, and education. It works like TCPDump, but Wireshark adds a great graphical interface that allows you to filter, organize and order the captured data so it takes less time to analyze it. A text-based version, called Tshark, features similar.

Wireshark uses ".**pcap** and **.pcapng**" files to store the captured packets.

The ability to view data in log and capture files and identify malicious activity in the data is a special skill requiring deep knowledge of network and application protocols. This article provides a brief introduction to networked forensic investigations of suspected illegal activity linked to IT. Criminals are hacking computer networks for a variety of purposes but primarily for economic advantage. Banking and other personal information stored on PCs and servers are among the most common targets that will help to complete fraudulent financial transactions. A specific skill requiring in-depth knowledge of network and application protocols is the ability to translate data into log and capture files and detect malicious activity in the data. This article includes a brief introduction to network based forensic investigations of alleged information technology-related criminal activity.

For additional information, please refer the Wireshark User Guide - Wireshark.org/download/docs/user-GUIde.pdf

Wireshark Basics

Installation:

Windows OS: Download the latest edition of the Wireshark from Wireshark's Official Website (Wireshark.org/#download). After downloading, executing it with administrative privilege. After that install wizard appeared then install it by clicking the "Next". For that time also install the "WinPcap" with it.

Linux OS: Some of the Linux distributions like CSI Linux, Kali Linux, Parrot Security OS comes with Wireshark already installed. But for rest of the Linux system you can use the following steps to install in your system.

a. Open Terminal
b. Add the Wireshark Package [sudo add-apt-repository ppa:Wireshark-dev/stable]
c. Update the Repository [**sudo apt-get update**]
d. Install the Wireshark [sudo apt-get install Wireshark]

How to Download and Install Wireshark

Wireshark can be downloaded for most Operating Systems. You will see the most recent stable release and the current release of the development. Unless you are an advanced user, get the stable version downloaded.

Download: wireshark.org/download.html

If prompted, during the Windows setup process, choose to install WinPcap or Npcap as these include the libraries required to capture live data.

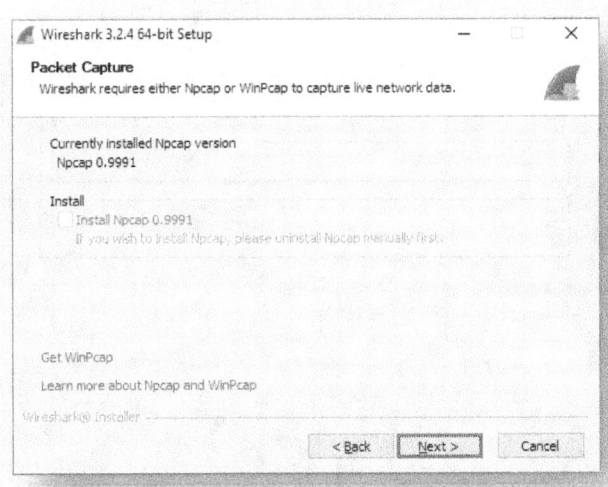
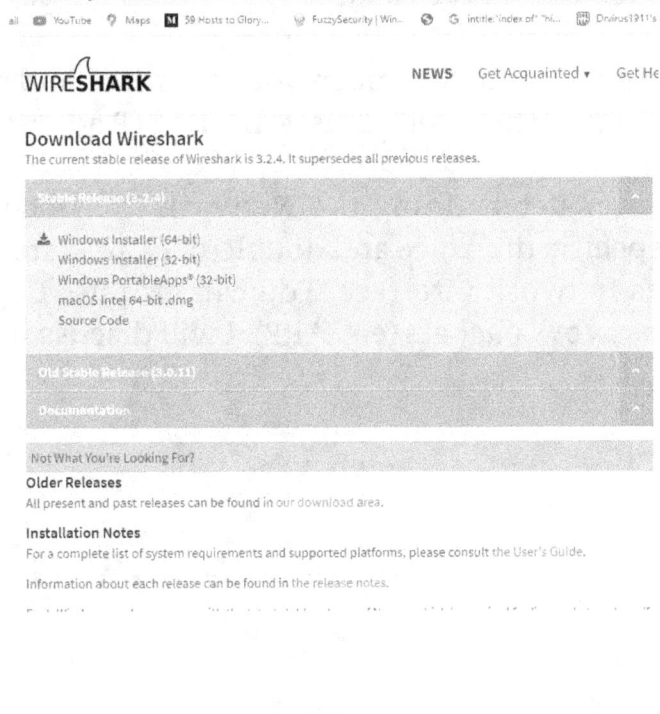

Wireshark is available through the Ubuntu Universe repository. You can enable repository in the universe and then install it like this:

Installation on Ubuntu

> **sudo add-apt-repository universe**
> **sudo apt install wireshark**

Installation on CentOS

> **yum install gcc gcc-c++ bison flex libpcap-devel qt-devel gtk3-devel rpm-build libtool c-ares-devel qt5-qtbase-devel qt5-qtmultimedia-devel qt5-linGUIst desktop-file-utils**
>
> **sudo yum install wireshark wireshark-qt**

User Interface:

Opening Wireshark

By Double clicking on the Wireshark shortcut (Windows) or type "**Wireshark**" on terminal (Linux) to execute the Wireshark.

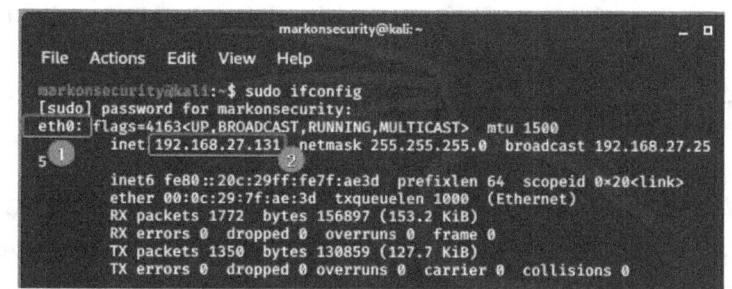

Fig 1: Internet Configuration details (ifconfig)

Before capturing, open your terminal and type '**ifconfig**' to know about your interface. For me, the interface is '**eth0**' and IP address is '**192.168.27.131**'.

After determining the Network Interface. Now open the Wireshark and choose the specific interface and double-click to start capture the traffic. In Figure 2, I choose **eth0** as network interface. You can also use Capture filter to capture only specific types of network packets (e.g. ARP). I will discuss in later section.

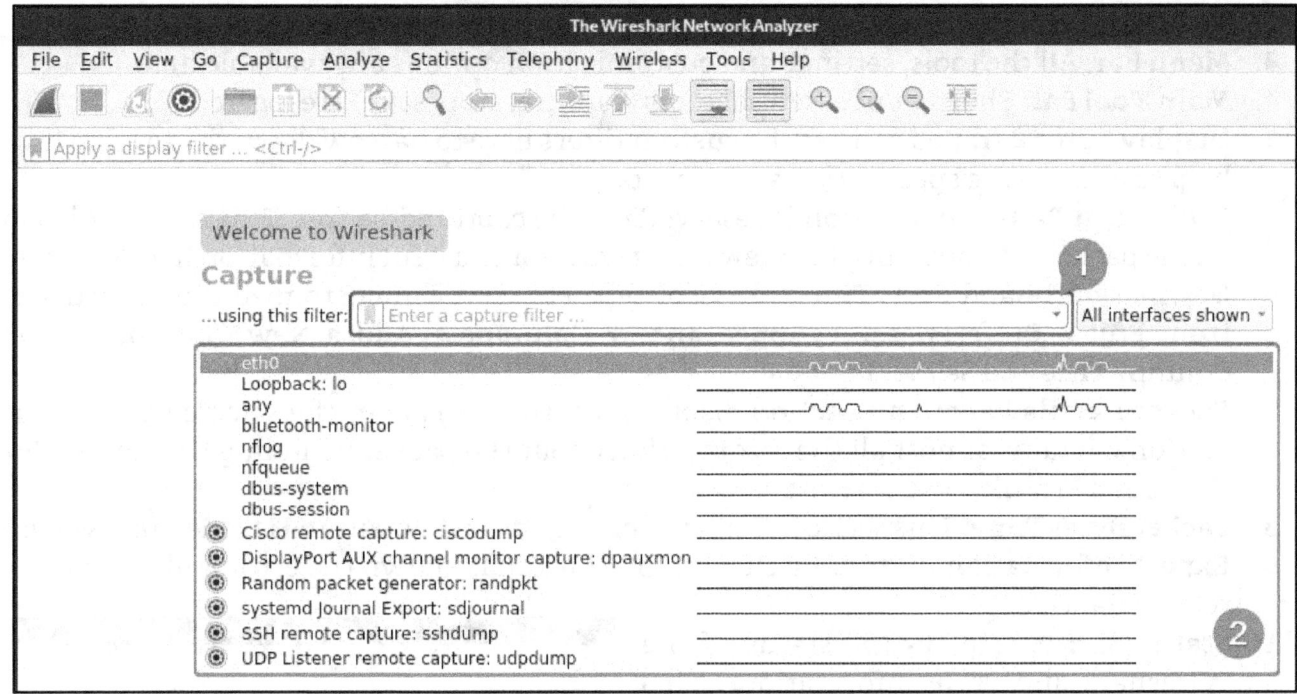

Fig 2: Basic Interface of Wireshark

The Graphical User Interface of Wireshark is shown in the following screenshot:

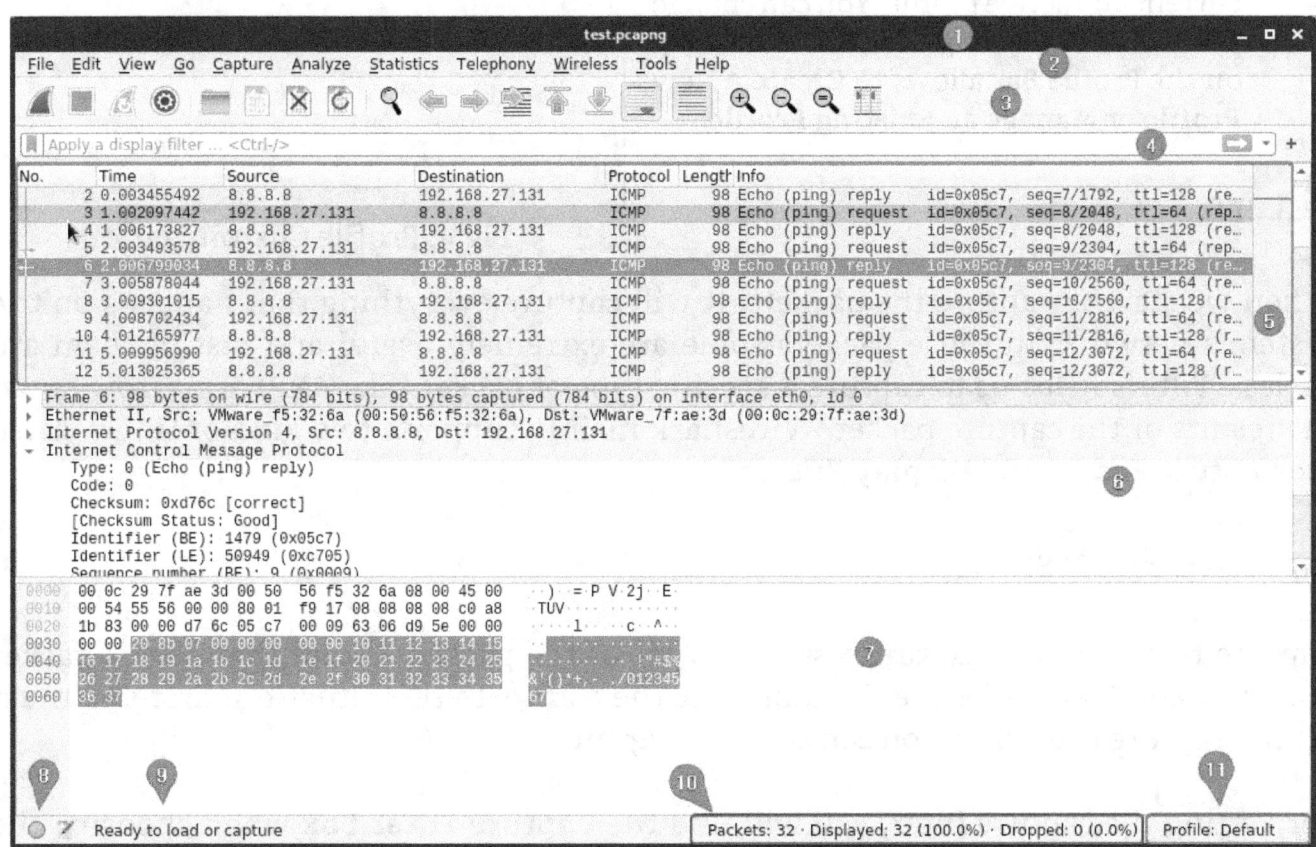

Fig 3: Main user interface of Wireshark

2. **Title Bar:** Display the packet title or Captured file name (test.pcapng)
3. **Menu Bar:** All the tools, settings and customization options are available here.
4. **Main Tool Bar:** Shortcut of essential tools (capture, stop, save) are located
5. **Display Filter Bar:** You can use the custom filters here to narrow down the results. It will help to analyze the specific types of packets.
6. **Packet List Pane:** This section is reserved for the captured packet. This section displays all the packets captured in a list view along with some useful information like Source and Destination IP and Port, Time, Protocol type etc. You can customize this information from **Edit** > **Preferences...** > **Appearance** > **Columns** > **Add a New Column** > Give a Column **Title** and Select the '**Type**'.
7. **Packet Details Pane:** This section displays information about the selected packet. This section contains almost all the information about the packet including IP Address, Port Number & Details, MAC address
8. **Packet Bytes Pane:** This section displays selected packet details in Hexadecimal view.
9. **Expert Information Button:** By clicking this button is shown the error and information related data etc.
10. **Status Bar:** It displays the status of the Wireshark and PCAP information. This section provides details about the total number of capture packets and related information.
11. **Profile Bar:** This section shown the current and active profile. You can change the profile by clicking on it. Right-clicking on the Profile Bar allows to **Create a New Profile** or **Manage an Existing Profile**.

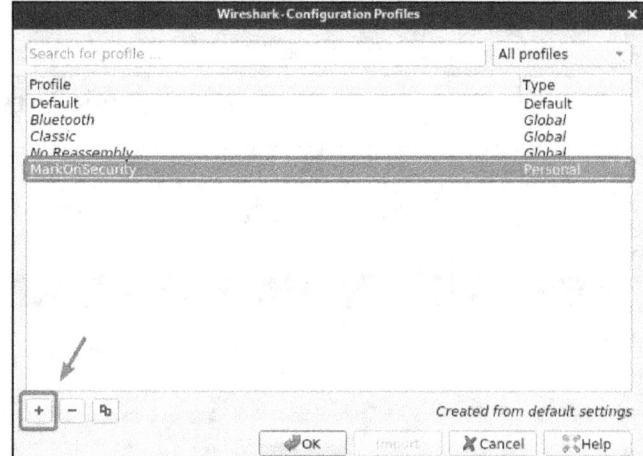

Fig 4: Profile Customization

Filters:

When we start to capture the packets. It will capture everything that happens on the system's network. In those packets some are extremely useful and rest of them are useless. Filters helps us to capture a specific type of packet (like ARP) or narrow down the results of the capture packet. Wireshark mainly supports two kind of filters those are **Capture Filters** and **Display Filters**.

Capture Filters:

Capture filter helps to capture a specific type of the packet. Except that others packet will ignored. It works before the capturing the traffic. In this situation, first you must set the capture filter then you can start the capture.

For Setting the capture filter, you will find the **Capture Filter Box** when choosing the Network Interfaces (Fig - 2, Mark-1). Or, Go to the **Capture** > **Capture Filters** > List of the Capture Filters. Here you can Add or Delete a custom capture filter also. **Resource:** wiki.Wireshark.org/CaptureFilters

Display Filters:

Display filters helps to narrow down the results from captured packets. It can also be used in running process of capturing. It locates above the packet list pane (Fig - 3, Mark - 4). When you type the filter in the box it will suggest some filter. If the box shown as red then the filter is incorrect, if it shown in green then the filter is correct.

It supports the Boolean expressions, that uses for specifying the data or combine two commands. These expressions are commonly used in display filters -

> **or** or || : OR
> **and** or && : AND
> **gt** or > : Greater than
> **lt** or < : Less than
> **eq** or == : Equals

Example of Display Filters:

> ARP Protocol Size - **arp.proto.size**
> TCP URG Flag - **tcp.flags.urg**
> Filter through IP Source and Destination address using Boolean operator -
> **ip.src == 192.168.27.31 or ip.dst == 10.42.30.67**

> **Resources:**
> packetlife.net/media/library/13/Wireshark_Display_Filters.pdf
> wiki.Wireshark.org/DisplayFilters
> Wireshark.org/docs/dfref

Other Useful Options:

Coloring Rules:

In Wireshark, colorizing a specific packet type is a effective method to identify and spot the packet of interest from the Packet List Pane.
Wireshark has its own predefined coloring rules. But you can add and delete the coloring rules as per your requirements. To add a new coloring rule go to **View** > **Coloring Rules...** to Add a new coloring rule click on '+' button to add a new rules and enter the Name of the rules and Filter. You can change the Foreground and the Background color is per your requirement.

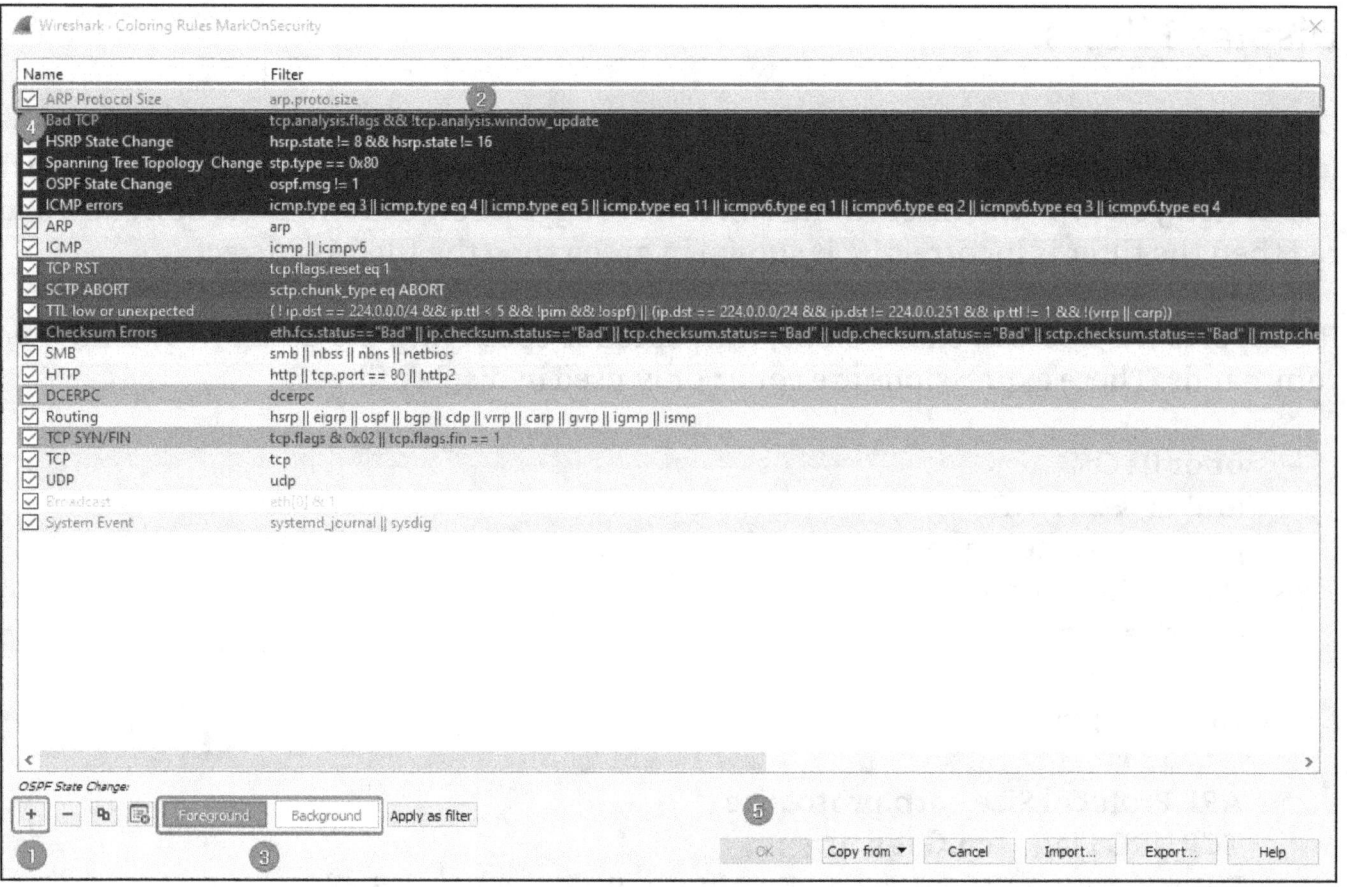

Fig 5: Coloring Rules

Network Statistics:

Wireshark provide us a huge range of network statistics features. It helps to gather the general knowledge about the captured or loaded packet file. It can be accessible from Menu Bar of the Wireshark named 'Statistics'.

From the Statistics menu you can do the following things –

1. **Capture File Properties:** It provides general information about the captured packet. Including Name, Length, Hash value, Hardware information, Interface details, Packet data statistics etc.
2. **Resolved Addresses:** Mapping all the IP addresses with the Domain Name.
3. **Protocol Hierarchy:** All the protocol that has been captured & percentage of the packets.
4. **Conversations:** All the conversations between Client A to Client B of the packets. Click on **Name Resolution** on Ethernet section it allows to reveal the domain names.
5. **Endpoints:** Like Conversations but only display the endpoint addresses.
6. **Packet Lengths:** Certain amount of packet length to the destination. Including packet count and percentages from total packet.
7. **IO graph:** Graphical representation of communication between two endpoints.
8. **DNS:** Reveals all the DNS services
9. **Flow Graph:** Reveals all the TCP packets in a Graphical manner.

10. **HTTP > Load Distribution:** Reveals what the servers and IP addresses served for this computer system.

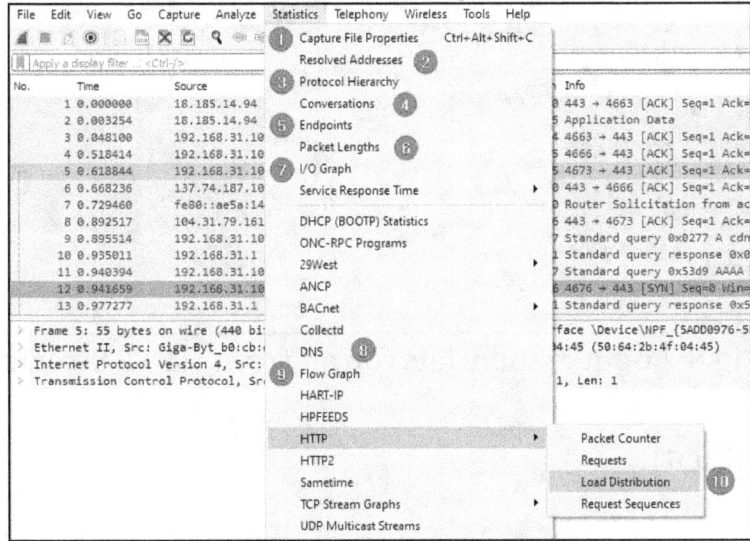

Fig 6: Network Statistics of Packets

Follow Stream:

Protocol stream following is one of the powerful features. It helps you to looking for crucial data from a stream. You can follow TCP, UDP, TLS, HTTP packets from packet list pane. It also allows you to identify the login credential from HTTP Packet.

You can follow the stream by two ways:

- Select a packet which you want to follow then Right-click > Follow > TCP / UDP/ TLS Stream
- Or go to Analyze > Follow > TCP / UDP/ TLS Stream

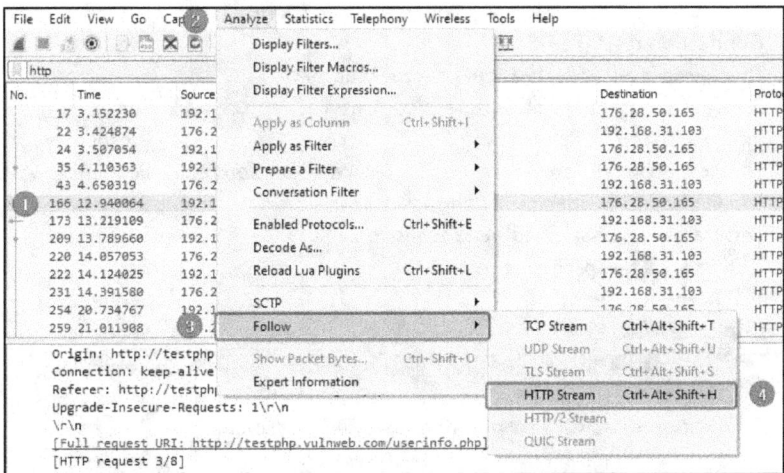

Fig 7: Following a HTTP Stream

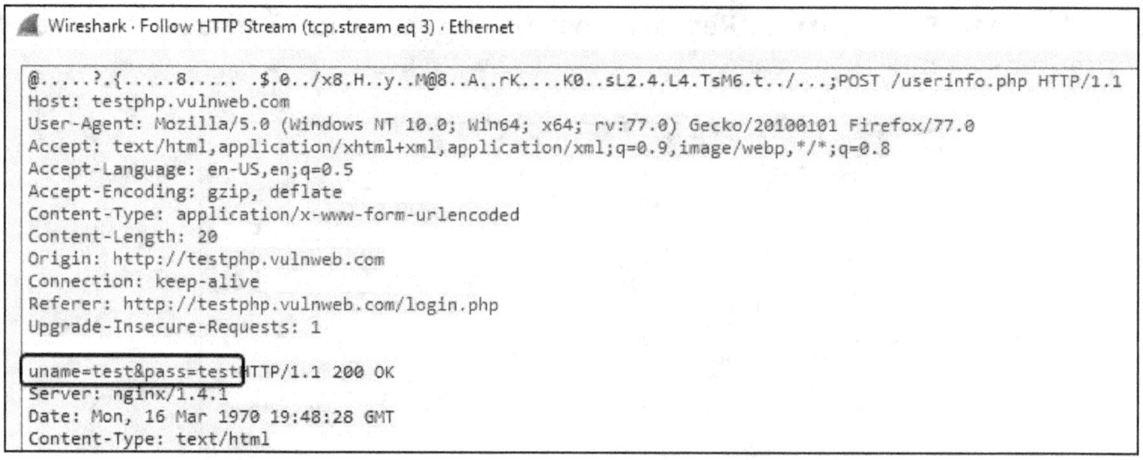

Wireshark · Follow HTTP Stream (tcp.stream eq 3) · Ethernet

```
@.....?.{.....8..... .$.0../x8.H..y..M@8..A..rK....K0..sL2.4.L4.TsM6.t../...;POST /userinfo.php HTTP/1.1
Host: testphp.vulnweb.com
User-Agent: Mozilla/5.0 (Windows NT 10.0; Win64; x64; rv:77.0) Gecko/20100101 Firefox/77.0
Accept: text/html,application/xhtml+xml,application/xml;q=0.9,image/webp,*/*;q=0.8
Accept-Language: en-US,en;q=0.5
Accept-Encoding: gzip, deflate
Content-Type: application/x-www-form-urlencoded
Content-Length: 20
Origin: http://testphp.vulnweb.com
Connection: keep-alive
Referer: http://testphp.vulnweb.com/login.php
Upgrade-Insecure-Requests: 1

uname=test&pass=testHTTP/1.1 200 OK
Server: nginx/1.4.1
Date: Mon, 16 Mar 1970 19:48:28 GMT
Content-Type: text/html
```

Fig 8: Login credentials found from HTTP Stream

Expert Information:

Expert Information provides the deeper information in a quick way. When it tracks down any abnormalities and area of interest it raises a flag for it. You can access expert information from **Analyze** > **Expert Information** or from the left corner of the buttom (Fig 3, Mark 8)

Red: Indicates for Malformed packets (Error)
Yellow: Indicates for any Warnings
Blue: Indicates for Information (Chat)
Cyan: Indicates for any events (Note)

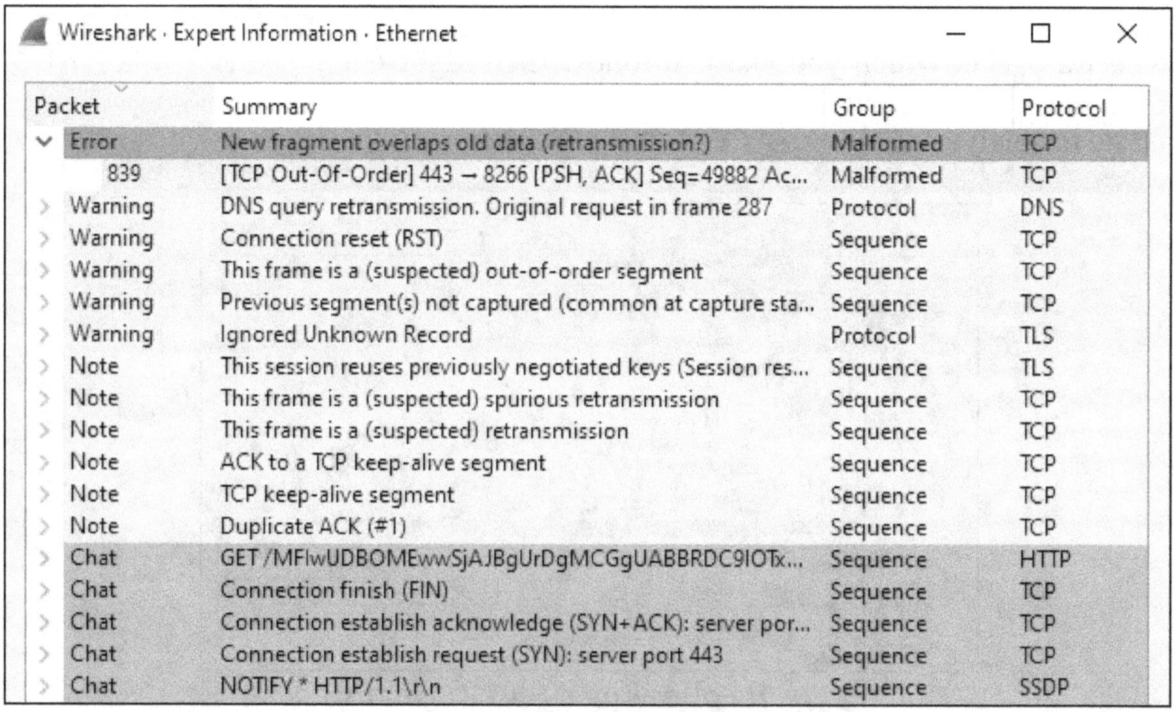

Wireshark · Expert Information · Ethernet

Packet	Summary	Group	Protocol
Error	New fragment overlaps old data (retransmission?)	Malformed	TCP
839	[TCP Out-Of-Order] 443 → 8266 [PSH, ACK] Seq=49882 Ac...	Malformed	TCP
Warning	DNS query retransmission. Original request in frame 287	Protocol	DNS
Warning	Connection reset (RST)	Sequence	TCP
Warning	This frame is a (suspected) out-of-order segment	Sequence	TCP
Warning	Previous segment(s) not captured (common at capture sta...	Sequence	TCP
Warning	Ignored Unknown Record	Protocol	TLS
Note	This session reuses previously negotiated keys (Session res...	Sequence	TLS
Note	This frame is a (suspected) spurious retransmission	Sequence	TCP
Note	This frame is a (suspected) retransmission	Sequence	TCP
Note	ACK to a TCP keep-alive segment	Sequence	TCP
Note	TCP keep-alive segment	Sequence	TCP
Note	Duplicate ACK (#1)	Sequence	TCP
Chat	GET /MFIwUDBOMEwwSjAJBgUrDgMCGgUABBRDC9IOTx...	Sequence	HTTP
Chat	Connection finish (FIN)	Sequence	TCP
Chat	Connection establish acknowledge (SYN+ACK): server por...	Sequence	TCP
Chat	Connection establish request (SYN): server port 443	Sequence	TCP
Chat	NOTIFY * HTTP/1.1\r\n	Sequence	SSDP

Fig 9: Expert Information Window

Saving a Captured Packets:

After capturing the network packets, you can also save those packets for further analysis. To save those packets go to the **File > Save (Ctrl+S) > Choose the Location > Give a 'Filename' > Choose the file type** (Default: .pcapng)

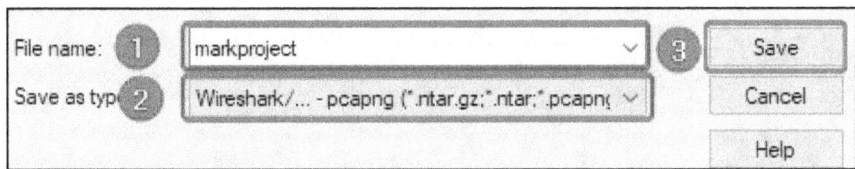

Fig 10: Saving a Network packets

This process helps you to save all the packet the captured. But sometimes the packet sizes are too huge, and you do not need all of those packets. In that scenario you choose your packet as per your needs and mark them by Right-click > Mark/ Unmark Packet or by pressing shortcut key [Ctrl+ M]. After the marking go to the **File > Export Specified Packets... >** Enter the **Name** & Choose the **File types > Save**.

Wireshark Data Taster for ARP Poisoning
Layer 2/3

By
Mossaraf Zaman Khan

Detection of ARP Poisoning

Introduction to ARP:

ARP stands for Address Resolution Protocol. It helps to mapping an Internet Protocol (IP) address to a Media Access Control (MAC) address i.e. machine address. IPv4 is 32bits long and the MAC address is 48bits long. So, it helps to translate 32bit address to 48bit addresses and vice versa. ARP works on layer 2 (Data link Layer) and layer 3 (Network Layer) of the OSI model.

How ARP works:

When User-A wants to establish the connection with User-B but User-A doesn't know about the User-B MAC address. The User-A sends an **ARP-Request** packet to the destination IP address (User-B's IP address). Because the destination IP address is indicating to User-B, so User-B will reply with the **ARP-Reply** packet, listening its MAC address. Now User-A has the required information to exchange the traffic with the User-B.

Ro view the ARP table:

   a. Open a command prompt
   b. type '**arp -a**'

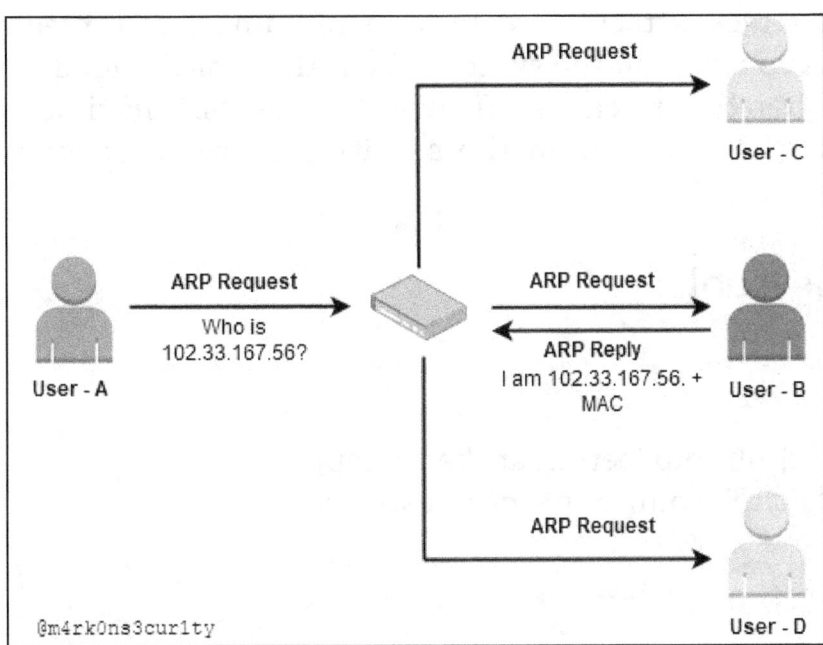

Fig 11: How ARP Works

ARP Poisoning:

ARP Poisoning is a type of attack, where attacker sends falsified ARP messages over the local host so attacker can link their MAC address with the victim's IP address. Once attacker's MAC is successfully authenticated with the victim's computer network, then the attacker can intercept, modify any communications to the legitimate MAC address. It is also known as Man-in-the-Middle (MITM) attack.

In Man-in-the-Middle attack attackers creates a connection between two users and intercept their communication by controlling the connection.

How ARP Poisoning Attack Works:

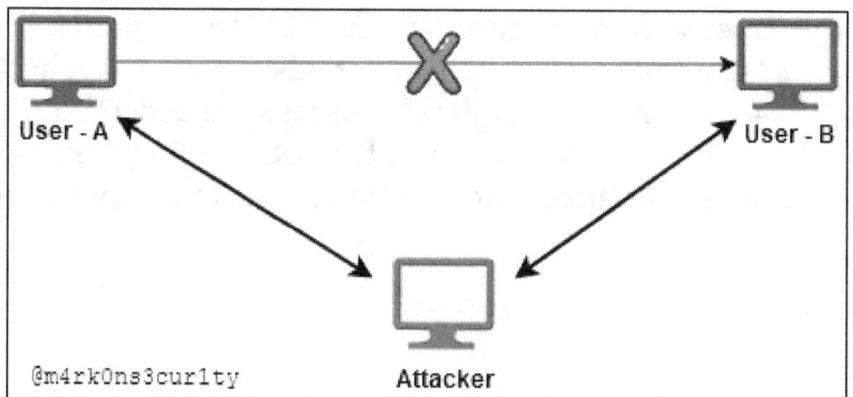

Fig 12: ARP Poisoning Attack

In ARP Poisoning attack, attacker creates a huge number of forged ARP-Request and ARP-Reply packets to overload the switch. Then ARP table is flooded with the spoofed ARP packets, and then the attacker sniff all of the packets. This time malicious attacker redirect traffic so they can obtain the sensitive information or prepare for more advanced attack.

ARP Poisoning Tools:

    Ettercap
    arpspoof
    Bettercap [github.com/bettercap/bettercap]
    Xerosploit [github.com/LionSec/xerosploit]

Detection of ARP Poisoning through Wireshark:

Lab Configuration:

Tool: Ettercap - GUI [for ARP Poisoning], Wireshark [Sniffing]
Victim Machine: Windows 7
Attacker Machine: Kali Linux

Configure the Wireshark:

Wireshark should be placed in Attacker's Machine i.e. Kali Linux
When there is a large number of falsified ARP request, this is an indication of an ARP storm. It could be detected easily through Wireshark. To detect this storm, go to **Edit** > **Preferences** > **Protocols** > **ARP/RARP** > [x] **Detect ARP request storms**.

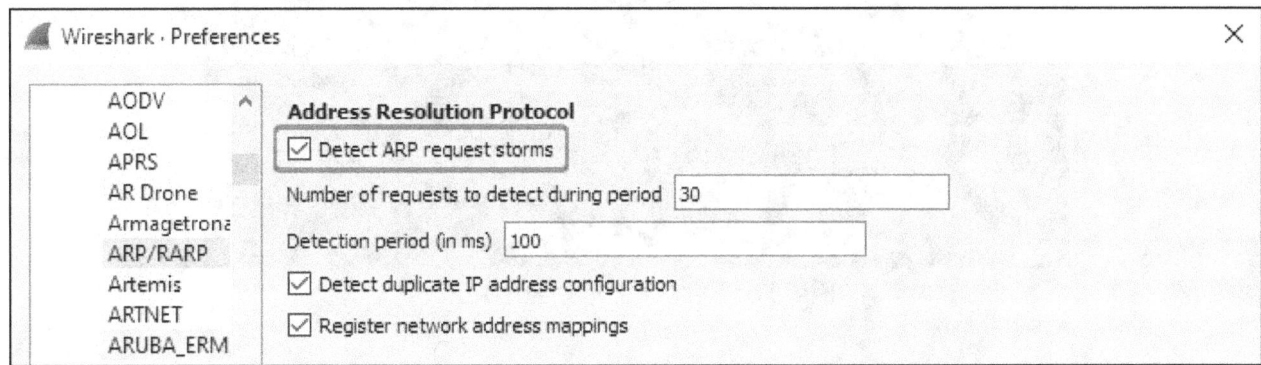

Fig 13: Detection of ARP request storms

Getting the Victim Machine IP:

Command Prompt > Type "**ipconfig**" to get the IP address of Victim Machine

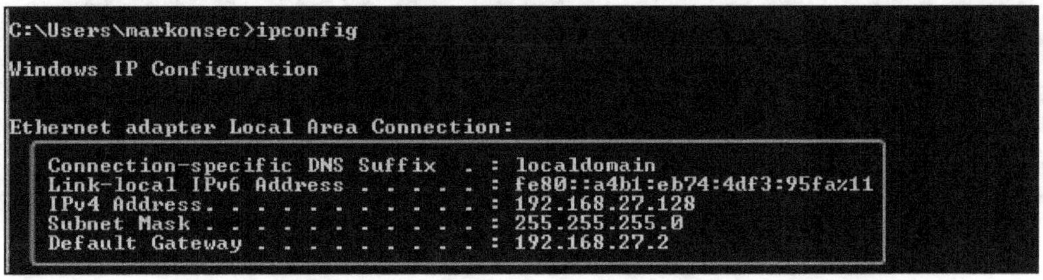

Fig 14: Windows 7 IP configuration (ipconfig)

So, Victim Machine (Windows 7): Target IP address is **192.168.27.128**

EtterCap Configuration & Launching Attack:

Step 1: Set System Configuration (**sysctl**) for forwarding IPv4 packet. This is allows to movement the packets through attacker's system.
sysctl -w net.ipv4.ip_forward=1

Fig 15: sysctl Configuration

Step 2: Search on Kali linux for Ettercap-graphical and execute it with root access.

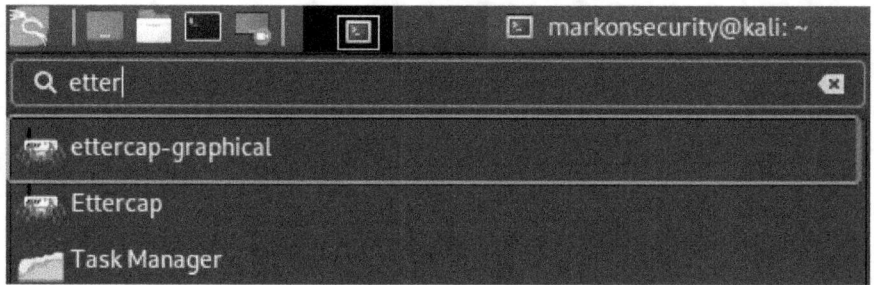

Fig 16: Ettercap Graphical

Step 3: Click on **Search** button. It will automatically search for the available host on the network. From Fig-14 we know our target IP is **192.168.25.128**. So set the IP for ARP Poisoning Attack.

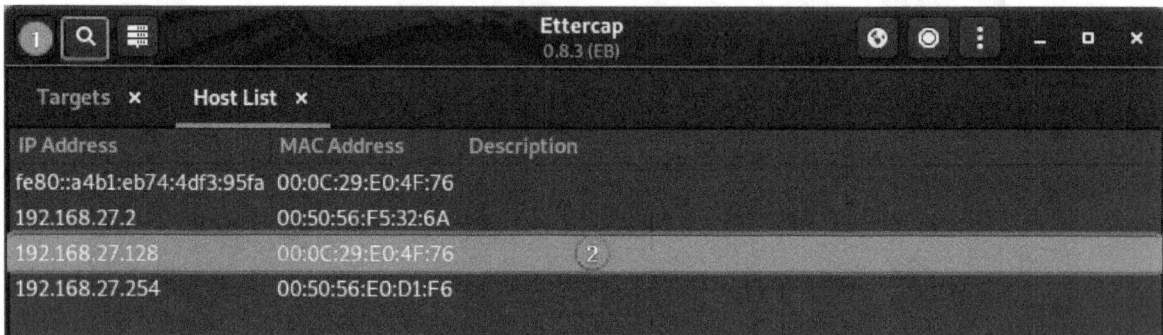

Fig 17: Gathering the Live Host

Step 4: Now choose the "**ARP Poisoning**" Attack from the drop-down menu and checkmark for the **Sniff Remote Connection**. Click OK to Continue

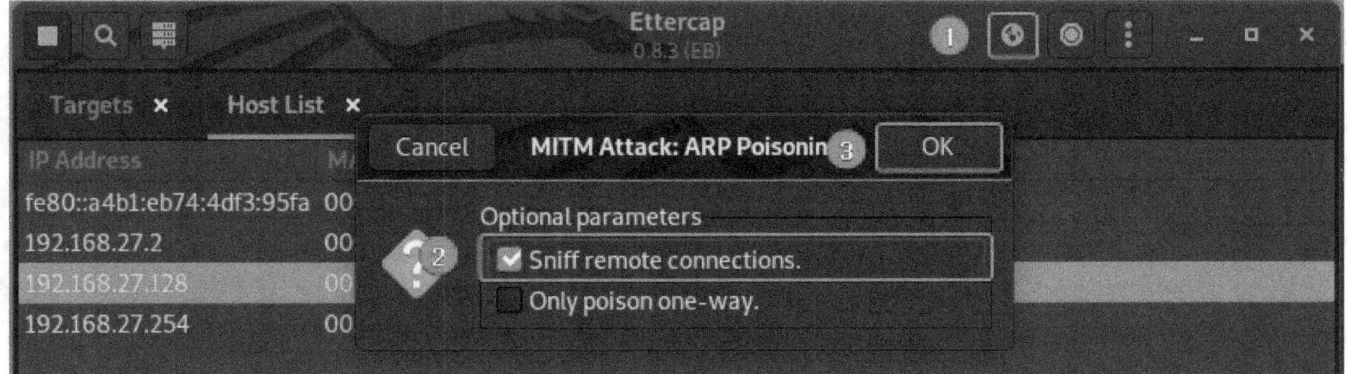

Fig 18: Selecting the Attack Type

Step 5: Start the Wireshark and choose the interface (eth0) and start capturing. The go back to Ettercap and click on red circle to start the attack.

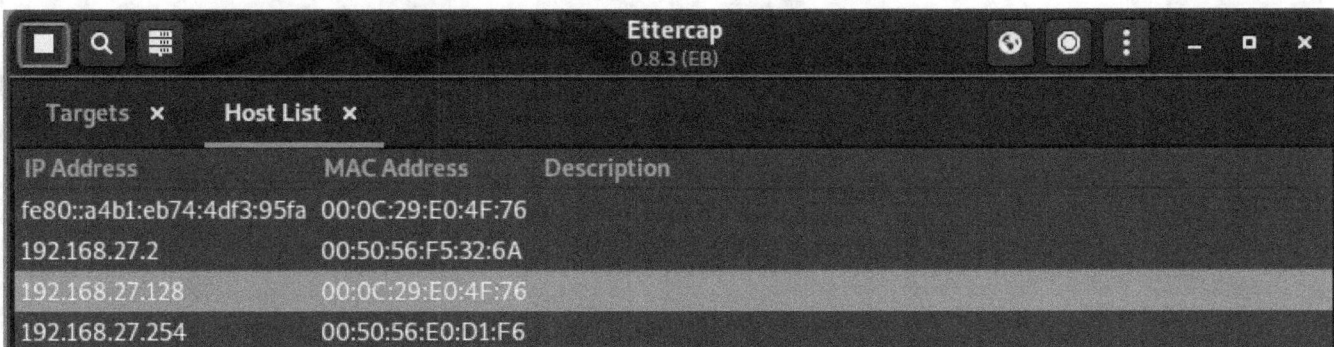

Fig 19: Launching the ARP Poisoning attack

Step 6: Now in Victim Machine (Win 7). Victim access the **testphp.vulnweb.com** site and enter the login credential. That also captured via the Ettercap.
Username: **test** & Password: **test**

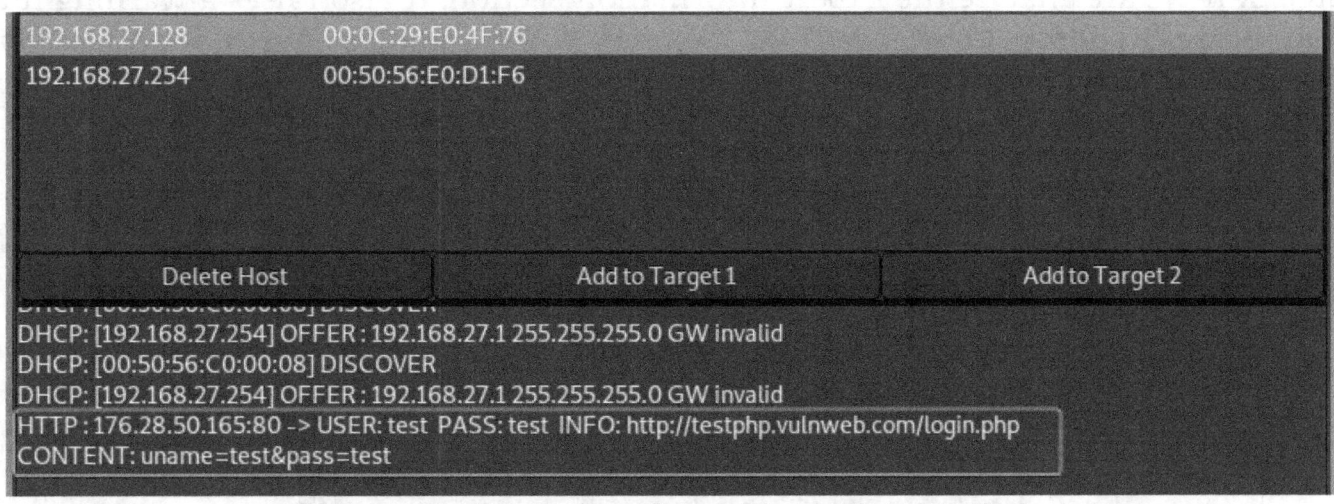

Fig 20: Gathering Credential by ARP Poisoning

Packet Analysis using Wireshark:

Step 1: After attacking, stop the packet capture in Wireshark and save into a pcap file for further investigation.

Step 2: Analyze the captured Packets using Wireshark. You will notice a flood of ARP packets are captured. And some packets also tells that "**duplicate use of 192.168.27.128 detected**". That's our victim's IP address. And it also tells us "**duplicate use of 192.168.27.2 detected**" that is our default gateway (shown in Fig 14). In Packet Details Pane tells us about the position where duplicate IP address is detected.

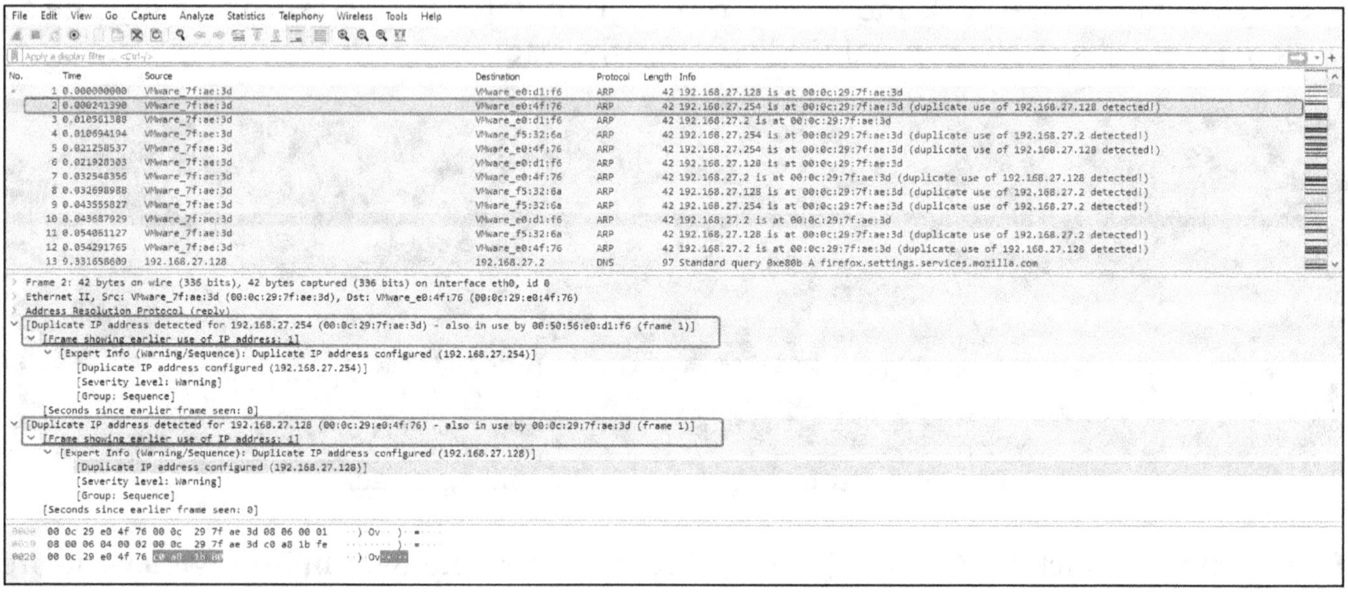

Fig 21: Packet Analysis using Wireshark

Step 3: If we are analyze the Expert Information Section. It also raises a warning for "**Duplicate IP address Configured**" for 79 times. By expanding this area, we can easily navigate to those packets where duplicate IP address was used. That is also a clear indication of ARP Poisoning.

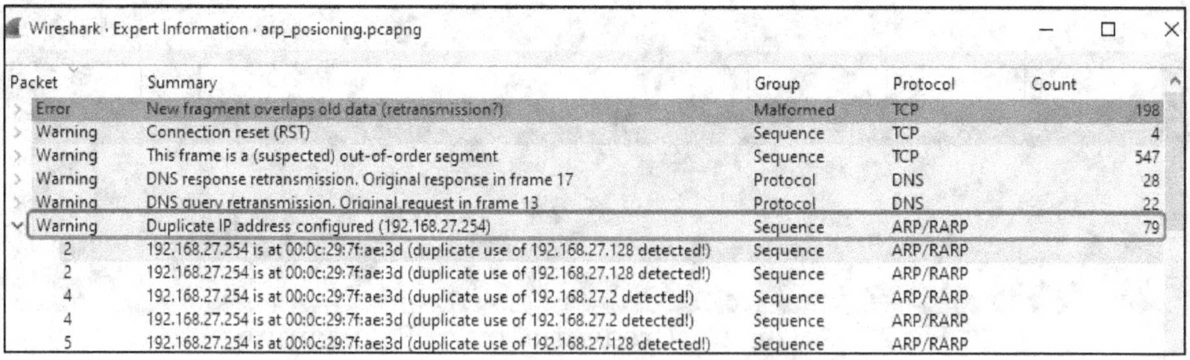

Fig 22: ARP Poisoning detection by Expert Information

The Delicious Network Layer
Layer 3

By
Nitin Sharma

Layer 3 – The Network Layer Explained

A quick review: In the seven-layer OSI model, Layer 3 is known as Network Layer. This layer is the part of Internet communication process where network-to-network connections occur, by sending packets of data back and forth between different networks. The network layer uses 4 basic processes [1]:

> **Addressing end devices** – In the same way, that a phone has a unique telephone number, end devices must be configured with a unique IP address for identification on the network. An end device with a configured IP address is referred to as a host.
>
> **Encapsulation** - The network layer receives a protocol data unit (PDU) from the transport layer. In a process called encapsulation, the network layer adds IP header information, such as the IP address of the source (sending) and destination (receiving) hosts. After header information is added to the PDU, the PDU is called a packet.
>
> **Routing** - The network layer provides services to direct packets to a destination host on another network. To travel to other networks, the packet must be processed by a router. The role of the router is to select paths for and direct packets toward the destination host in a process known as routing. A packet may cross many intermediary devices before reaching the destination host. Each route the packet takes to reach the destination host is called a hop.
>
> **De-encapsulation** - When the packet arrives at the network layer of the destination host, the host checks the IP header of the packet. If the destination IP address within the header matches its own IP address, the IP header is removed from the packet. This process of removing headers from lower layers is known as de-encapsulation. After the packet is de-encapsulated by the network layer, the resulting Layer 4 PDU is passed up to the appropriate service at the transport layer.

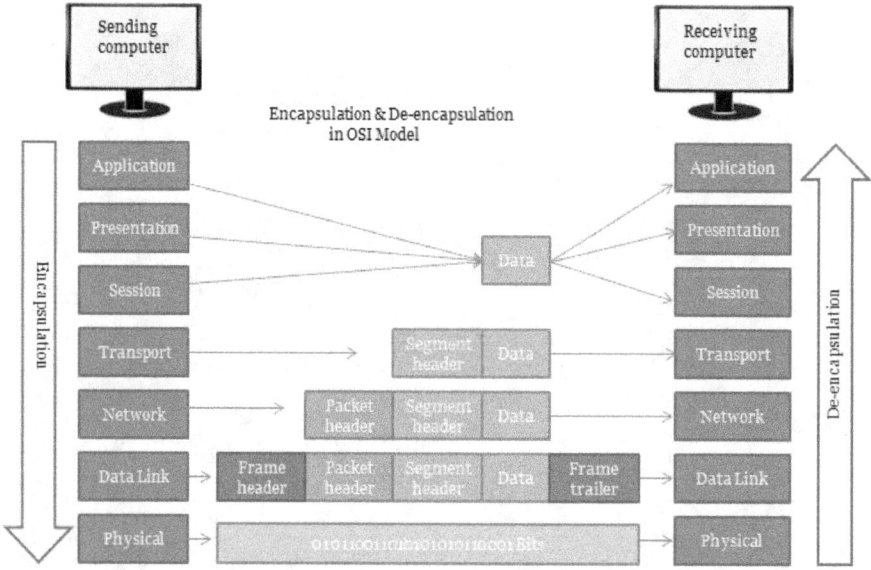

Data Encapsulation at OSI Layers [2]

Network Layer Protocols

There are several protocols operating at the Network Layer protocol suite which includes CLNS, DDP, EGP, EIGRP, etc. However, some commonly implemented protocols that are utilized more often include:

1. Internet Protocol (IPv4 and IPv6)
2. Internet Message Control Protocol (ICMP)

IP Protocol

Host-to-Host network-layer delivery protocol for the internet with the following properties:

- Connectionless – No connection with the destination is established before sending data packets.
- Best Effort (unreliable) – Does its best to deliver packet but packet delivery is not guaranteed. Limited error controls and corrupted packets are discarded.
- No flow-control.
- Must be paired with a reliable transport – TCP and/or application layer protocol to ensure reliability.
- Encapsulate the Transport Layer "Segment" by adding an IP header.

Offsets	Octet	0								1								2								3							
Octet	Bit	0	1	2	3	4	5	6	7	8	9	10	11	12	13	14	15	16	17	18	19	20	21	22	23	24	25	26	27	28	29	30	31
0	0	Version				IHL				DSCP						ECN		Total Length															
4	32	Identification																Flags			Fragment Offset												
8	64	Time To Live								Protocol								Header Checksum															
12	96	Source IP Address																															
16	128	Destination IP Address																															
20	160	Options (if IHL > 5)																															
24	192																																
28	224																																
32	256																																

32-bit IPv4 Header [3]

Internet Protocol Version 4 (IPv4)

An IP packet consists of a header section and a data section. An IP packet has no data checksum or any other footer after the data section. Typically, the Data Link Layer encapsulates IP packets in "Frames" with a CRC footer that detects most errors, and typically the end-to-end TCP layer checksum detects most other errors.

Significant fields in IPv4 header include:

1. **Version** - Contains a 4-bit binary value identifying the IP packet version. For IPv4 packets, this field is always set to 0100.
2. **Differentiated Services** - Formerly called the *Type of Service (ToS)* field, the DS field is an 8-bit field used to determine the priority of each packet. The first 6 bits identify the Differentiated Services Code Point (DSCP) value that is used by a quality of service (QoS) mechanism. The last 2 bits identify the explicit congestion notification (ECN) value that can be used to prevent dropped packets during times of network congestion.
3. **Time-to-Live (TTL)** - Contains an 8-bit binary value that is used to limit the lifetime of a packet. It is specified in seconds but is commonly referred to as hop count. The packet sender sets the initial time-to-live (TTL) value and is decreased by one each time the packet is processed by a router or hop. If the TTL field decrements to zero, the router discards the packet and sends an Internet Control Message Protocol (ICMP) Time Exceeded message to the source IP address. The traceroute command uses this field to identify the routers used between the source and destination.
4. **Protocol** - This 8-bit binary value indicates the data payload type that the packet is carrying, which enables the network layer to pass the data to the appropriate upper-layer protocol. Common values include ICMP (1), TCP (6), and UDP (17)
5. **Source IP Address** - Contains a 32-bit binary value that represents the source IP address of the packet (Identifies where the packet is from)
6. **Destination IP Address** - Contains a 32-bit binary value that represents the destination IP address of the packet. (Identifies where the packet is going)

The remaining fields are used to identify and validate the packet, or to reorder a fragmented packet. These include:

1. **Internet Header Length (IHL)** - Contains a 4-bit binary value identifying the number of 32-bit words in the header. The IHL value varies due to the Options and Padding fields. The minimum value for this field is 5 (i.e., 5×32 = 160 bits = 20 bytes) and the maximum value is 15 (i.e., 15×32 = 480 bits = 60 bytes).
2. **Total Length** - Sometimes referred to as the Packet Length, this 16-bit field defines the entire packet (fragment) size, including header and data, in bytes. The

minimum length packet is 20 bytes (20-byte header + 0 bytes data) and the maximum is 65,535 bytes.
3. **Header Checksum** - The 16-bit field is used for error checking of the IP header.

The checksum of the header is recalculated and compared to the value in the checksum field. If the values do not match, the packet is discarded.

A router may have to fragment a packet when forwarding it from one medium to another medium. When this happens, fragmentation occurs and the IPv4 packet uses the following fields to keep track of the fragments:

1. **Identification** – This 16-bit field uniquely identifies the fragment of an original IP packet.
2. **Flags** – The 3-bit field identifies how the packet is fragmented. It is used with Fragment Offset and Identification fields to help reconstruct the fragment into the original packet.
3. **Fragment Offset** – This 13-bit field identifies the order in which to place the packet fragment in the reconstruction of the original unfragmented packet.

Types of IPv4 Addresses

1. **Public Addresses** – Designated for use in networks that are accessible on the Internet.
2. **Private Addresses** – Blocks of Addresses that are used in networks that require limited or no Internet Access. [per RFC 1918]
    a. 10.0.0.0 to 10.255.255.255 (10.0.0.0/8)
    b. 172.16.0.0 to 172.31.255.255.255(172.16.0.0/12)
    c. 192.168.0.0 to 192.168.255.255(192.168.0.0/16)

Note: Per RFC 6598, IANA reserved another group of addresses know as shared address space intended for use in service provider networks with address block 100.64.0.0/10

Special Use IPv4 Addresses

1. **Network and Broadcast Addresses** –
    a. First address of Network → Network Address
    b. Last address of Network → Broadcast Address
2. **Loopback Address** – For testing purposes, this is a special address to direct traffic to itself. [127.0.0.1]
3. **Link Local Addresses** – Address block 169.254.0.0 to 169.254.255.255 [169.254.0.0/16] are designated as link-local addresses. These addresses can be

automatically assigned to the local to the local host by the operating system in environments where no IP configuration is available.

4. TEST-NET Addresses – Address block 192.0.2.0 to 192.0.2.255 (192.0.2.0/24) is set aside for teaching and learning purposes. Can be used in documentation and network examples with domain names example.com or example.net in RFCs, vendor docs, etc.

5. Experimental Addresses – The addresses in the block 240.0.0.0 to 255.255.255.254 are listed as reserved for future use (per RFC 3330)

Legacy Classful Addressing

Per RFC 1700 Assigned Numbers, the unicast ranges are grouped into specific sizes called Class A, Class B, and Class C addresses. Use of single such address space for complete network is referred to as classful addressing.

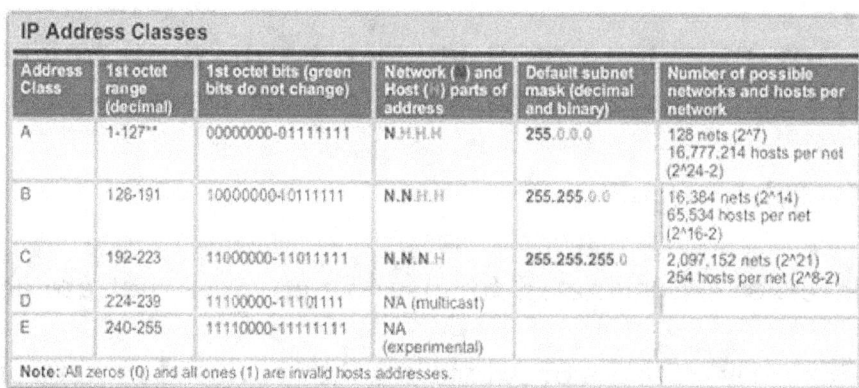

IP Address Classes [4]

Limitations of IPv4

1. IP Address Depletion (Limited IPv4 availability while internet connected devices still increasing)
2. Internet Routing Table Expansion (IPv4 routes consume a great deal of memory and processor resources on the Internet routers)
3. Lack of end-to-end connectivity (Public IPv4 is shared while internal NAT IPs remain hidden which is problematic for technologies that require end-to-end connectivity)

Internet Protocol Version 6 (IPv6)

Improvements over IPv4 includes increase in address space, improved packet handling, NAT elimination and integrated security.

4 bits Version	4 bits Priority	24 bits Flow Label	
16 bits Payload Length		8 bits Next Header	8 bits Hop Limit
128 bits Source Address			
128 bits Destination Address			

128-bit IPv6 Header [5]

1. **Version** - This field contains a 4-bit binary value identifying the IP packet version. For IPv6 packets, this field is always set to 0110.
2. **Traffic Class** - This 8-bit field is equivalent to the IPv4 Differentiated Services (DS) field. It also contains a 6-bit Differentiated Services Code Point (DSCP) value used to classify packets and a 2-bit Explicit Congestion Notification (ECN) used for traffic congestion control.
3. **Flow Label** - This 20-bit field provides a special service for real-time applications. It can be used to inform routers and switches to maintain the same path for the packet flow so that packets are not reordered.
4. **Payload Length** - This 16-bit field is equivalent to the Total Length field in the IPv4 header. It defines the entire packet (fragment) size, including header and optional extensions.
5. **Next Header** - This 8-bit field is equivalent to the IPv4 Protocol field. It indicates the data payload type that the packet is carrying, enabling the network layer to pass the data to the appropriate upper-layer protocol. This field is also used if there are optional extension headers added to the IPv6 packet.
6. **Hop Limit** - This 8-bit field replaces the IPv4 TTL field. This value is decremented by one by each router that forwards the packet. When the counter reaches 0 the packet is discarded and an ICMPv6 message is forwarded to the sending host, indicating that the packet did not reach its destination.
7. **Source Address** - This 128-bit field identifies the IPv6 address of the sending host.
8. **Destination Address** - This 128-bit field identifies the IPv6 address of the receiving host
9. **Extension Headers** – Optional and are placed between the IPv6 header and the payload. EHs are used for fragmentation, security, etc.

IPv6 Address and Prefix Notation

The IPv6 convention is different from dotted decimal address notation of IPv4. The 128 bits in the IPv6 address [6]:

1. Are written as eight 16-bit hexadecimal blocks separated by colons (not case sensitive)
2. Use abbreviations to simplify the notation
3. Omit (optionally) leading zeroes.
4. Use double colons (::) to replace consecutive zeros (or leading or trailing zero strings), but never more than once per address.

So, an address like: **2eba:0000:0000:0000:0241:cbfa:8bc5:0000** can be written as: **2eba:0:0:0:0241:cbfa:8bc5:0** or **2eba::0241:cbfa:8bc5:0**

but not as: **2eba::0241:cbfa:8bc5::**

Routers seldom have to worry about complete ("host") addresses because their routing tables (and the forwarding tables they are based on) usually employ a prefix and examine only the number of bits that match the longest entry in the table. This is the "longest match" rule, and ensures that a 64-bit prefix (if present) is preferred over a 32-bit prefix; when the first 32 bits of a packet's destination address are the same in both table entries (longest match wins). Prefixes used for routing are defined in IPv6 by RFC 4291. So, the IPv6 address:

2eba:0000:0000:0000:0241:cbfa:8bc5:5c85/64 has as a 64-bit prefix of 2bfc:0000:0000:0000:

ICMP (Internet Control Message Protocol)

The Internet Control Message Protocol is a layer 3 protocol used by network devices to diagnose network communication issues. The ICMP packet is encapsulated in an IPv4 packet. The ICMP packet consists of header and data sections [7].

ICMP Header Format

Offsets	Octet	0								1								2								3							
Octet	Bit	0	1	2	3	4	5	6	7	8	9	10	11	12	13	14	15	16	17	18	19	20	21	22	23	24	25	26	27	28	29	30	31
0	0	Type								Code								Checksum															
4	32	Rest of Header																															

The ICMP header starts after the IPv4 header and is identified by IP protocol number '1'. All ICMP packets have an 8-byte header a variable-sized data section.

   a. TYPE – ICMP type
   b. CODE – ICMP subtype
   c. Checksum – Internet checksum for error checking, calculated from the ICMP header and data with value 0 substituted for this field.
   d. Rest off Header – Four bytes field, contents based on the ICMP type and code.

Primary Use Case: Error Reporting. To determine whether or not data is reaching its intended destination in a timely manner.

Supporting use cases include:

1. **Source Quench Message**: ICMP will take source IP from the discarded packet and informs to source by sending this message. (to reduce speed of transmission)
2. **Parameter Problem**: ICMP will take source IP from the discarded packet and informs to source by sending parameter problem message. (Calculated Header Checksum mismatched to Received Header Checksum)
3. **Time Exceeded Message** - ICMP will take source IP from discarded packet and informs to the source, of discarded datagram due to time to live field reaches to zero, by sending time exceeded message
4. **Destination Unreachable**: This is generated by host or its inbound gateway to inform the client that the destination is unreachable for some reason
5. **Redirection Mess**age: Redirect requests data packets be sent on an alternate route. The message informs to a host to update its routing information (to send packets on an alternate route)

Routing Basics

A host can send a packet to:

1. **Itself** – Pinging itself by sending a packet to special IPv4 address of 127.0.0.1 which is referred to as the loopback interface. [Direct Connection]
2. **Local Host** – This is a host on the same network as the sending host. The hosts share the same network address. [Local Network Route]
3. **Remote Host** – This is a host on a remote network which do not share the same network address. [Local Default Route]

Default Gateway

The default gateway is the device that routes traffic from the local network to devices on remote networks. In a home or small business network, the default gateway is often used to connect the local network to the Internet.
Note: A host device does not maintain routing information beyond the local network, to reach remote destinations. This is done by default gateway by maintaining a route table.

IPv4 Routing Table

Running the "**netstat -r**" or "**route -n**" command over a Linux host displays the host route table.

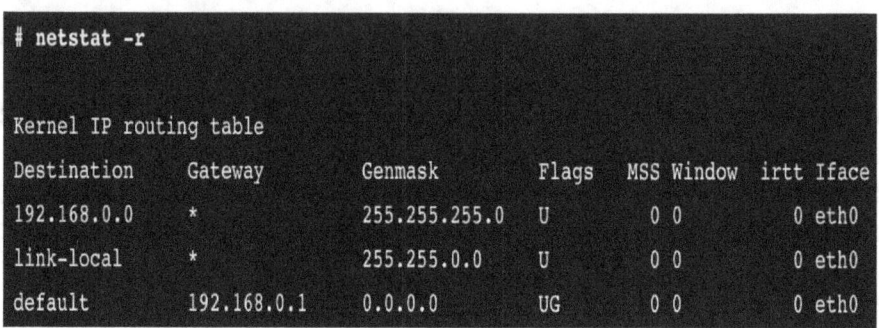

Routing Table: Linux

1. **Destination** – Lists the reachable networks.
2. **Gateway** – Lists the address used by the local computer to get to a remote network destination.
3. **Genmask/Netmask** – Lists a subnet mask that informs the host how to determine the network and the host portions of the IP address.
4. **Flags** – U➔Route is Up, G➔Route is to Gateway, H➔Route is to Host, D➔Route is created by Redirect, M➔Route is modified by Redirect.
5. **MSS** – Max. Segment Size field for TCP header specify the largest amount of data in bytes that a computer can receive in a single TCP segment.
6. **Window** – TCP Window Size in bytes.
7. **irtt** – Initial Round Trip Time for TCP connections over this route.
8. **Iface** – Outbound NIC name.

Router: Introduction

A router is a computer, L3 device. There are many types of infrastructure routers available. Cisco routers are designed to address the needs of:

1. Branch – Teleworkers, small business, and medium-size branch sites, Includes Cisco 800, 1900, 2900, and 3900 Integrated Series Routers (ISR) G2 (2nd generation)
2. WAN – Large businesses, organizations, and enterprises. Includes the Cisco Catalyst 6500 Series Switches and the Cisco Aggregation Service Router (ASR) 1000.
3. Service Provider – Large service providers. Includes Cisco ASR 1000, Cisco ASR 9000, Cisco XR 12000, Cisco CRS-3 Carrier Routing System, and 7600 Series routers.

The focus of CCNA certification is on the Branch family of routers. Regardless of their function, size or complexity, all router models are essentially computers. Routers also require:

- Operating System (OS) – Required to provide routing and switching functions. The Cisco Internetwork Operating System (IOS) is the system software used for most Cisco devices regardless of the size and type of the device.
- Central Processing Unit (CPU) – To execute OS instructions such as System Initialization, routing functions, and switching functions.
- Random Access Memory (RAM) – To store various applications and processing including: Cisco IOS, Running configuration files, IP routing table, ARP cache, Packet Buffer, etc.
- Read Only Memory (ROM) – To store bootup instructions, basic diagnostic software and Limited backup version of the OS.

Memory	Volatile / Nonvolatile	Stores
RAM	Volatile	Running IOS Running Configuration IP Routing and ARP tables Packet Buffer
ROM	Nonvolatile	Bootup instruction Basic diagnostic software Limited IOS
NVRAM	Nonvolatile	Startup configuration file
Flash	Nonvolatile	IOS Other system files

Router Memory

IPv4 vs IPv6

Basis	IPv4	IPv6
Size of IP Address	IPv4 has 32-bit address length.	IPv6 has 128-bit address length.
Addressing Method	IPv4 utilizes dotted decimal notation.	IPv6 utilizes hexadecimal convention with colon separation.
Number of Header Fields	14	8
Length of Header Fields	20	40
Checksum	Yes	No
Type of Addresses	Unicast, Broadcast and Multicast	Unicast, Multicast and Anycast
Example	192.168.34.21	2839:0dfc:0000:0000:ff53:0043:5aea:00ed
No. of Classes	5 [A→E]	IPv6 allows storing an unlimited no. of IP Address.
Configuration	Required for newly installed system.	Optional
VLSM Support	Yes	No
Fragmentation	Done by sending and forwarding routes.	Done by sender.
Routing Information Protocol	Yes	No. Only Static routes.
NAT	Yes	No. Only Direct addressing.
Address Mask	Yes	No
SNMP Support	Yes	No
Security	Dependent on applications.	IPSec built in. Needs to be enabled.
Authentication	No	Yes
Encryption	No	Yes
QoS Handling Packet Header	No	Yes

IP to MAC resolution	Broadcast ARP	Multicast Neighbor Solicitation
Local Subnet Group Mgmt.	IGMP	MLD
Mapping	ARP	NDP

Network Layer: Attacks and Security Measures

There are several attacks that could be performed to compromise/disrupt the Network Layer. As we know, the main responsibility of the network layer is to transmit the packets from the source to the destination by finding the best route, which is the route that has the lowest cost and shortest path between source and destination, the major goal is to disrupt this path. Some of the attacks related to network layer are discussed below [8].

1. IP Spoofing Attack: Used to gain unauthorized access to the servers when attacker spoofed its own IP address with a "trusted" IP address such that victim will not understand the source of traffic is malicious. The main root cause of DDoS attacks is IP spoofing.

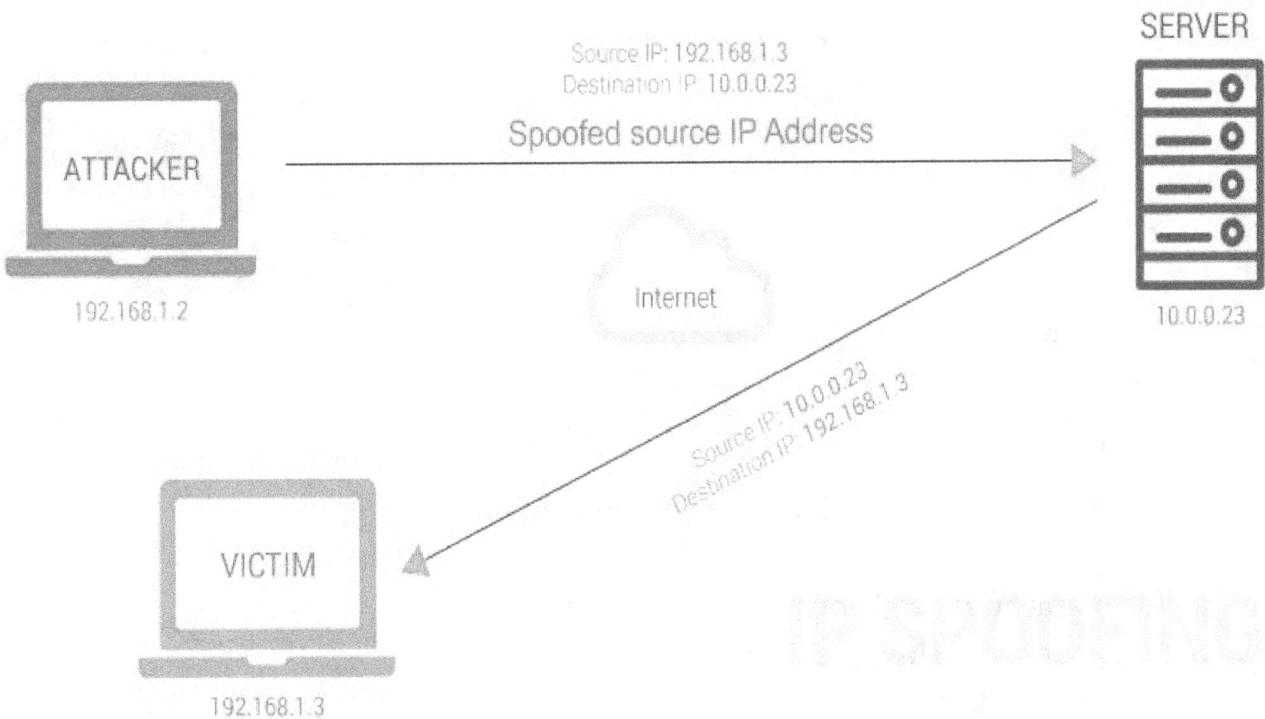

Security Measures to mitigate IP Spoofing:

a. Use AUTH(N) based on Key Exchange between the machines on your network; IPv6 has IPSec built-in that can significantly cut down the risk of IP Spoofing.
b. Use of an ACL to deny private IP addresses on the downstream interfaces.
c. Implementing filters on both Inbound and Outbound traffic.
d. Configure Routers and Switches to reject packets originating from outside of local network that claim to originate from within.
e. Enable encryption sessions on the routers so that trusted hosts outside the network can securely communicate with the local hosts.

2. **Hijacking Attack**: The basic idea for this attack is to disrupt a session between client and server and take over the IP address of the trusted client. In the next step, the attacker will discontinue the communication between the server and the trusted client and create a new session with server pretending to be the trusted client. This might require additional capture efforts for information like authentication cookie, session IDs, BGP etc. along with trusted IP.

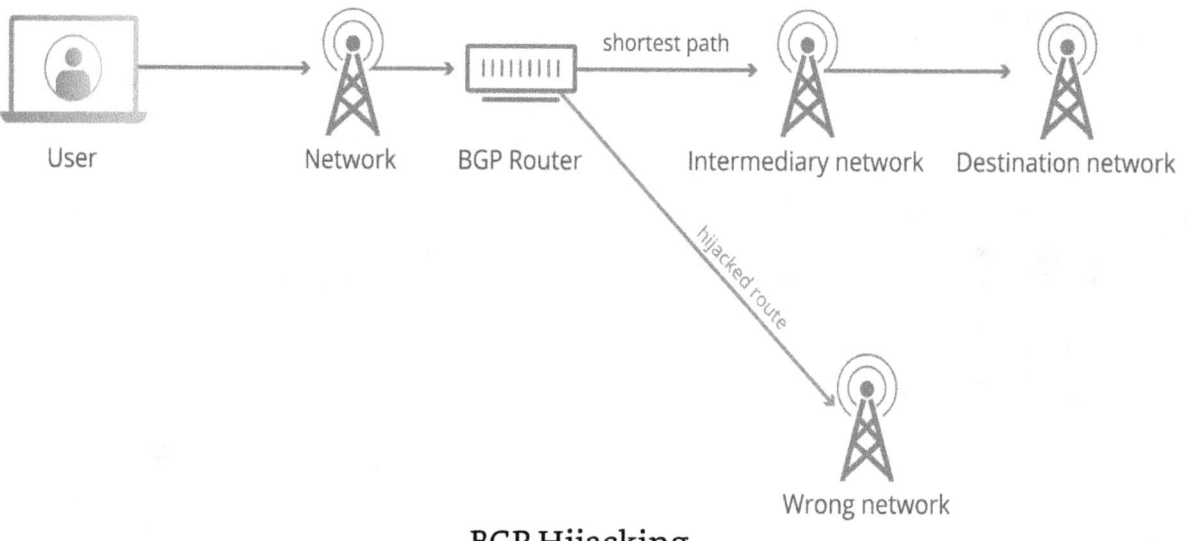

BGP Hijacking

Security Measures to mitigate Hijacking Attack:

a. Utilizing advanced encryption methods,
b. Different AUTH(N) mechanisms.
c. IP Prefix Filtering
d. BGP Hijacking Detection.

3. The Smurf Attack: The attacker will send a high number of packets from a spoofed IP address to the server in order to disable the service provided by the network. An example of this attack will be similar to ICMP request flooding or ping flood by using an IP broadcast address. The slight difference is due to an amplification attack vector that boosts its damage potential by exploiting characteristics of broadcast network.

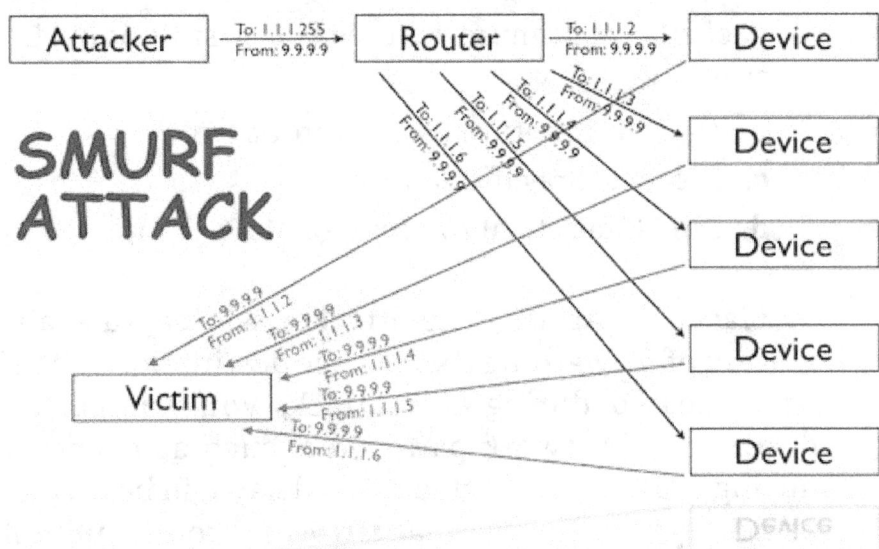

Security Measures to mitigate Smurf Attacks and Ping Floods:

a. Blanket Block pings from outside networks.
b. Deploy DDoS protection solution

4. Wormhole Attacks: Wormhole nodes fake a route that is shorter than the original one within the network to confuse routing mechanisms which rely on distance between the nodes. The attackers will record the packets at one point of the network and retransmits them to another point of the network using private highspeed network, and then replays them into the network from that point. Such kind of attacks are a serious threat against network routing protocols. Mostly seen in wireless sensor networks.

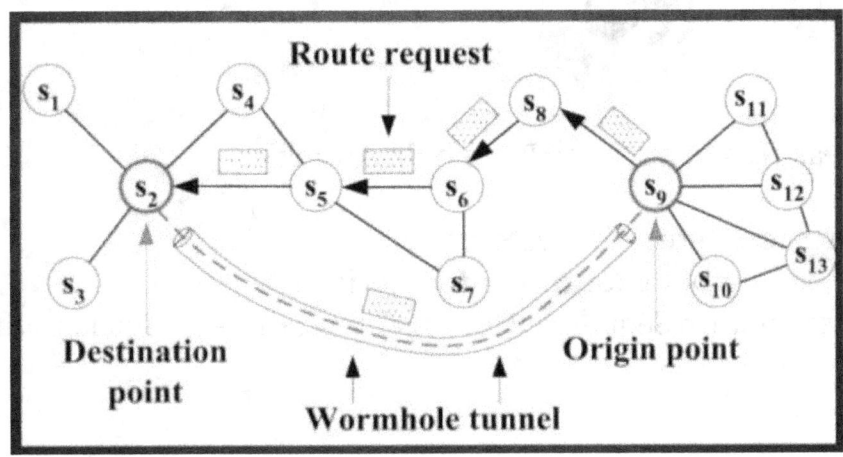

Security Measures to mitigate Wormhole Attack:

a. A leash is any information that is added to a packet designed to restrict the packet's maximum allowed transmission distance. Use Geographical and Temporal Leashes.
b. Digital Signature Based Approach
c. Protocol Specific Solutions
d. SAM (Statistical Analysis of Multipath)

5. **Blackhole Attack:** The attacker will capture all the packets and discard them instead of forwarding them to the destination. The effectiveness of the network will be decreased during this attack, while important packets will not reach the destination. Network parameters such as delay and throughput will be changed during the blackhole attack. The delay will be increased because the packets will not be delivered to the destination. The throughput will become very less, while it will be used from the blackhole attacker. It's a kind of DoS Attack. It is also known as Packet Drop Attack.

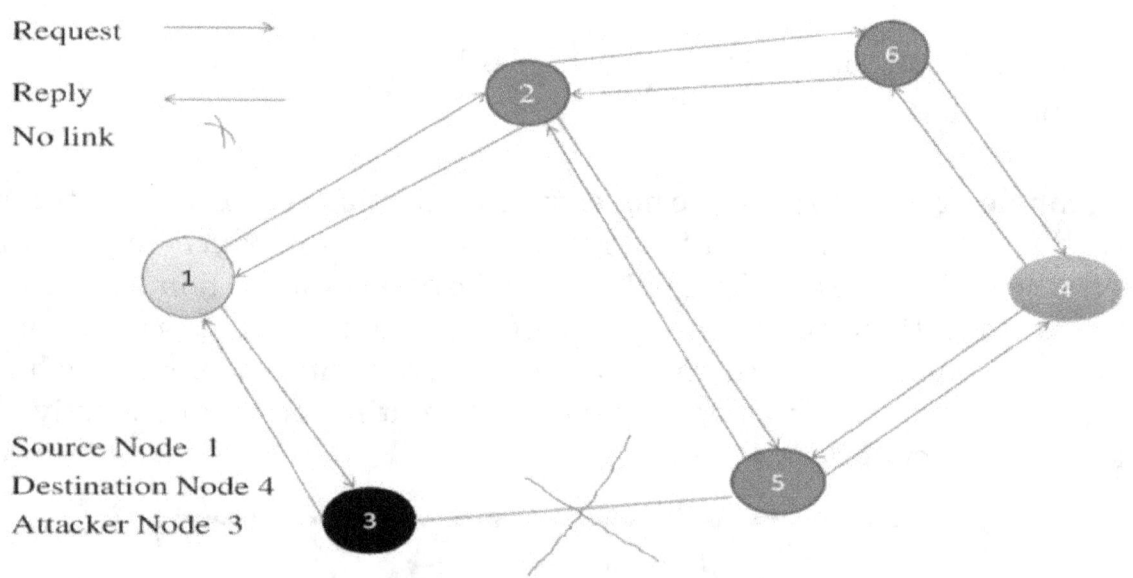

Security Measures to mitigate Blackhole Attack:

a. IDS (Intrusion Detection System)
b. Cross Checking Data Routing Information (DRIs)
c. Using Destination Sequence No. Parameter of Reply Packet with threshold.

References

[1] Network Layer, Data Communication, TeachWeb Milinis Reference. Accessed on 14th June 2020.
Link: teachweb.milin.cc/datacommunicatie/tcp_osi_model/network_layer.htm

[2] Data Encapsulation and De-encapsulation Explained [Image] Accessed on 16th June, 2020.
Link: computernetworkingnotes.com/ccna-study-GUIde/data-encapsulation-and-de-encapsulation-explained.html

[3] IPv4 [Image], Wikipedia. Accessed on 14th June 2020.
Link: en.wikipedia.org/wiki/IPv4

[4] Legacy Classful Addressing [Image], IPv4, Network Layer, TCP OSI Model, TeachWeb Millinis Reference. Accessed on 14th June 2020
Link: teachweb.milin.cc/images/datacommunicatie/introduction_to_networks/8.1.4.4_legacy_classful_addressing_small.jpg

[5] IPv6 Packet Format, Network Layer and Routing, Computer Networking [Image]. Accessed on 14th June 2020.
Link: expertsmind.com/CMSImages/426_IPv6%20packet%20Format.png

[6] Differences in Addressing Between IPv4 and IPv6, Juniper Networks. Accessed on 15th June 2020.
Link: juniper.net/documentation/en_US/learn-about/ipv4-ipv6-differences.pdf

[7] Datagram Structure, ICMP, Wiki. Accessed on 16th June 2020.
Link: en.wikipedia.org/wiki/Internet_Control_Message_Protocol

[8] A review of Network Layer and Transport Layer Attacks on Wireless Networks, Edvald Sula, International Journal of Modern Engineering Research (IJMER), 9th Feb, 2019. Accessed on 16th June 2020.
Link: ijmer.com/papers/Vol8_issue12/D0812012327.pdf

Taking a Bigger Bite With Wireshark
Layer 3/4

By
Ambadi MP

Packet Capturing With WireShark

Click on the Wireshark icon after downloading and installing Wireshark and start Wireshark.

This screen allows you to select the network interface you wish to capture the packets from. As you can see, Wireshark has detected all interfaces.

- Ethernet,
- Local Area Connection 2
- Bluetooth Network Connection
- Wi-Fi

Depending on the network interfaces of your system yours may appear differently.

Windows Analysis

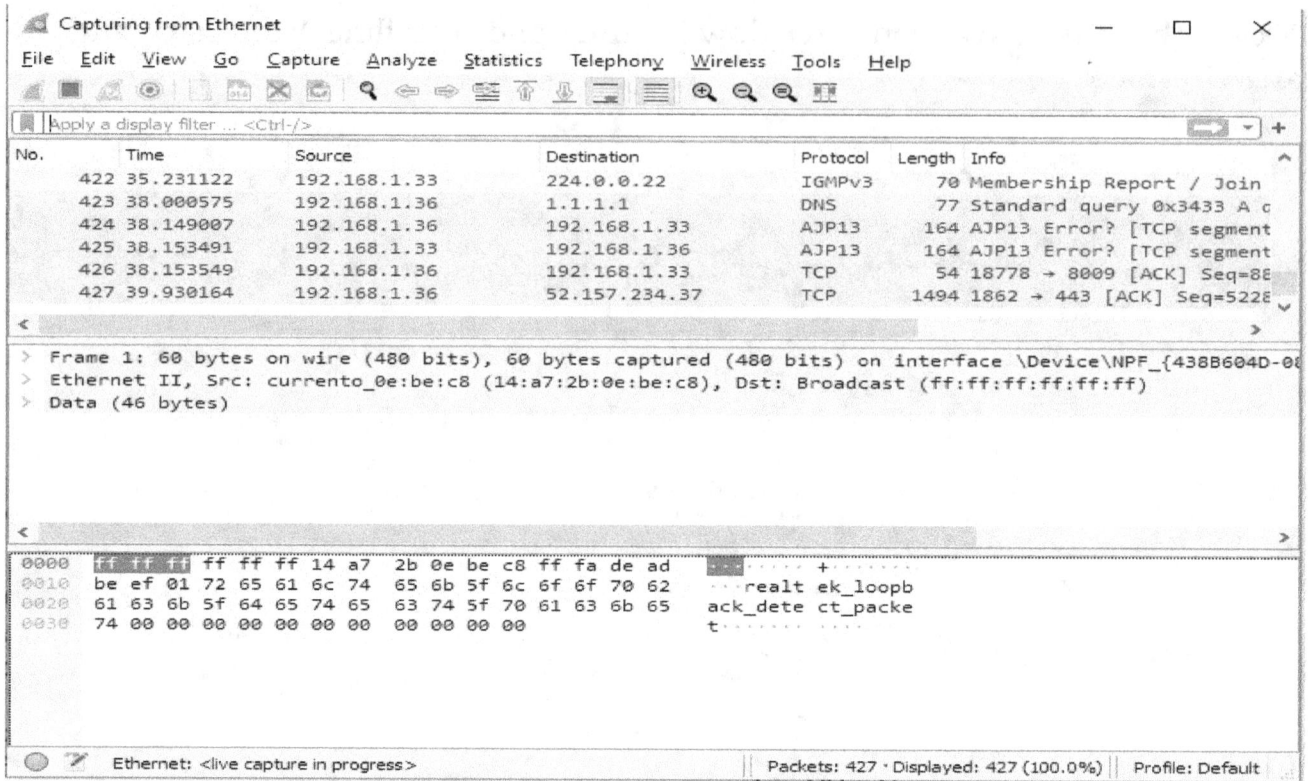

Wireshark will start capturing and packaging packets in .pcap format from your network interface. This is the standard packet capture file format (you'll find it's used in products like Snort, aircrack-ng and many more across our industry).

You will see three different windows for review in Wireshark. The top window in the following screenshot is known as the Packet List Pane, labeled # 1. Color coded packets should be seen moving through that window in real time.

The middle window is called the Packet Details Panel, labeled as # 2. This pane gives us header details from a selected packet in Window # 1.

Finally, Packet Bytes Pane, Window # 3 provides you with information about payload in both left hexadecimal format and right ASCII format.

Create Filter

Overall, there will be much too much information to carry out a realistic study. Packs fly by hundreds or tens of thousands per minute. To make effective use of Wireshark, we need to filter the traffic to see only those packets we want. Wireshark has a simple filtering language to use effectively and effectively, which you should understand in a forensics investigation.

There are many different protocols to the packets which fly through our interface. Perhaps the first filter we want to add is a protocol filter. Know, TCP / IP is a suite of protocols and we would like to concentrate on only a few of them in our study.

Type "tcp" in the filter window. Note that it turns green showing that your syntax is correct (if your syntax is wrong, it remains pink). Now, to add the filter, press the arrow button at the far right of the filter window.

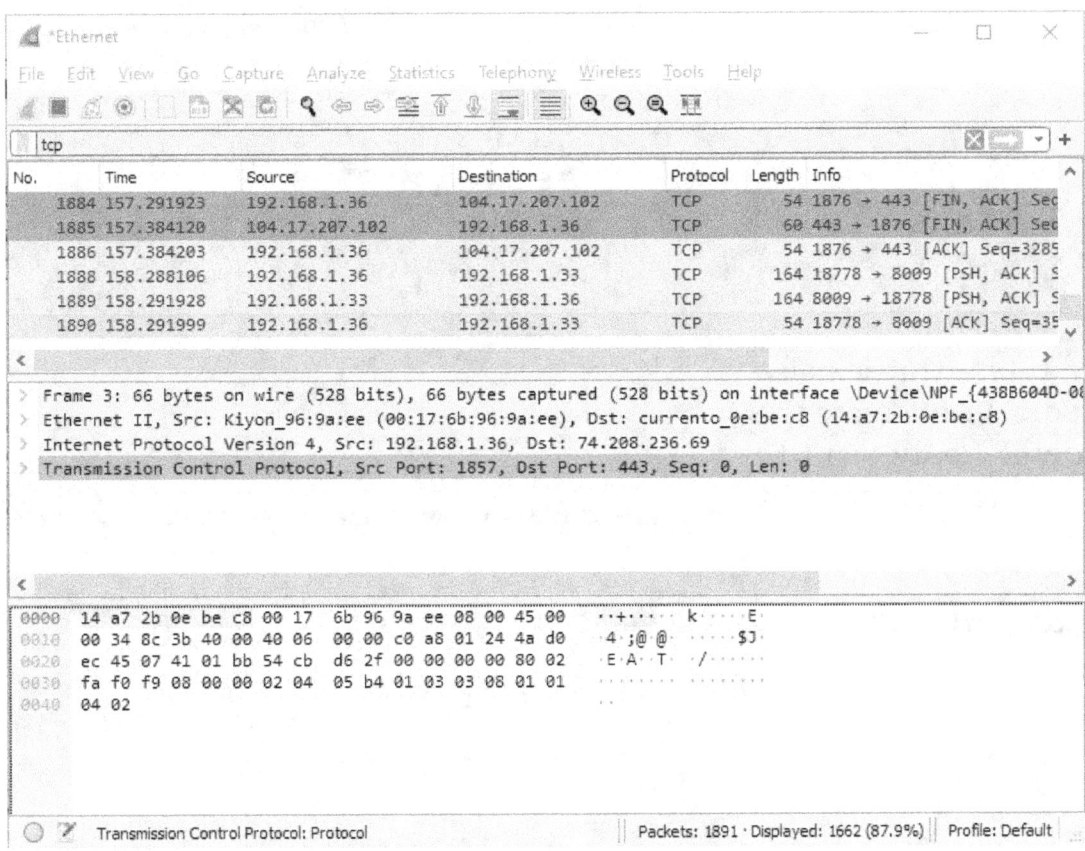

When you do that, Wireshark will filter out all traffic but the tcp traffic will. You can do just about the same for any protocol like "http," "smtp," "udp," "dns," etc. Try some and see what kind of traffic is going through your interface.

If we only want to see traffic from a particular IP address, we can create a filter that only displays traffic from or from that address. We can do this by logging into the filter window.

    ip.addr==<IP address>

Notice double equal sign (==) in Wireshark filter syntax. A single = will not function in that syntax.

Want to see traffic coming in or going to the IP address 192.168.1.36, make a filter like this.

ip.addr == 192.168.1.36

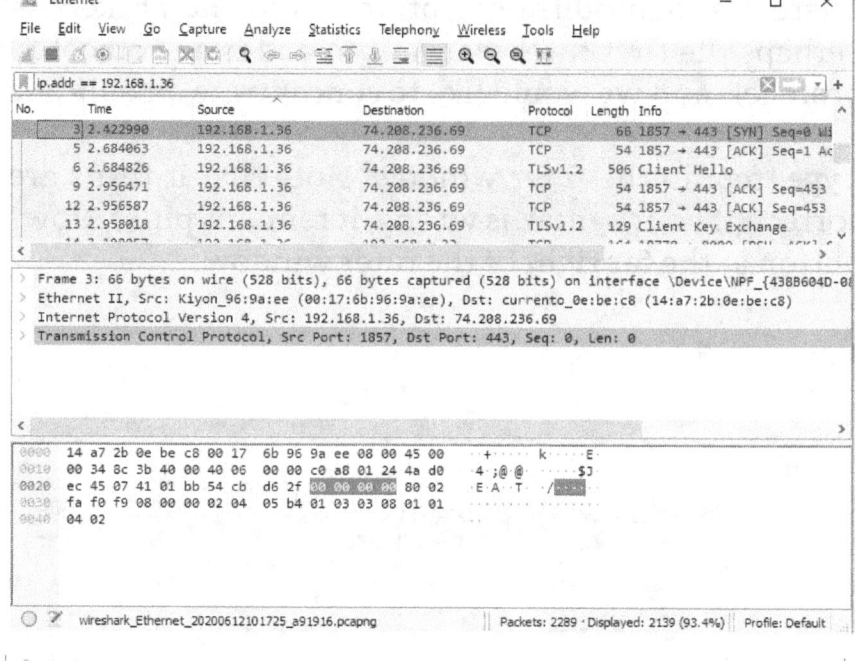

We can filter traffic also through port. I can create the filter below if I only want to see TCP traffic destined for port 80;

tcp.dstport==80

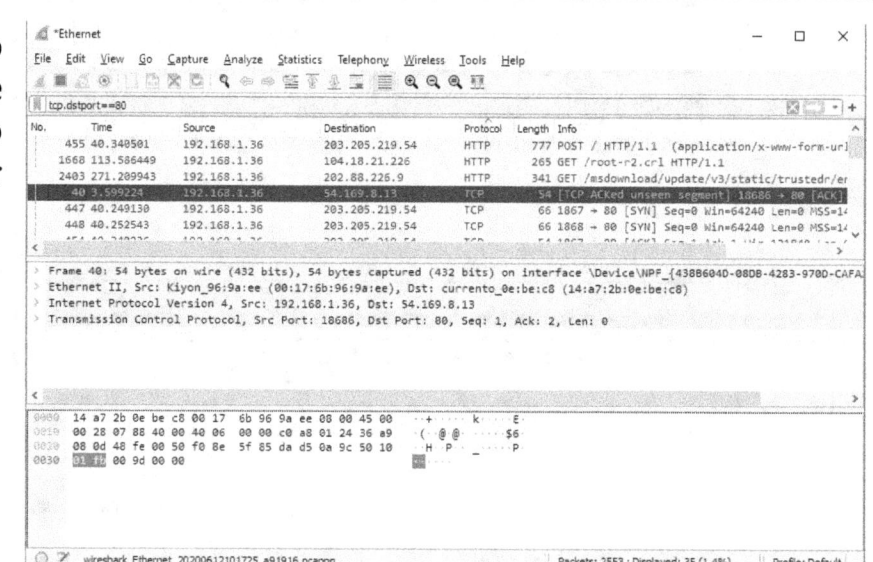

When creating filters, we will most often use = = as the operator in our filter (see others below). This works fine if we are looking for one of the many fields of protocol. If we are looking for payload strings, we must use the "contains" operator. So, if I were looking for packets with the Facebook word in them, I could create filters like this below.

tcp contains youtube

As you can see above, with the word Facebook it has found just two packets in the payload and we can see the word Facebook in the # 3 pane of the ASCII window.

Finally, we can find filter expressions on

View → Internals → Supported Protocols

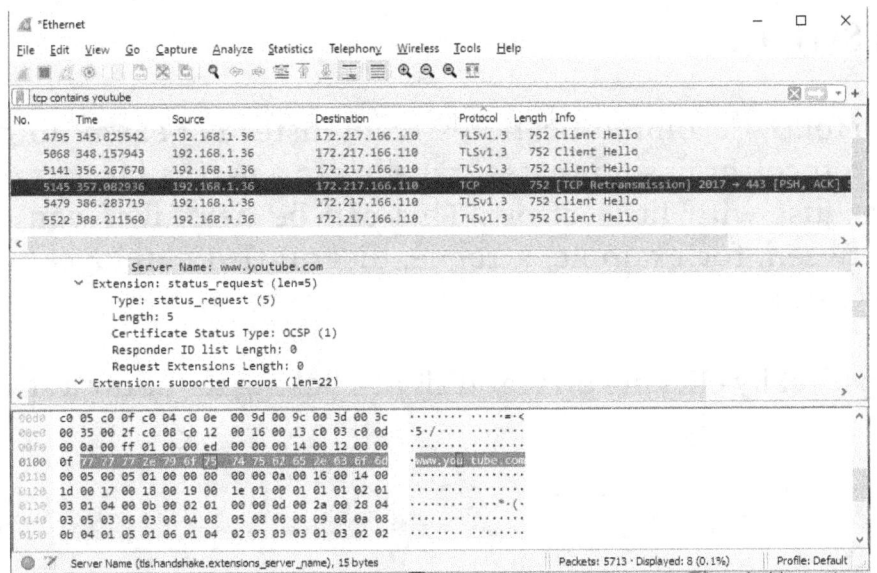

it will open the window for Wireshark Filter Expressions as below.

This window lists all filters. These are hundreds of protocols, and they include fields. You can extend a protocol and select all its fields of interest.

Operator Description

==		Equal to
!=		Not equal to
>		Greater than
<		Less than
>=		Greater than or equal to
<=		Less than or Equal to
contains		Protocol or Field contains a value
matches		Protocol or text field matches a regular expression

Try building filters using some of these other operators and fields to get a feel for what Wireshark can do for you.

Following a Stream

You will want to follow a communication stream instead of examining all the packets of a particular protocol, or in some cases traveling to a particular port or IP. Wireshark lets you do that just with little effort. This can be helpful if you try to follow a conversation between, for example, a rogue, disgruntled employee who is trying to damage your network

Simply select a packet by clicking on it and right-clicking to follow a stream.

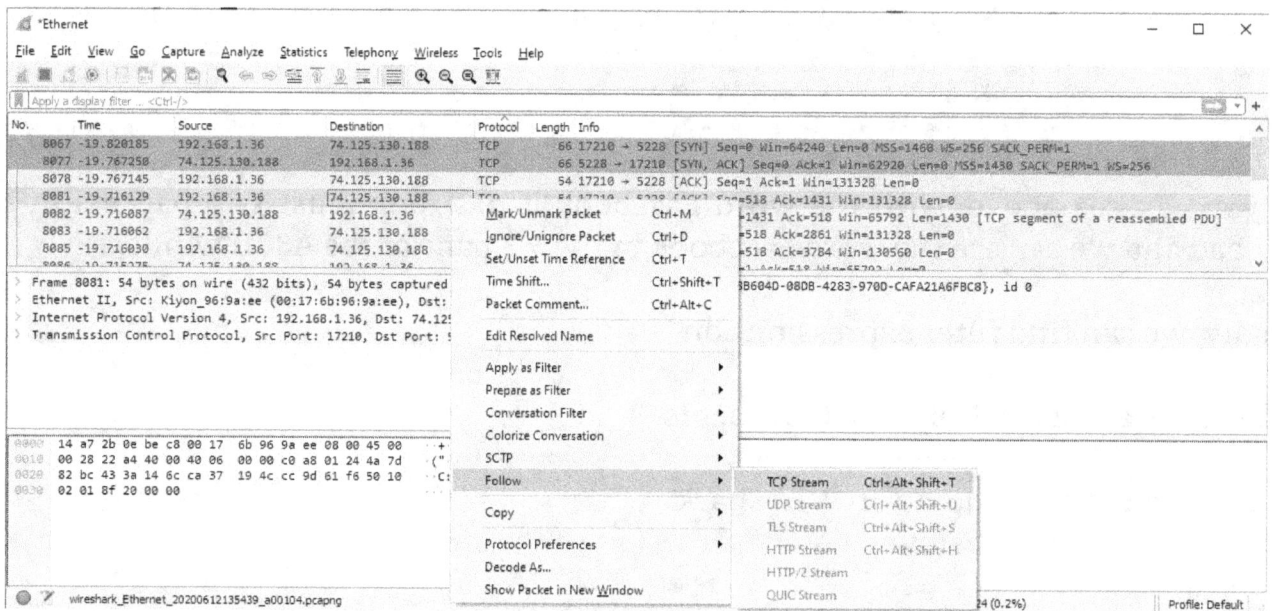

This will open a window as above pull down. Click "Follow" then click "TCP Stream."

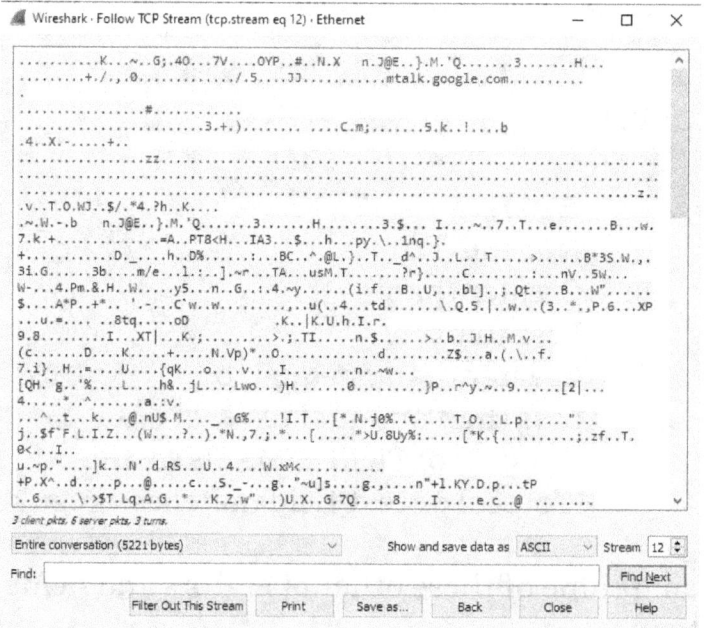

137

This opens a window that includes all the packets and their contents in this stream. Note the statistics at the bottom of the window to the far left (5221 bytes) and the method for displaying content (ASCII).

Statistics

Finally, we would want to gather statistics about our packet capture. This may be particularly useful when creating a standard baseline for traffic. Just click the Statistics tab at the top of Wireshark and a pull-down menu will appear. In our case, let's browse down to IPv4 Statistics, and then to all addresses.

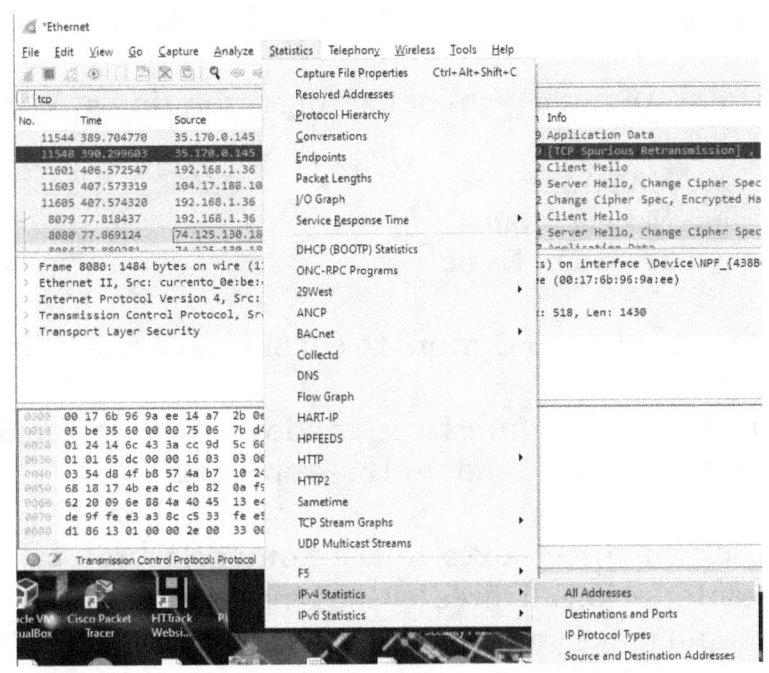

As we click, there is a window that displays statistics for every and every IP address in our packet capture

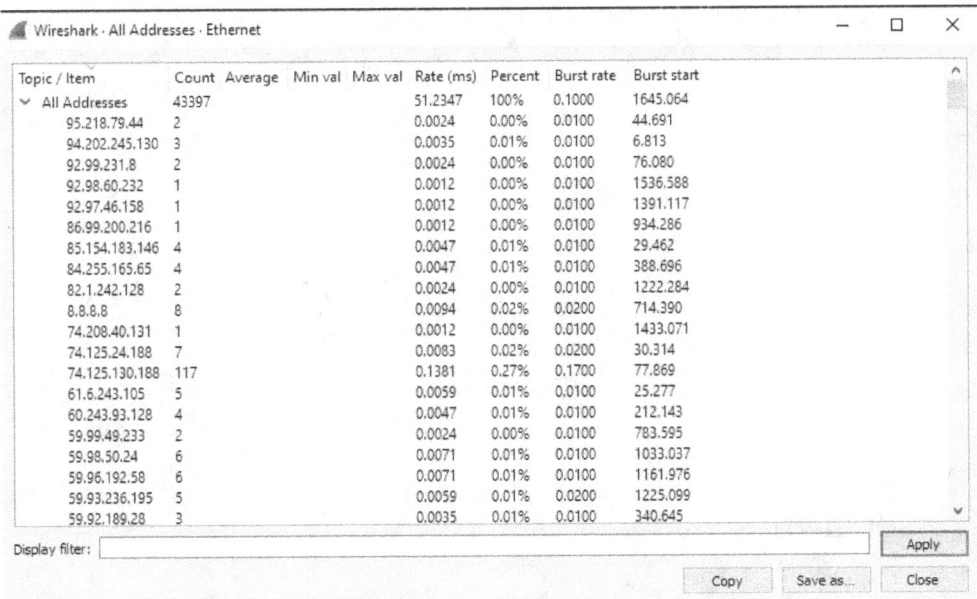

We're going to try to advance your knowledge and understanding of Wireshark to the level where you can use many features in an actual forensic investigation network.

Name Resolution

The data that you are analyzing on any network often have indecipherable names. IPv4 addresses are 4 bytes of decimal data such as 192.168.1.101 and 6 hexadecimal addresses such as "**00.AA.CD.11.EF.23**." Sometimes this data becomes easier to decode and interpret if it is translated to a human-readable name rather than a number, just as DNS does to us when we browse the Internet.

There are three types of naming resolution at Wireshark.

- MAC Addresses
- Network Name
- Transport Name

Go to Capture → Options to enable name resolution (the capture must stop first).

In the Capture Interfaces window, click on the 3rd tab, Options. It will show "Name Resolution" box, and the three options.

Click all three boxes to see nomenclature resolution on all three levels. This definitely should make your analysis a bit easier.

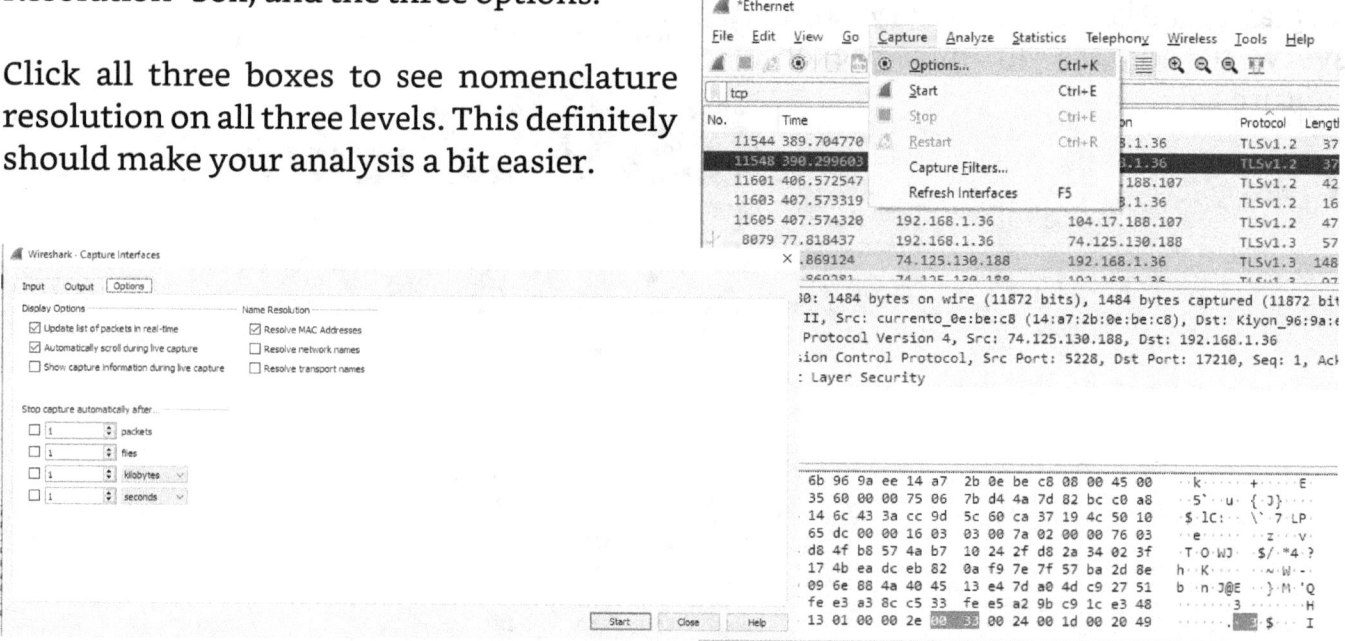

Protocol Dissection

Analysis of network traffic will require a certain dissection of the protocol to illuminate what really happened on the network. We may want to see for example which IP packets are broken, or which TCP packets a has the RST flag collection. We can do this by creating the appropriate filter and dissecting those packets using the middle window in Wireshark.

For example, if we want to see which IP packets have been fragmented, we want to create a field filter in the IP header that is also called flags or more fragments (MF). When setting this flag, it means the packet has been broken and the target network needs to be reassembled (attackers also break packets in an effort to bypass firewalls and IDS's).

On the Filter Expression we can find fragmented packets as below.

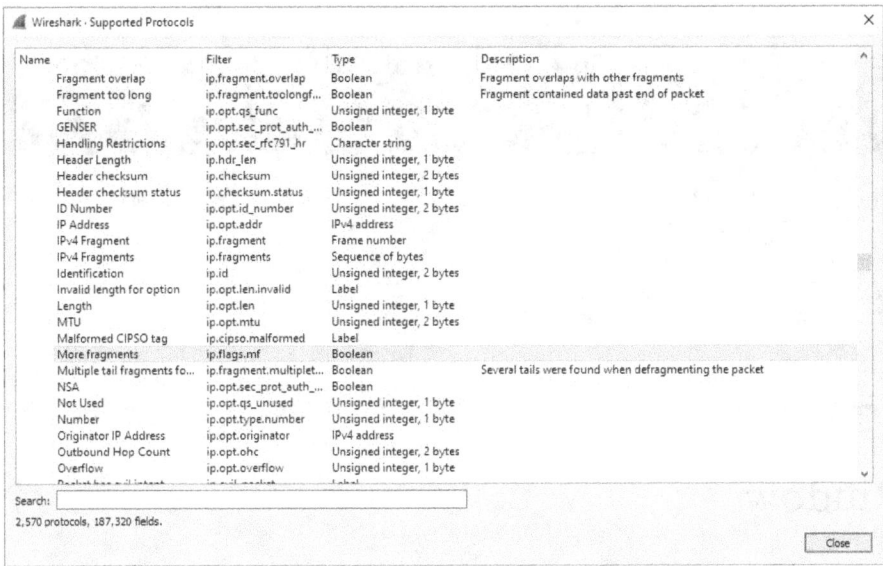

ip.flags.mf==1

Here the IP protocol can be selected and expanded until we find the ip.flags.mf, then select = = and set the value to 1. Now Wireshark can only show packets which have the IP flag set for MF or fragmented packets. The shown packets are broken packets. This may occur during the usual transmission process or could be an indicator that an attacker is attempting to bypass IDS or firewall detection.

Unlike IP flag TCP has its own flags. These flags signal the intent of the TCP packet sender, for example initiating a connection (SYN) or breakdown of a session (FIN). If we want to see all the packets starting a TCP session, we can set the Wireshark filter to;

tcp.flags.syn == 1

This filters packets out except those initiating a TCP session. When we pick one of those packets, we can dissect it in the middle window and see it has the SYN flag set.

The same is true for either of the six TCP flags (SYN, ACK, FIN, PSH, URG, RST). TCP uses the RST flag to signal a "strong" link termination, or a packet has entered the wrong port or IP. The following filter can be used to find certain packets.

tcp.flags.reset==1

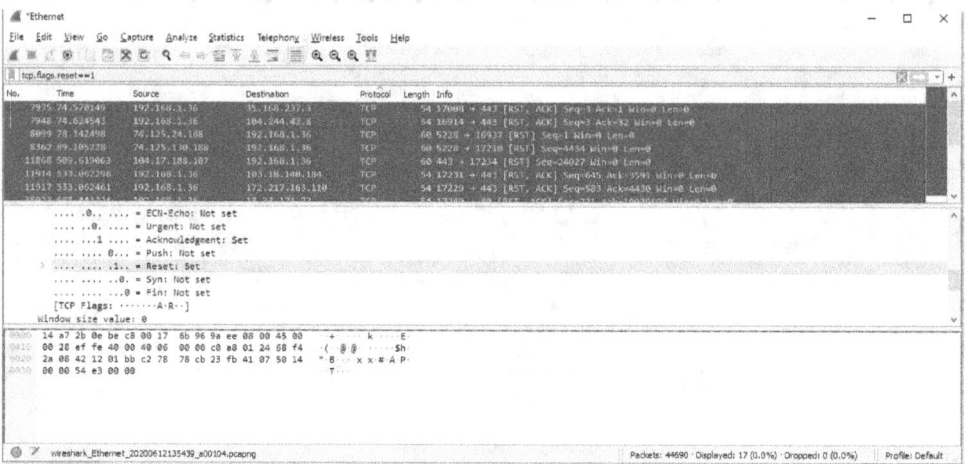

Statistics Window

Using each protocol such as TCP, UDP, DNS, ICMP etc., statistics are often useful when we analyze large amounts of data. This can be a useful technique for creating a reference snapshot of what your usual traffic looks like to promote the detection of anomalous traffic when a question occurs.

Click on the Statistics tab at the top menus to view the protocol statistics, and then select Protocol Hierarchy.

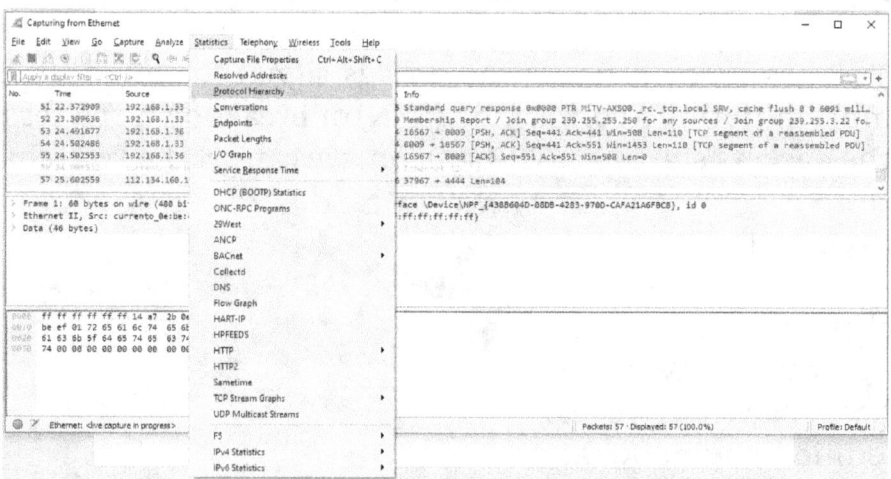

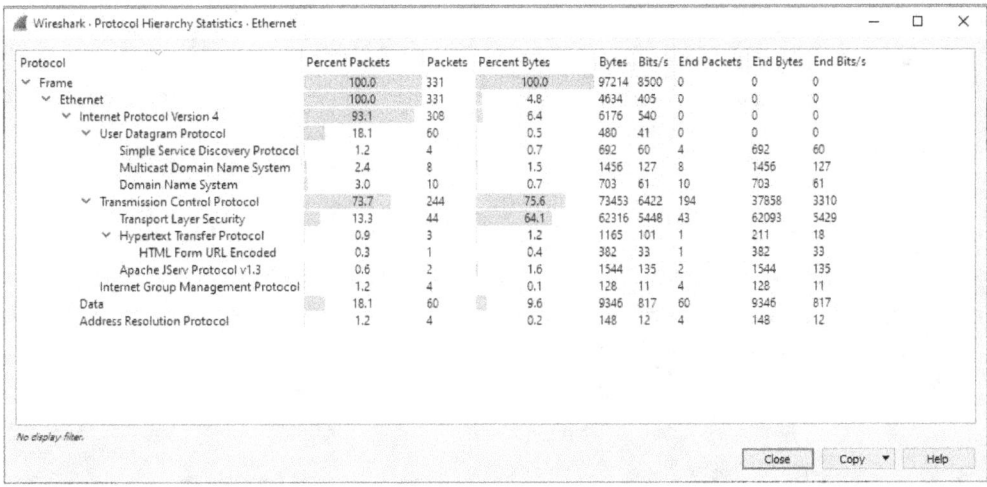

Wireshark creates a display window with all the data concerning the various protocols. If you have this data from regular traffic before problems occur, you can take another snapshot when problems emerge and compare them to try and recognize changes and probably the cause of the problem or issue.

Analyzing Endpoints Using Wireshark

Sometimes we want to see where the traffic ends when doing the traffic analysis. We would like to see the endpoints of communication, in other words. This could be an IP or MAC address.

We can select Statistics, and then Endpoints, to see the communication endpoints with their statistics.

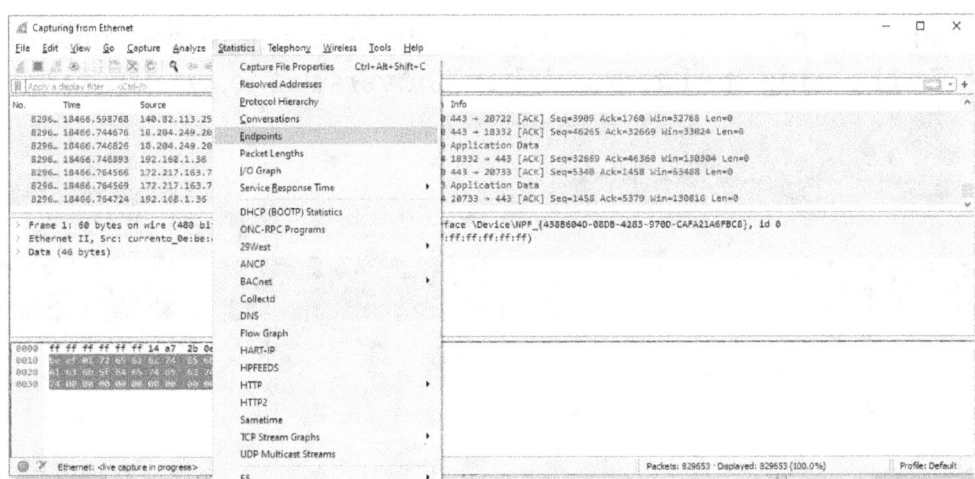

Additionally, by clicking the Endpoint Types button in the bottom right corner and selecting the protocol we want to filter for, we can filter these data by protocol.

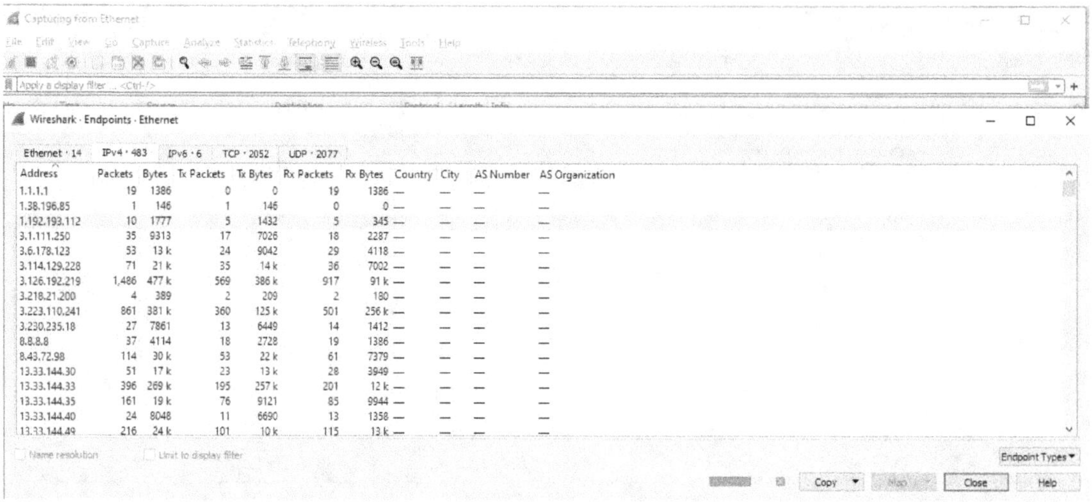

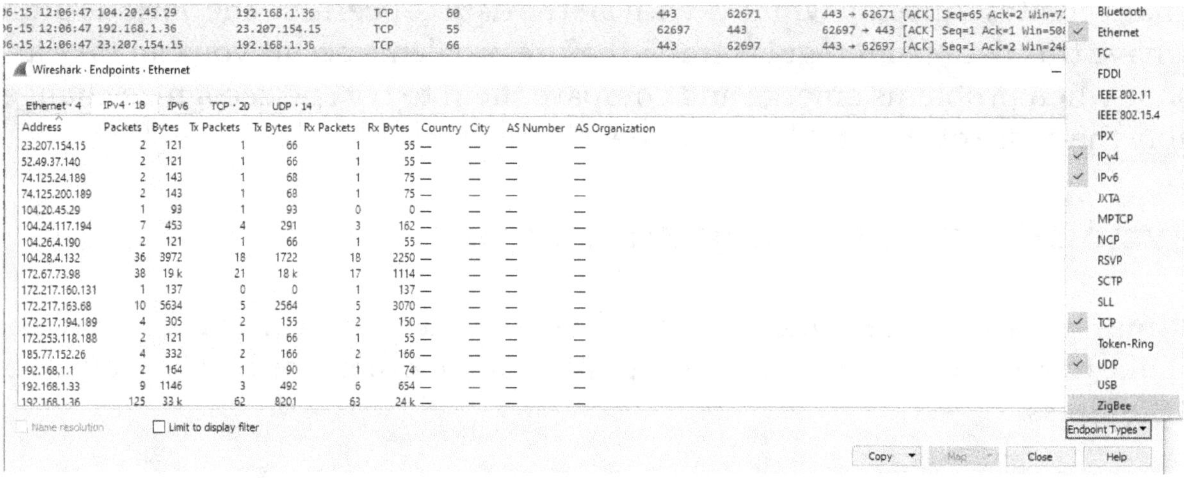

Analyzing Conversations

While analyzing network traffic, we may at times want to see data on a two-end conversation. By choosing Statistics and then Conversations, we can do that.

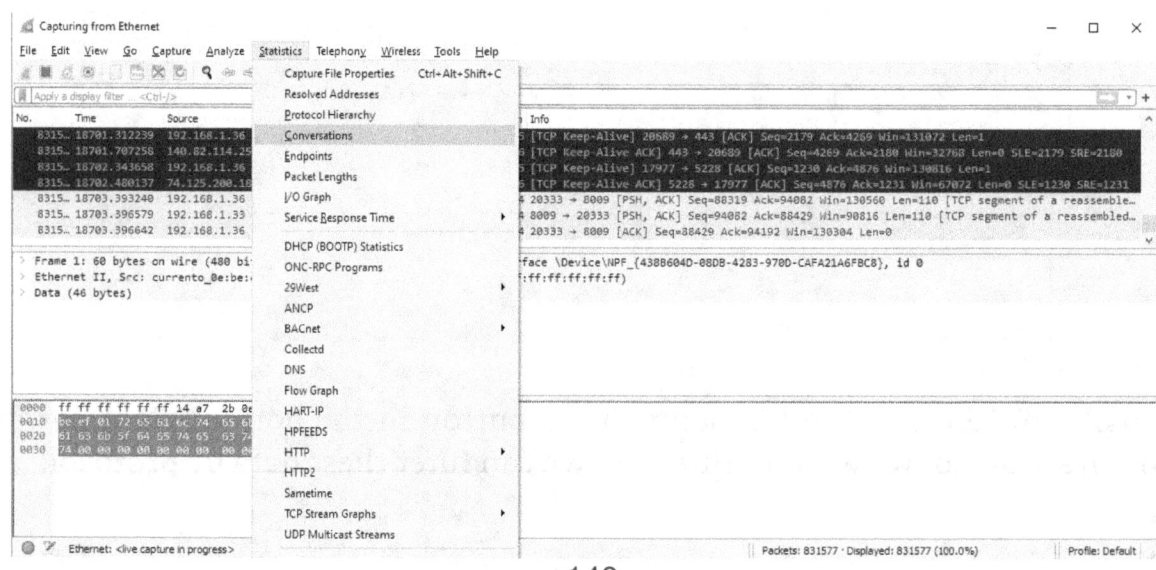

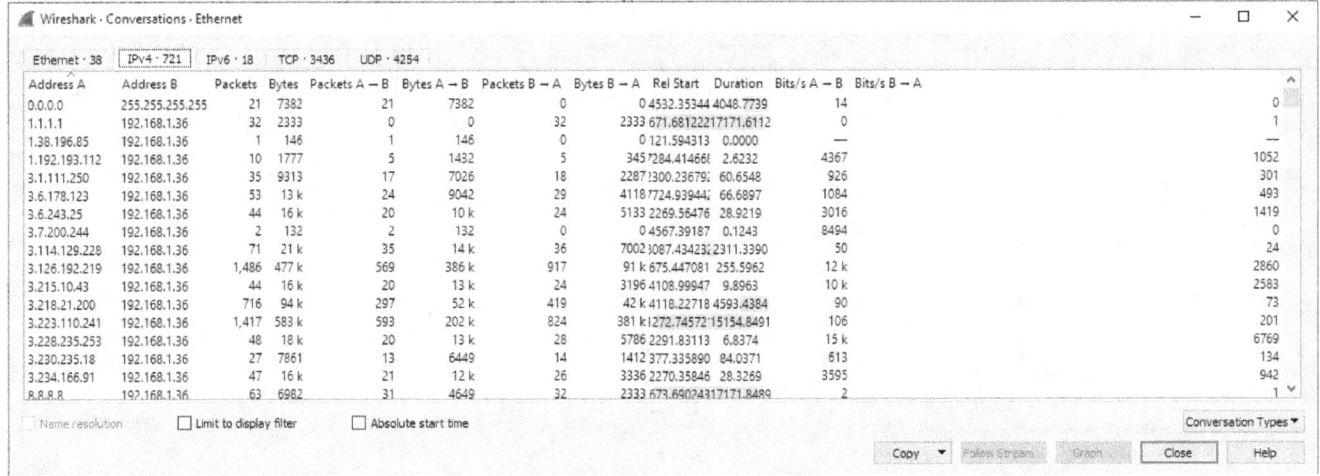

Wireshark will open a window like this, showing every conversation and then statistics related to that conversation that includes number of packets, bytes, duration of the conversation etc.

Analyzing traffic graphs

It is best to work with graphs when dealing with huge amounts of traffic, instead of scrolling down thousands of captured packets to identify errant packets. There are a couple of graphs within Wireshark which can be used.

IO graphs

These graphs can be used to evaluate highs and lows in traffic. This is very important in tracking matters. To use an IO graph, select a packet and click "IO Graph" under "Statistics." Select "Statistics," then "IO Graph," to create an IO Graph.

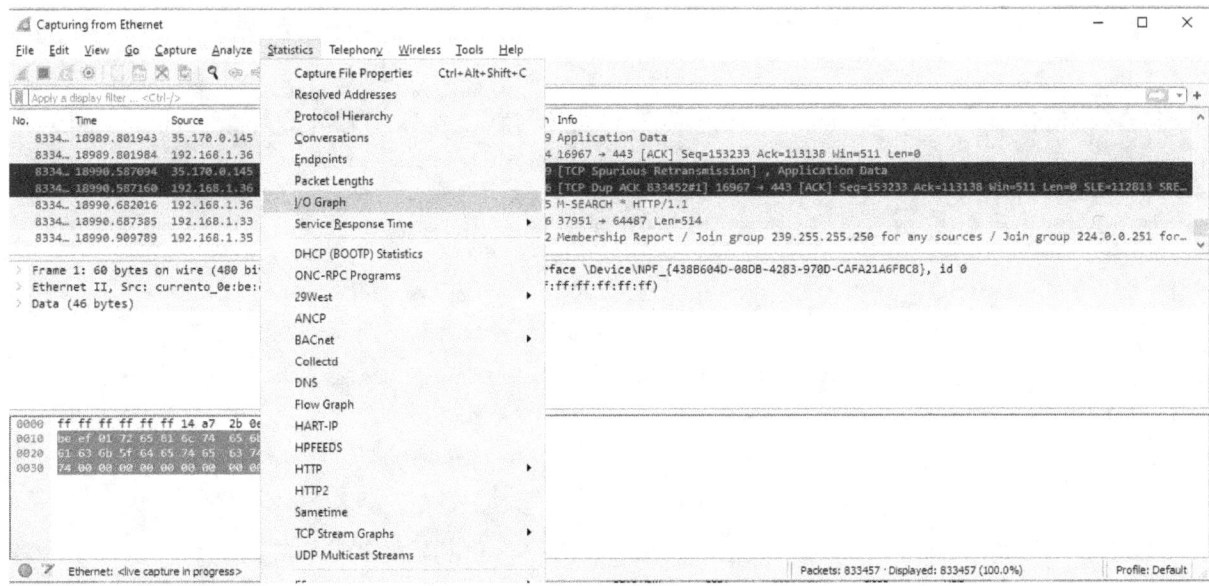

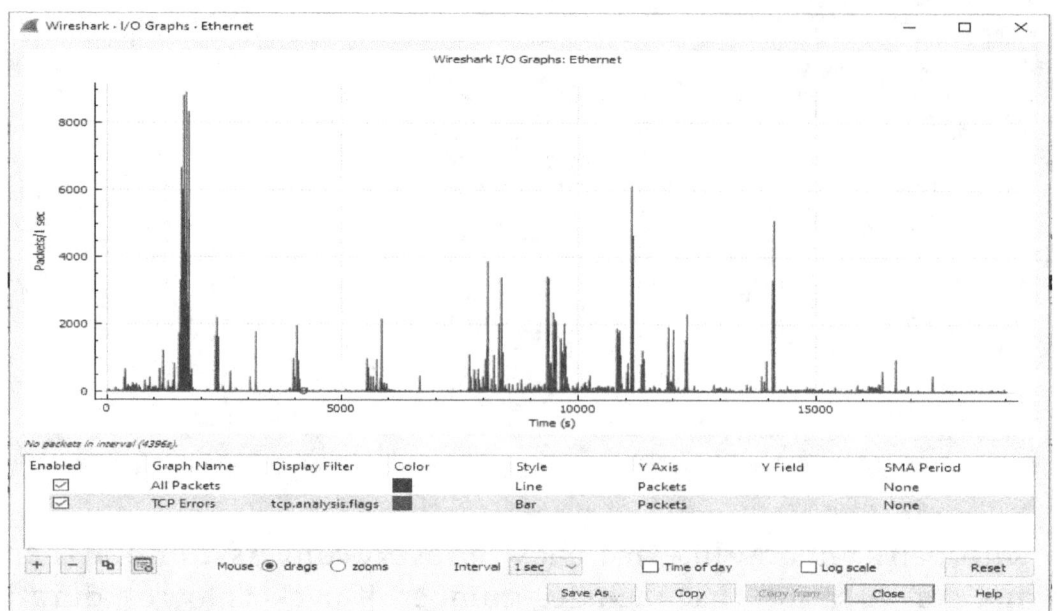

The data in the x-axis is the time in seconds, and the data in the y-axis, according to the graph above, represents the packets per tick. You can filter the graph to display graphs based on the daytime, interval and log scale, and you can even reset applied settings back to normal.

Flow graphs

This gives us a column-type graph showing which connections we might use to troubleshoot, missing frames, retransmission traffic and much more. We can export those results in a text-based production. To construct a flow graph, pick "Statistics," and then "Flow Graph.". By doing so we were able to produce the graph below.

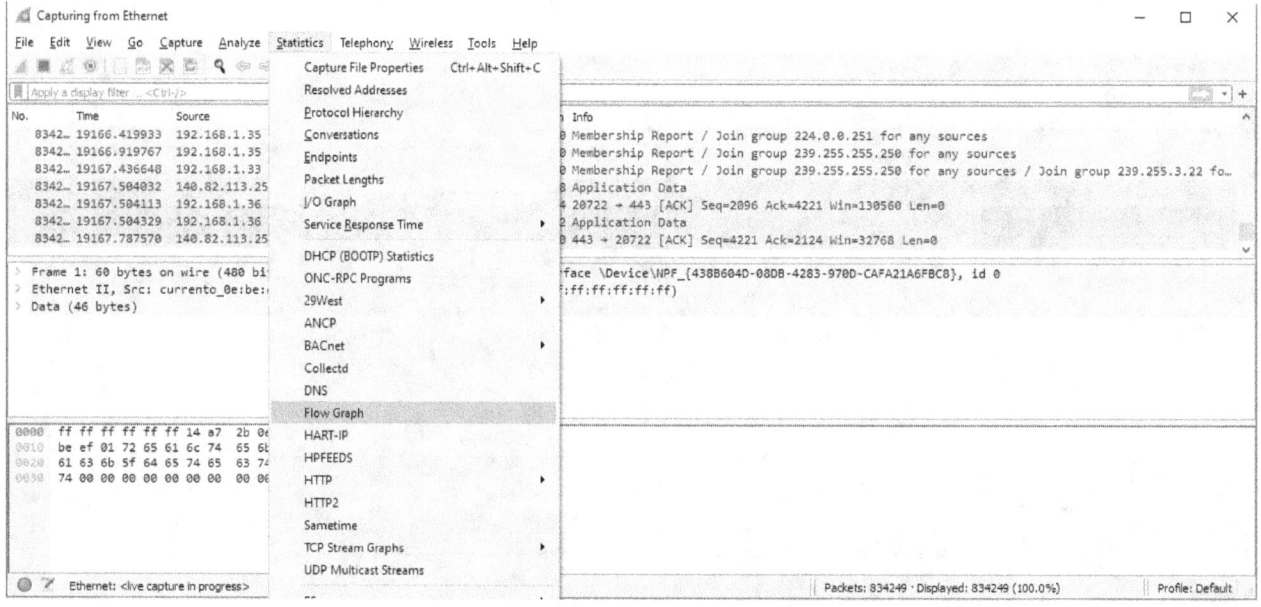

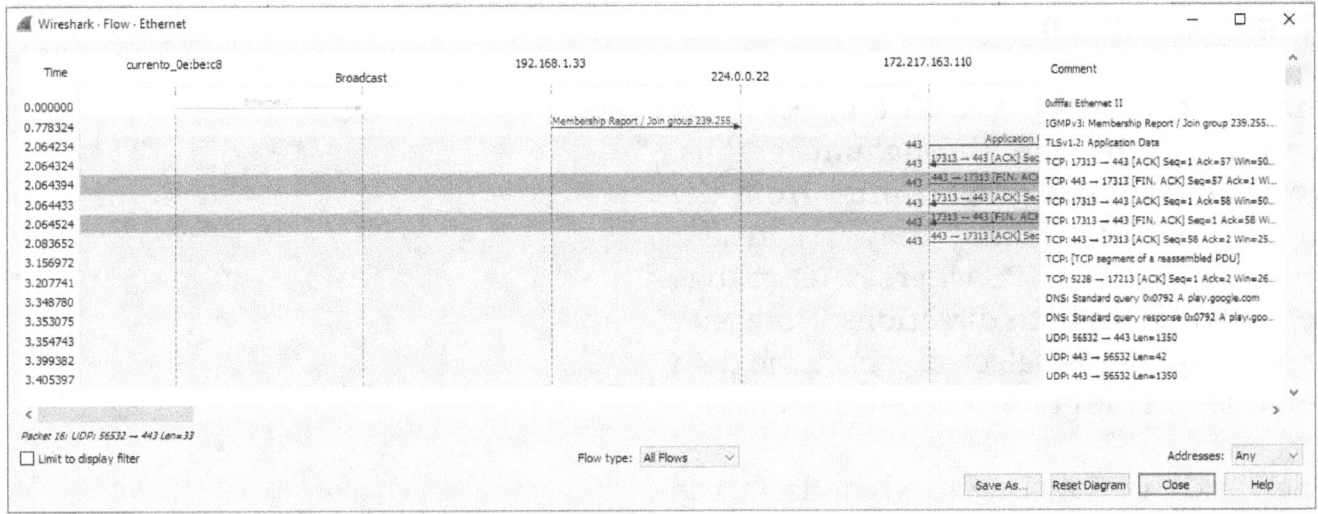

TCP stream graphs

These are a set of graphs representing network traffic in a graphical style distinct from the graphs above. Let's take a look:

Round-trip time graphs

The round trip time is the amount that the ACK would receive for a packet sent. This occurs within TCP communication, where an ACK is received for every packet sent, confirming a packet delivery. Choose a packet, then navigate to "Statistics," then pick "TCP Stream Graph," then "Round Trip Time Graph" to construct a round trip time graph.

A couple of things to note:

The x-axis is the TCP sequence number and in seconds the y-axis is the RTT

The dots on the graph represent a packet's RTT. An empty graph can mean you have selected a packet in the opposite direction

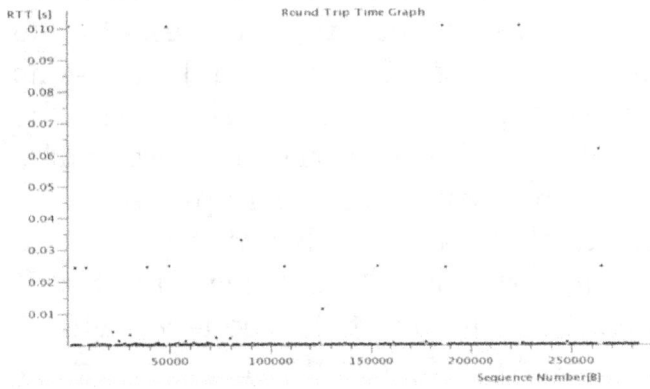

You should look for a vertical line of plotted RTT points to define the latency. This could either suggest that the sending device has a queued-up packet, or duplicate ACKs that are suffering.

Throughput graphs

Similar to IO graphs, traffic direction is represented by the throughput graphs. Nonetheless, these graphs differ from the IO graphs in that they represent unidirectional traffic, whereas IO graphs depict traffic in both directions. Note that depending on the selected packet the data you'll see on the graph will be different.

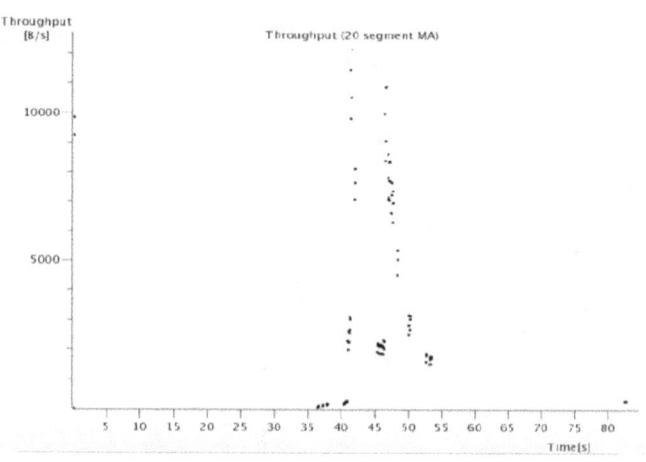

The x-axis is the time in seconds in the graph, and the y-axis represents the bytes per second throughput.

Time-sequence graph (tcptrace)

Using this graph portrays the TCP traffic flow with time. The traffic is unidirectional, just as the throughput graphs are. Use this graph to inform you about segments currently moving, the acknowledgement of segments we have provided, and the buffer area that the customer can carry.

Open the capture or trace file

Choose any TCP packet (various will offer different results)

Select the option 'Statistics,' then select 'TCP Stream Graphs,' then select 'Time Series Graph (tcptrace)'

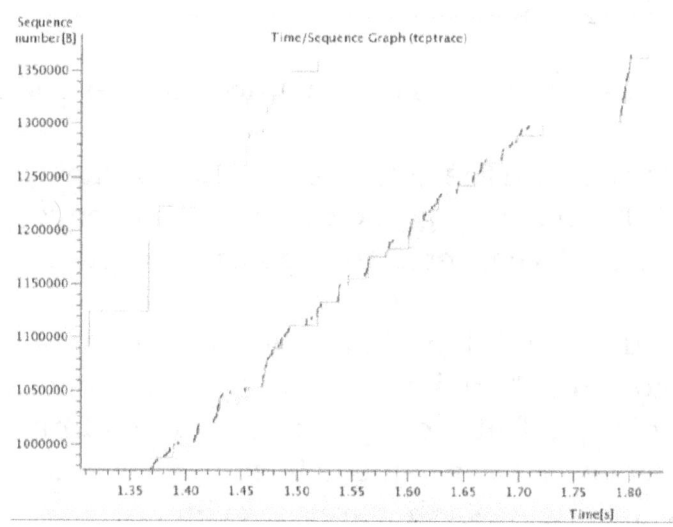

The y-axis in the graph represents the number of the TCP series, and the x-axis represents the time in seconds. The numbers of the TCP series are increased by the bytes sent with each packet. This means that if the number of the sequence is 1 and the packet sent has 10 bytes of data, the number of the sequence will be increased by 10, making the next number 11.

Customizing Display column according to our preferences

Default column display does not work effectively for the type of analysis, it's better to customize according to our preferences

Wireshark 's default columns: Number, Time, Source, Destination, Protocol, Length, and Info

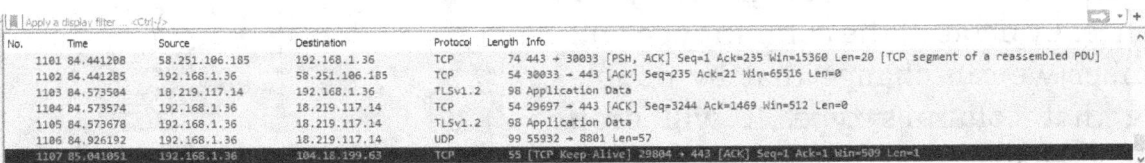

We can change this by go to Edit → Preferences

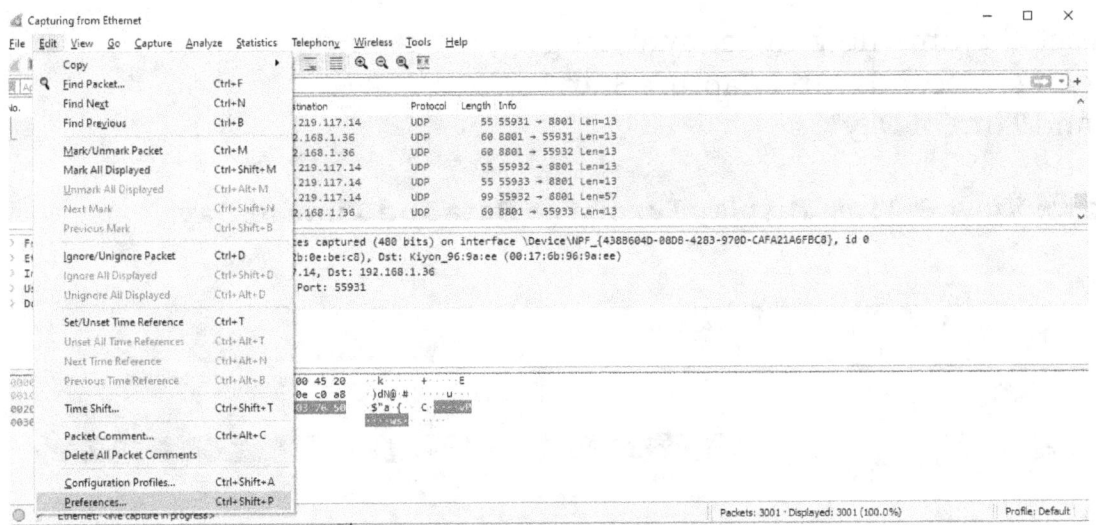

On there, extend Appearence → Columns
We can see the columns that appeared on wireshark analysis window there.

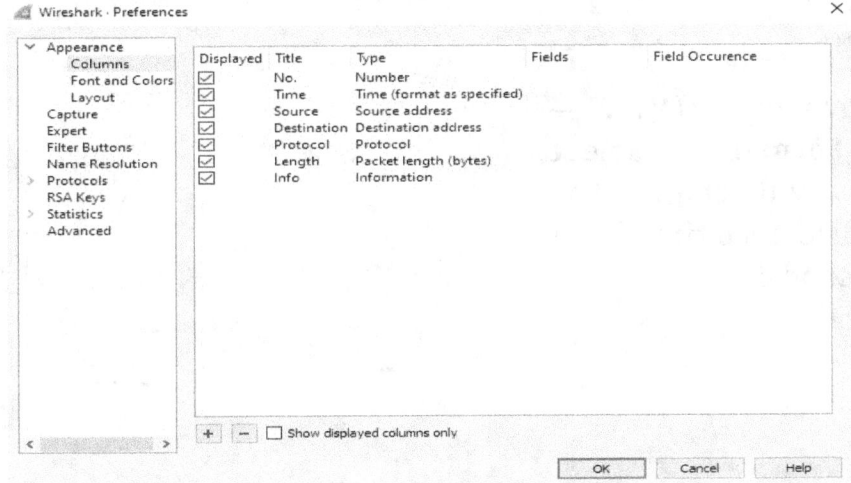

There is an option of adding and deleting columns

+ for adding Columns
- for deleting columns

When we click on +, it will add a new column

Name that column according to your preference. By default, the column type will be Number we can change that by double clicking that column's type. It will drop down all available types.

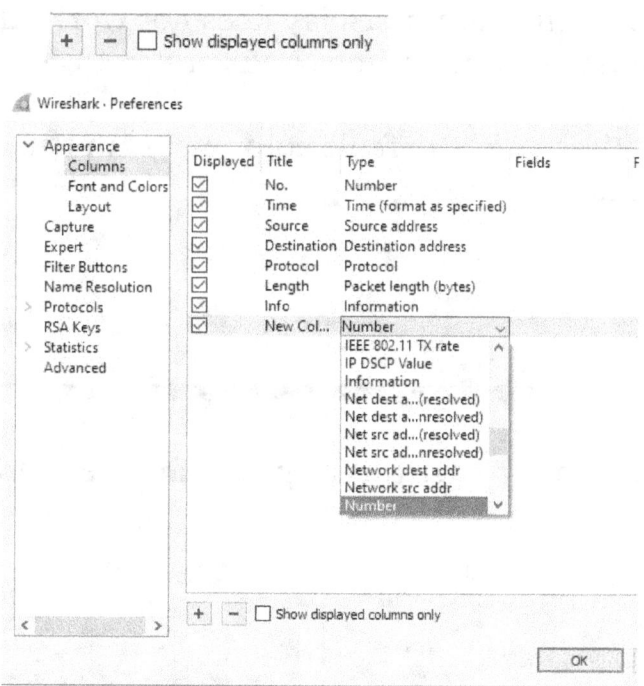

Clicking – will delete that column.

Let us reset the time now to get analyzing easier. Change "Seconds After Capture Start" to "Date and Time of Day"

Go to: **View → Time Display Format → Date and Time of Day.**

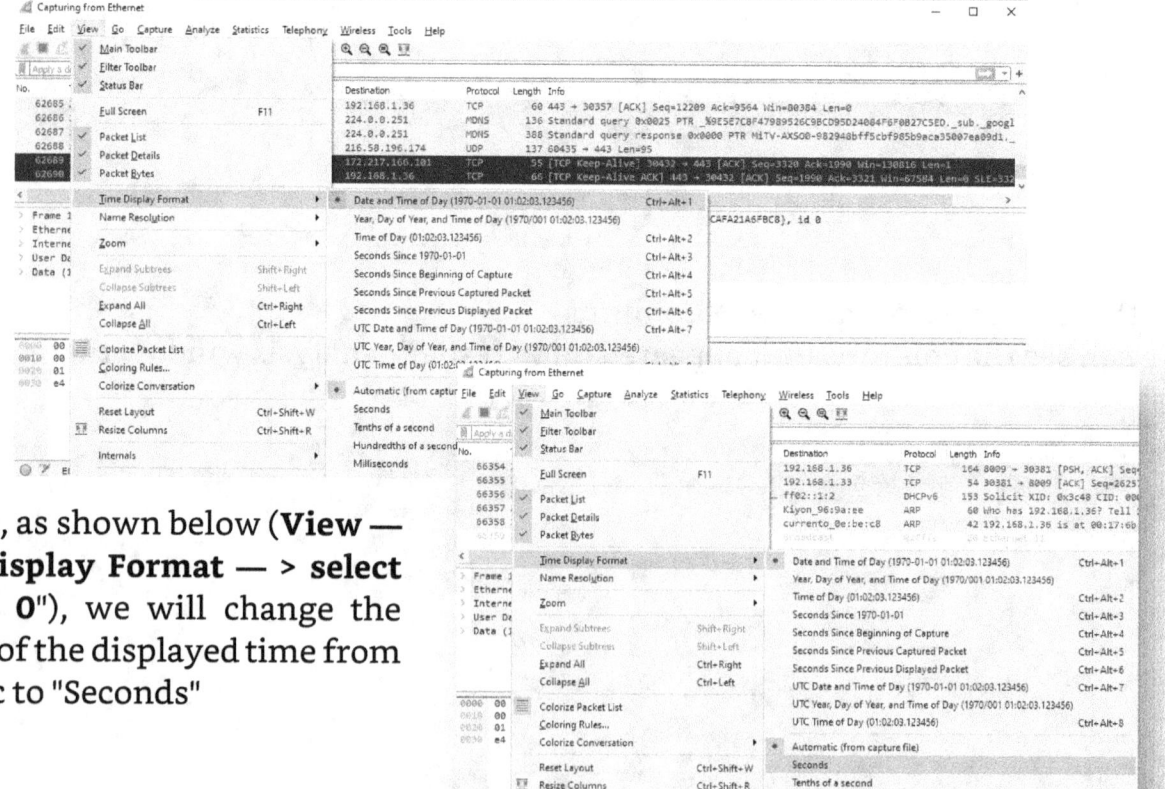

After that, as shown below (**View —> Time Display Format — > select "Seconds: 0"**), we will change the precision of the displayed time from automatic to "Seconds"

149

Many of the columns are aligned to the right and can be corrected by right clicking the column and selecting the correct alignment

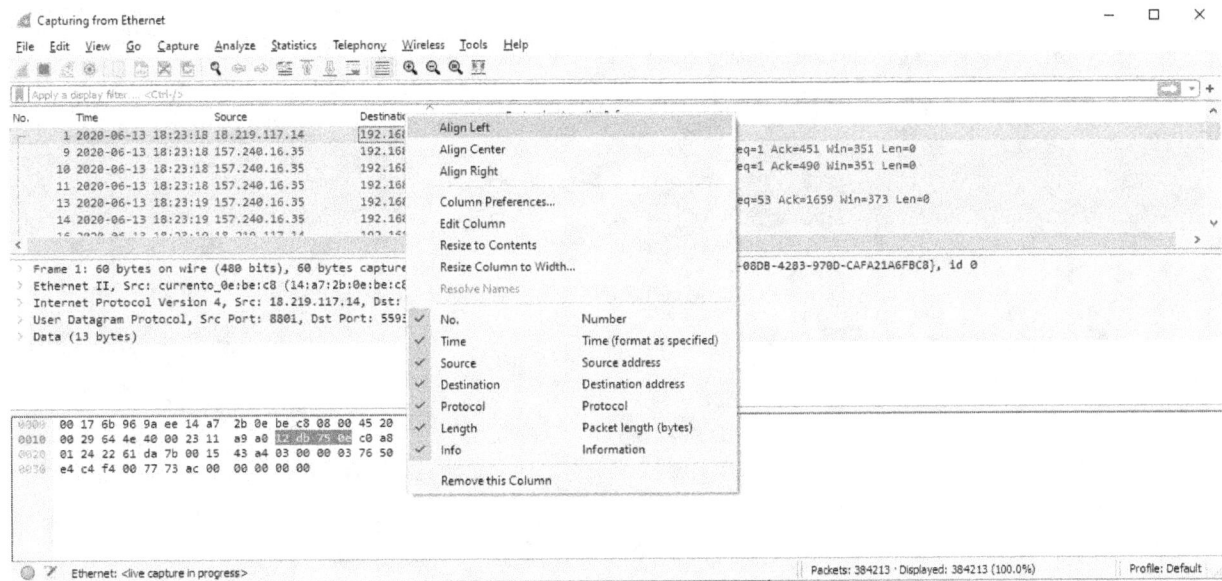

We can add Hosts to our panel. For that, filter on http.request, so we're only seeing the HTTP requests.

Right Click on **Host → Apply as Column**

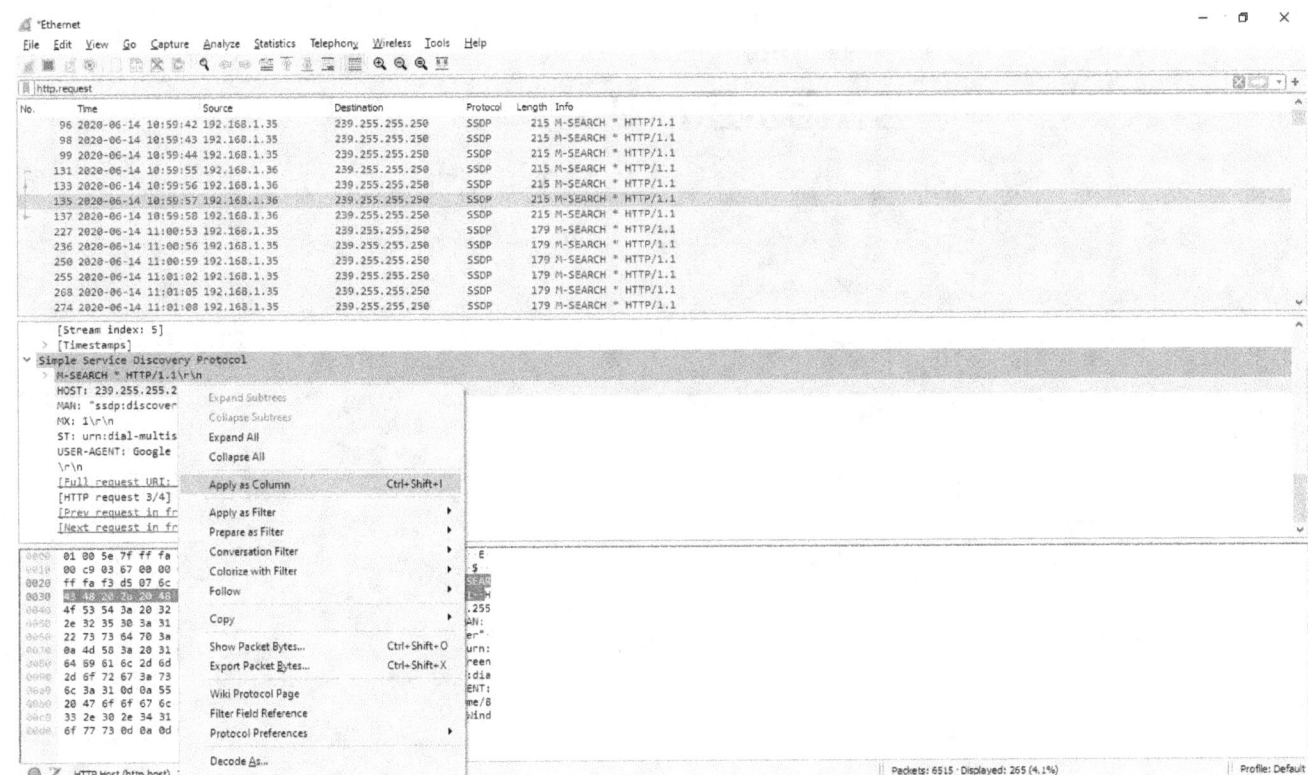

Analysing the Application Layer
Layer 6/7

By
Ambadi MP

Analyzing malware traffic through Wireshark

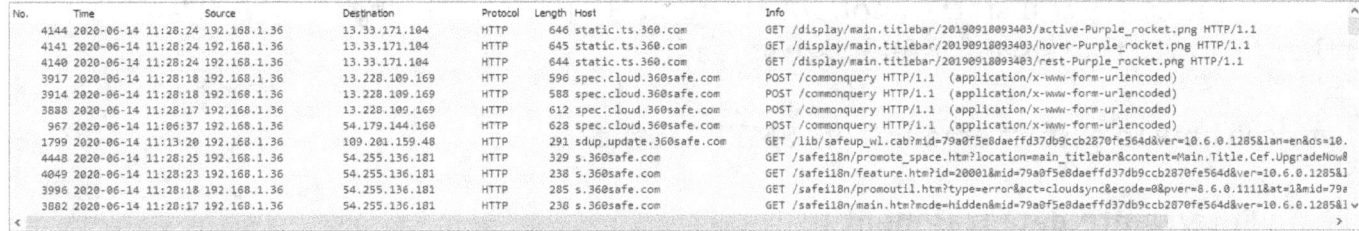

Extracting Objects from HTTP Traffic

Spreading of malware on networks is quite common. So, Security professionals may need to export objects from the pcaps for closer examination when reviewing packet captures (pcaps) of suspicious activity.

Let us see how to extract objects using Wireshark

For extracting files go to File → Export Objects
We can see DICOM , HTTP , IMF , SMB , TFTP protocols there
For files from HTTP Traffic

    File → Export Objects → HTTP

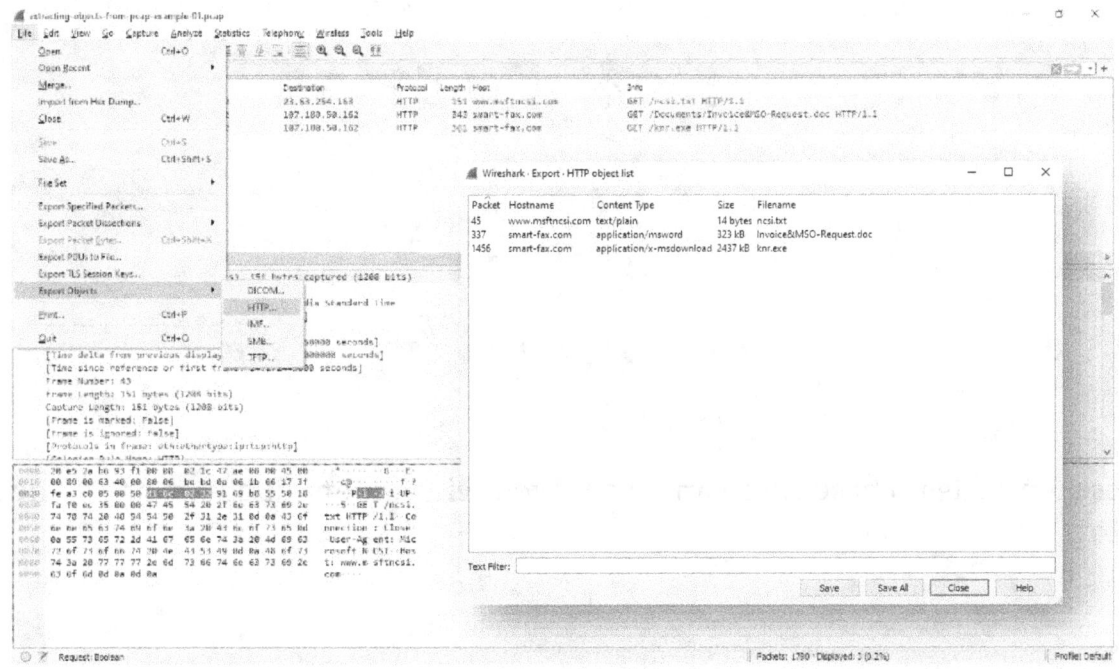

Click Save All. Choose Location For saving those files.
Files will be extracted and saved there.

Extracting Objects from SMTP Traffic

But malwares are transferred not only though HTTP. SMTP is the other protocol that used for malware spreading.

Let's see how to extract emails from SMTP Traffic.

Filter: **smtp.data.fragment**

Click on File → Export Objects → IMF

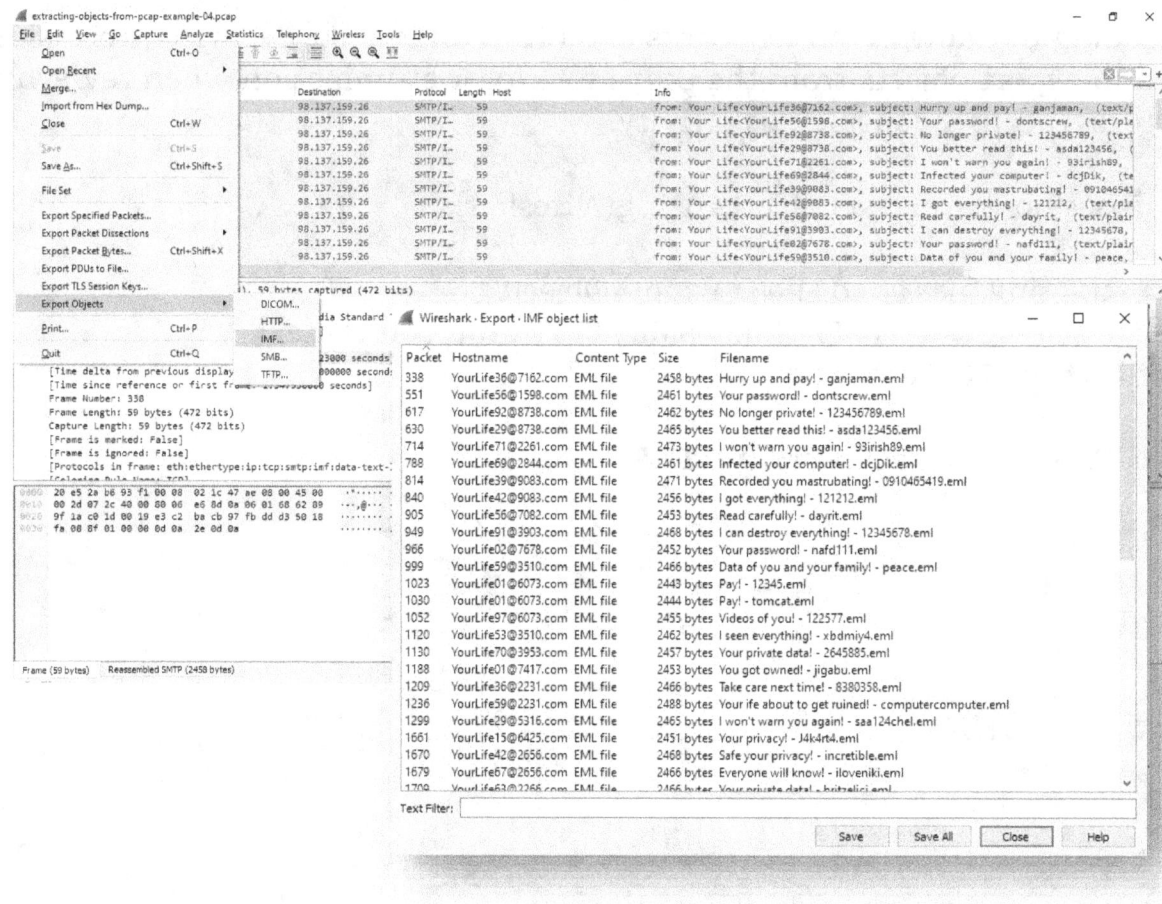

Save these .eml files. These files can be checked with an email client or examined in a text editor.

Extracting Objects from FTP Traffic

During malware infections some malware families are using FTP. Our malware executables retrieved from an FTP server, followed by information sent back to the same FTP server from the infected Windows Host.

    Filter: **ftp.request.command**

We can see Username, Password, and files in traffic using this filter.

We know which of the files that have been retrieved and sent, we can use an ftp-data filter to analyze traffic from the FTP data channel.

In Wireshark, we cannot use the feature Export Objects to export such objects. We may therefore follow the TCP stream for each from the data channels. To select one of the TCP segments, left-click on any of the lines ending with (SIZE q.exe) Then right-click to open menu and click Follow → TCP stream

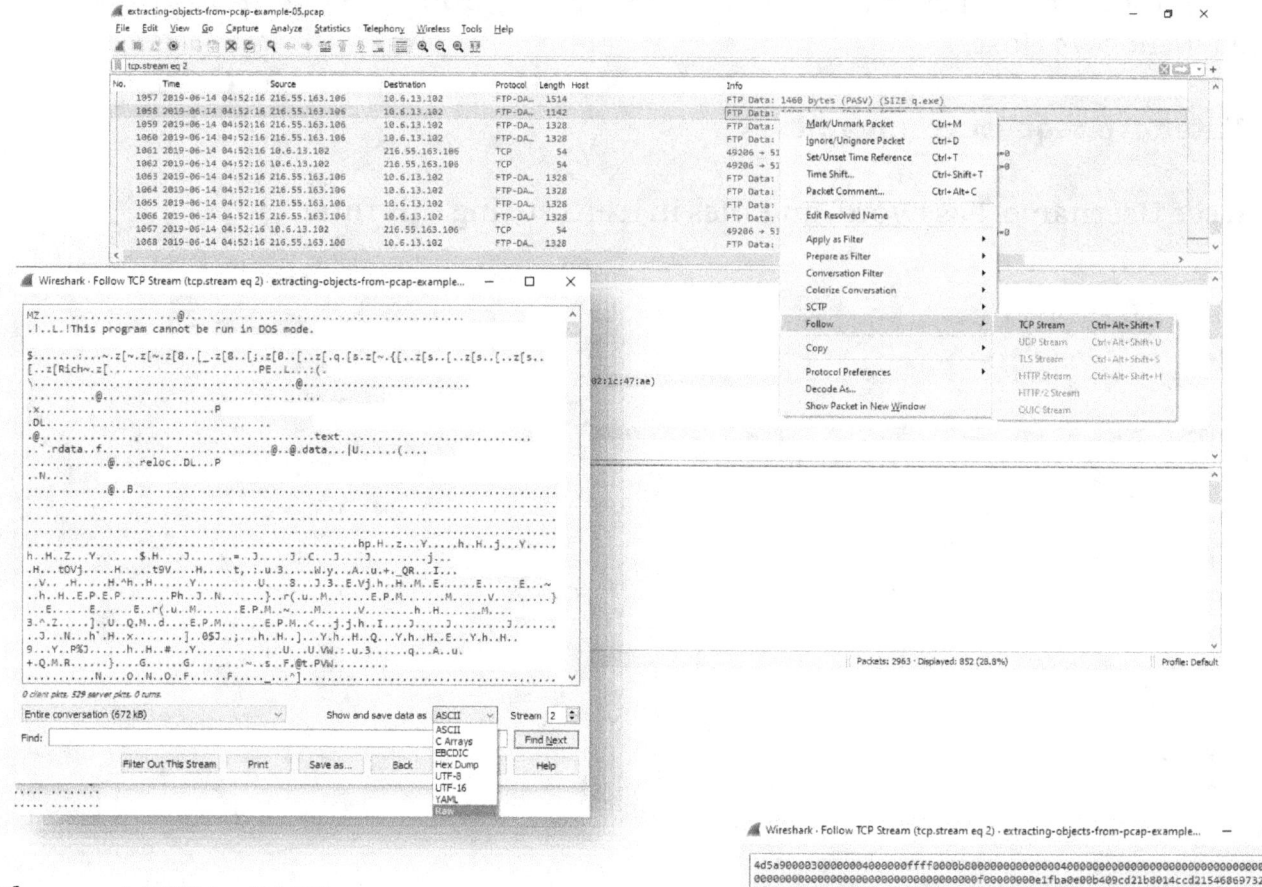

Change ASCII to RAW

Now save it as q.exe

Follow this step to extract rest of the files.

For getting SHA256 hash of these executable file use this command on terminal.

shasum -a 256 filename

eg: shasum –a 256 q.exe

ca34b0926cdc3242bbfad1c4a0b42cc2750d90db9a272d92cfb6cb7034d2a3bd

Search on Virus Total with that file's hash.

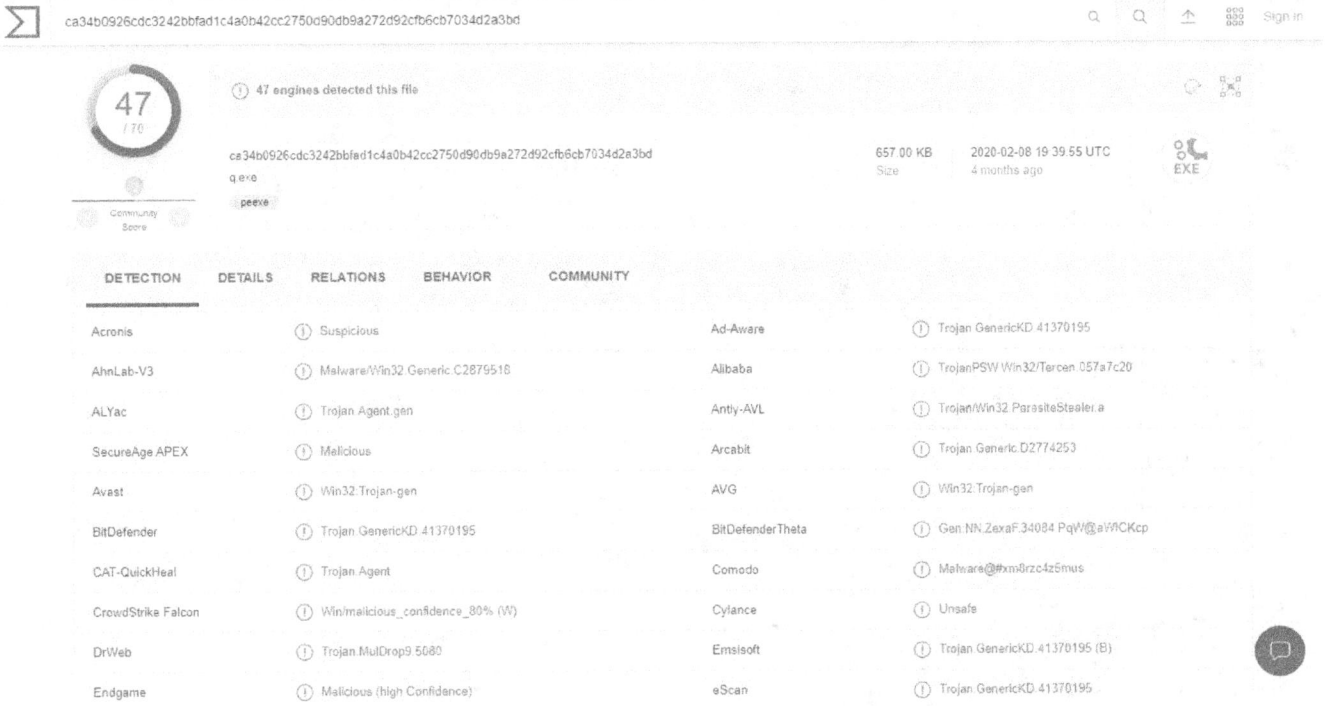

When exporting the HTML files sent back to the FTP server from the infected Windows host we need to search more precisely. Why? For what? Because each time the same name for the file is used. Use filter ftp.request.command, select, and scroll to the end. We will see the same file name used to store stolen data (STOR) as an HTML to the FTP server

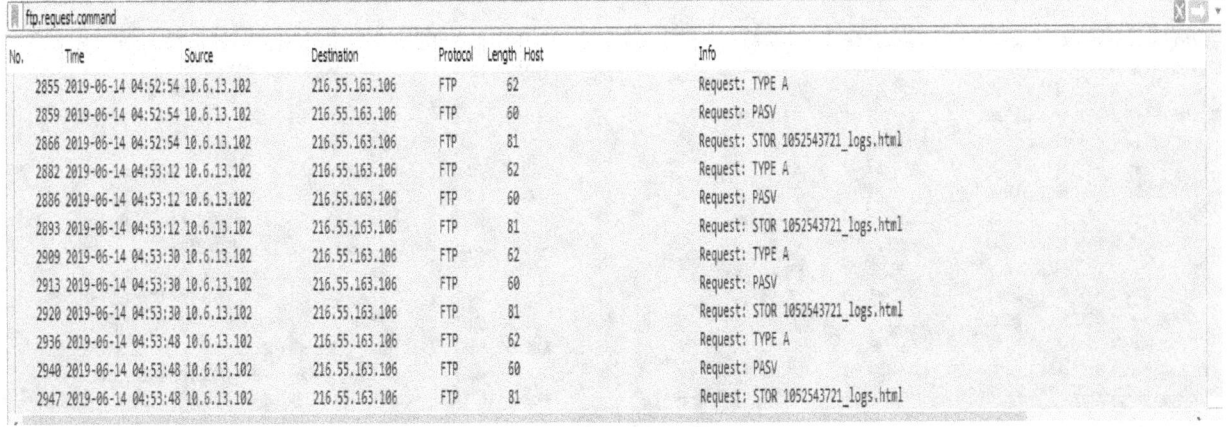

Use the filter ftp-data.command contains .html to see the associated files sent over the ftp data channel.

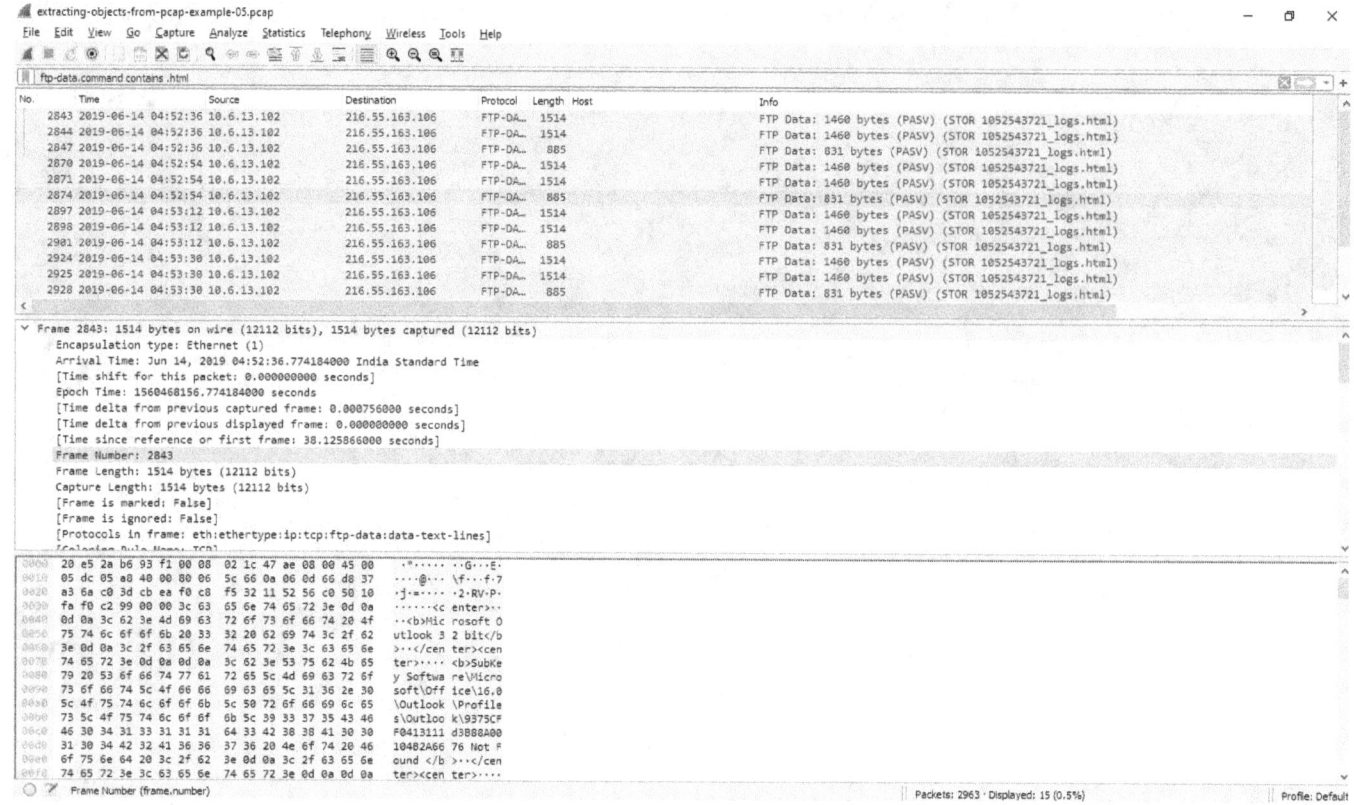

The destination port changes to the FTP server each time the file (STOR) is stored. TCP port 52202 is used for the first time. TCP port 57791 is for the second time. Has TCP port 55045 for the third time. It has 57203 for the fourth time. And 61099 the fifth time.

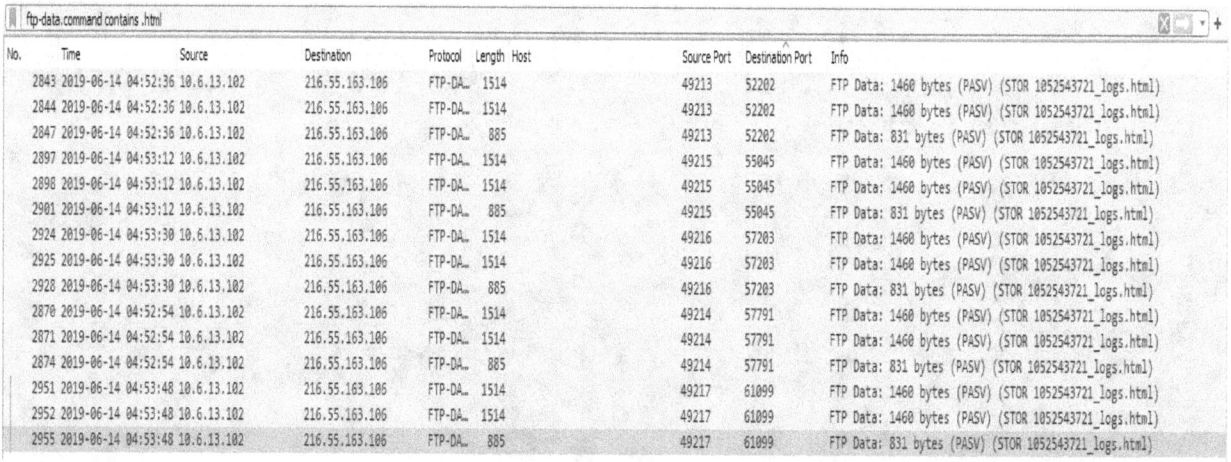

We're using the same process as we used to. Instead of concentrating on the file names, focus on the TCP ports. To any TCP line use port 52202 to follow the TCP stream. Change "Show and save data as" to "Raw" in the TCP stream window, then save that file.. Do the same in case of HTML file over TCP port 57791.

Analyzing Torrent Traffic

Let us see how to analyze a torrent traffic and gather information. Before starting I'll explain what is BitTorrent?

BitTorrent is a file-distribution protocol. It identifies URL content and is designed to seamlessly integrate with the web. Its advantage over plain HTTP is that when multiple downloads of the same file occur simultaneously, the downloaders upload to each other, allowing the file source to support very large numbers of downloaders with only a modest increase in their load.

These entities comprise a distribution of BitTorrent files:

- A web server
- A static 'metainfo' file
- A Tracker
- An 'original' downloader
- End user's web browsers
- End user's downloaders

It is a great ability to either identify malicious activity or someone using your network for the wrong reasons (even if it is harmless) to be able to track BitTorrent activity Actually, In fact, if you have people who use it to download things like the Linux distribution that was seceded, you might want to allow BitTorrent on your network. If it means a user downloads copyrighted material or malware, you might not want to allow that either.

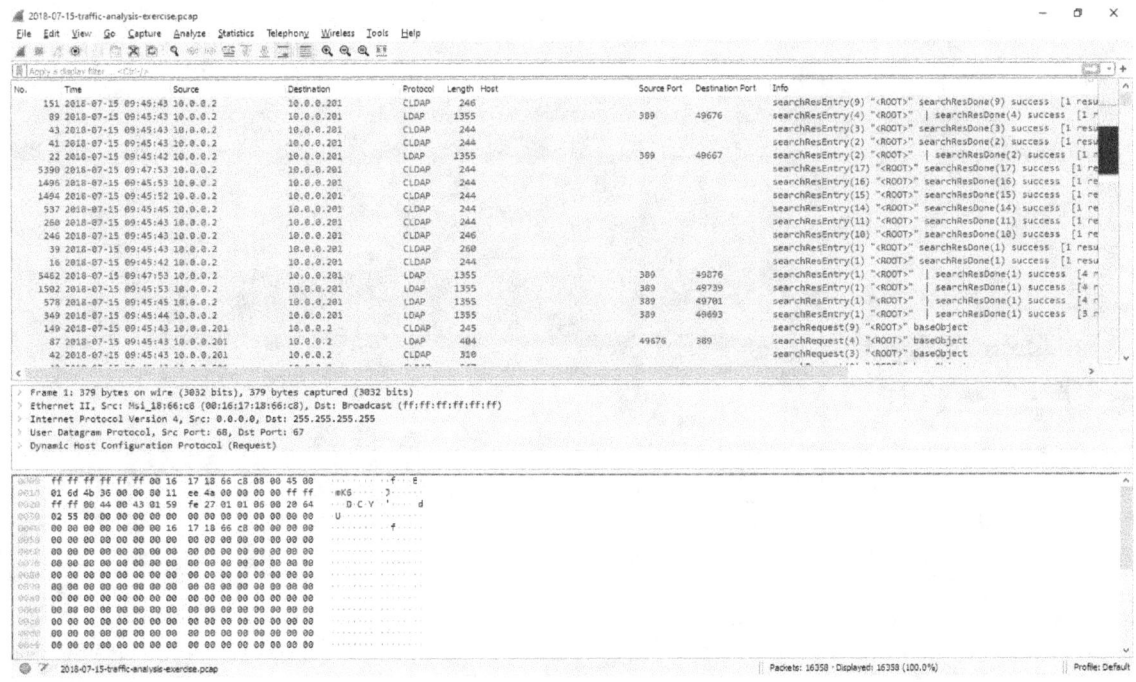

Use filter **bittorrent** for filtering BitTorrent requests.

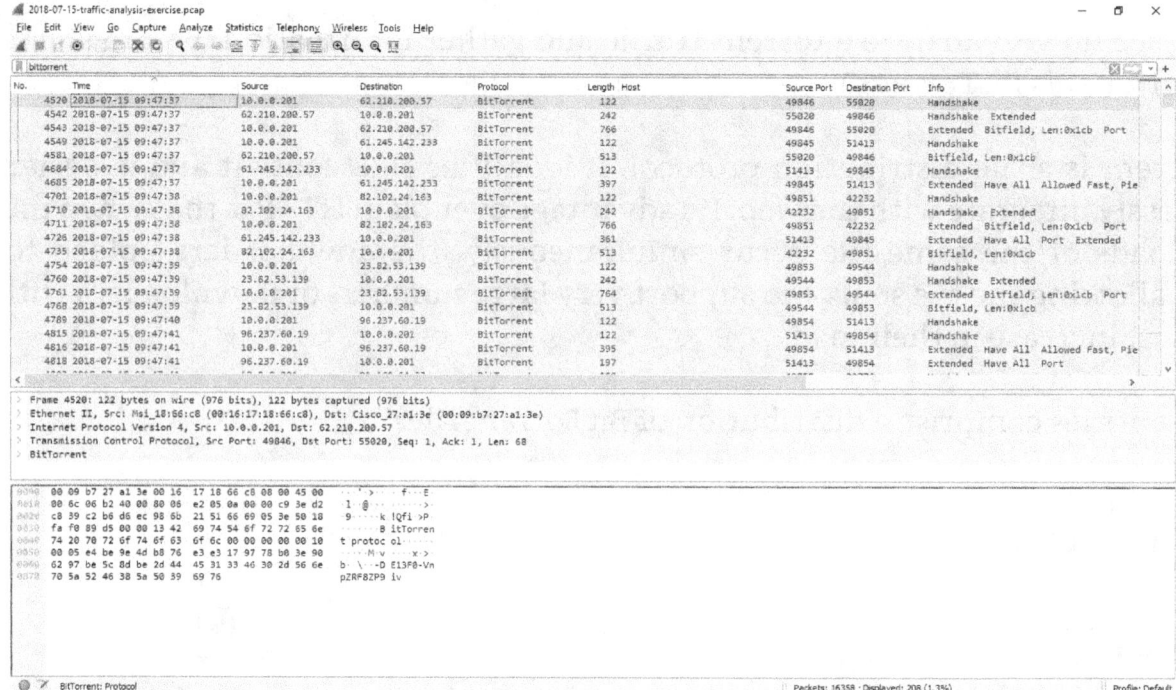

We want to know which file is downloaded, use this filter:

http.request.uri contains .torrent

It means filter all urls with .torrent files.

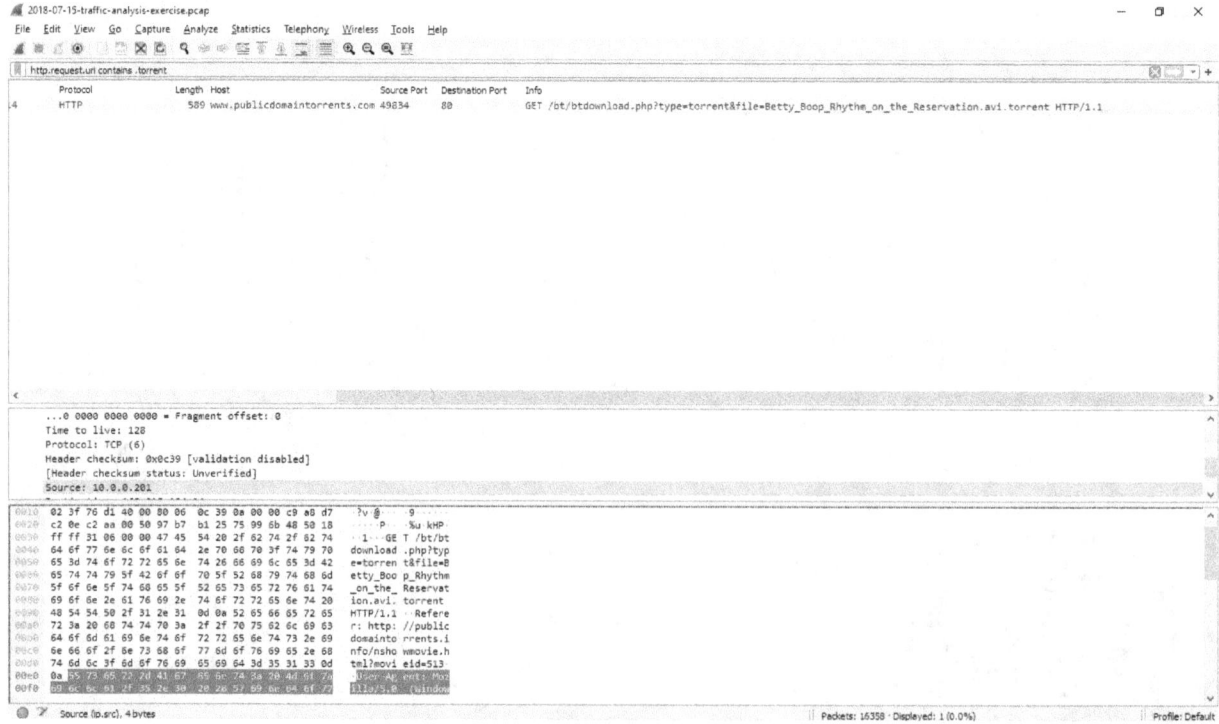

Now Right Click on that and **Follow → TCP Stream**

By analyzing the tcp stream .torrent file name is
Betty_Boop_Rhythm_on_the_Reservation.avi.torrent

In HTTP, we may search for "announce" or "scrape" URLs for finding torrent tracker traffic and seeing if any other files are torrenting.

For that use filters

    http.request.uri contains announce
    http.request.uri contains scrape

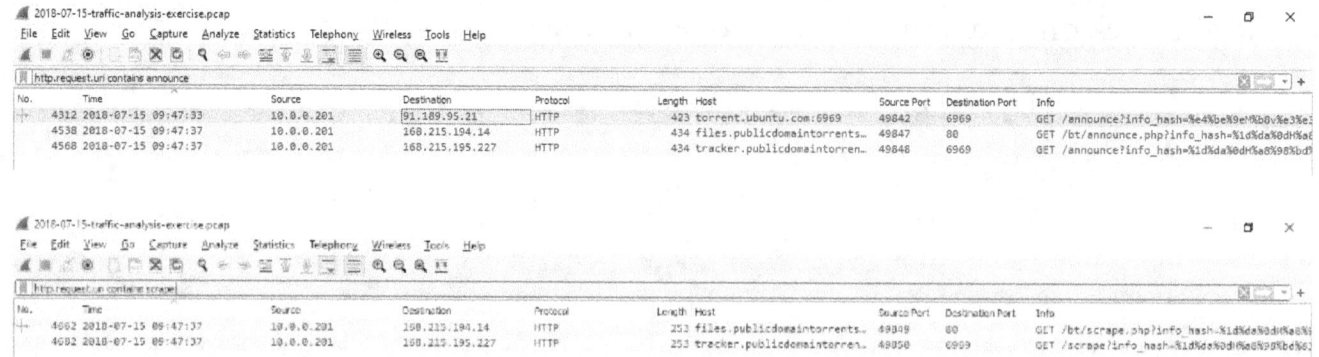

HTTP request headers from tracker traffic should also give us the torrent client in the UserAgent string.

In addition to tracker traffic to two publicdomaintorrents.com domains, the results also show tracker traffic to torrent.ubuntu.com.

Length	Host	Source Port	Destination Port	Info
423	torrent.ubuntu.com:6969	49842	6969	GET /announce?info_hash=%e4%b
434	files.publicdomaintorrents.com	49847	80	GET /bt/announce.php?info_has
434	tracker.publicdomaintorrents.com:6969	49848	6969	GET /announce?info_hash=%1d%d

Length	Host	Source Port	Destination Port	Info
253	files.publicdomaintorrents.com	49849	80	GET /bt/scrape.php?info_hash=
253	tracker.publicdomaintorrents.com:6969	49850	6969	GET /scrape?info_hash=%1d%da

The results also show the tracker traffic to two publicdomaintorrents.com domains Tracker to Torrent.ubuntu.com.

For the first HTTP request, follow the TCP stream, of torrent.ubuntu.com. Check out the User-agent string, it is Deluge 1.3.15.(Deluge is a torrent client deluge-torrent.org/)

What is tracking that traffic? You can find out that from the value of info hash. Select the value right after info hash= in the same HTTP GET request

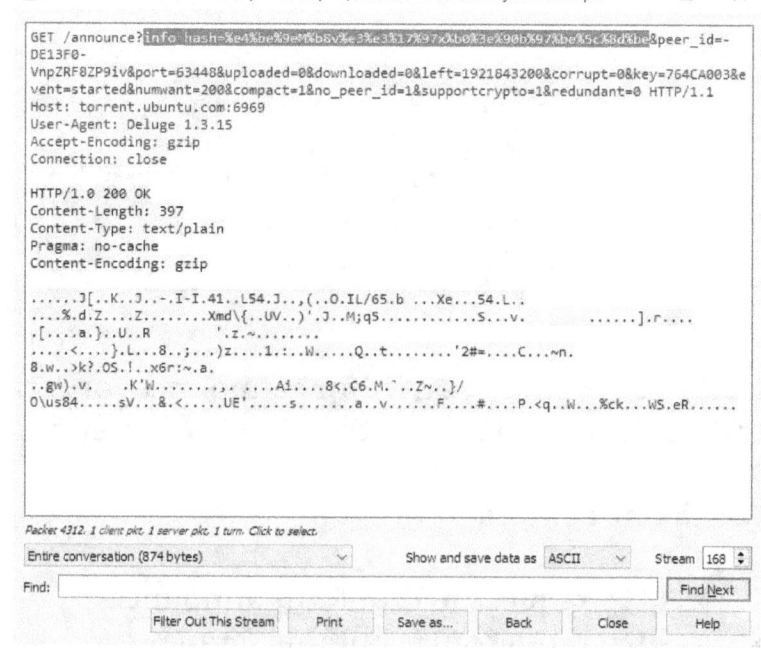

info_hash=%e4%be%9eM%b8v%e3%e3%17%97x%b0%3e%90b%97%be%5c%8d%be

after decoding url encoding the hash will be:
e4be9e4db876e3e3179778b03e906297be5c8dbe

Search that hash on Google and it comes up with:

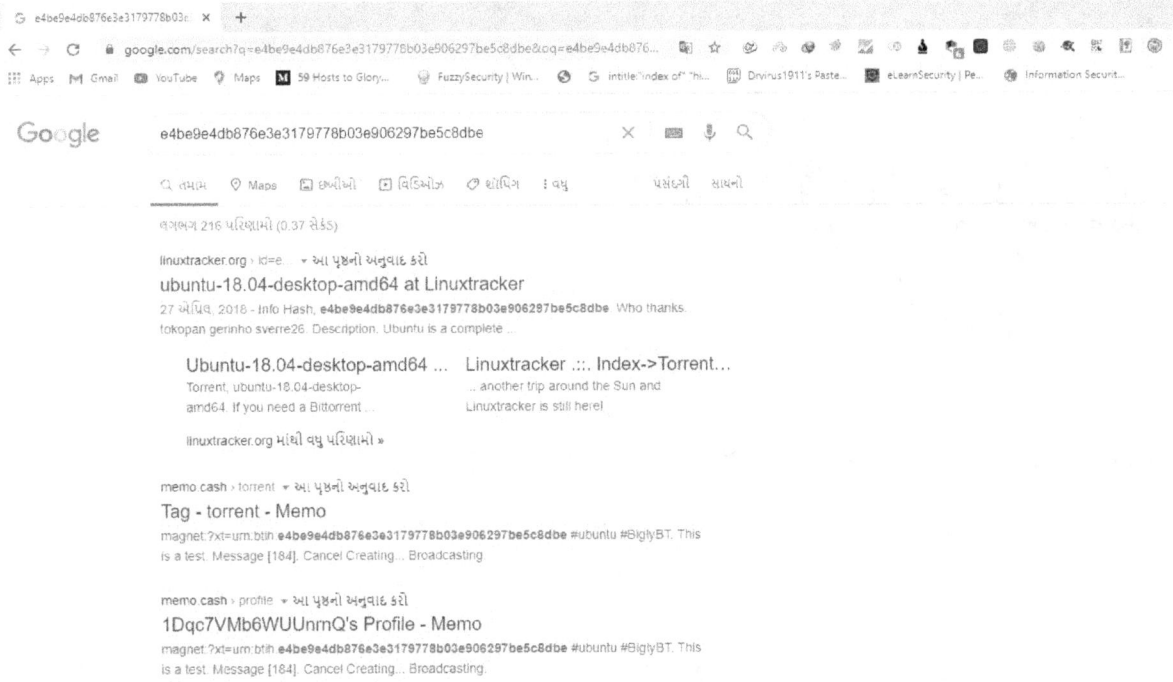

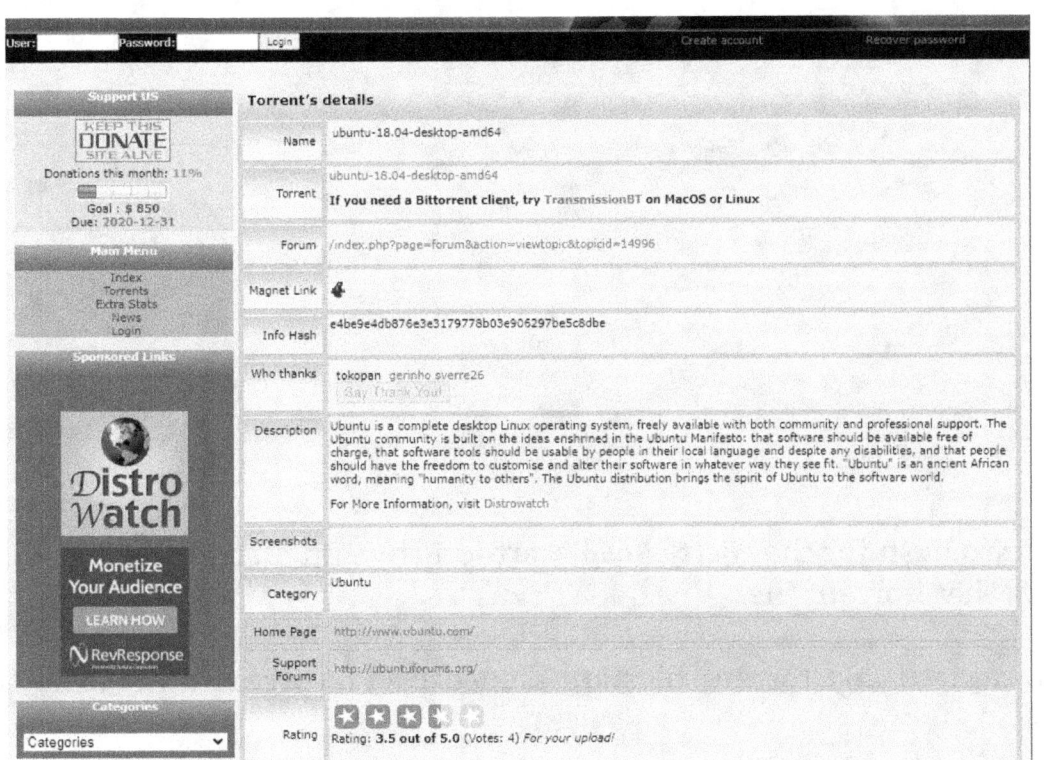

It is an ubuntu18.04-desktop-and64.iso file let us decode it using url decoder

Use the same for tracker traffic on the other HTTP requests.

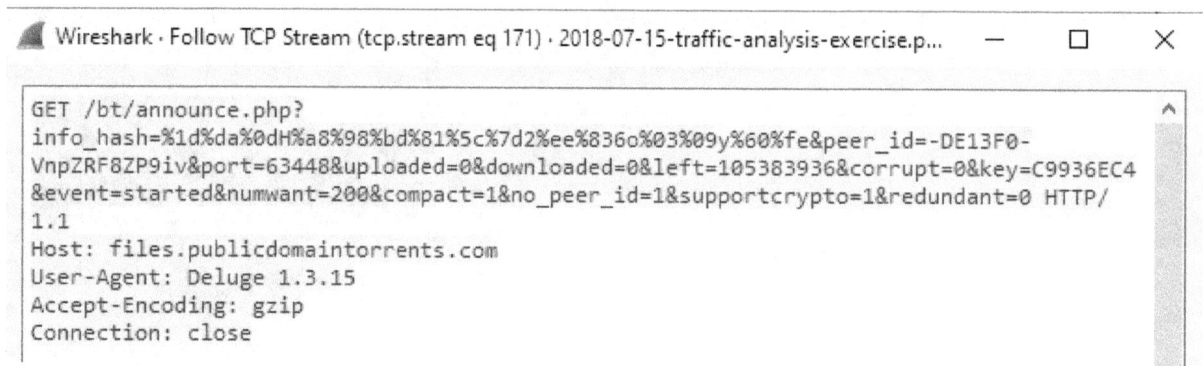

Hash is **1dda0d48a898bd815c7d32ee83366f03097960fe**

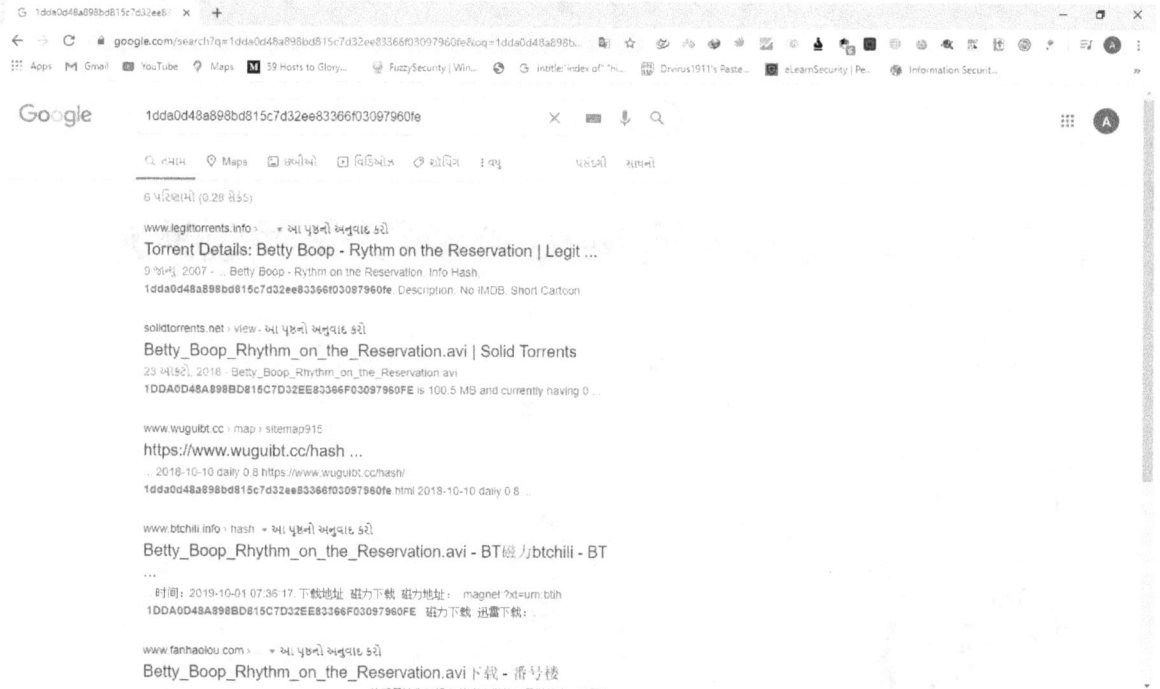

That is an info hash for the **"Betty Boop"** cartoon rhythm on the reservation we found earlier from that .torrent file.

For determining if any torrent files are seeded by BitTorrent .info_hash filtering in Wireshark

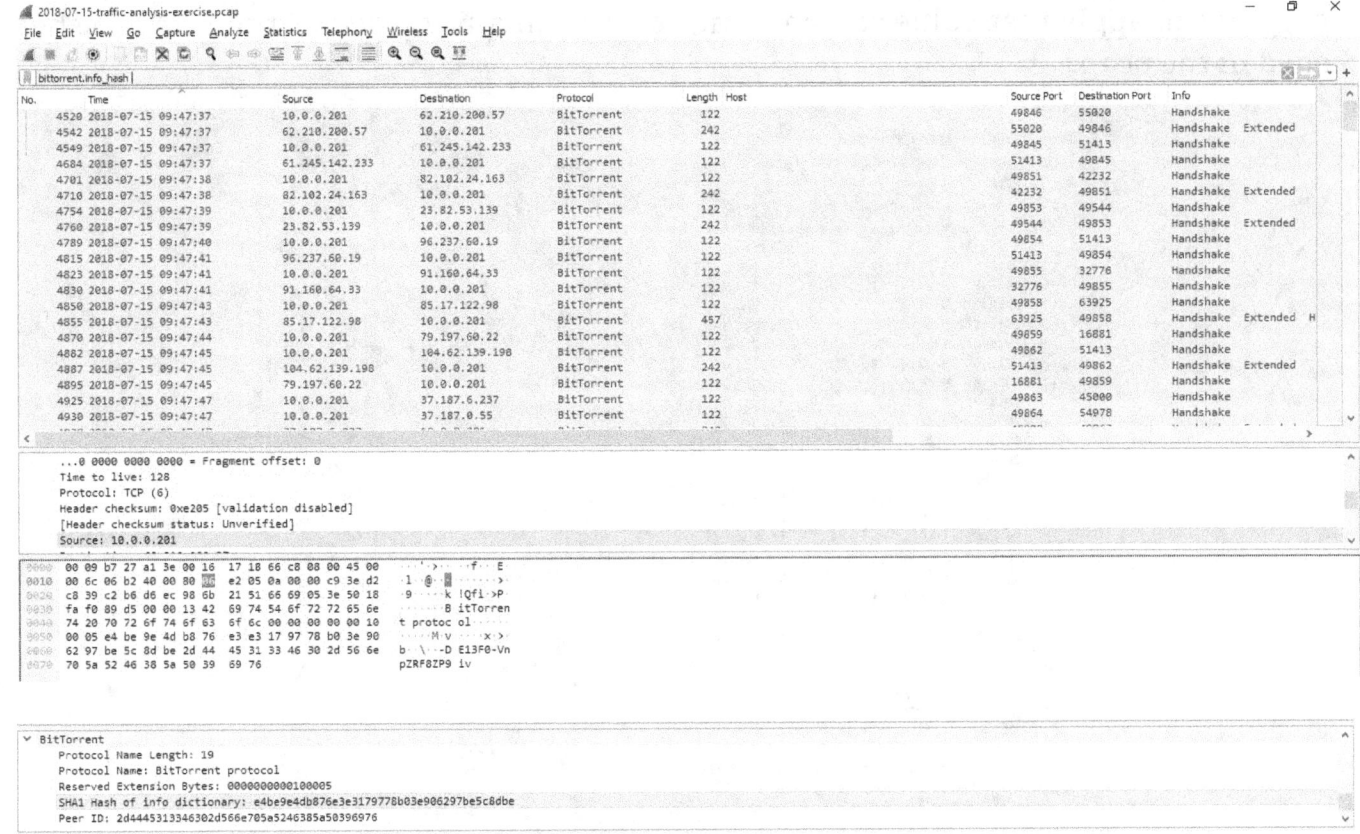

You can copy that field's hexadecimal value by copying it as a hex-stream. Then, if needed, paste it into a Google search. In this case it is the same SHA1 hash we found earlier for the Ubuntu 18.04 ISO package.

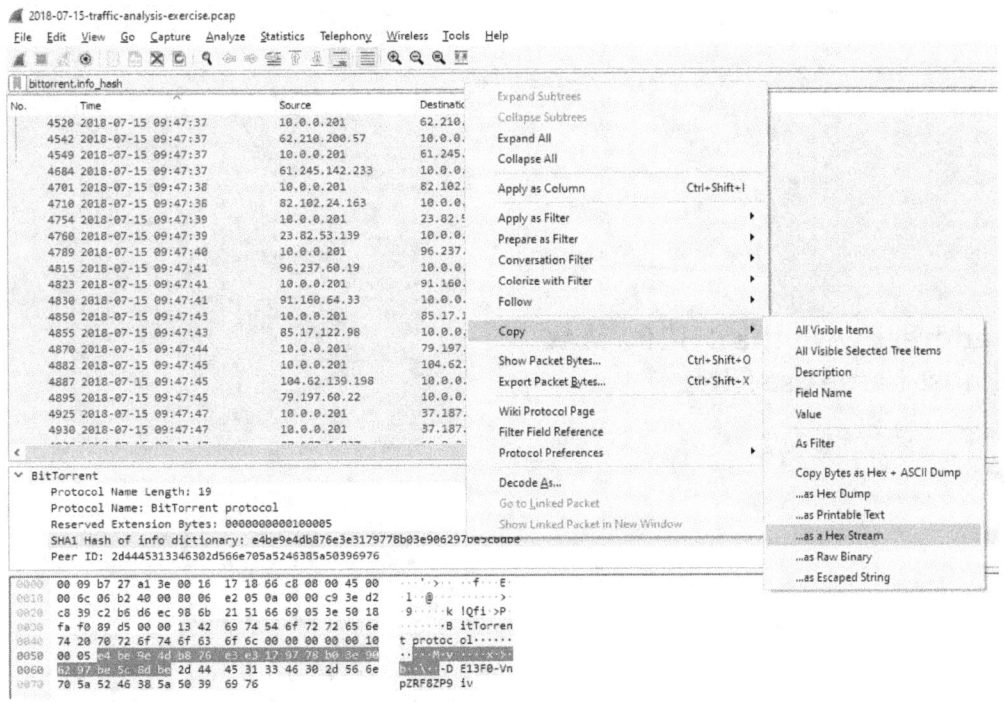

Also, you can apply that value as a column, so you can quickly see all the SHA1 hashes seeded in the pcap.

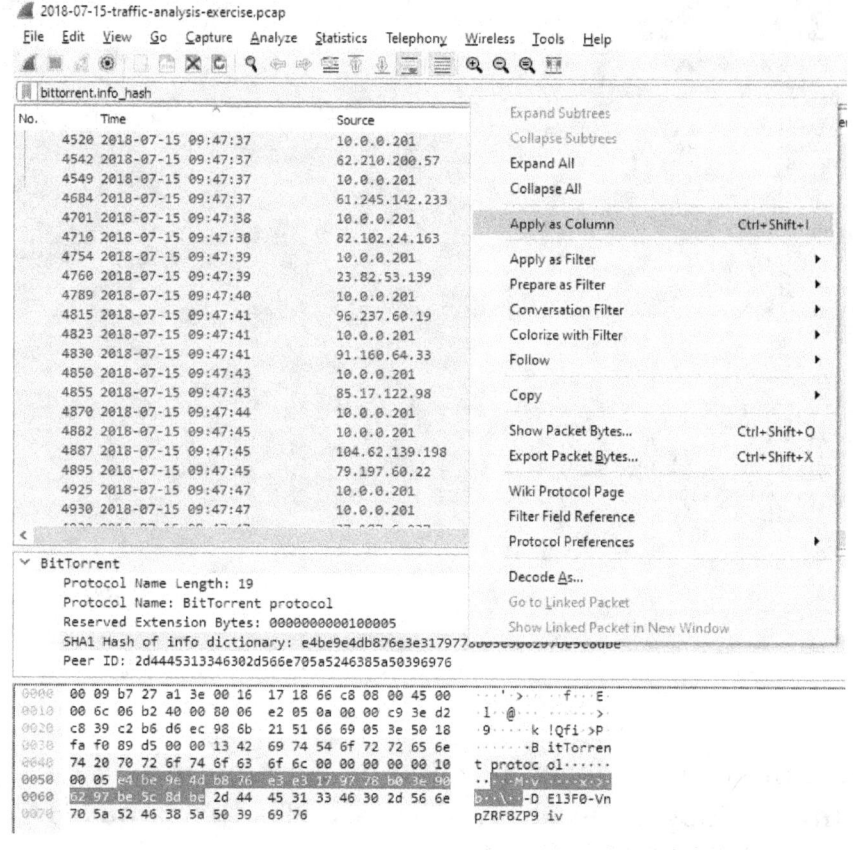

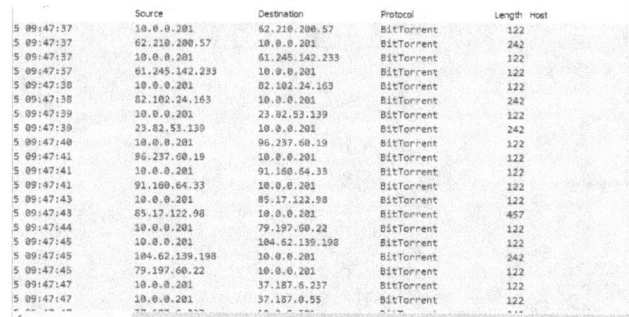

To locate IP address with the DHCP's MAC address and host name use filter

Bootp

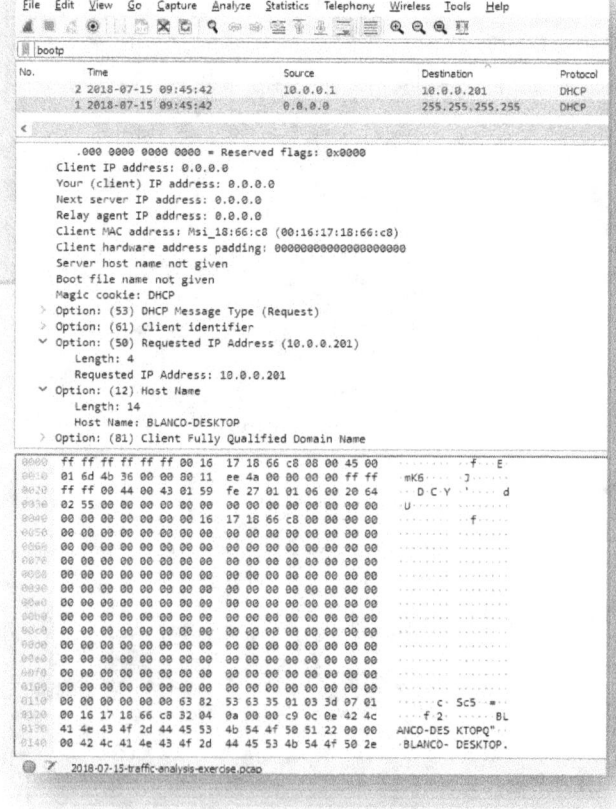

The Bootstrap Protocol (BOOTP) is a computer networking protocol used by Internet Protocol networks to automatically assign an IP address from a configuration server to the network devices.

From this filter we can see:

> **MAC Address: 00:16:17:18:66:c8**
> **IP Address: 10.0.0.201**
> **Host Name: BLANCO-DESKTOP**
>
> Use filter **kerberos.CnameString**

To find the name of a Windows user account.

Windows host names and user account names are represented by the **CNameString** values. Upon location of any **CNameString** value in the frame details panel, add it as A column, so you can find your associated user account quickly from your column display.

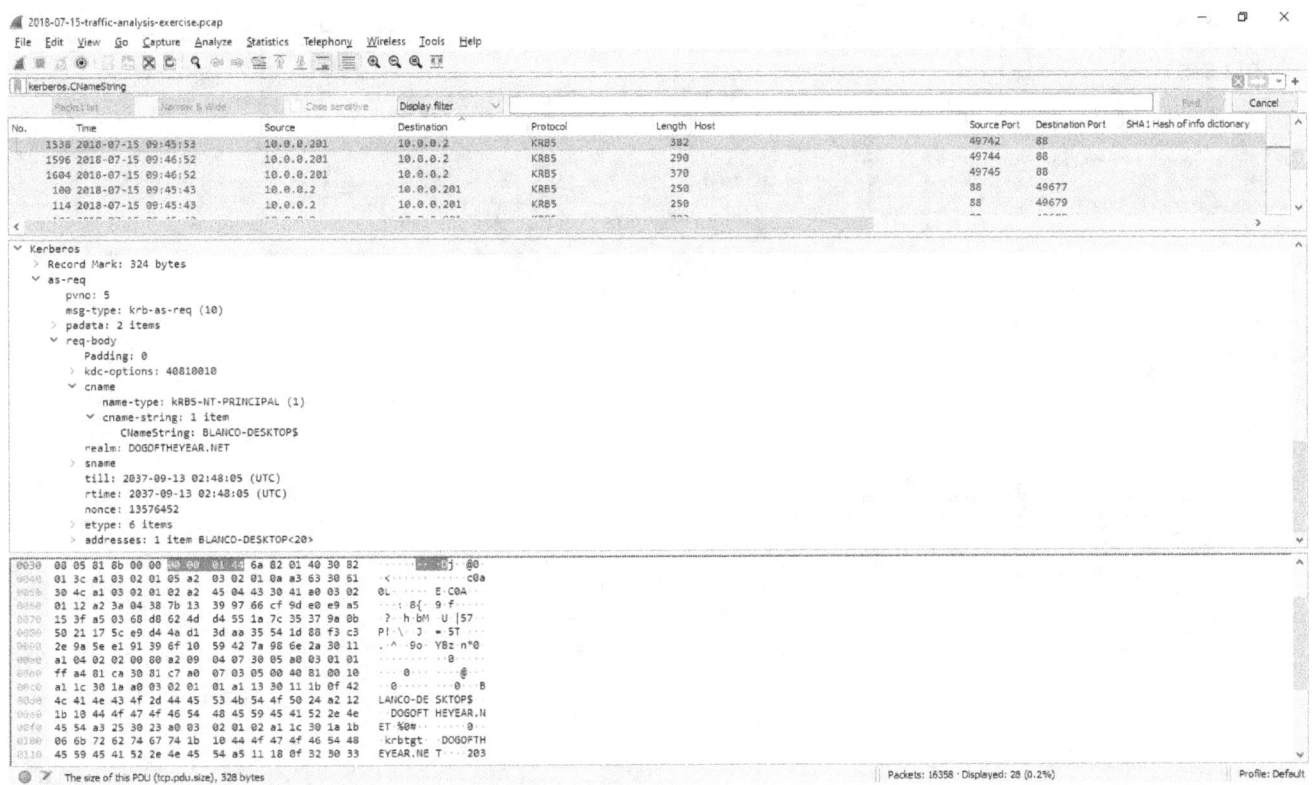

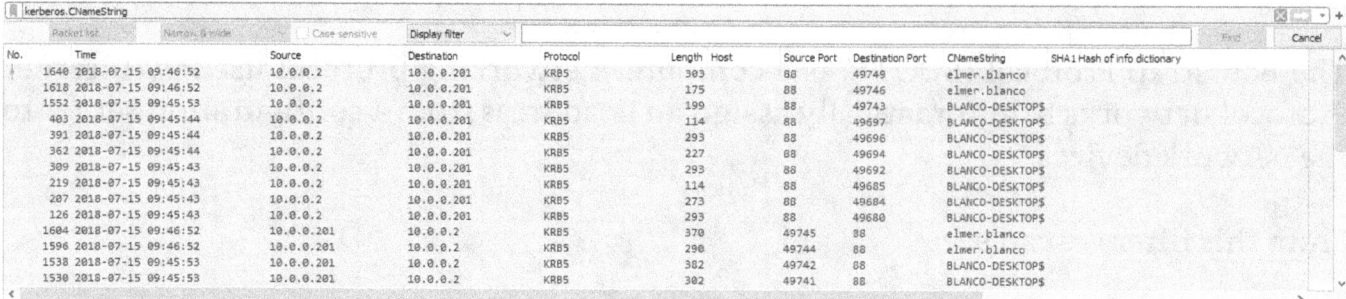

- Host names are end with $.
- User account names are without the $ sign at the end.

User: elmer.blanco
Host: BLANCO-DESKTOP

For finding which version of Windows is host running use filter, check the User-Agent string for normal web browsing traffic in the HTTP request headers.

We can filter For finding which version of Windows is host running by **http.request and! (udp.port eq 1900)**

To view publicdomaintorrents.info viewed by the user. Then, Right click and Follow TCP stream.

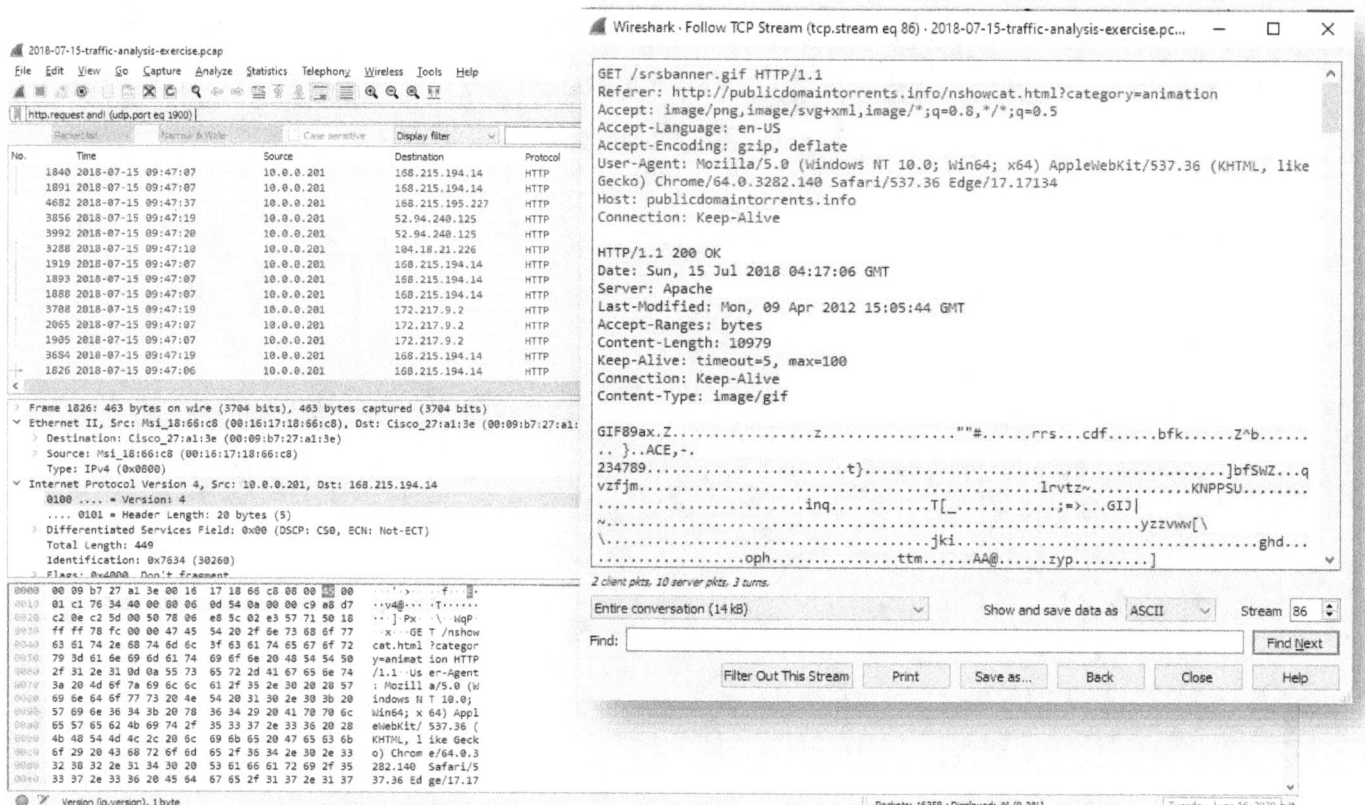

The User-Agent reveals this is a 64-bit Windows 10 host

Analyzing a MODBUS DoS attack on SCADA

Attacks on SCADA / ICS systems are not intended for confidential information, but for the process itself. While a DDoS attack on a web server can be costly and inconvenient, a DDoS attack on a SCADA system may be life threatening!

Another key difference between the traditional IT systems and SCADA systems is the communication protocol. SCADA / ICS is composed of existing seria protocols such as modbus and DNP3. While now encapsulated for external communication in TCP / IP, internally they are still very simple serial protocols.

Finding modbus Traffic

Let's analyze and separate SCADA/ICS traffic using WireShark. Let's look at the ubiquitous modbus over TCP packet, perhaps the SCADA/ICS protocol most widely used. While modbus was originally designed for use on a serial medium such as RS232 or RS485, it was modified for use over TCP / IP networks.

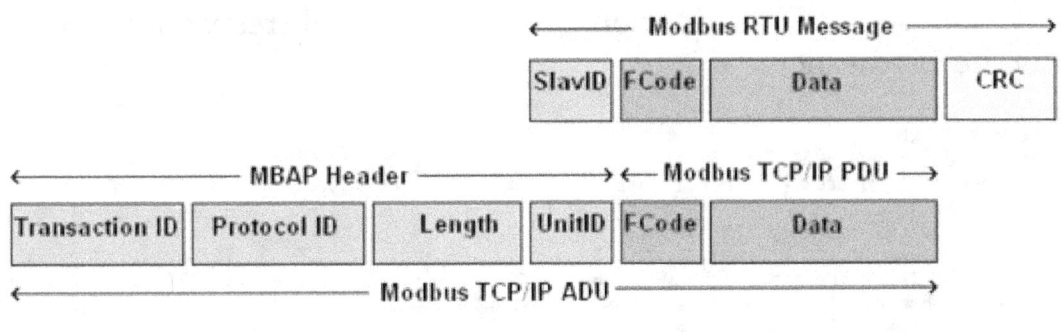

hackers-arise.com

Let's open some sample modbus traffic using Wireshark. We'll be using a pcap file of some modbus test data in this tutorial. To open this, use Wireshark to open modbus test data part1.pcap (File —> Open).

Now that we've loaded this capture file, we can use Wireshark to do research. First, let's create some modbus-traffic filters. The most basic filter in modbus would be;

mbtcp

This would filter all traffic, but the TCP traffic modbus over.

```
Filter: mbtcp                                    Expression... Clear Apply Save

Time        Source      Destination   Protocol Length Info
15.266493   10.0.0.57   10.0.0.3      Modbus   66   Query:    Trans:    0; Unit:  10, Func:  8/  1: Force L
15.268405   10.0.0.3    10.0.0.57     Modbus   63   Response: Trans:    0; Unit:  10, Func:  8: Diagnostics
15.268888   10.0.0.57   10.0.0.3      Modbus   66   Query:    Trans:    0; Unit:  10, Func:  8/  1: Force L
15.271020   10.0.0.3    10.0.0.57     Modbus   63   Response: Trans:    0; Unit:  10, Func:  8: Diagnostics
15.271447   10.0.0.57   10.0.0.3      Modbus   66   Query:    Trans:    0; Unit:  10, Func:  8/  1: Force L
15.273608   10.0.0.3    10.0.0.57     Modbus   63   Response: Trans:    0; Unit:  10, Func:  8: Diagnostics
25.889380   10.0.0.57   10.0.0.3      Modbus   66   Query:    Trans:    0; Unit:  10, Func:  8/  1: Restart
25.891231   10.0.0.3    10.0.0.57     Modbus   63   Response: Trans:    0; Unit:  10, Func:  8: Diagnostics
25.891714   10.0.0.57   10.0.0.3      Modbus   66   Query:    Trans:    0; Unit:  10, Func:  8/  1: Restart
25.893737   10.0.0.3    10.0.0.57     Modbus   66   Response: Trans:    0; Unit:  10, Func:  8/  1: Restart
```

⊞ Frame 8: 66 bytes on wire (528 bits), 66 bytes captured (528 bits)
⊞ Ethernet II, Src: Runtop_00:62:0d (00:20:78:00:62:0d), Dst: Intel_ce:70:51 (00:02:b3:ce:70:51)
⊟ Internet Protocol Version 4, Src: 10.0.0.57 (10.0.0.57), Dst: 10.0.0.3 (10.0.0.3)
    Version: 4
    Header length: 20 bytes
 ⊞ Differentiated Services Field: 0x00 (DSCP 0x00: Default; ECN: 0x00: Not-ECT (Not ECN-Capable Transport))
    Total Length: 52
    Identification: 0x8583 (34179)
 ⊞ Flags: 0x02 (Don't Fragment)
    Fragment offset: 0

```
0000  00 02 b3 ce 70 51 00 20  78 00 62 0d 08 00 45 00   ....pQ.. x.b...E.
0010  00 34 85 83 40 00 80 06  61 05 0a 00 00 39 0a 00   .4..@... a....9..
0020  00 03 0a 12 01 f6 61 97  f1 83 70 f1 ad 1b 50 18   ......a. ..p...P.
0030  fa f0 19 52 00 00 00 00  00 00 00 06 0a 08 00 04   ...R.... ........
0040  00 00                                              ..
```

hackers-arise.com

Clicking on any of those packets will allow us to start a more detailed review of the packets. We can see their destination port and protocol (respectively 502 and mbap), expanding the TCP header.

    [Source GeoIP: Unknown]
    [Destination GeoIP: Unknown]
⊟ Transmission Control Protocol, Src Port: mbap (502), Dst Port: rvs-isdn-dcp (2578), Seq: 49, Ack: 73, Len: 12
    Source port: mbap (502)
    Destination port: rvs-isdn-dcp (2578)
    [Stream index: 1]
    Sequence number: 49   (relative sequence number)
    [Next sequence number: 61   (relative sequence number)]
    Acknowledgment number: 73   (relative ack number)
    Header length: 20 bytes
 ⊞ Flags: 0x018 (PSH, ACK)
    window size value: 65463
    [Calculated window size: 65463]
    [Window size scaling factor: -2 (no window scaling used)]
 ⊟ Checksum: 0x1416 [validation disabled]

```
0000  00 20 78 00 62 0d 00 02  b3 ce 70 51 08 00 45 00   . x.b... ..pQ..E.
0010  00 34 ff ea 40 00 80 06  e6 9d 0a 00 00 03 0a 00   .4..@... ........
0020  00 39 01 f6 0a 12 70 f1  ad 4b 61 97 f1 cb 50 18   .9....p. .Ka...P.
0030  ff b7 14 16 00 00 00 00  00 00 00 06 0a 08 00 01   ........ ........
0040  00 00                                              ..
```

hackers-arise.com

If we scroll down a bit, we will get into the fields of Modbus and Modbus / TCP and read their values there.

```
        [Bad Checksum: False]
      [SEQ/ACK analysis]
         [This is an ACK to the segment in frame: 20]
         [The RTT to ACK the segment was: 0.001776000 seconds]
         [Bytes in flight: 12]
         [PDU Size: 12]
   Modbus/TCP
      Transaction Identifier: 0
      Protocol Identifier: 0
      Length: 6
      Unit Identifier: 10
   Modbus
      Function Code: Diagnostics (8)
      Diagnostic Code: Restart Communications Option (1)
      Restart Communication Option: Leave Log (0x0000)
0000  00 20 78 00 62 0d 00 02  b3 ce 70 51 08 00 45 00   . x.b... ..pQ..E.
0010  00 34 ff ea 40 00 80 06  e6 9d 0a 00 00 03 0a 00   .4..@... ........
0020  00 39 01 f6 0a 12 70 f1  ad 4b 61 97 f1 cb 50 18   .9....p. .Ka...P.
0030  ff b7 14 16 00 00 00 00  00 00 00 06 0a 08 00 01   ................
0040  00 00                                              ..
```

hackers-arise.com

Click on the Expression tab next to the filter window to add more complex modbus filters and open the Expression Creator. Within the field name sub-window we will scroll down to the M's before we get to modbus.

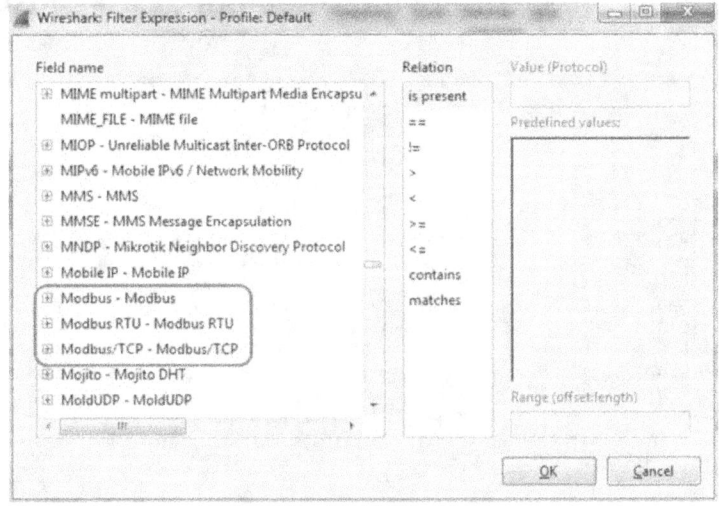

hackers-arise.com

As you can see above there are three (3) field names with modbus within them. Let's extend each and every one and see what they contain. The Modbus / TCP filter includes only fields special to the TCP implementation of modbus. In the original modbus protocol all fields are found in the Modbus protocol.

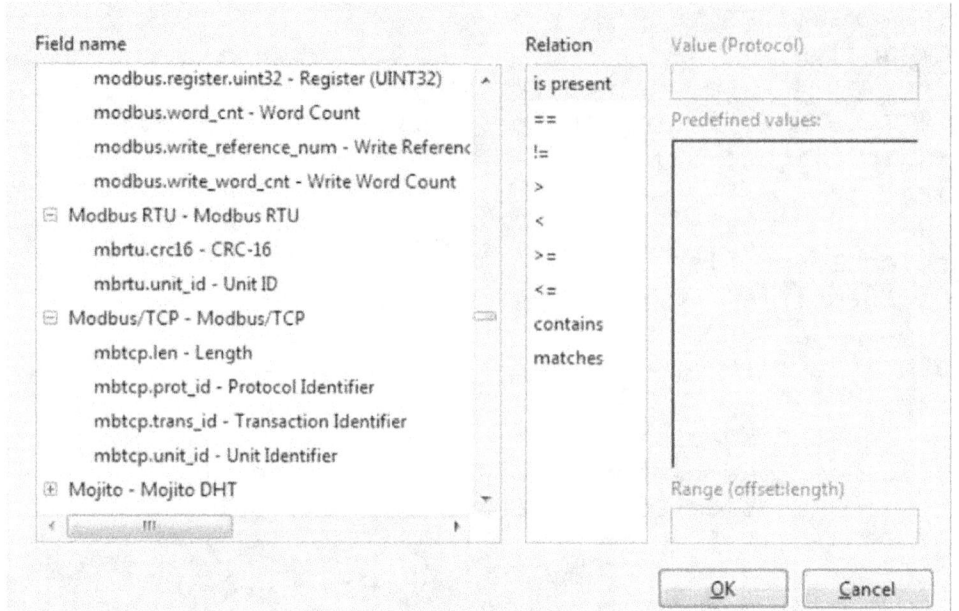

hackers-arise.com

If we are searching for different fields in the Modbus protocol, we will use these fields instead of modbus implementing TCP / IP.

Modbus Diagnostic Codes Filtering

We can do that by entering; in the filter window, **modbus.diagnostic** code

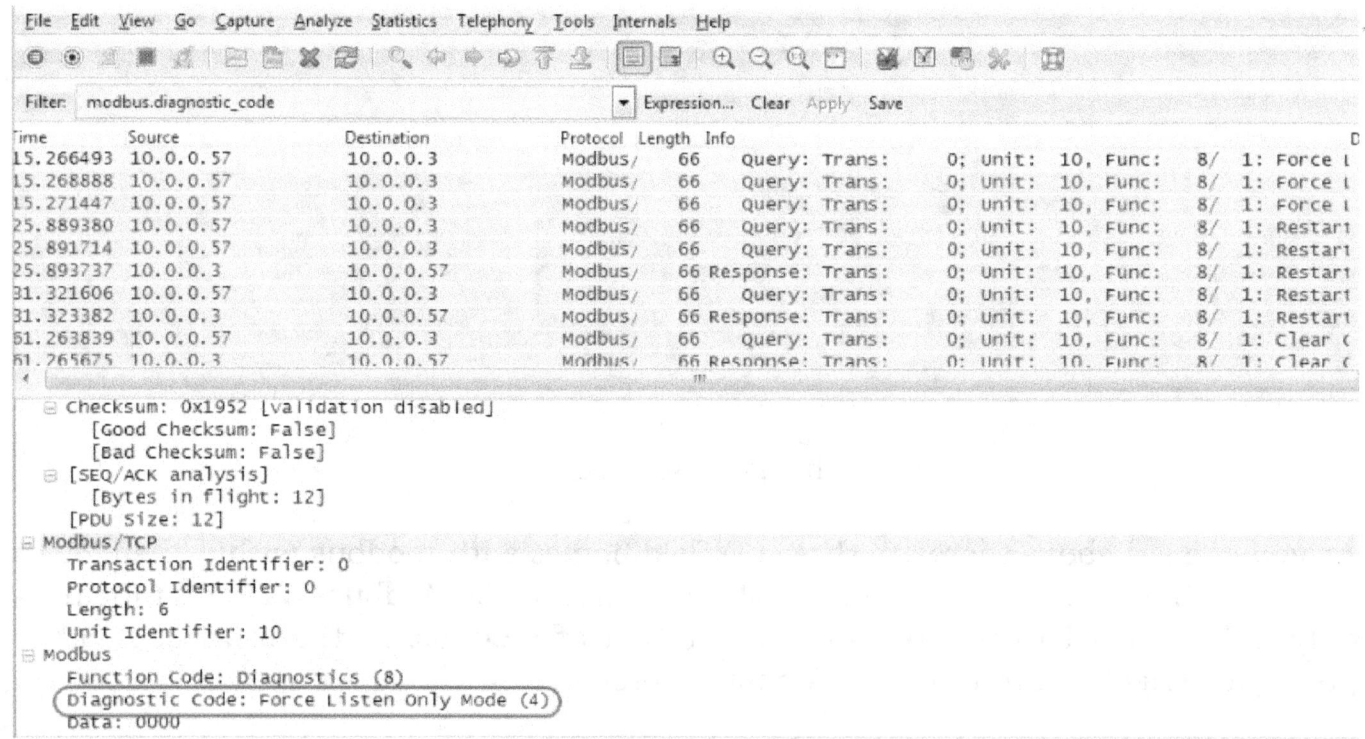

hackers-arise.com

Wireshark retrieves all packets of modbus filled in with diagnostic code If we analyze one of those packets and scroll down to Modbus protocol fields, you can see that this one has a Diagnostic Code = 4 or "Force Listen Only Mode" We might filter on and search for packets with that Diagnostic Code only by creating such a filter;

modbus_diagnostic_code ==4

Wireshark found that only 3 packets contained Diagnostic Code.

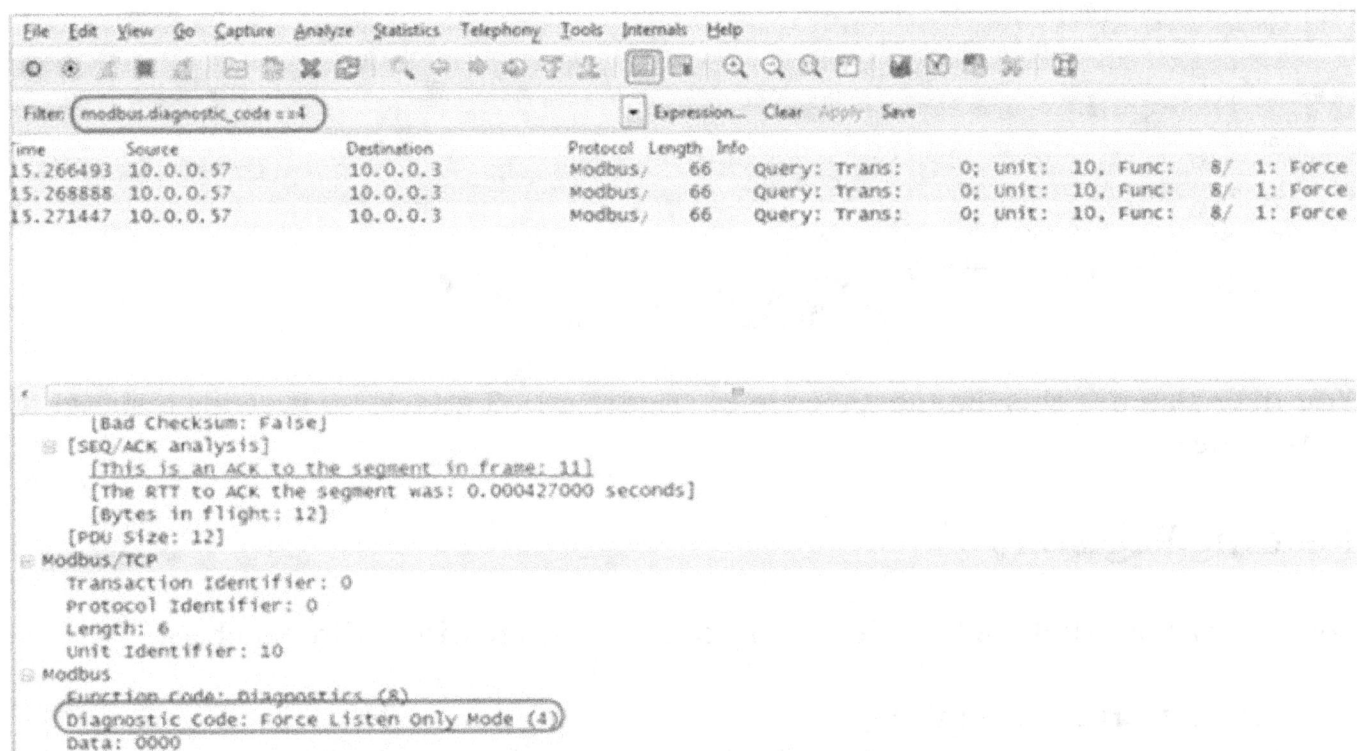

hackers-arise.com

In some SCADA DoS attacks, the modbus frame with this diagnostic code was used, as it sends a signal to "Power Listen Only" to the PLC and does not send data to the actuators, alarms or other PLCs with which it communicate.Could have disastrous consequences!

Filtering Suspicious Modbus Packets

We can build a lot of different filters that are looking for packets that meet certain field criteria. Here we search for "restart communications" by creating the following filter;

modbus.diagnostic_restart_communication_option

```
Filter: modbus.diagnostic.restart_communication_option

Time        Source      Destination   Protocol  Length  Info
25.889380   10.0.0.57   10.0.0.3      Modbus/   66      Query: Trans:    0; Unit: 10, Func:  8/ 1: Restart
25.891714   10.0.0.57   10.0.0.3      Modbus/   66      Query: Trans:    0; Unit: 10, Func:  8/ 1: Restart
25.893737   10.0.0.3    10.0.0.57     Modbus/   66      Response: Trans: 0; Unit: 10, Func:  8/ 1: Restart
31.321606   10.0.0.57   10.0.0.3      Modbus/   66      Query: Trans:    0; Unit: 10, Func:  8/ 1: Restart
31.323382   10.0.0.3    10.0.0.57     Modbus/   66      Response: Trans: 0; Unit: 10, Func:  8/ 1: Restart
```

```
Checksum: 0x1931 [validation disabled]
    [Good Checksum: False]
    [Bad Checksum: False]
[SEQ/ACK analysis]
    [Bytes in flight: 12]
    [PDU Size: 12]
Modbus/TCP
    Transaction Identifier: 0
    Protocol Identifier: 0
    Length: 6
    Unit Identifier: 10
Modbus
    Function Code: Diagnostics (8)
    Diagnostic Code: Restart Communications Option (1)
    Restart Communication Option: Leave Log (0x0000)
```

hackers-arise.com

You may also use this diagnostic code to trigger a DoS attack, as it sends a signal to restart the PLC.

Reading Registers

Look for packets that read 16-bit registry contents by creating a filter such as;

modbus.register.uint16

```
[SEQ/ACK analysis]
    [This is an ACK to the segment in frame: 57]
    [The RTT to ACK the segment was: 0.001987000 seconds]
    [Bytes in flight: 13]
    [PDU Size: 13]
Modbus/TCP
    Transaction Identifier: 1
    Protocol Identifier: 0
    Length: 7
    Unit Identifier: 10
Modbus
    Function Code: Read Holding Registers (3)
    Byte Count: 4
    Register 0 (UINT16): 9
    Register 1 (UINT16): 24
```

hackers-arise.com

These packets indicate that an attacker attempts to read the data values in the register to understand its pre-attack role (a form of recognition) or add them to something with malicious content and effect.

With Wireshark we can catch data packets to allow a more thorough analysis. This tool is geared towards tracking data traffic within a network. Such a tool allows the user to scan for network protocol errors and issues on his / her own computer. Accordingly, Wireshark is also gaining popularity within information technology and network-internal communication, as the identification of irregularities will prevent risks to the Computer and its components. From a security perspective it must be considered that such a system is helpful in detecting and preventing hacker attacks. Especially among people working in the industry, this can be beneficial if sensitive data are stored on their computer which should never touch third parties.

Wireshark can also be used to assess SCADA / ICS attacks if you know what to look for. Any security engineer working in SCADA / ICS technology must be knowledgeable in Wireshark or other Protocol Analyzers along with the details of the communication protocol used at their facility for this type of research to be properly prepared. This strong approach helps us analyze network traffic to the finest degree in granular. Improving your understanding of this process will have to pay major dividends in your forensic career!

References

hackers-arise.com. (n.d.).
    Retrieved from hackers-arise.com/post/2018/09/27/network-forensics-part-2-detecting-and-analyzing-a-scada-dos-attack.

malware-traffic-analysis (n.d.).
Retrieved from malware-traffic-analysis.net/

hackers-arise.com. (n.d.).
Retrieved from hackers-arise.com/post/2018/10/31/network-forensics-wireshark-basics-part-2

hackingarticles.in. (n.d.).
    Retrieved from hackingarticles.in/network-packet-forensic-using-wireshark/

kunbus.com. (n.d.).
    Retrieved from kunbus.com/wireshark.html.

nystec.com. (n.d.).
    Retrieved from nystec.com/insights/network-forensics-101/

resources.infosecinstitute.com. (n.d.).
    Retrieved from resources.infosecinstitute.com/category/certifications-training/network-traffic-analysis-for-incident-response/how-to-use-traffic-analysis-for-wireshark/.

resources.infosecinstitute.com. (n.d.).
    Retrieved from resources.infosecinstitute.com/category/certifications-training/network-traffic-analysis-for-incident-response/how-to-use-traffic-analysis-for-wireshark/.

Analyzing the Trickbot Malware
Layer 3/4

By
Nitin Sharma

> "If you know the enemy and know yourself, you need not fear the result of a hundred battles."
> - The Art of War, Sun Tzu

In the modern world, Cybercrime landscape has changed a lot considering the cyber-warfare from malware perspective. Early malwares were primitive, often spreading entirely offline via floppy disks carried from computer to computer by human hands. As networking and the Internet matured, malware authors were quick to adapt their malicious code and take advantage of the new communication medium.

Photo by The Digital Artist, Pixabay [1]

It is getting more and more difficult to devise strategies for detection of malwares in the computer systems. There are so many phishing campaigns, botnets, C2 servers currently interacting with numerous legit systems in an unauthorized manner. Creating a havoc in the business world, these sophisticated pieces of malware can do even more damage when combined with each other. One such wreaking example is "Emotet, Ryuk, Trickbot: Loader-Ransomware-Banker Trifecta" [2]. This has already caused millions of dollars in damages and ransoms paid.

In this paper, we will be discussing about Trickbot malware as a banking trojan, its spamming and malware delivery process, detection, confinement strategies and much more. Evolution of Trickbot till date to its latest version and modular enhancements will be the focus for this paper.

Trickbot: The Beginning

First seen in 2016, Trickbot is a malware that steals system information, login credentials and other sensitive data from vulnerable Windows hosts.

Trickbot is one of the most recent banking trojans with many of its original features inspired by Dyre, another banking Trojan. According to Fidelis Cybersecurity [3], the loader for Trickbot, which has been around since at least September 2016, uses the same custom crypter as Cutwail, a favorite of the group which spread Dyre via spam and social engineering campaigns. The loader is responsible for determining whether it's running on a 32- or 64-bit system. After conducting a bit check, it downloads the resources necessary to load up the Trickbot malware.

Trickbot: Capabilities

Trickbot has evolved a lot since its first appearance in 2016.

1. Stealing banking credentials (man-in-the-browser attack).
   a. Static Injection – Involves replacing the banking site's legitimate login page with a fake one that looks almost exactly like it.
   b. Dynamic Injection/Server-Side Injection – Redirects the web browser to a server under the trojan operator's control whenever the user enters the URLs for the targeted banking sites.
2. Stealing from Bitcoin Wallets.
3. With the help of different modules, can get local and other user account details, tax information, system, and network information and so on.
4. Connecting infected devices to malicious, criminally controlled networks over the Internet, giving criminals full control of them
5. Spread across a victim's network by infecting other devices, including those on trusted domains (known as lateral movement), often using SMB shares.
6. Downloading further malicious files such as Remote Access Tools, VNC clients and ransomware.

Trickbot: Infection Vectors

According to Malpedia [4], the important infection vector paths for Trickbot are:

1. Phish ➔ Link MS Office ➔ Macro Enabled ➔ Downloader ➔ Trickbot
2. Phish ➔ Attached MS Office ➔ Macro Enabled ➔ Downloader ➔ Trickbot
3. Phish ➔ Attached MS Office ➔ Macro enabled ➔ Trickbot installed

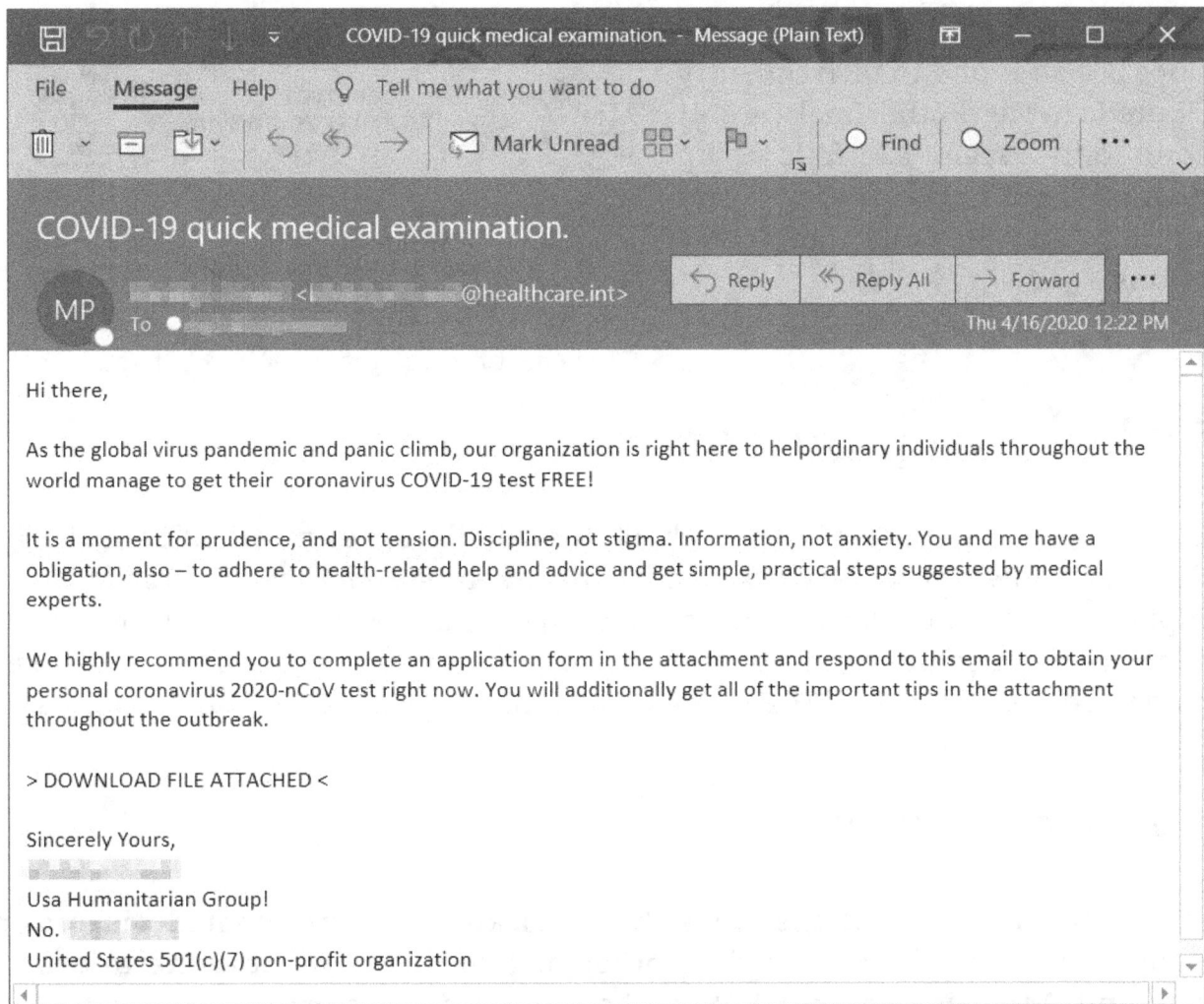

Trickbot Phishing Mail based on Office 365 ATP data, Microsoft Security Intelligence [5]

Trickbot is often distributed through malspam. Emails from these campaigns contain links to download malicious files disguised as invoices, images, or documents. These files may be Windows executable files for Trickbot, or they may be some sort of downloader for the Trickbot executable. In some cases, links from these emails return a zip archive that contains a Trickbot executable or downloader [6]. There are a lot of malspam campaigns seen luring COVID-19. According to Microsoft Security Intelligence, Trickbot is the most prolific malware operation using COVID-19 themed lures. They have used several hundreds of unique macro-laced document attachments in emails that pose as message from a non-profit offering free COVID-19 test.

It has been found that the macro uses CHOICE.EXE to wait 20 seconds before downloading the info-stealing payload. Trickbot campaigns are known to delay malicious activities to evade emulation or sandbox analysis.

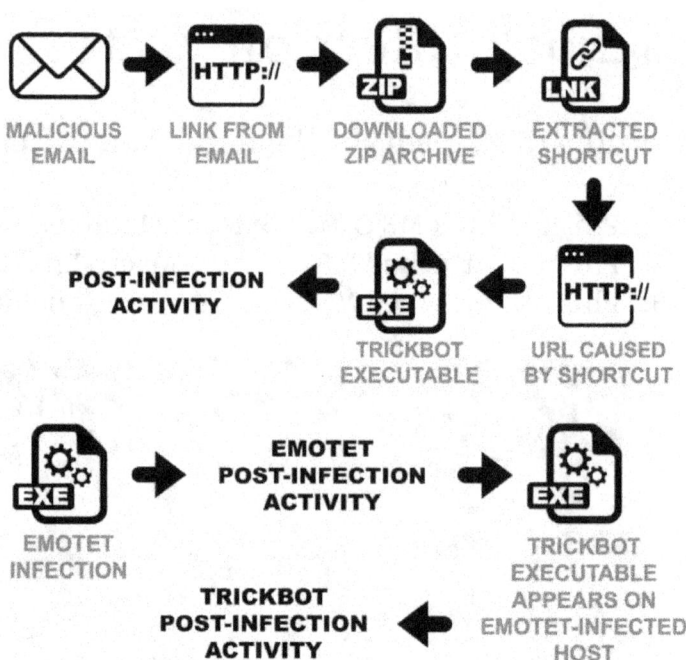

Flowchart from a Trickbot infection from malspam in September 2019 [6]

Trickbot is also found to be frequently distributed through other malware. It is commonly seen as follow up malware to Emotet infections and sometimes from IcedID and Ursnif infections.

Flowchart for Emotet with Trickbot activity [6]

Trickbot: Symptoms of Infection

Once an endpoint is infected with Trickbot, there will not be any significant change to be observed. However, a network admin will likely see changes in traffic flows or attempts to reach out to blacklisted IPs and domains, as the malware will communicate with Trickbot's C2 server to exfiltrate data and receive tasks. The traffic with C2 server is found to be encrypted over TCP port 443, 447, or 449 being GET/POST requests.

How Trickbot works

We have already observed the ways, how Trickbot is disseminated via malspam campaigns and secondary payload by other malwares. The Multi-State Information Sharing and Analysis Center (MS-ISAC) has released a security primer on Trickbot malware [7].

The malspam campaigns that deliver Trickbot use third party branding familiar to the recipient. The emails typically include an attachment, such as a Microsoft Word or Excel document. The opened attachment will prompt the user to enable macros, which executes a VBScript to run a Powershell script to download the malware. Trickbot runs checks to ensure it is not in the sandbox environment and then attempts to disable antivirus programs, such as Microsoft's Windows Defender. Once executed, Trickbot redeploys itself in the "%AppData%" folder and creates a scheduled task that provides persistence [8].

Trickbot sends HTTP requests to the following websites to determine the infected host's public IP address:

- hxxp://myexternalip.com/raw
- hxxp://api.ipify.org
- hxxp://icanhazip.com
- hxxp://bot.whatismyipaddress.com
- hxxp://ip.anysrc.net/plain/clientip

At this point, Trickbot starts receiving instructions from the command and control (C2) server and is ready to download modules which are sent with a configuration file. The modules are delivered as Dynamic Link Libraries. After receiving the infected host's system information, the initial Trickbot C2 sends an expiration time and a new IP address that will be used to download further modules. The C2 servers constantly change and the Trickbot infection is updated with this new information. Trickbot uses HTTP/HTTPS GET and POST requests to download modules and report stolen information/credentials to the C2 server. Trickbot uses web injects - Static and Dynamic (as already discussed in Trickbot Capabilities) to steal financial information from online banking sessions to defraud its victims. Trickbot's distributors are using group tags (gtags) to uniquely identify specific Trickbot campaigns. The gtag and a unique bot identifier are included in the URIs when Trickbot communicates with its C2 servers.

Visual Representation of Trickbot and its modules [9]

The following is an overview of common Trickbot modules and configuration files, but this not an exhaustive list since Trickbot is constantly adding new features.

Artifacts for Trickbot modules on an infected Windows 7 client [10]

- Banking Information Stealers
    - ***LoaderDll/InjectDll*** – Monitors for banking website activity and uses web injects (e.g. pop ups and extra fields) to steal financial information.
    - ***Sinj*** – This file contains information on the online banks targeted by Trickbot and it uses redirection attacks (also known as web fake injections).
    - ***Dinj*** – This file contains information on the online banks targeted by Trickbot and it uses server-side web injections. (See more in Trickbot Targeting)
    - ***Dpost*** – Includes an IP address and port for stolen banking information. If the user enters banking information for one of the listed banks, the information is sent to the dpost IP address. Most of the data exfiltrated by TrickBot is sent to the dpost IP address.

- System/Network Reconnaissance
    - ***Systeminfo*** – Harvests system information so that the attacker knows what is running on the affected system.
    - ***Mailsearcher*** – Compares all files on the disk against a list of file extensions.
    - ***NetworkDll*** – Collects more system information and maps out the network.

- Credential and User Information Harvesting
    - ***ModuleDll/ImportDll*** – Harvests browser data (e.g. cookies and browser configurations)
    - ***DomainDll*** – Uses LDAP to harvest credentials and configuration data from domain controller by accessing shared SYSVOL files.
    - ***OutlookDll*** – Harvests saved Microsoft Outlook credentials by querying several registry keys.
    - ***SqulDll*** – Force-enables WDigest authentication and utilizes Mimikatz to scrape credentials from LSASS.exe. The worming modules use these credentials to spread Trickbot laterally across networks.
    - ***Pwgrab*** – Steals credentials, autofill data, history, and other information from browsers as well as several software applications.

- Network Propagation
    - ***WormDll and ShareDll*** – These are worming modules that abuse Server Message Block (SMB) and Lightweight Directory Access Protocol (LDAP) to move laterally across networks.
    - ***TabDll*** – Uses the EternalRomance exploit (CVE-2017-0147) to spread via SMBv1.

New modules are constantly seen in progress e.g. Nworm replacing mworm.

TRICKBOT PROPAGATION TO DOMAIN CONTROLLER FROM SEPTEMBER 2019 THROUGH MARCH 2020

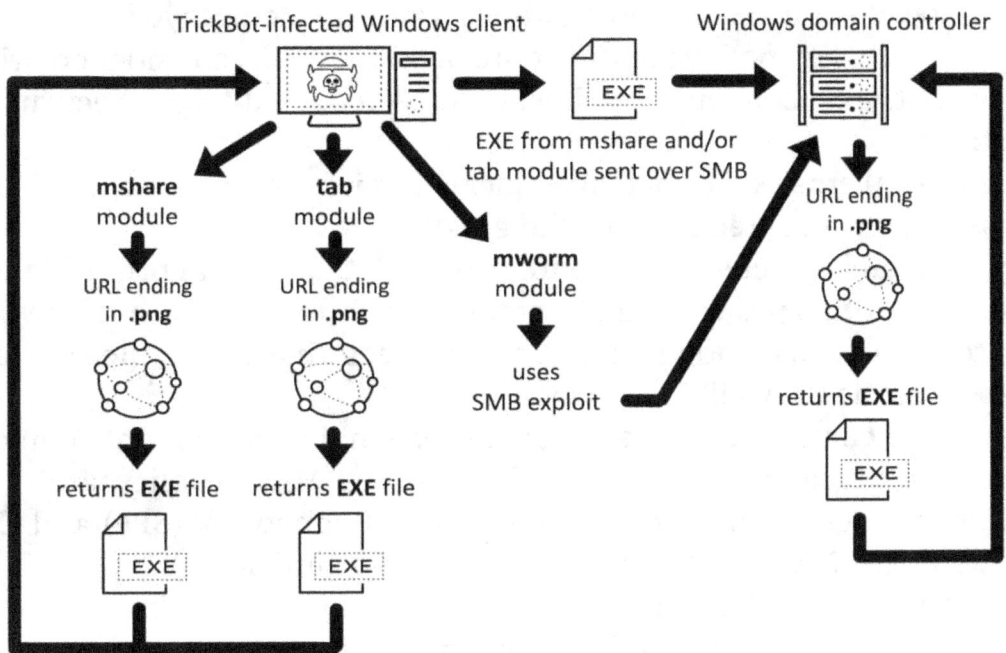

Trickbot Propagation Flow Chart [11]

Trickbot Targeting

Trickbot target information has been revealed in a research by @GarWarner [12], where the configuration files of Trickbot were decoded to see what the current collection of URLs in the DINJ file is targeting. The DINJ file for Trickbot contain lists of URL patterns labeled with markup tags. There were 84 "igroups" containing 329 URL patterns, targeting 131 named domains.

DINJ file breakdown [12]

- The most common target was Japanese banks and financial institutions. US Banks were second in popularity and then the German Banks.
- Many other targets were found related to Brokerages, Big Retails, Crypto-Currency Exchanges/Companies, Payroll companies, etc.

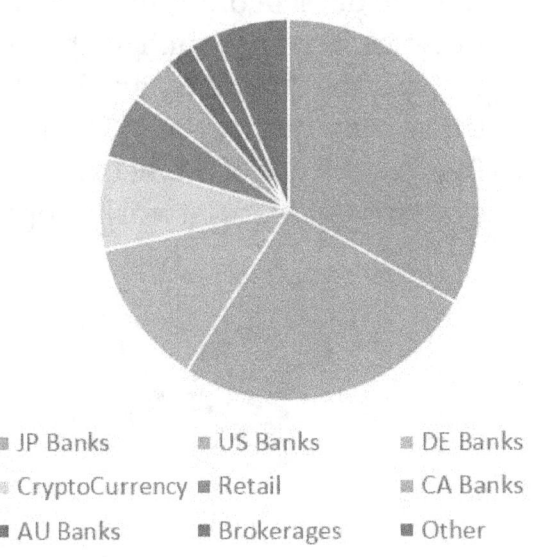

Trickbot DINJ Targets - 04MAR2020

- JP Banks
- US Banks
- DE Banks
- CryptoCurrency
- Retail
- CA Banks
- AU Banks
- Brokerages
- Other

Preventive Actions for Trickbot Infection

- Provide social engineering and phishing training to employees.
- If you do not have a policy regarding suspicious emails, consider creating one and specify that all suspicious emails should be reported to the security and/or IT departments.
- Mark external emails with a banner denoting it is from an external source. This will assist users in detecting spoofed emails.
- Apply applicable patches and updates immediately after appropriate testing.
- Implement filters at the email gateway for emails with known malspam indicators, such as known malicious subject lines, and block suspicious IP addresses at the firewall.
- To lower the chance of spoofed or modified emails, implement Domain Message Authentication Reporting and Conformance (DMARC) policy and verification, starting by implementing the Sender Policy Framework (SPF) and the Domain Keys Identified Mail (DKIM) standards. (CIS Subcontrol 7.8)
- Organizations should consider using application whitelisting technology on all assets to ensure that only authorized software executes, and all unauthorized software is blocked from executing on assets (CIS Subcontrol 2.7). Organizations should also ensure that the application whitelisting software only allows authorized, digitally signed scripts (such as *.ps1, *.py, macros, etc.) to run on a system (CIS Subcontrol 2.9).
- Adhere to the principal of least privilege, ensuring that users have the minimum level of access required to accomplish their duties. Limit administrative credentials to designated administrators.
- Implement a centrally managed, up-to-date anti-malware solution (CIS Subcontrol 8.2). In addition to valuable preventive and corrective capabilities, detective controls provided by anti-malware software are beneficial in providing awareness of any threats which may become active within the environment.
- If not already being done, consider implementing an Intrusion Detection System (IDS) to detect command and control (C2) activity and other potentially malicious network activity, such as the MS-ISAC's Albert system.
- Ensure that systems are hardened with industry-accepted guidelines, such as those provided by the CIS Benchmarks division. (cisecurity.org/cis-benchmarks/)
- Disable the use of SMBv1 across the network and require at least SMBv2 to harden systems against Network Propagation modules used by TrickBot.

How to tackle Trickbot Infections

- Disable Internet access at the affected site to help minimize the extent of exfiltration of credentials associated with external, third-party resources.
- Review impacted subnets to identify multi-homed systems which may adversely impact containment efforts. Also, consider temporarily taking the network offline to perform identification, prevent reinfections, and stop the spread of the malware.
- Identify, shutdown, and take the infected machines off the network.
- Heighten monitoring of SMB communication or outright block it between workstations and configure firewall rules to only allow access from known administrative servers.
- Assess the need to have ports 445 (SMB) open on systems and, if required, consider limiting connections to only specific, trusted hosts.
- Start with remediation of multi-homed systems (e.g. Domain Controller, File Server) as these can communicate across Virtual Local Area Networks (VLANs) and can be a potential means for spreading malware.
- Create clean VLANs that do not have access to infected VLANs. After the systems have been reimaged or restored from a known good backup, place them on the clean VLAN.
- Do not login to infected systems with domain or shared local administrator accounts. This is the best remediation strategy since TrickBot has several ways of gaining access to credentials.
- As TrickBot is known for scraping both domain and local credentials, it is recommended that a network-wide password reset take place. This is best done after the systems have been cleaned and moved to the new VLAN. This is recommended so new passwords are not scraped by the malware.
- Apply host-based isolation via Windows Firewall Group Policy Objects (GPOs), host-based intrusion detection system/network intrusion detection system (HIDS/NIDS) products, a Private Virtual Local Area Network (pVLAN), or similar means to help mitigate propagation.
- Determine the infection vector (patient zero) to determine the root cause of the incident.

Walkthrough: Trickbot PCAP Analysis

In this walkthrough, we will discuss about Wireshark GUI briefly and analyze a small PCAP file for Trickbot examination. Feel free to go through the previous in-depth article about Trickbot malware.

Pre-requisites for this walkthrough to follow along:

1. Kali Linux VM where Wireshark comes inbuilt.
    a. Kali 2019 (5.2.0-kali2-amd64)
    b. Wireshark 3.0.3
2. Trickbot PCAP Exercise – Catbomber [13]

Wireshark is a free and open-source packet analyzer release under the terms of GNU General Public License, used for network troubleshooting, analysis, software and communications protocol development, and education. It is a cross platform tool designed with Qt widget toolkit widely used to analyze PCAP files in its GUI version. There is also a terminal-based (non-GUI) version called TShark. [14]

Wireshark Calibration

Before starting with Trickbot PCAP analysis, we need to calibrate the Wireshark GUI platform with specific attributes/fields.

1. Start with checking Wireshark version. For this walkthrough, we prefer to go with 3.x versions as there are some differences with older 2.x versions.

2. For calibration process, we will set the capture to "eth0" interface of our VM. Double click on "eth0" and proceed.

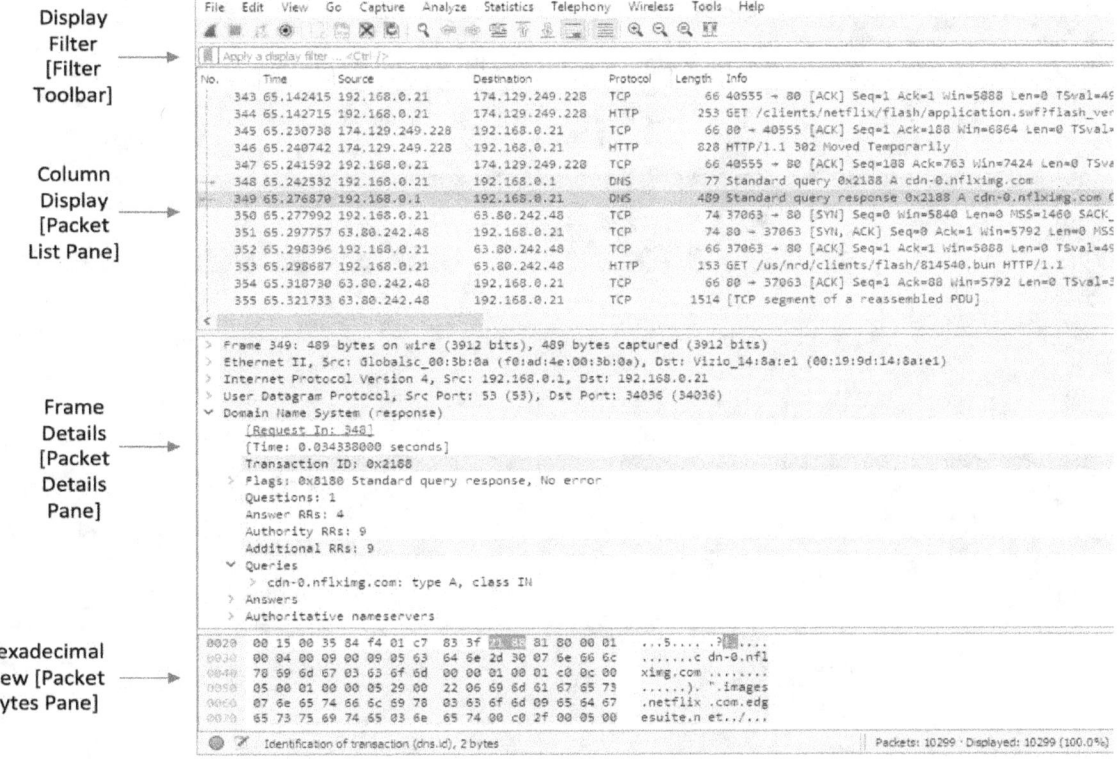

3. In the Firefox Browser of Kali VM, I have searched for some websites like, "informationwarfarecenter.com", "cve.circle.lu", "Netflix", etc. to generate some dummy traffic for adjusting attributes in Wireshark.

4. In the Column Display, right click on any of the column header to bring up the column header menu and set/check the display to show only following attributes: Time, Source, Destination, and Info.

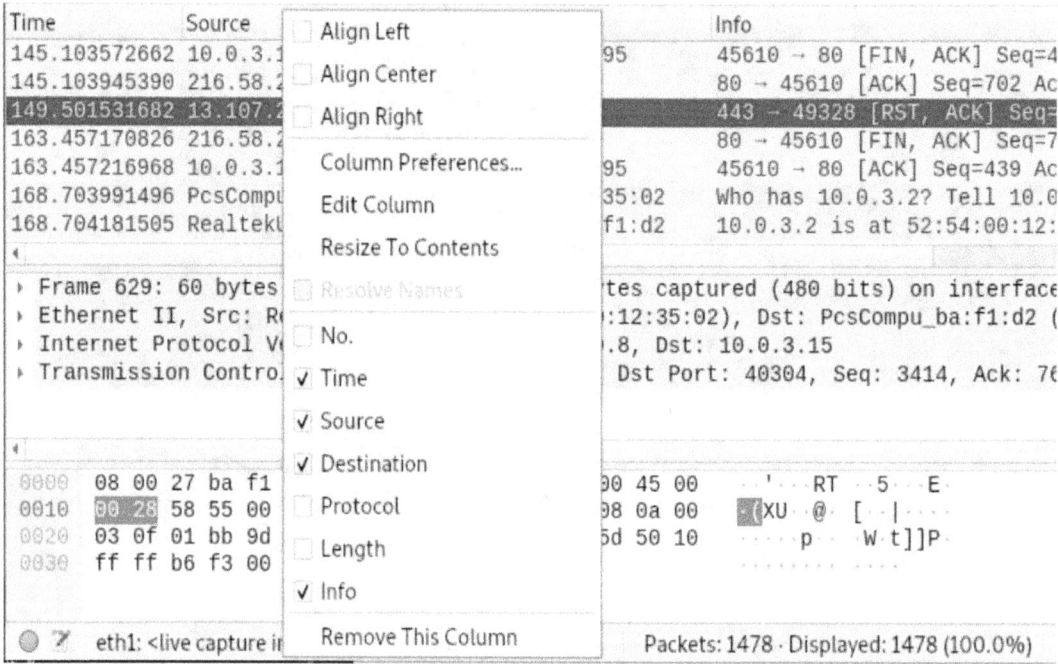

5. In the same menu, select "Column Preferences" then "Columns". Click on "+" button to add new columns for "Source Port" and "Destination Port".

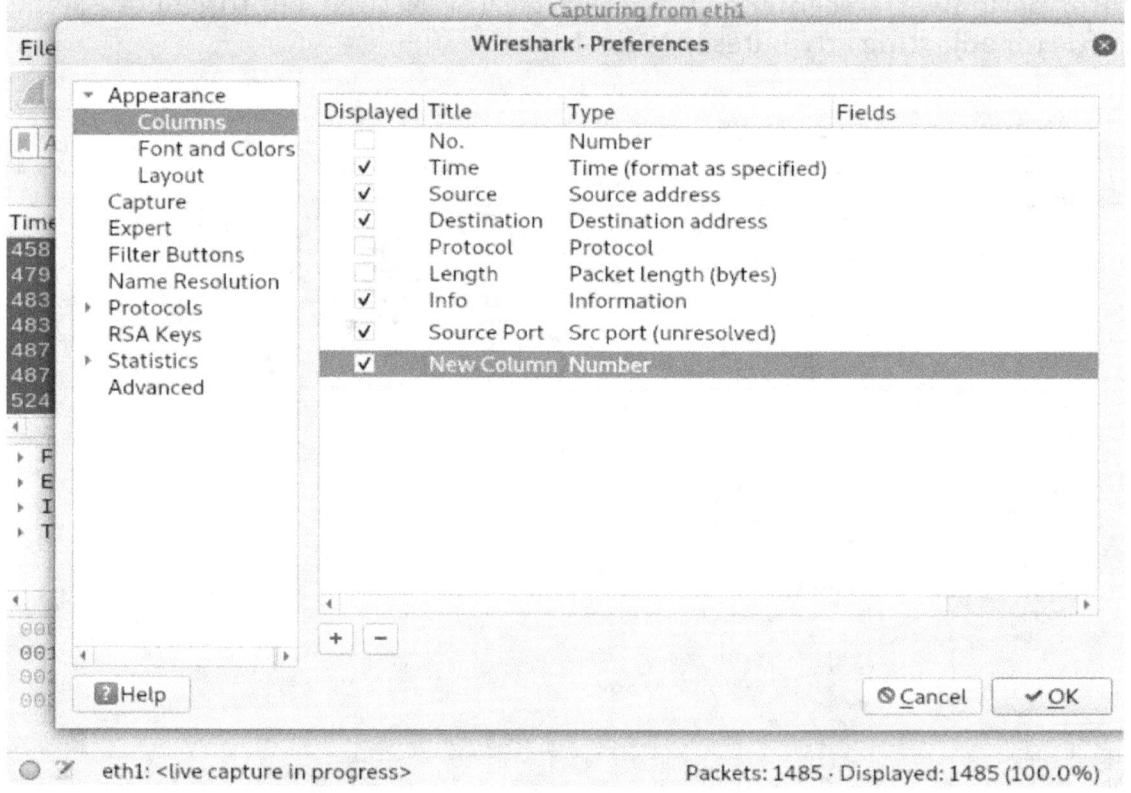

a. Rename the "New Column" title as "Source Port" and select "Src port (unresolved)" from the "Type" drop down where "Number" is present.
b. Similarly, add new column using "+" button, rename the column title as "Destination Port" and select "Dest port (unresolved)"

After completing this step, you will be able to see the Column Display Headers as below.

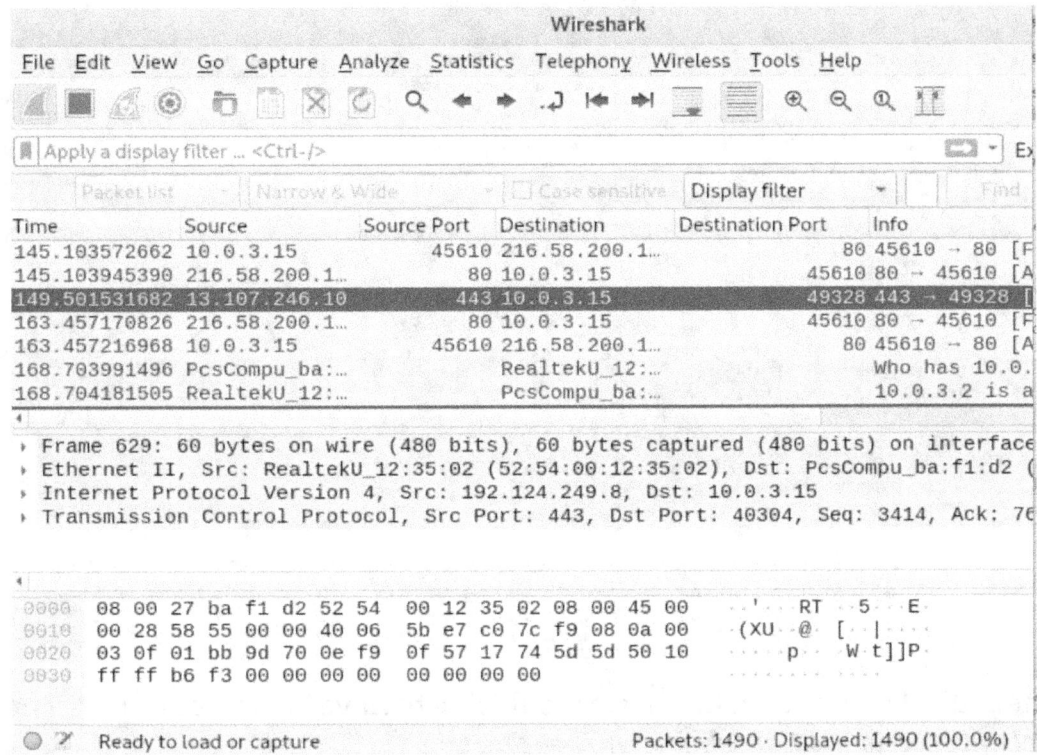

6. Now, let us change the Time Column format. Click "View" →"Time Display Format".
   a. Select "UTC Date and Time of Day (1970-01-01 01:02:03.123456)" and "Seconds".

188

7. There is an important custom column we require to get the Host information. For this, apply a display filter as "*http.request*" and examine the frame for "Hypertext Transfer Protocol". Expand the same to reveal "Host:" which is HTTP host name. Right click the same and select "Apply as Column" in menu appeared.

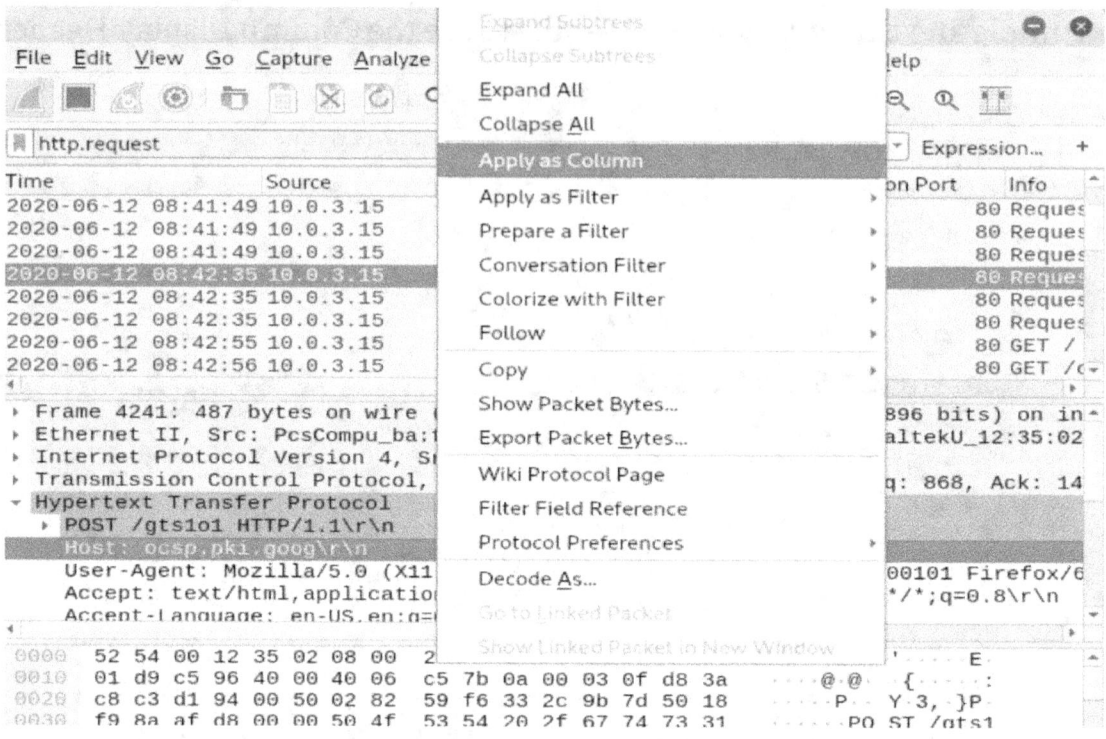

8. The next display header column, we would like to have is "Server Name". For this, apply a display filter as "*tls.handshake.type == 1*".

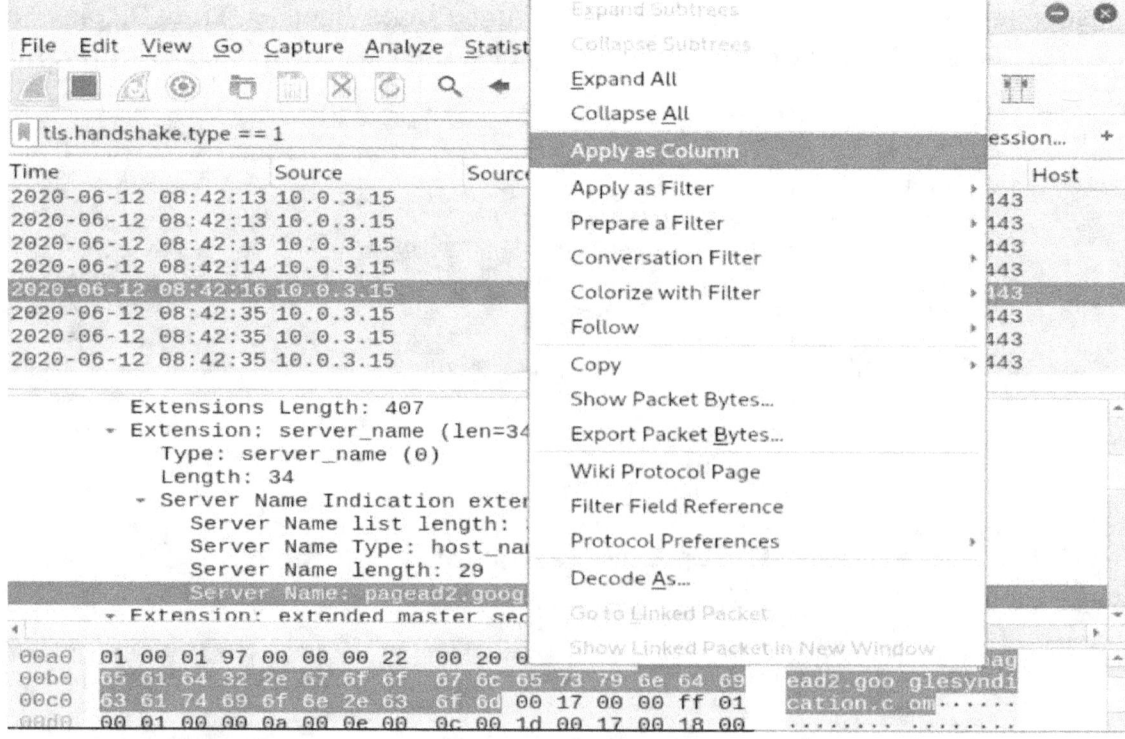

b. Examine the frame details for "Handshake Protocol: Client Hello" → "Extension: server_name" → "Server Name Indication extension" → "Server Name:". Apply this "Server Name:" as column by right click in the appeared menu as above.

```
http.request or tls.handshake.type == 1
Title: me  Type: Custom                              Fields: me  Occurrence: 0   Cancel

tion Port  Host                          Server Name              Info
     80    informationwarfarecenter.com                           GET /Images/header-
     80    ir-na.amazon-adsystem.com                              GET /e/ir?t=cyberse
     80    informationwarfarecenter.com                           GET /video/IWC-Red-
     80    ocsp.pki.goog                                          Request
    443                                  adservice.google.com     Client Hello
    443                                  apis.google.com          Client Hello
    443                                  cve.circl.lu             Client Hello
    443                                  cve.circl.lu             Client Hello
```

c. The calibration is complete now. Stop the capture pushing the red square "Stop Capturing" button from the Main Toolbar. We are ready to ride the Wireshark fun.

Trickbot PCAP Analysis – Scenario

There is a Trickbot infection in an Active Directory (AD) environment where the infection spreads to the Domain Controller (DC).

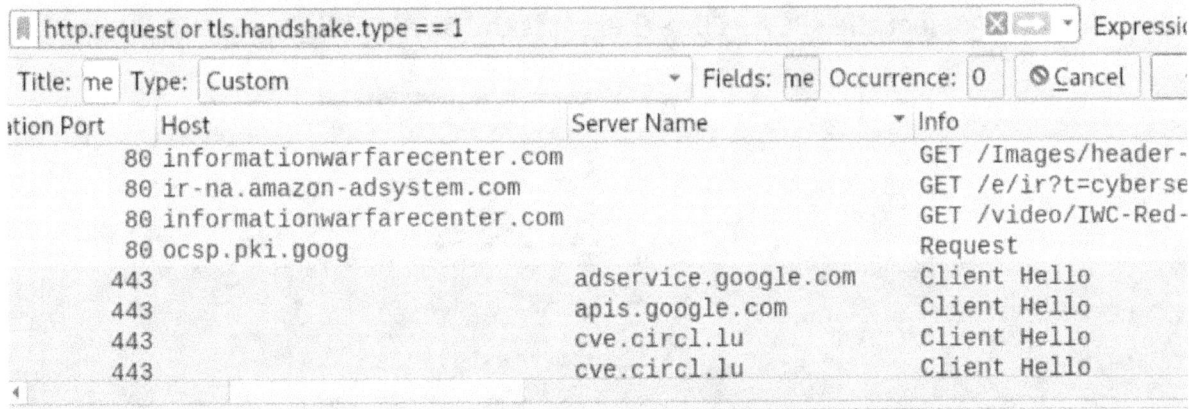

LAN segment data:

- LAN segment range: 10.5.28.0/24
- Domain: catbomber.net
- Domain Controller: 10.5.28.8 – Catbomber–DC
- LAN segment gateway: 10.5.28.1
- LAN segment broadcast address: 10.5.28.255

Questions:

1. Based on the Trickbot infection's HTTP POST traffic, what is the IP address, hostname and user account name for the infected Windows client?
2. What is the other user account name and other Windows client host name found in the Trickbot HTTP POST traffic?
3. What is the infected user's email password?
4. Two Windows executable files are sent in the traffic. What are the SHA256 file hashes for these files?

Analysis:

2. Load the PCAP file into Wireshark.
    a. Click "File" → "Open" → <PCAP File>
    b. Select the <PCAP File> (here it is the one highlighted in blue) and open it.
    c.

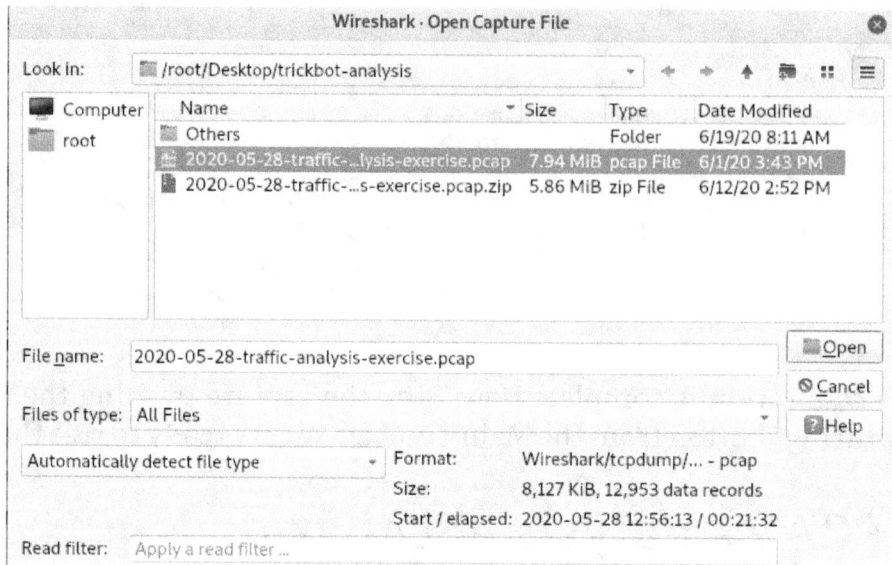

3. Apply "basic" filter → "(http.request or tls.handshake.type == 1) and !(ssdp)" and observe the traffic.
    a. HTTPS/SSL/TLS traffic over TCP port 447 and 443 (in the purple highlight)

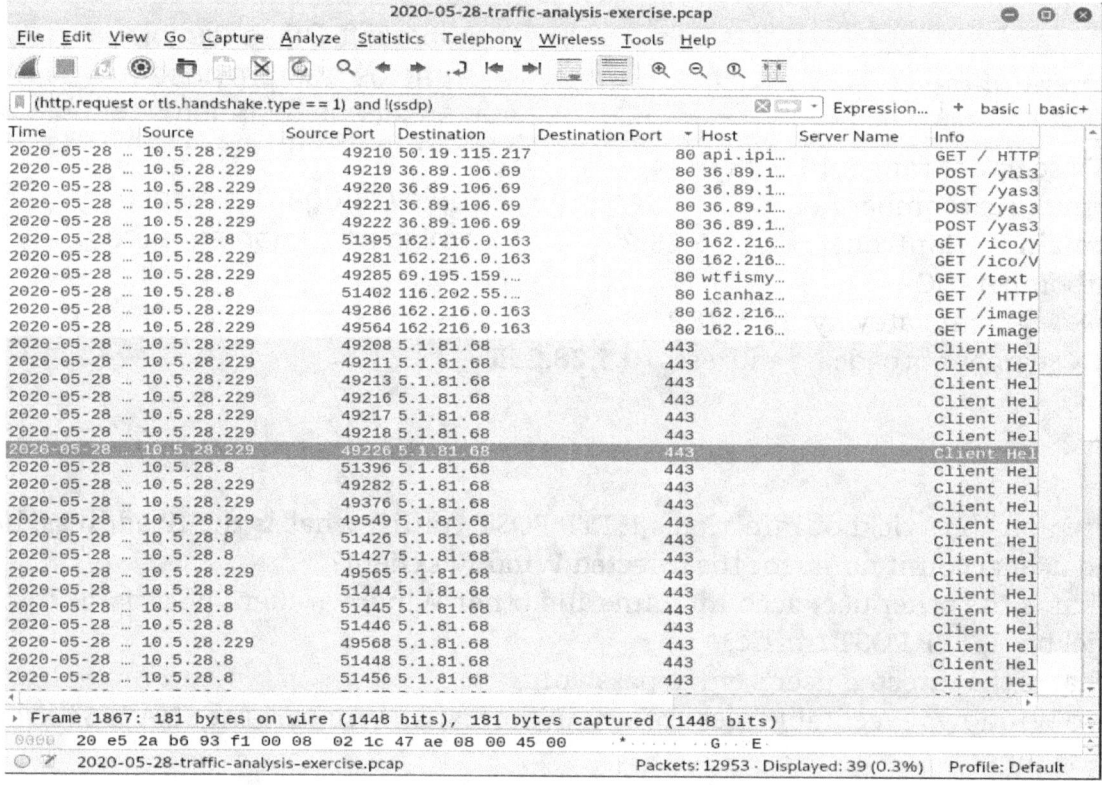

b. HTTP traffic over TCP port 8082 (at the bottom in green highlight)

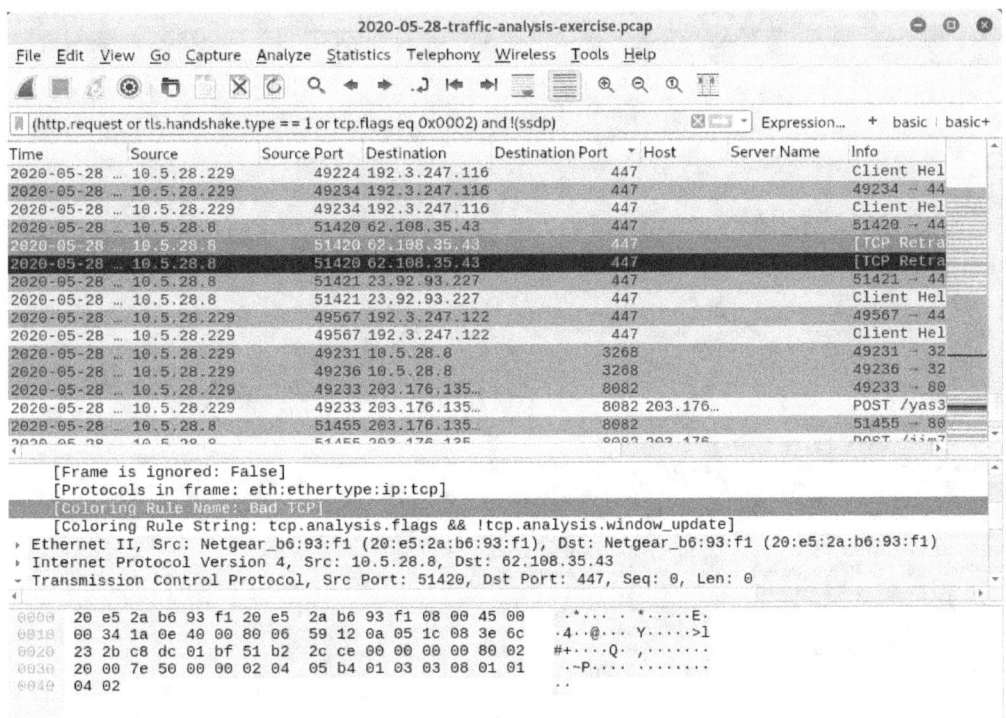

4. Apply "basic+" filter → "(http.request or tls.handshake.type == 1 or tcp.flags eq 0x0002) and !(ssdp)" and observe the traffic.
    a. We found some "Bad TCP" requests with TCP port 447 in black color in Column Display. Looking at the last two lines in the Frame's Packet Details pane confirms about the coloring rule and string.

5. Analyze the POST requests made over TCP port 8082 found via "basic" filter results.
   a. Filter the requests with "(http.request and tcp.port eq 8082)".

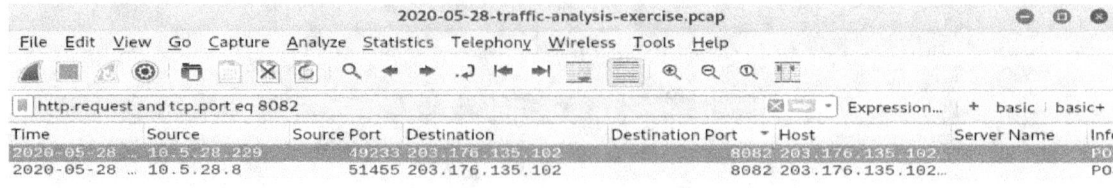

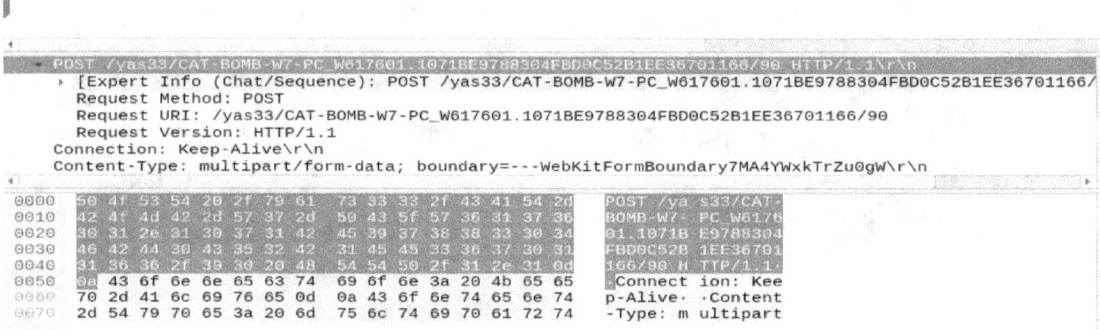

   b. Follow the TCP stream for all the requests found. [Several machine details and other user details found!]

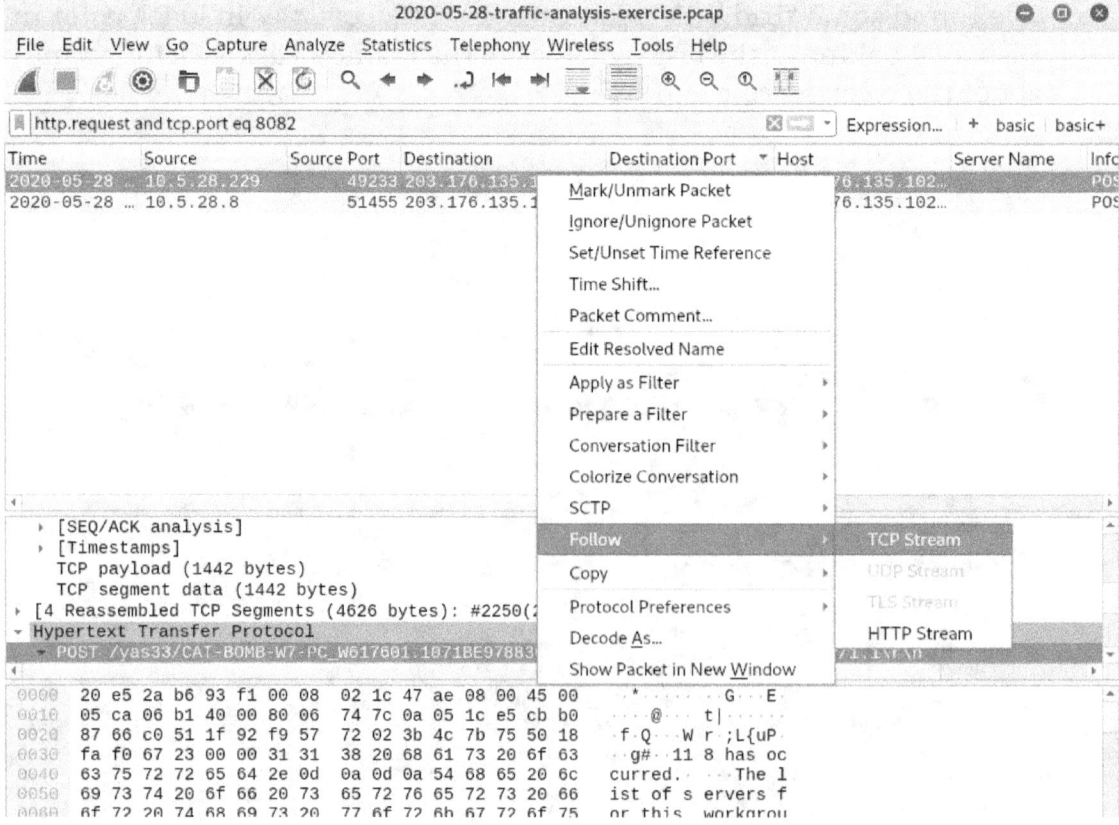

c. Process list information found.

d. Other User's detail and Local Machine data found.

6. Analyzing traffic for mail related information sent out via a POST request.
    a. Filter the requests with "http.request and ip contains mail".

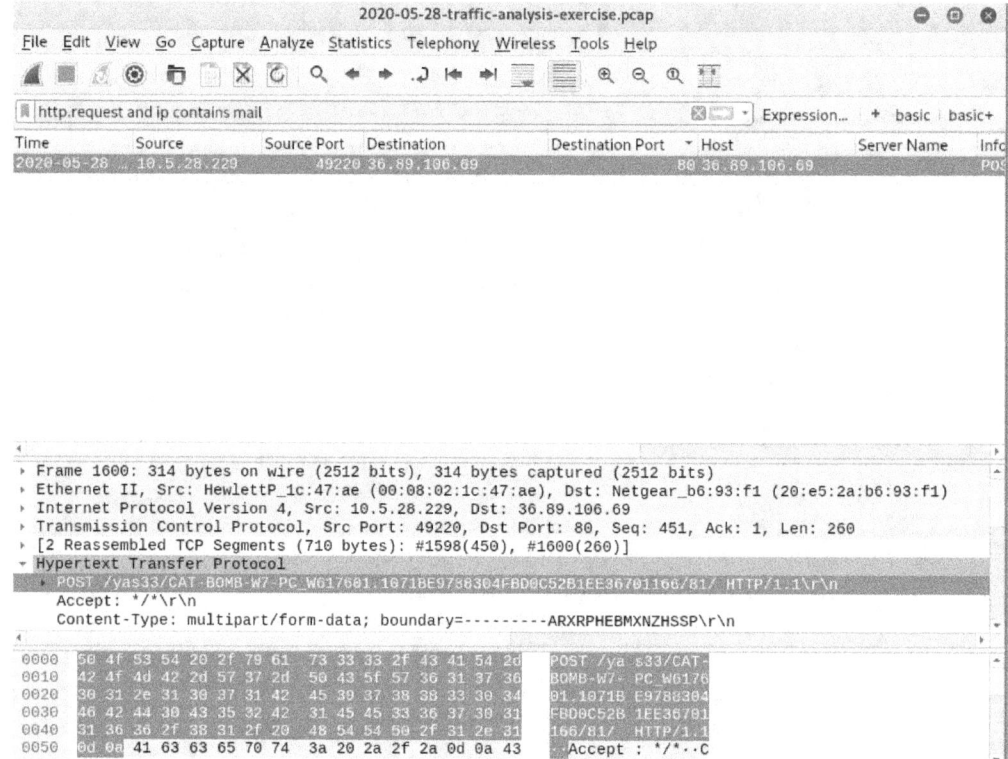

    b. Follow the TCP stream for further analysis. [Credential exfiltration: Password found!]

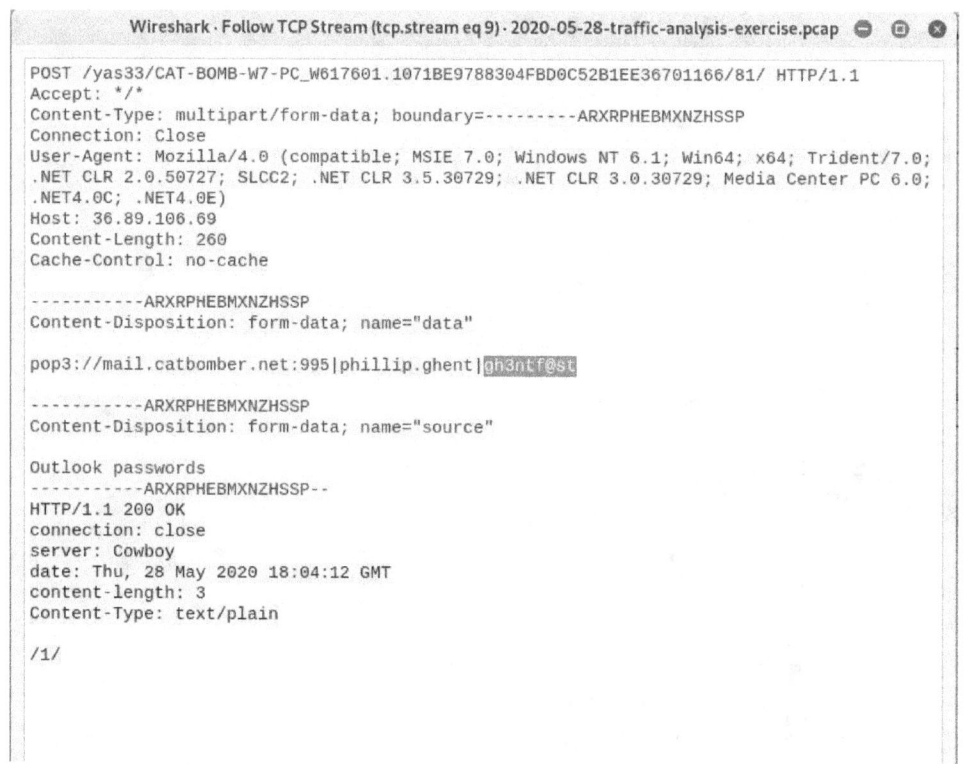

7. Analyzing traffic for any Windows executable files in this PCAP.
    a. Filter this using → ***http contains "DOS mode"*** and look for Request URI in the Hypertext Transfer Protocol in Frame Details. [The suspicious files found are is imgpaper.png and cursor.png]

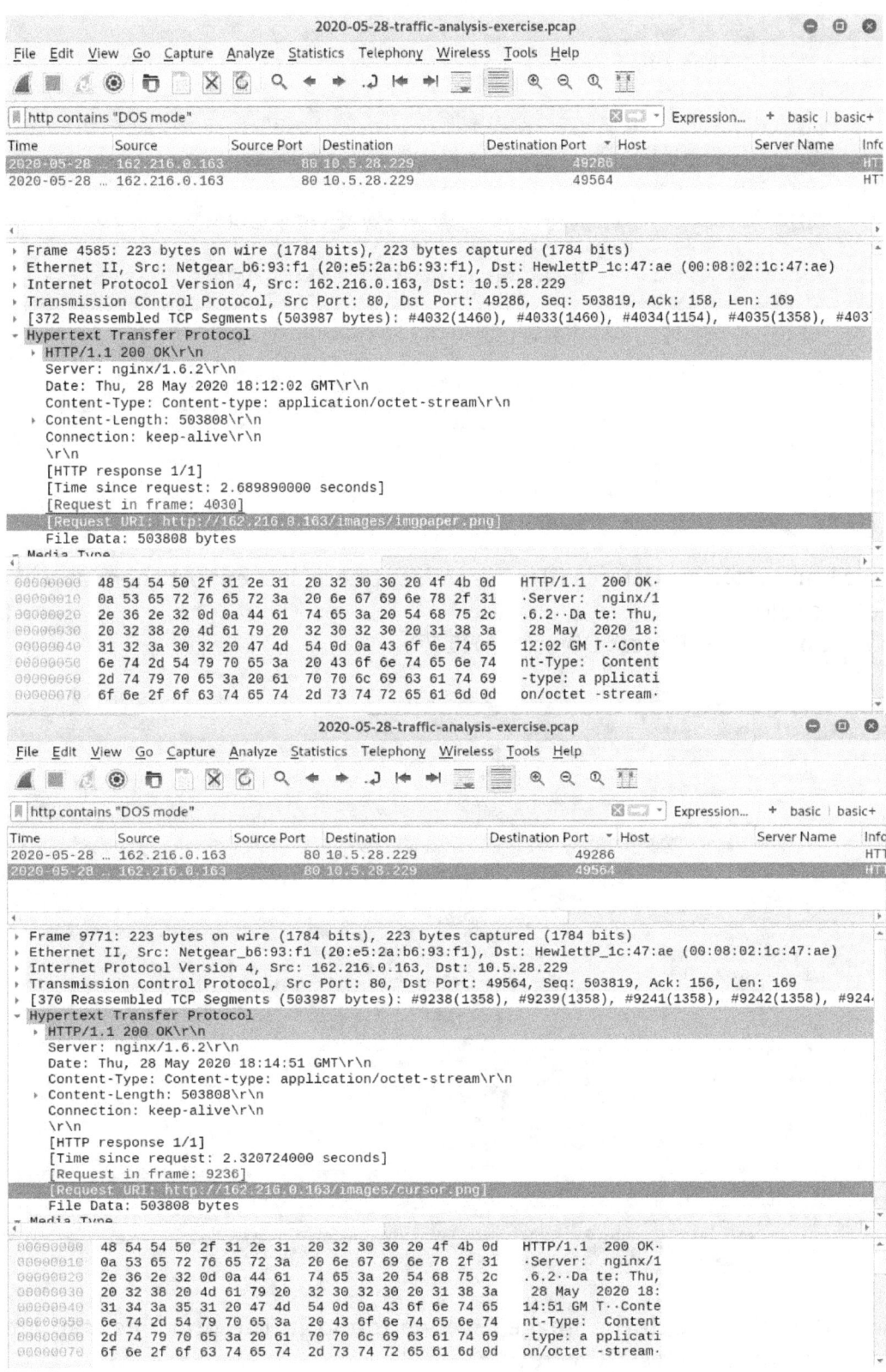

b. Follow TCP stream. [MZ is the header for executable file format.]

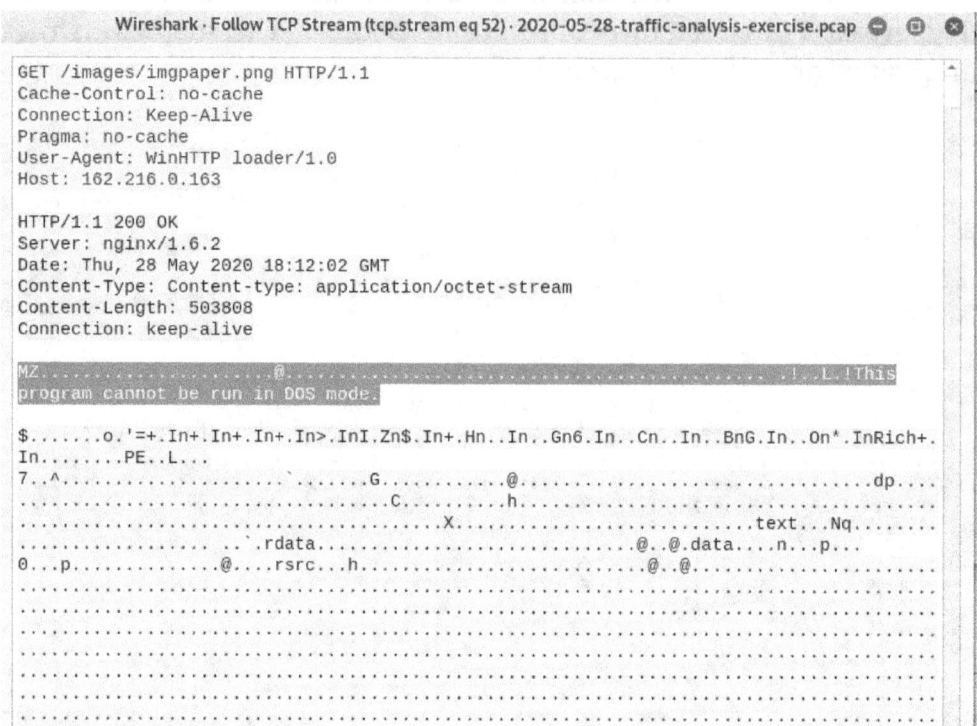

8. As we know, two executable files are present here, lets export them and save in Trickbot Analysis folder.
    a. Go to File →Export Objects →HTTP.

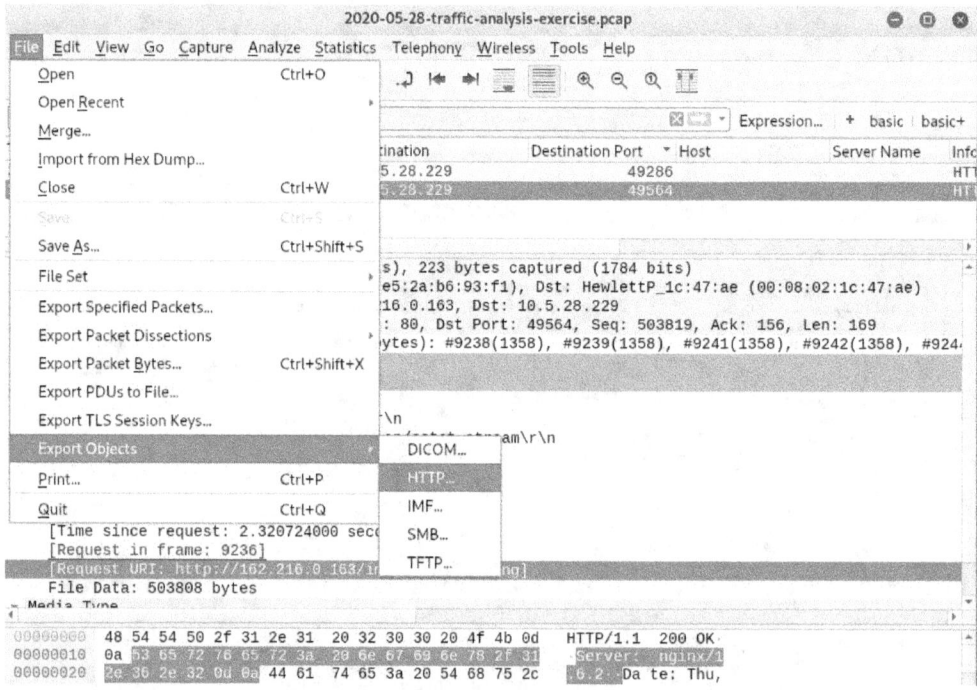

    b. Download both the image files we found in the previous step and save in our Trickbot-analysis directory.

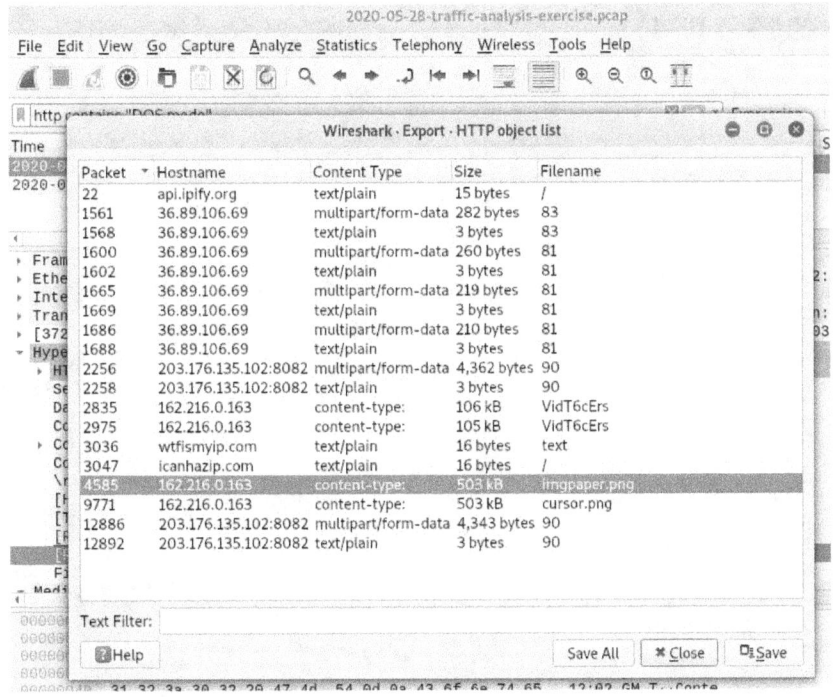

9. Calculate the hash for both image files using **shasum** utility.

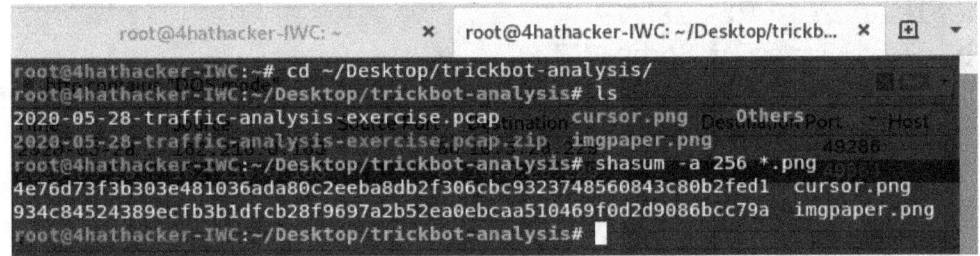

10. Check the hash values in Virus Total or Recorded Future.
    a. Cursor.png

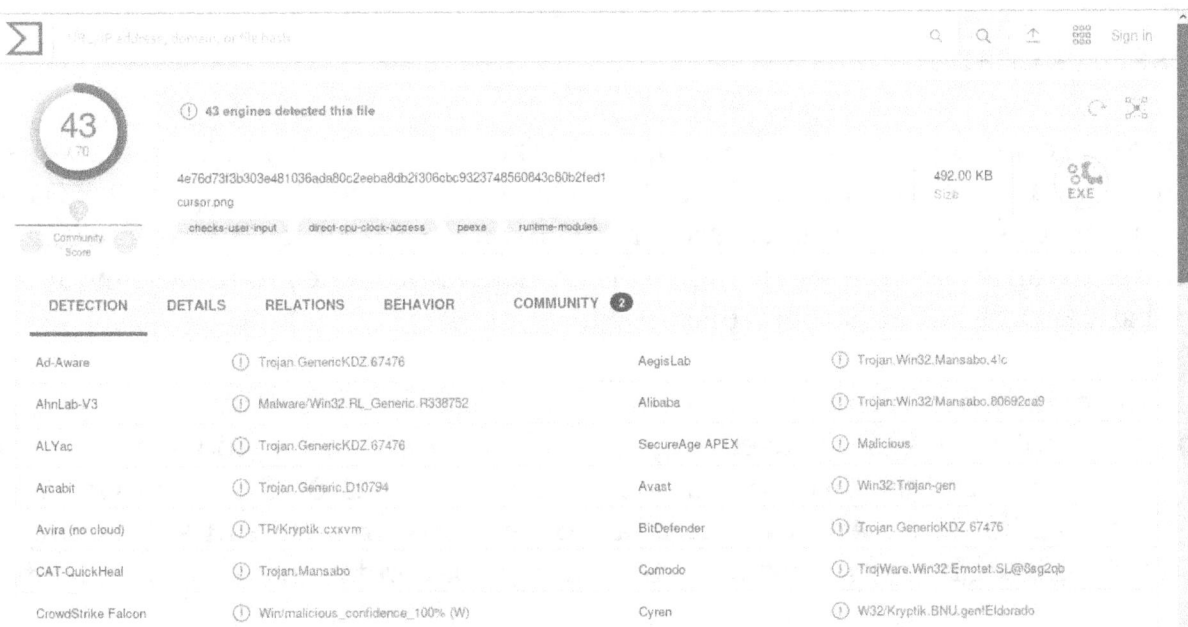

b. Imgpaper.png

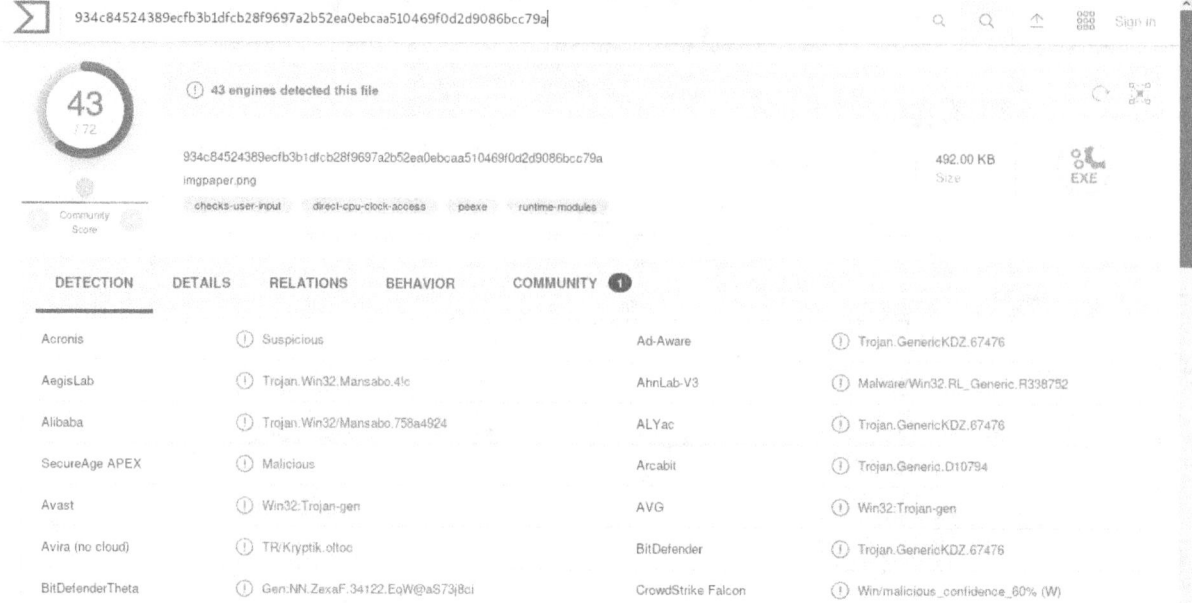

Answers:

1. Infected Windows Client Details:
    a. IP Address: 10.5.28.229
    b. Host Name: Cat-Bomb-W7-PC
    c. User Account Name: phillip.ghent
2. Another user account:
    a. Host Name: CAT-BOMB-W10-PC
    b. User Account Name: timothy.sizemore
3. Infected user's email password: gh3ntf@st
4. SHA256 hashes for the two EXE files:
    a. 4e76d73f3b303e481036ada80c2eeba8db2f306cbc9323748560843c80b2fed1
    b. 34c84524389ecfb3b1dfcb28f9697a2b52ea0ebcaa510469f0d2d9086bcc79a

Lessons Learnt

Network Forensics encompasses law, cyber-crime, technology and even business firms. It has equal importance in Govt. Investigations as well as Business Data Breach Investigations. We have discussed about different forms of investigations based on different frames of time and mindset. Technical approaches to handle evidence and its legal advantage have also been discussed.

The difference between network flow analysis and packet capture analysis is unique however both should be used together along with other tools and processes to withstand modern scenarios of threats and cyber-crimes. Similar to what we have seen during Trickbot PCAP Analysis, there are other Ransomware and APTs ready to attack your system or already have disguised you to go beyond your firewall and defenses.

References

[1] Ransomware-cyber-crime-malware-2321110 [Photograph], TheDigitalArtist, Pixabay. Last accessed on June 21, 2020. - pixabay.com/illustrations/ransomware-cyber-crime-malware-2321110/

[2] Emotet, Ryuk, Trickbot: Loader-Ransomware-Banker Trifecta, Mathew J. Schwartz, Data Breach Today. Published on April 15, 2020. Last Accessed on June 21, 2020. - databreachtoday.com/emotet-ryuk-trickbot-loader-ransomware-banker-trifecta-a-14126

[3] TrickBot: We missed you, Dyre, Threat Research Team. Published on Oct. 15, 2016. Last Accessed on June 21, 2020. Link: fidelissecurity.com/threatgeek/archive/trickbot-we-missed-you-dyre/

[4] TrickBot, Malpedia. Last Accessed on June 21, 2020. – malpedia.caad.fkie.fraunhofer.de/details/win.trickbot

[5] Microsoft Security Intelligence (@MsftSecIntel) [Photo], Twitter. Published on Apr 17, 2020. Last Accessed on June 21, 2020. -twitter.com/MsftSecIntel/status/1251181180281450498/photo/2

[6] Wireshark Tutorial: Examining Trickbot Infections, Brad Duncan, Unit 42, Palo Alto Networks. Published on Nov. 8, 2019. Last Accessed on June 21, 2020.
Link: unit42.paloaltonetworks.com/wireshark-tutorial-examining-trickbot-infections/

[7] MS-ISAC Releases Security Primer on Trickbot Malware, Current Activity Landing, National Cyber Awareness System, US-CERT. Published on Mar. 14, 2019. Last Accessed on June 21, 2020. – us-cert.gov/ncas/current-activity/2019/03/14/MS-ISAC-Releases-Security-Primer-TrickBot-Malware

[8] Security Primer – Trickbot, White Papers, Center for Internet Security. Last Accessed on June 21, 2020. - cisecurity.org/white-papers/security-primer-trickbot/

[9] A visual representation of Trickbot and its modules [Photo], Goodbye Mworm, Hello Nworm: Trickbot Updates Propagation Module, Brad Duncan, Unit 42, Palo Alto Networks. Published on May 28, 2020. Last Accessed on June 21, 2020. - unit42.paloaltonetworks.com/wp-content/uploads/2020/05/Figure-1.-A-visual-representation-of-TrickBot-and-its-modules..jpeg

[10] Example of artifacts for Trickbot modules on an infected Windows 7 client [Photo], Goodbye Mworm, Hello Nworm: Trickbot Updates Propagation Module, Brad Duncan, Unit 42, Palo Alto Networks. Published on May 28, 2020. Last Accessed on June 21, 2020. - unit42.paloaltonetworks.com/wp-content/uploads/2020/05/Figure-2.-Example-of-artifacts-for-TrickBot-modules-on-an-infected-Windows-7-client..jpeg

[11] Trickbot propagation flow chart from September 2019 through March 2020 [Photo], Goodbye Mworm, Hello Nworm: Trickbot Updates Propagation Module, Brad Duncan, Unit 42, Palo Alto Networks. Published on May 28, 2020. Last Accessed on June 21, 2020. - unit42.paloaltonetworks.com/wp-content/uploads/2020/05/Figure-3.-TrickBot-propagation-flow-chart-from-September-2019-through-March-2020..jpeg

[12] What sites is Trickbot targeting, CyberCrime & Doing Time, Gary Warner. Published on Mar 5, 2020. Last Accessed on June 21, 2020. - garwarner.blogspot.com/2020/03/what-sites-is-trickbot-targeting.html

[13] The History of Computing Project, Timeline: Chronology of the history of computing, The History of Computing Foundation, Maurik, The Netherlands, 2010. Last Accessed on June 18, 2020. - thocp.net/timeline/timeline.htm

[14] Mark Pollitt. A History of Digital Forensics. 6th IFIP WG 11.9 International Conference on Digital Forensics (DF), Jan 2010, Hong Kong, China. pp.3-15, ff10.1007/978-3-642-15506-2_1ff. ffhal-01060606f. Last Accessed on June 18, 2020. - hal.inria.fr/hal-01060606/document

[15] University of Washington [Photo], Seattle, United States, Taylor Vick, Unsplash. Last Accessed on June 18, 2020. - unsplash.com/photos/M5tzZtFCOfs

[16] Guide to Integrating Forensic Techniques into Incident Response, Timothy Grance, Suzanne Chevalier, Karen Kent Scarfone, Hung Dang, Special Publication (NIST SP) – 800-86, Published on September 1, 2006. Last Accessed on June 18, 2020. - nist.gov/publications/guide-integrating-forensic-techniques-incident-response

[17] Introduction to Network Forensics Handbook Final V1.1, Cybersecurity ENISA Training, Published August 2019. Last Accessed on June 18, 2020. - enisa.europa.eu/topics/trainings-for-cybersecurity-specialists/online-training-material/documents/introduction-to-network-forensics-handbook.pdf

[18] A Framework of Network Forensics and its Application of Locating Suspects in Wireless Crime Scene Investigation, Junwei Huang, Yinjie Chen, Zhen Ling, Kyungseok Choo, Xinwen Fu University of Massachusetts Lowell, USA + Southeast University, China. Last Accessed on June 18, 2020. - pdfs.semanticscholar.org/10b8/8debc818ca1da825fb9848cfaf8dccf2aa9f.pdf

[19] Privacy and Search, Expectation of Privacy, Wikipedia. Last Accessed on June 18, 2020. - en.wikipedia.org/wiki/Expectation_of_privacy#Privacy_and_search

[20] H. Marshall Jarrett and Michael W. Bailie, Searching and Seizing Computers and Obtaining Electronic Evidence in Criminal Investigations (Washington, DC: Office of Legal Education Executive Office, 2009). Last Accessed on June 18, 2020. - justice.gov/sites/default/files/criminal-ccips/legacy/2015/01/14/ssmanual2009.pdf

[21] Stored Communications Act (SCA, codified at 18 U.S.C. Chapter 121 2701-2712), Wikipedia. Last Accessed on June 18, 2020. - en.wikipedia.org/wiki/Stored_Communications_Act

[22] Legal Considerations, Guidelines for Evidence Collection and Archiving, RFC3227. Last Accessed on June 18, 2020. - tools.ietf.org/html/rfc3227

[23] Network Forensics, Wikipedia. Last accessed on June 19, 2020. - en.wikipedia.org/wiki/Network_forensics#Overview

[24] Flow Analysis Versus Packet Analysis, What should you Choose, Netfort.com. Last Accessed on June 19, 2020. - netfort-prod.k8s.corpwebsite.gcp.rapid7.com/content/uploads/PDF/WhitePapers/NetFlow-Vs-Packet-Analysis-What-Should-You-Choose.pdf

[25] Traffic analysis exercise – Catbomber, Malware-traffic-analysis.net. Published on May 28, 2020. Last Accessed on June 19, 2020. - malware-traffic-analysis.net/2020/05/28/index.html

[26] Wireshark, From Wikipedia, the free encyclopedia. Last Accessed on June 19, 2020. - en.wikipedia.org/wiki/Wireshark

Email Forensic Analysis
Lyer 6

By
Nitin Sharma

"Like almost everyone who uses e-mail, I receive a ton of spam every day. Much of it offers to help me get out of debt or get rich quick. It would be funny if it weren't so irritating."
- Bill Gates

Communication is one of the most important art one should possess, especially in business context. It impacts every aspect regarding the relationship with employees, suppliers and customers. 90% of messages are conveyed through non-verbal communication, while most companies utilize email or other forms of electronic messaging as a means of written communication.

Email communication is the mode of written communication which provides more formal structure and official perspective. Attackers find business emails as the easiest medium to spread malware through deceptive spam emails convincing target victims to click open the attachments or links that comes along. By opening the link or attachments, the users are directed to malicious websites or end up opening a malicious document by this way the attackers install the malware from backend on to the user's system and therefore gains access to business network resulting a security breach.

Necessity of securing emails therefore arises, and businesses should validate their email security services. In this paper, email forensics has been discussed thoroughly for malicious email header detection in spam and illicit emails. At the end, a practical walkthrough is included with some email hygiene and security best practices.

Photo by @bermixstudio, unsplash.com [1]

Email: OSI Perspective

Email runs on SMTP (Simple Mail Transfer Protocol) which is Layer 7 (Application Layer) protocol.
When an email is sent, the data passes through all the layers to the physical layer where the data is put onto the network cabling, and then sent to the receiving computer where the process reverses and the data travels up through the layers to the

application layer of the receiving computer.

In this process, Layer 6 (Presentation Layer) introduces a set of syntax and semantics to the information transmitted through the lower protocol layer that will be the focus of upcoming discussion. Please see below the flow of sending email from Alice to Bob with OSI Layer functions.

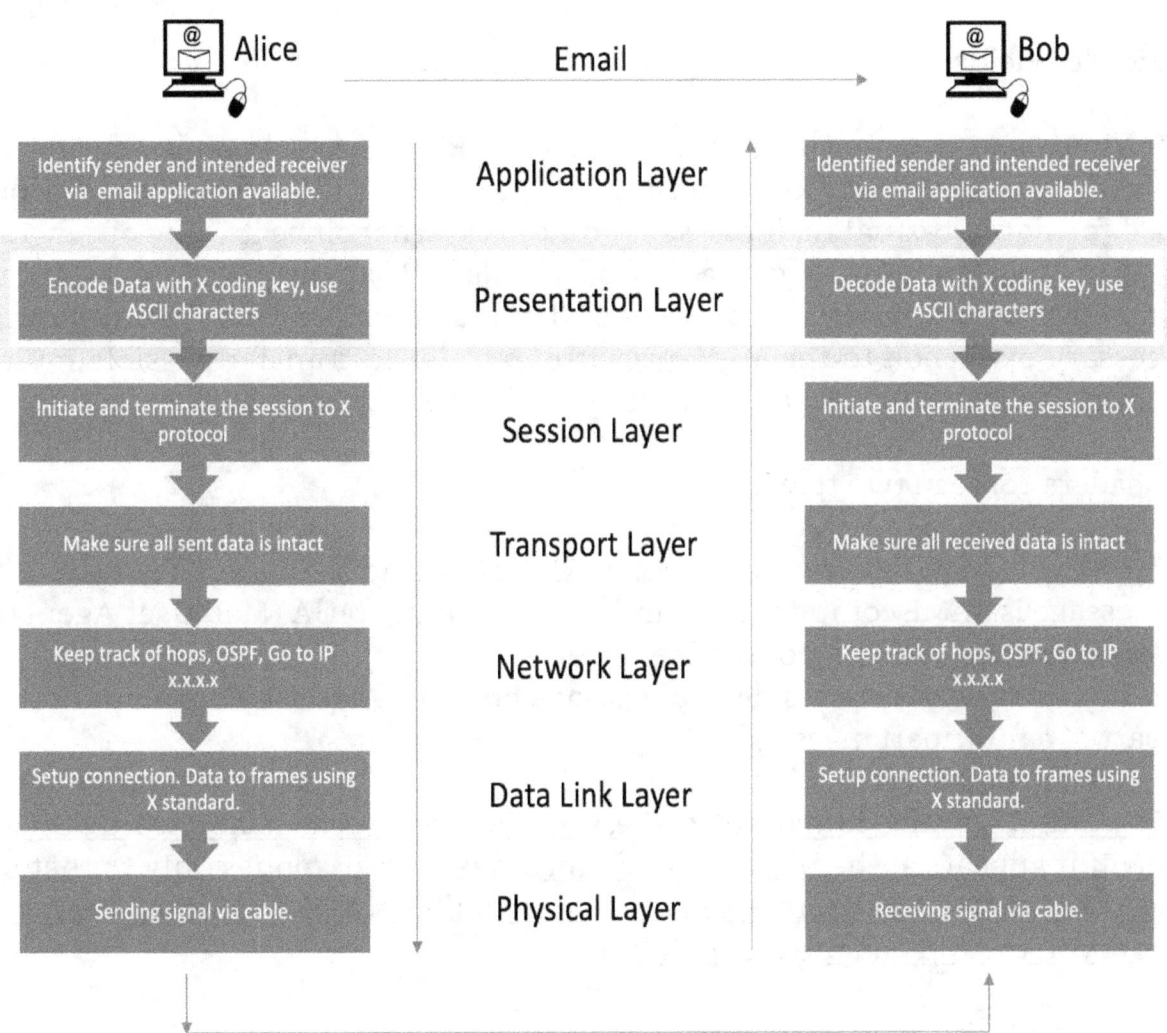

Email Headers

An Email message consists of a number of header fields and a body (optional). Header fields consist of name-value pairs that are delimited by a colon. Mandatory headers provide information on the sender and the recipient of the message and the date the message was sent. Other headers may give information on the subject or contents of the message and how it was routed through the Internet. The blank line separating the header fields from the body is an ASCII carriage return character (CR) followed by an ASCII linefeed character (LF) on a line by itself.

1. Mandatory Headers – Date, From, To.
2. Optional Headers – Subject, Comment, Keywords, Encrypted, CC and BCC.

Other headers include Dynamic and User Defined headers usually written for custom email applications.

MIME Header Fields

The Multipurpose Internet Mail Extensions (MIME) protocol is an extension to the Standard for the Format of ARPA Internet Text Messages. This protocol has defined the standard format of textual mail messages on the Internet since it came out in 1982. It describes the format of message headers but it tells little about the content of the body of the message which is limited to 7-bit ASCII characters. The MIME protocol provides the necessary extension to the MAIL protocol in order to transfer possible multi-part textual and non-textual data object in the body of a MAIL message. [2]

MIME headers come in two flavors:

1. **MIME message headers** – additional RFC 822-style headers. They denote that a message is MIME compliant and inform a receiving MUA (Mail User Agent) of the structure and encoding of the message.
2. **MIME part headers** – reside in a message body and describe the contents of each part of a multipart message.

Note: If a MIME header is part of a message header block, it applies to the entire message. If it appears at the beginning of a message part, it applies only to that part. A Mail User Agent (MUA) also referred to as an email client, is a computer application that allow you to send and retrieve email.

MIME message headers are [3]:

1. MIME Version – To declare the version of the Internet message body format standard in use. e.g. MIME-Version: 1.0
2. Content-Type – Specifies the nature of the data in the body of an entity by giving media type and subtype identifiers, and by providing auxiliary information that may be required for certain media types. Top Level media types are: text, image, audio, video, application, multipart, message.
3. Content-Transfer-Encoding – Shows the type of encoding performed on a message or message part and therefore gives information on how to decide it. The SMTP limits email messages to US-ASCII 7-bit characters and lines of fewer

than 998 data characters, per RFC 821. Content-Transfer-Encoding values can be: 7bit, 8bit, binary, quoted-printable, base64, Custom, or user-defined schemes. The first three do not require any decoding.
  4. Content-ID – This header is uncommon and optional but becomes mandatory if a Content-Type of message/external-body is used. This is also used to augment the multipart/alternative media type.
  5. Content-Description – It is an optional header to add textual description to file attached to an email.

MIME Encoding

When creating a mail message, one must decide how to encode each part of the message.

1. 7-bit data – It is simple US-ASCII text, with the restrictions placed on it by RFC 821. No octets with ASCII decimal values of zero or more than 127 are allowed. No encoding required.
2. 8-bit data – Decimal values over 127 are also allowed. Allowable on some systems but might get translated to 7-bit by intervening mail servers if any. When creating a mail destined to route directly onto the Internet, don't use this encoding type.
3. Binary data – It may contain any type of octets, irrespective of their possible translation to ASCII. The same restrictions and notes for 8-bit data apply to binary. Do not use this encoding type for Internet use via SMTP. Translate binary data into Base64 encoding type.
4. Quoted-Printable – Should be used for data that is nominally text and human-readable but not "7-bit clean". The simple rules that follow quoted printable method are,
   a. Convert the original data into an octet stream by ensuring that the bits are in big endian format.
   b. Any octet, except a CRLF line-break in the original data, may be changed to an equal sign (=) followed by a two-character hexadecimal representation of the octet's character value. An octet must be so changed unless another rule allows an alternative method.
   c. Octets with ASCII decimal values of 33 through 60 and 62 through 126 may be represented as their ASCII character representations.
   d. Whitespace (tabs, ASCII decimal value 9, and spaces, ASCII decimal value 32) may be left as those values unless they would fall at the end of a line, then they must be encoded by 4a.
   e. Line breaks in the original data should be converted to the CRLF form.
   f. No line may be longer than 76 characters, not including the ending CRLF characters. If the original data includes lines longer than 76 characters, a

"soft" line-break may be added by ending a line with an equal sign (=) followed by the normal CRLF sequence.
5. <u>Base64</u> – This encoding takes three octets (24 bits) and maps them into four 6-bit blocks, then represents each 6-bit block with a character in a 64-character alphabet ($2^6 = 64$). Because of this mapping, base 64 encoded information is about one-third larger than the original data. The complete rule set for base64 encoding looks like this,
    a. Convert the original data into an octet stream by ensuring that the bits are in big-endian format.
    b. If the data to be encoded is textual, line breaks must be converted to CRLF form first.
    c. Remove three octets at a time from the stream and convert them into four 6-bit indexes into the base64 alphabet.
    d. Convert the four 6-bit indexes into four characters from the base64 table.
    e. Ensure that each line of encoded information is less than 76 characters long, not including the terminating line break (CRLF).
    f. When you reach the end of the original data, you may have one or two octets left over. If octets are left over, you will have to "pad" the encoding. If the number of octets in the original data was divisible by 3, no padding is necessary.
    g. To pad the encoding, add zero bit onto the end of the stream until you have an integral number of 6-bit blocks. Apply 5c, to get the base64 characters, as normal. Then add either one or two equal signs (=) onto the end of the encoding until the total number of characters is evenly divisible by 4.

Advantages of MIME

1. It is able to send multiple attachments with a single message.
2. Unlimited message length.
3. Binary attachments (executables, images, audio, or video files) which may be divided if needed.
4. MIME provided support for varying content types and multi-part messages.

Email Authentication

Email authentication is used to block harmful or fraudulent uses of email such as phishing and spam.
In general, the email authentication works like below, [4]

1. A business or organization that sends email establishes a policy that defines rules by which email from its domain name can be authenticated.
2. The email sender configures its mail server and other technical infrastructure to implement and publish these rules.
3. A mail server that receives email authenticate the message it receives by checking details about an incoming email message against the rules defined by the domain owner.
4. The receiving mail server acts upon the results of this authentication to deliver, flag or even reject the message.

The most commonly used email authentication standards are,

a. **SPF - Sender Policy Framework** (Allows senders to define which IP addresses are allowed to send mail for a particular domain i.e., Path Based Authentication).

   Example: SPF Record

   TXT @ "v=spf1 a include:_spf.google.com ~all"

   Explanation:

   TXT [The DNS zone record type; SPF records are written as TXT records]
   @ [In a DNS file, the "@" symbol is a placeholder used to represent the "current domain"]
   v=spf1 [Identifies the TXT record as an SPF record, utilizing SPF Version 1]
   a [Authorizes the host(s) identified in the domain's A record(s) to send e-mail]
   include: [Authorizes mail to be sent on behalf of the domain from google.com]
   ~all [Denotes that this list is all inclusive, and no other servers are allowed to send e-mail]

b. **DKIM – Domain Keys Identified Mail** (Provides an encryption key and digital signature that verifies that an email message was not faked or altered i.e., Content Based Authentication).

Example: DKIM Record

dk1024-2012._domainkey.xyzpath.com.   600   IN   TXT   "v=DKIM1\;
p=MIGfMA0GCSqGSIb3DQEBAQUAA4GNADCBiQKBgQC1TaNgLlSyQMNWVL
NLvyY/neDgaL2oqQE8T5illKqCgDtFHc8eHVAU+nlcaGmrKmDMw9dbgiGk1o
cgZ56NR4ycfUHwQhvQPMUZw0cveel/8EAGoi/UyPmqfcPibytH81NFtTMAx
UeM4Op8A6iHkvAMj5qLf4YRNsTkKAV;"

Explanation:

dk1024-2012 [Indicates the selector record name used with the domain to locate the public key in DNS. The value is a name or number created by the sender]

xyzpath.com [Indicates the domain used with the selector record to locate the public key]

DKIM1 [Optional tag representing the version of DKIM record]

MIGfMA0GCSqGSIb3DQEBAQUAA4GNADCBiQKBgQC1TaNgLlSyQM
NWVLNLvyY/neDgaL2oqQE8T5illKqCgDtFHc8eHVAU+nlcaGmr
KmDMw9dbgiGk1ocgZ56NR4ycfUHwQhvQPMUZw0cveel/8EAG
oi/UyPmqfcPibytH81NFtTMAxUeM4Op8A6iHkvAMj5qLf4YRNs
TkKAV [Required tag representing the public key used by a mailbox provider to match to the DKIM signature generated using the private key. It is generated along with its corresponding private key during the DKIM set-up process]

c. **DMARC – Domain-based Message Authentication, Reporting and Conformance** (utilizes the SPF and DKIM authentication mechanisms into a common framework and allows domain owners to declare how they would like email from that domain to be

Explanation:

v=DMARC1 [DMARC Protocol version]

p=reject [Protocol for domain, reject will cancel the message at SMTP layer]

pct=100 [Percentage of message subjected to filtering]

rua=mailto:postmaster@dmarcdomain.com [Reporting UTI of aggregate report]

Note: These standards were deigned to supplement SMTP, the basic protocol used to send email, because SMTP does not itself include any AUTH(N) mechanisms.

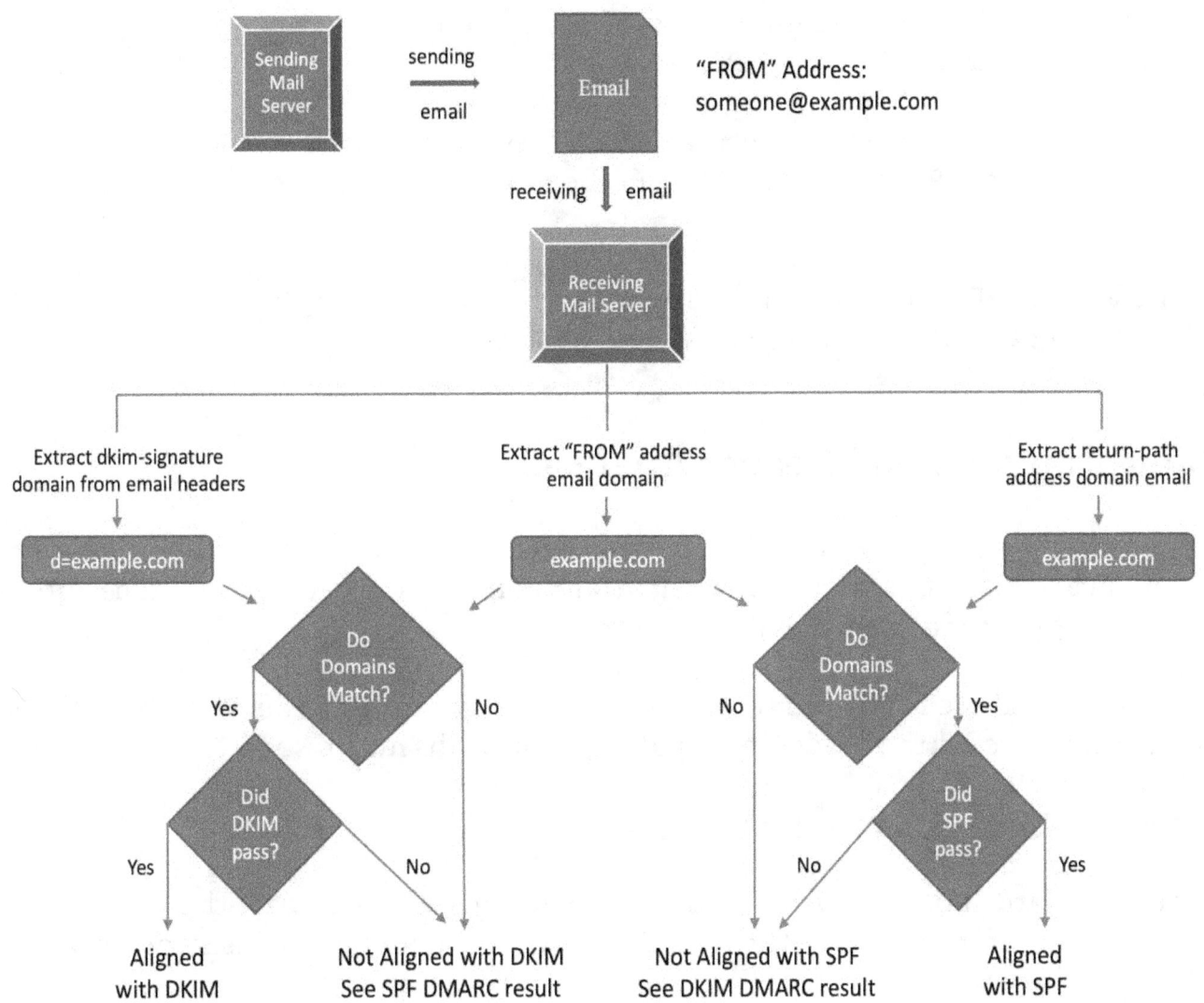

Authentication Work Flow:

With SPF and DKIM, it is up to the ISP to decide what to do with the results. DMARC takes it a step further and gives the org/company full control to set a policy to approve, reject or quarantine emails from sources the org/company do not know or trust, all based on the results of DKIM and SPF. [5]

For Example, ABC company publish a DMARC record that says if DKIM or SPF fails, reject the message. Participating ISPs will look at this policy and discard the emails that fail.

DMARC lets the ABC company tell ISPs how they want them to behave if SPF and DKIM fail or are not present. The flow chart above explains this.

Walkthrough: Email Header Analysis

In this walkthrough, we will go through a malicious email sent by unknown person. This email also has a text file attachment. You can follow the exercise by proceeding in a similar fashion for any email within your mailbox.

Pre-requisites: There is no specific pre-requisites to go through this walkthrough. We will be going to cover the header information we have discussed so far.

A. Capturing Headers from Malicious Email

1. The Standard Email Header details shown below describes the source and destination information for the mail. However, the source email is very suspicious with spelling errors and the destination e-mail is different from my email.

Note: Many spam mails will have "From:" and "To:" addresses we have never heard of. My email address might have been covered in the BCC (Blind Carbon Copy).

2. To get all the header details, Click the three dots at right side of mail window and select "Show Original".

3. All the details of Original Message and respective email header will appear as shown below. Save the header information in a text file.

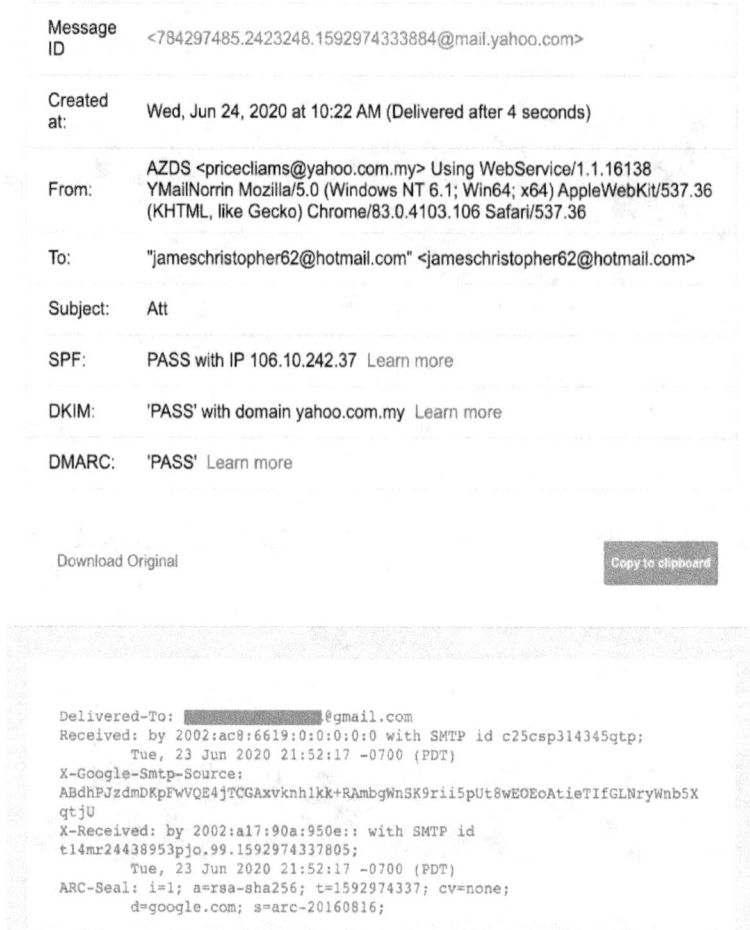

B. Analyzing Details from Header Information using MxToolBox

1. Copy the saved header details and paste them in MxToolBox Email Analyzer [6]. And Click "Analyze Header".

Email Header Analyzer

Paste Header:

```
Content-Type: text/plain
Content-Transfer-Encoding: base64
Content-Disposition: attachment; filename="-1.txt"
Content-ID: <31fc33ff-26c7-2f8f-76ff-48d6121427ef@yahoo.com>

SGkgU2lyL01hDQpJIHdhbnQgdG8gcGFydG5lcnNoaXAgd2l0aCB5b3UgaW4gdHJhbnNmZXIgb2Yg
ozMsNTE3LDAwMC4wMCEgQ29udGFjdCBtZSBmb3IgbW9yZSBkZXRhaWxzIG15ICBpZDogamFtZXNj
aHJpc3RvGhlcjYyQGhvdG1haWwuY29tICAgDQpUaGFua3MNCk1yIEphbWVzIENocmlzdG9waGVy

------=_Part_2423247_202191035.1592974333884--
```

[Analyze Header]

2. The result here, shows us that the delivery is not DMARC Compliant which is due to failure of SPF AUTH(N) and DKIM AUTH(N).

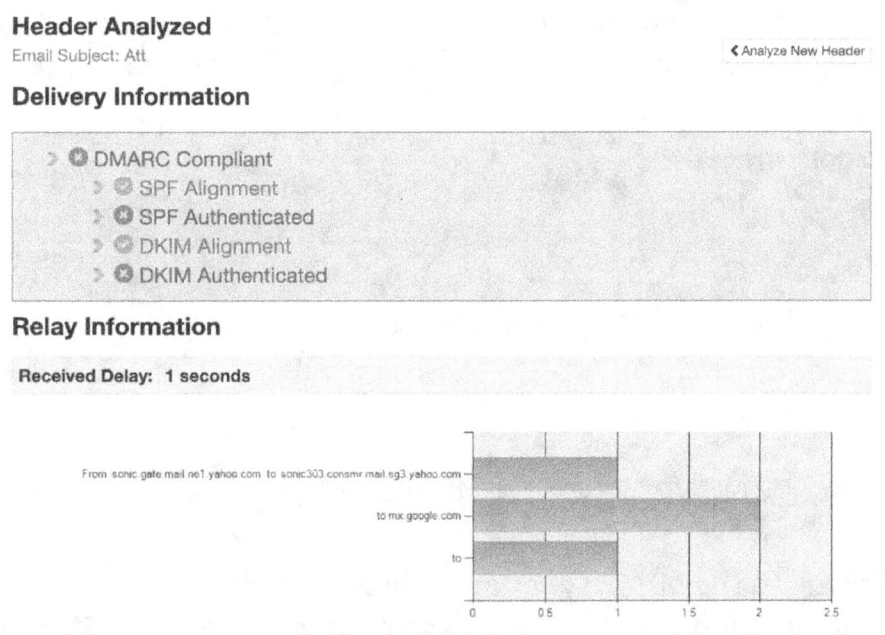

3. The SPF Authentication Failure means the IP address 106.10.242.37 is not authorized to send from the domain. The SPF record does not contain the sending server or IP address used for sending email to the mailbox provider. Notice the hops in between From and To Address also as above. And the result below where, IP Address is not present in the SPF record. You can even compare the results for SPF Lookup to find this IP.

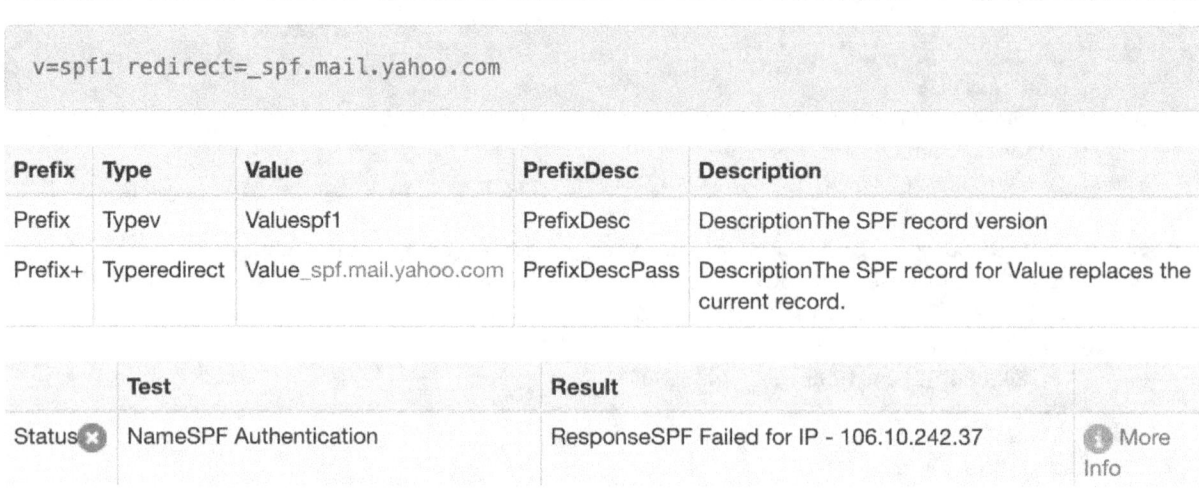

4. The DKIM Authentication Failure means the body hash verification fails, the computed hash of the message body does not agree with the body hash value stored in the "bh=" tag of the DKIM signature. [Note: The reasons for such failure might be the email body modification or wrong public key in DKIM-Signature Header/DNS]

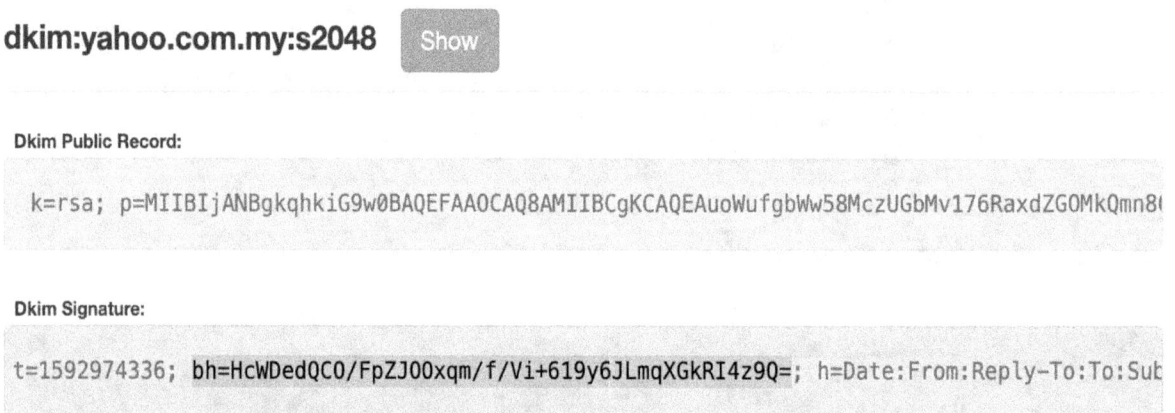

5. Now, we will come to the MIME types and the mail body.
    a. All the red highlights in the image shown below are MIME details.
    b. There are five **Content-Type** headers in this email example. The one on the message header is a composite type (multipart/mixed), allowing it to have message parts under it.
    c. The second **Content-Type** (multipart/alternative) is syntactically identical to previous one (multipart/mixed). In particular, each of the parts is an "alternative" version of the same information. The user agent should either choose the "best" type based on the user's environment and preferences or offer the user the available alternatives. We have here, text/plain and text/html.
    d. The last **Content-Type** is for the TXT document file attached, as we can see **Content-Disposition: attachment**.

e. The green box highlight actually contains the text message in **base64 encoded format**.

```
Date: Wed, 24 Jun 2020 04:52:13 +0000 (UTC)
From: AZDS <pricecliams@yahoo.com.my>
Reply-To: AZDS <pricecliams@yahoo.com.my>
To: "jameschristopher62@hotmail.com"
<jameschristopher62@hotmail.com>
Message-ID: <784297485.2423248.1592974333884@mail.yahoo.com>
Subject: Att
MIME-Version: 1.0
Content-Type: multipart/mixed; boundary="----=_Part_2423247_202191035.1592974333884"
References: <784297485.2423248.1592974333884.ref@mail.yahoo.com>
X-Mailer: WebService/1.1.16138 YMailNorrin Mozilla/5.0 (Windows NT 6.1; Win64; x64) AppleWebKit/537.36 (KHTML, like Gecko) Chrome/83.0.4103.106 Safari/537.36
Content-Length: 1096

------=_Part_2423247_202191035.1592974333884
Content-Type: multipart/alternative; boundary="----=_Part_2423243_1077152613.1592974333850"

------=_Part_2423243_1077152613.1592974333850
Content-Type: text/plain; charset=UTF-8
Content-Transfer-Encoding: 7bit




------=_Part_2423243_1077152613.1592974333850
Content-Type: text/html; charset=UTF-8
Content-Transfer-Encoding: 7bit

<html><head></head><body><div class="yahoo-style-wrap" style="font-family:Helvetica Neue, Helvetica, Arial, sans-serif;font-size:13px;"><div><br></div></body></html>
------=_Part_2423243_1077152613.1592974333850--
------=_Part_2423247_202191035.1592974333884
Content-Type: text/plain
Content-Transfer-Encoding: base64
Content-Disposition: attachment; filename="-1.txt"
Content-ID: <31fc33ff-26c7-2f8f-76ff-48d6121427ef@yahoo.com>
```

```
SGkgU2lyL01hDQpJIHdhbnQgdG8gcGFydG5lcnNoaXAgd2l0aCB5b3UgaW4gdHJhb
nNmZXIgb2Yg
ozMsNTE3LDAwMC4wMCEgQ29udGFjdCBtZSBmb3IgbW9yZSBkZXRhaWxzIG15ICBpZ
DogamFtZXNj
aHJpc3RvcGhlcjYyQGhvdG1haWwuY29tICAgDQpUaGFua3MNCk1yIEphbWVzIENoc
mlzdG9waGVy
```

```
------=_Part_2423247_202191035.1592974333884--
```

6. We can get the actual message from text file attachment without opening the file by decoding the Green box text at base64decode.org [7].

Decode from Base64 format

Simply enter your data then push the decode button.

```
SGkgU2lyL01hDQpJIHdhbnQgdG8gcGFydG5lcnNoaXAgd2l0aCB5b3UgaW4gdHJhbnNmZXIgb2Ygozmsnte3ldawmc4wmcegq29udgfjdcbtzsbmb3igbw9yzsbkzxrhawxzig15icbpzdogamftzxnjahjpc3rvcghlcjyyqghvdg1hawwuy29ticagdqpuagfua3mnck1ylephbwvziencmlzdg9wagvy
```

ⓘ For encoded binaries (like images, documents, etc.) use the file upload form a bit further down on this page.

[UTF-8 ▼] Source character set.

☐ Decode each line separately (useful for multiple entries).

◉ Live mode OFF   Decodes in real-time when you type or paste (supports only UTF-8 character set).

[‹ DECODE ›]   Decodes your data into the textarea below.

```
Hi Sir/Ma
I want to partnership with you in transfer of 3,517,000.00! Contact me for more details my  id: jameschristopher62@hotmail.com
Thanks
Mr James Christopher
```

C. IP Blacklist Check

1. Checking the email origin IP Address in publicly available blacklists is also a way to find out spam. Many of the lists have already been prepared with the help of different reporting procedures.

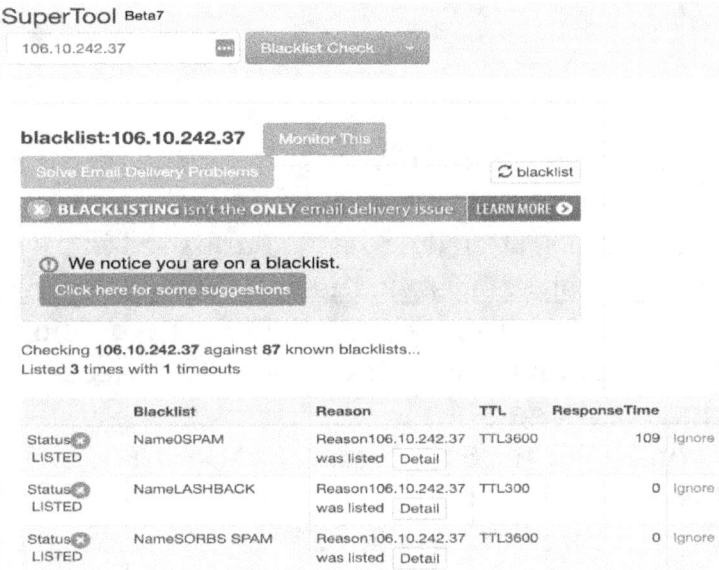

Best Practices for Email Security

1. Use strong passwords with upper and lower-case letters, numbers and special characters, random numbers, avoiding common-letter substitutions.
2. Use multi-factor authentication while logging in your email.
3. For emails received from unknown senders, do not click any link, or open the attachments downloading to your system.
4. Use spam filters, antivirus, and antimalware solutions.
5. Do not use your business email addresses for personal outcomes like online shopping, online gaming, etc.
6. Never access company email from public Wi-Fi without using a VPN.
7. Never click "Unsubscribe" link in spam emails. It might steal some information from your system or create a backdoor.
8. Use SPF, DKIM and DMARC as a part of business email setup.
9. Security Awareness training is the best way to ensure safety recommendations provided to the business folks.
10. Exercise caution when enabling Macros in Office Suite from the email attachments.

Lessons Learnt

Email forensics and security is very important in order to keep an organization as well as individual safe from spam and phishing. We have covered here OSI Email perspective, Message encoding schemes, MIME types and their importance, Email authentication methods and a simple walkthrough for Email Header Analysis. Following a set of guidelines and adoption of security best practices can help to tackle email compromise in modern digital and connected world.

References

[1] Anonymous computer hacker in white mask and hoodie [Photo], Bermix Studio, Unsplash. Last Accessed on June 23, 2020.- images.unsplash.com

[2] Presentation Layer Protocols, Henrik Frystyk, Published in July, 1994. Last Accessed on June 23, 2020. - w3.org/People/Frystyk/thesis/Presentation.html

[3] Multipurpose Internet Mail Extensions (MIME) Part One: Format of Internet Message Bodies, RFC-2045, Published in Nov., 1996. Last Accessed on June 23, 2020. - tools.ietf.org/html/rfc2045#page-8

[4] Email Authentication basics for SaaS teams, Sparkpost.com. Last Accessed on June 23, 2020. - sparkpost.com

[5] DMARC: Monitor and secure your email delivery, Chris Nagele, Postmarkapp.com. Published on June 2, 2020. Last Accessed on June 23, 2020. - postmarkapp.com/guides/dmarc

[6] MXtoolbox Email Header Analyzer [Online Tool], Last Accessed on June 23, 2020. - mxtoolbox.com/EmailHeaders.aspx

[7] Base64 – Decode and Encode [Online Tool], Last Accessed on June 23, 2020. - base64decode.org/

Kibana, ElasticSearch, and Logstash
Visualizing your Data
Layer 2/3/4/5/6/7

By
Richard Medlin

The Kibana Dashboard is used for searching, visualizations, and maps for you to view any type of data that you ship to ElasticSearch. The dashboard gives you the ability to look at data in as much depth as you configure it to go. The dashboard itself gives you a lot of flexibility for performing analysis of information in a side-by-side manner. Once you make dashboards you can edit and view the data that is displayed, or you can use some of the preconfigured dashboard visualizations that are already built into Kibana. You can customize the visualizations to set up a custom SIEM to monitor events on your network. Kibana provides an interface for you to see what is happening in your network environment, and can be used to display the information in a way that is quick and easy to drill down on anomalies in system and network behavior, while also providing signature based detection of potential malicious activity on the network.

Once you import data into ElasticSearch — using whatever method you decide — Kibana can take that data and provide multiple formats to visualize your data. You can use pie-charts, bar-charts, sunbursts, heat, region and coordinate maps, data tables, tag clouds, and histograms to name a few. Kibana allows you to add controls, radio sliders, and filters — this makes for a very versatile option when viewing data. Kibana uses metric aggregation and bucket aggregation to match search criteria in documents. Once you setup your desired dashboard panel using the visualization method, you can save the result and build a dashboard that you can access anytime.

In this section of the write-up we are going to cover how to make a Kibana Dashboard. In order to create a dashboard, you need to first create visualizations. The visualizations will be the different panes that will make up your dashboard. We are going to cover some of the basics for creating a dashboard similar to the one built for CSI Linux that can be downloaded at csilinux.com. Go ahead and launch ELK stack and ensure you have collected some logs with Zeek (Bro). At this point you should be in your web browser and open up Kibana by using the IP address for your SIEM.

This write-up will cover the following:
- Creating Visualizations for the SIEM Dashboard
- GeoHeat Map
- Saving Visualizations
- Viewing the Newly Created Visualization
- GeoIP Unique Count
- Top Network Traffic Generation, Network Applications, and Traffic Destination
- Average Missed Bytes
- Sum of Bytes
- Notices Generated
- Building the Dashboard

Creating Visualizations for the SIEM Dashboard

GeoHeat Map

We will start by creating a heat map that shows the location of external network traffic. This will allow you to see where your network communications are coming from externally, and where your internal network nodes are sending traffic to. This is helpful for identifying malicious traffic, and you can also setup caching for your proxy server if you have one on the network. That will help cut down some of the wait times for your network nodes and allow you to optimize your network speeds.

Left Click on **Visualize**:

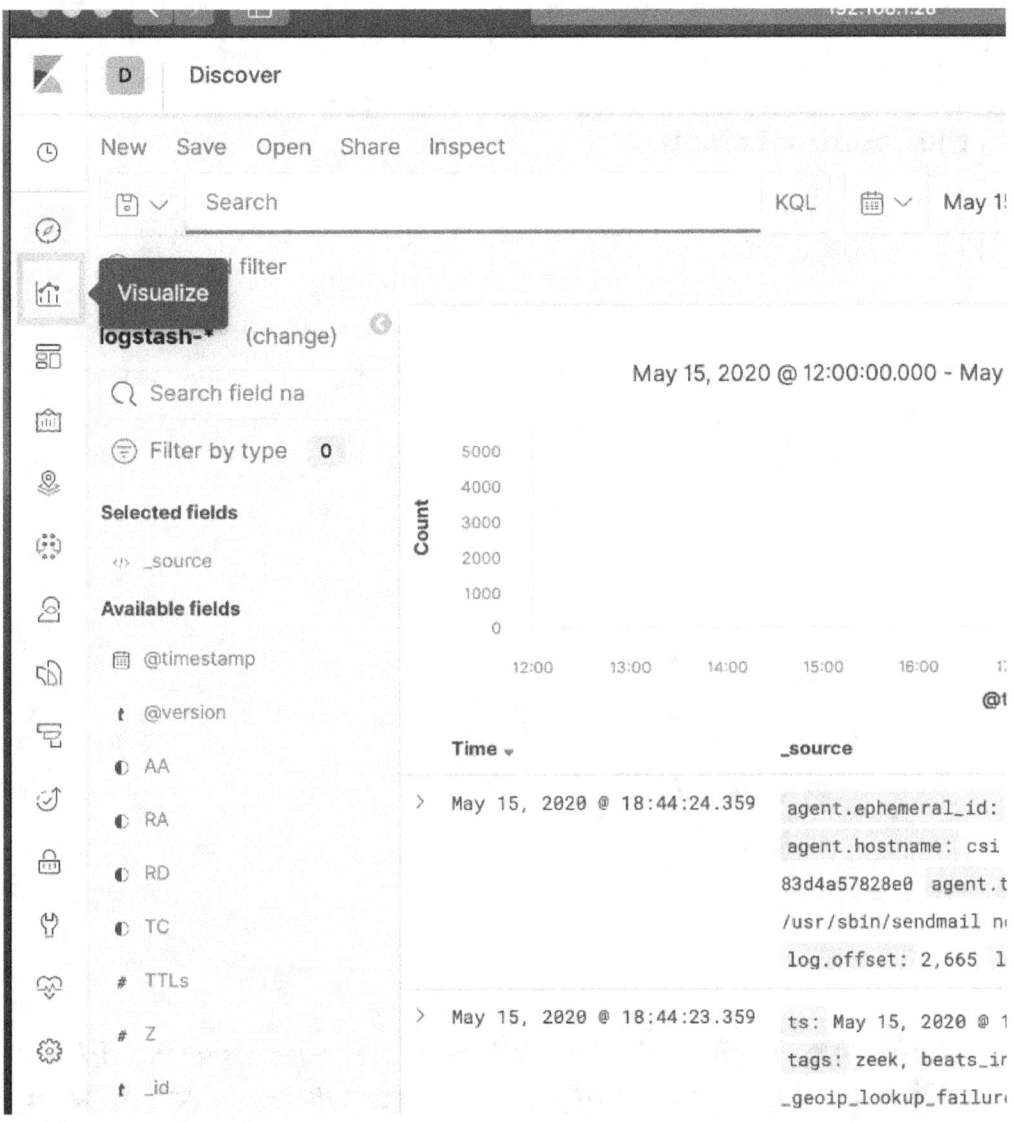

Left Click on **Create Visualization**:

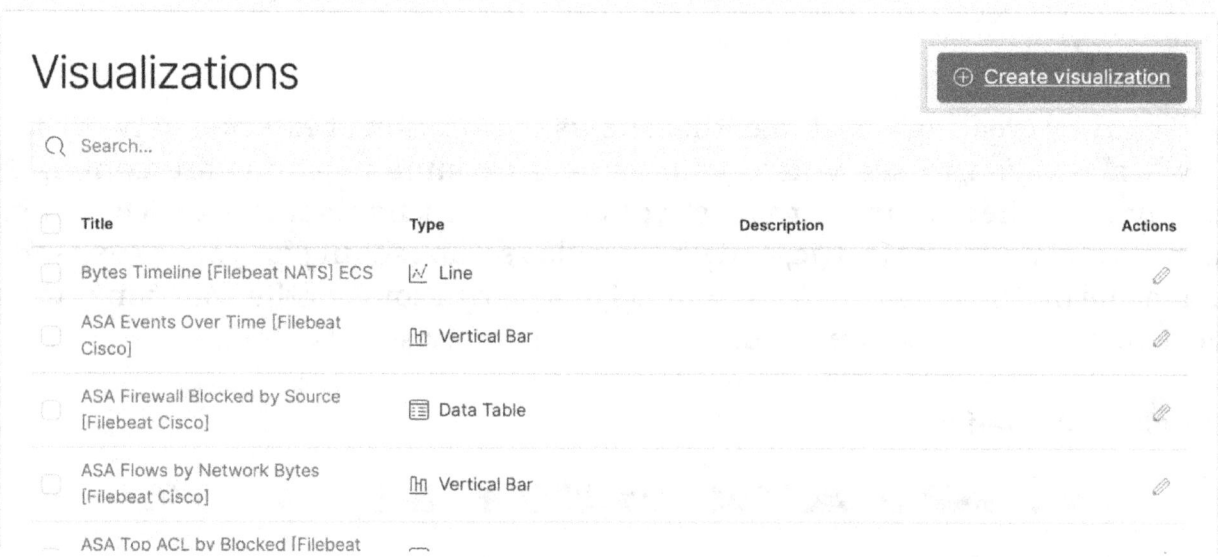

Left Click on the **Coordinate Map** icon:

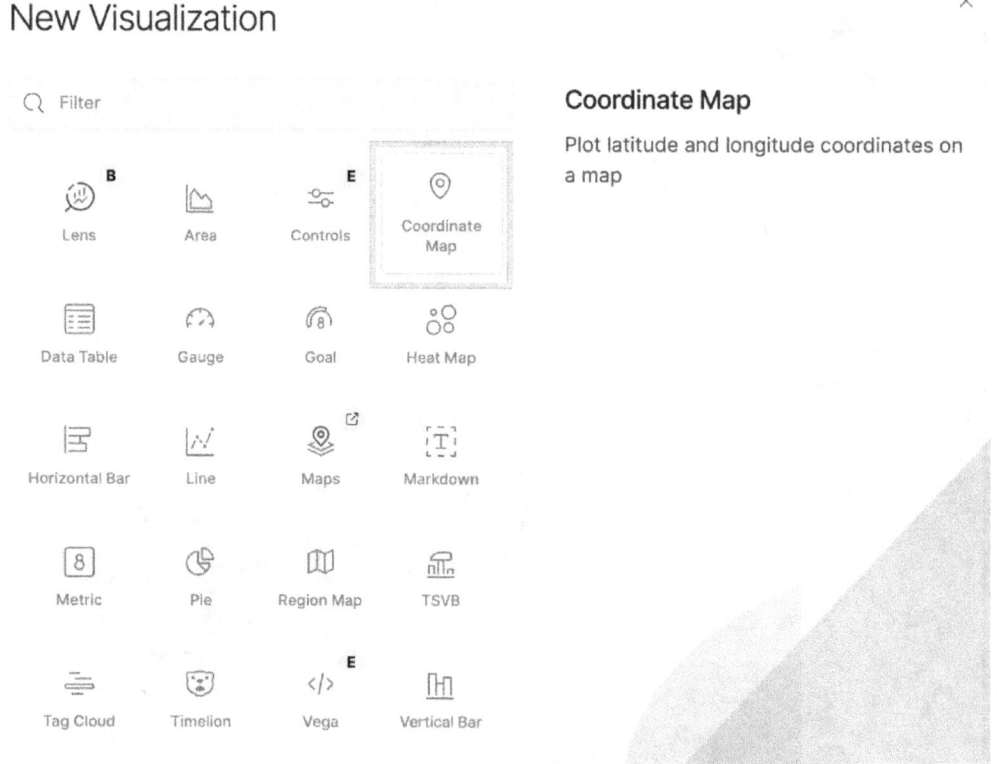

Note: Take a minute to explore the Visualization area and see the different types of panels you can create. There is a lot of flexibility for what you can do with the Kibana visualization dashboard.

Type log - or **logstash** and **Left Click logstash-*:**

Left Click the **+ Add** selection under Buckets and click Geo coordinates:

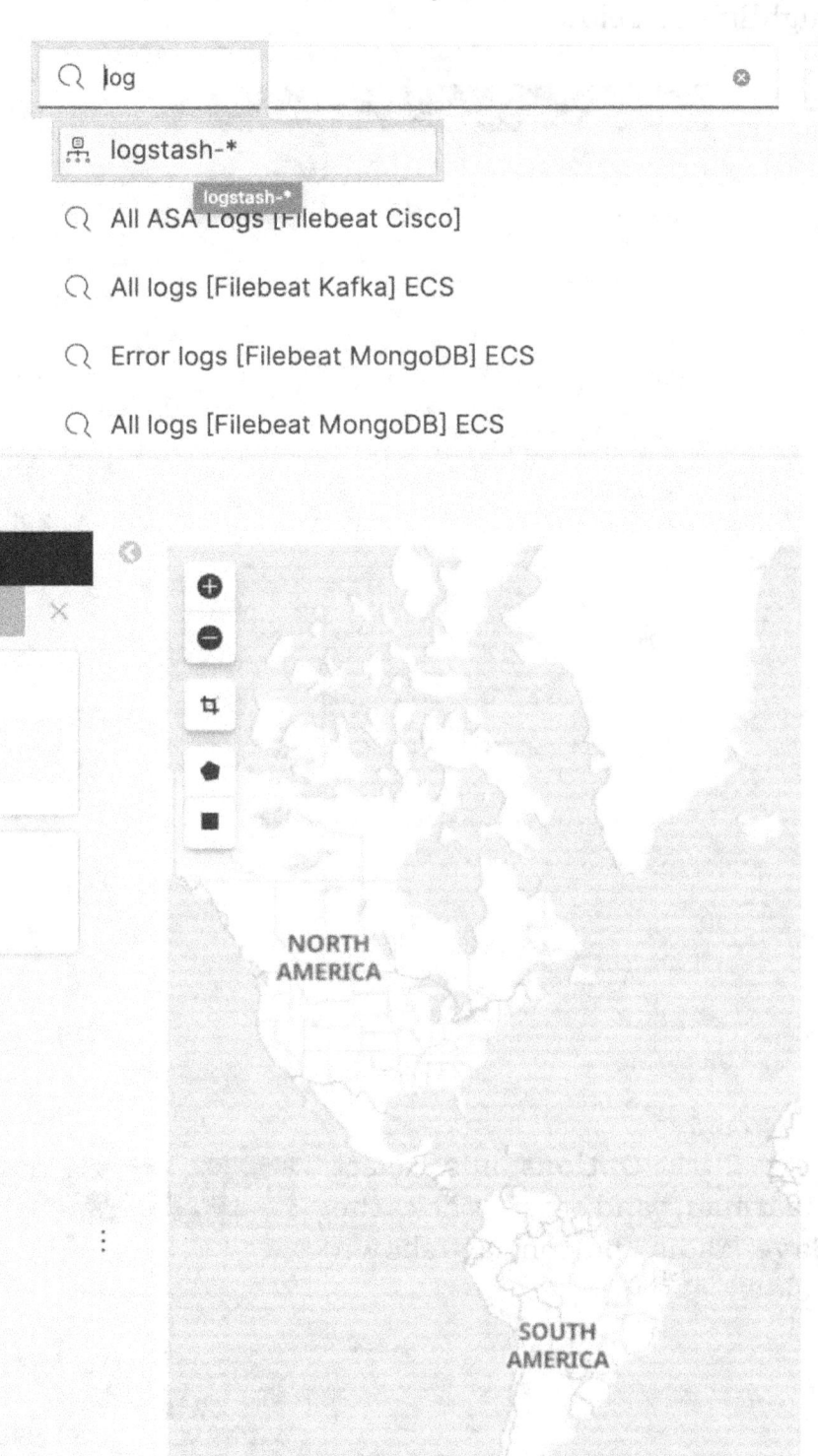

Left Click the Aggregation drop down and **select Geohash** — **Left Click** the **Field** drop down and **Left Click geo.iplocation**, and the **Left Click** the **play** radio button as highlighted below:

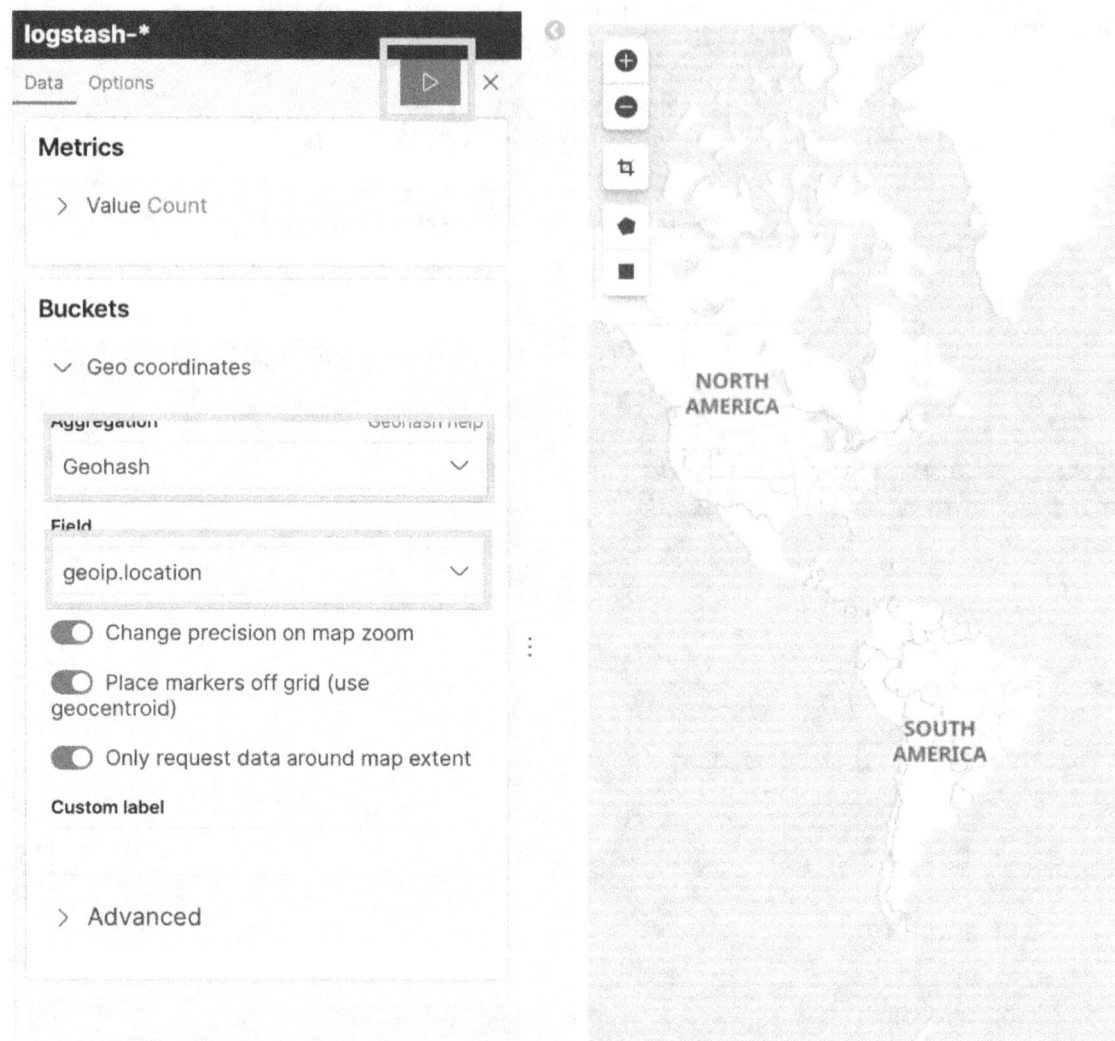

Left Click Options and select **Heatmap**, and then click the **Save** radio button as shown below:

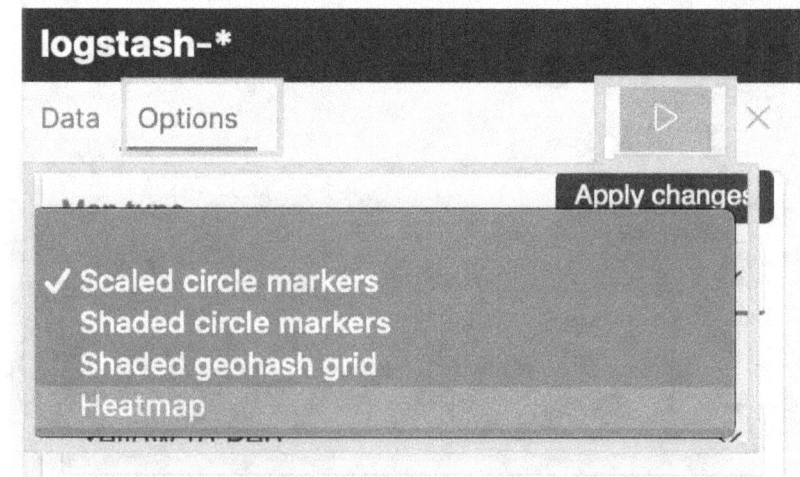

225

> *Note: If you use a WMS Map Server you can have the selected data display over that map, you just need to click the radio button to turn that on and enter you WMS URL, along with the appropriate layers, version, and format. Assign WMS Attribution strings, and then you can use comma separated lists of WMS Server supported styles if you use them, but you can leave that blank as well. Some servers use transparent layers, so you will need to use a png file type for the WMS Format if that is the case, or it will be transparent and won't display very clearly.*

You should now have an output like the following. Remember, you can adjust the cluster size in the options pane if you want to make the heatmap circles larger — it's a preference for how you would like to see the heat map. Next, we need to save the Visualization — I will detail how to do that, and once you do one, you can repeat the same process each time. In the steps after this one, I will just display how to generate the visualization to save space.

Refer back to the following steps to save your visualizations. The rest of these visualizations will give you a great idea of how to make your own custom visualizations. Feel free to play around with different visualizations and create a dashboard that works for you. I will provide the basic dashboard that I found important for my setup.

Saving Visualizations

Left Click Save:

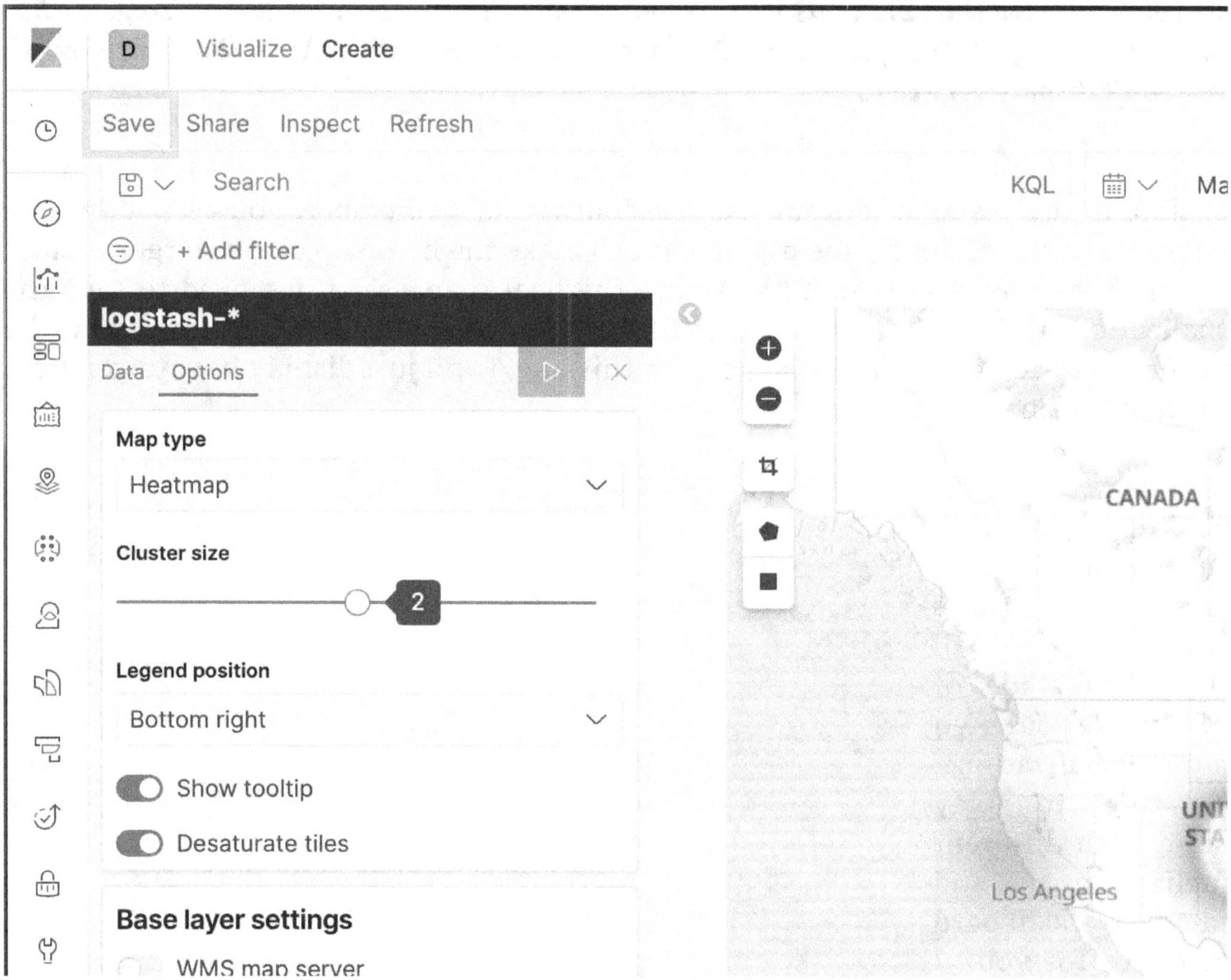

Fill out the **Title** Information that you want to name the Visualization, the **description** and **Left Click Save** in the lower right corner.

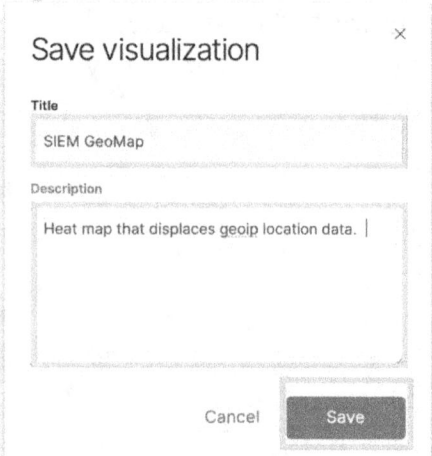

Note: You should get a pop up in the lower right corner of the Kibana page that shows saved and the name of the visualization.

View the Newly Created Visualization

Left Click Visualizations:

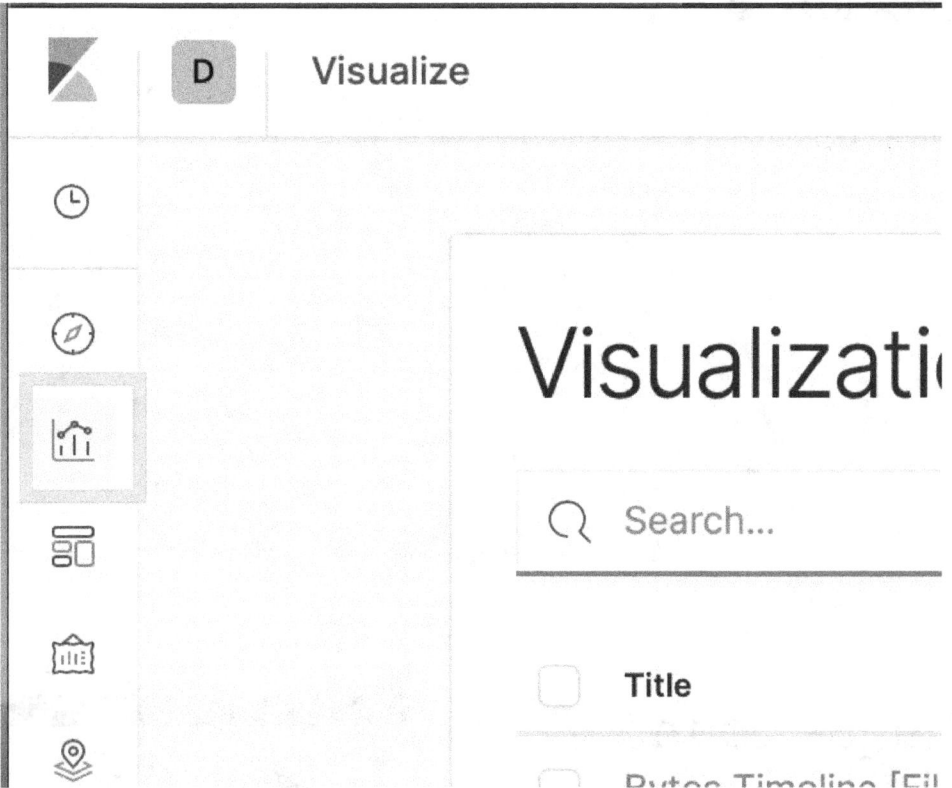

Type the name of the Visualization that you created and **Left Click** it from the list provided:

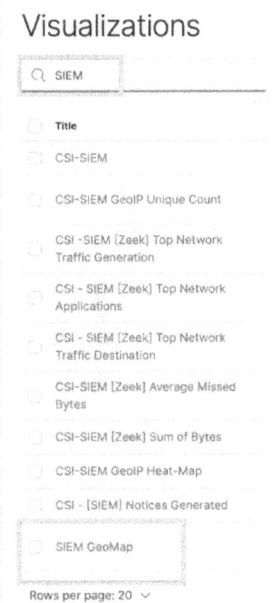

Note: *Once you select the Visualization you will be back at the editing menu for it. This is how you can go back and change your Visualization. We will go over how to do this from your dashboard as well, but you can change any specific Visualization and it be relayed to the dashboard because the dashboard is built off the Visualization itself, so if it's change, the dashboard will reflect too.*

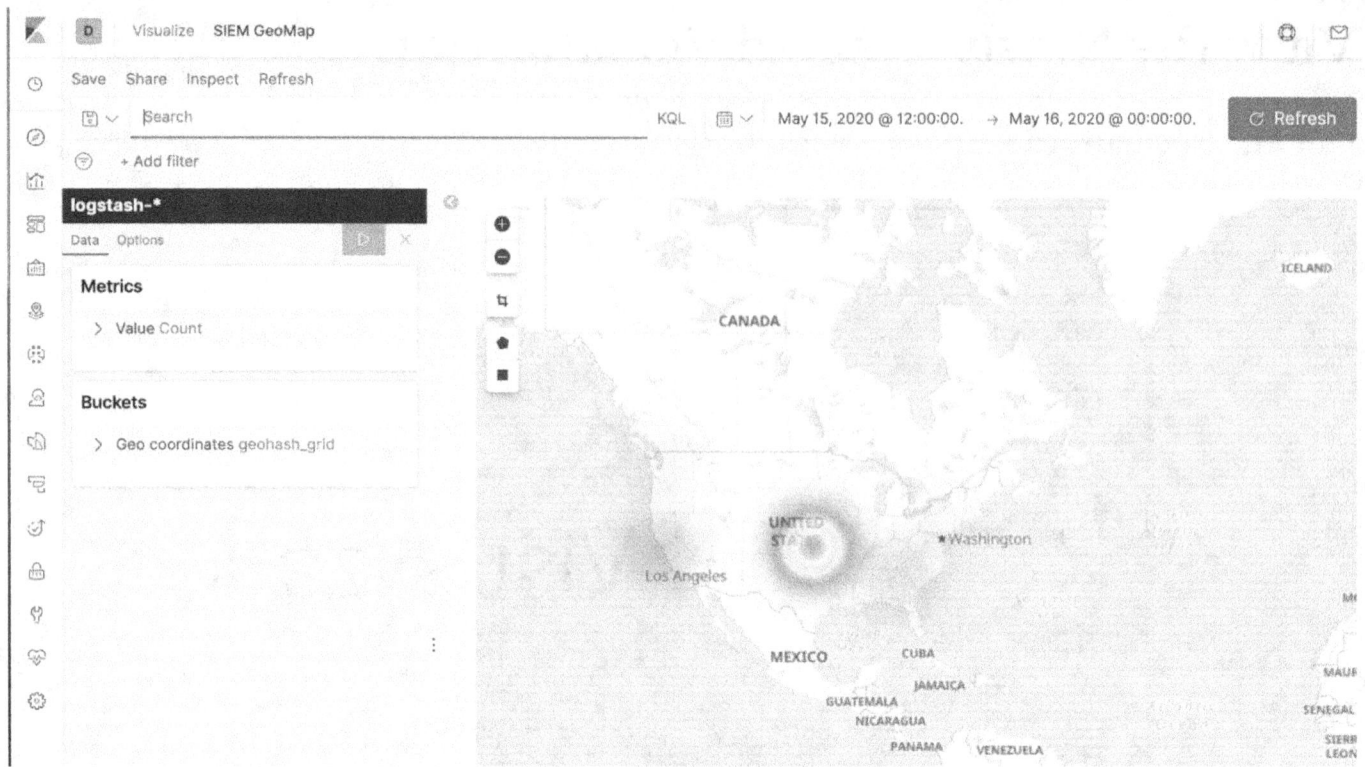

GeoIP Unique Count

This Visualization is going to allow you to show the specific unique counts of network traffic that correlates to your heat map you just created. The heatmap shows the large area of usage, while this will show specific counts based off of a color chart.

Left Click on **Visualize**:

Left Click on **Create Visualization**:

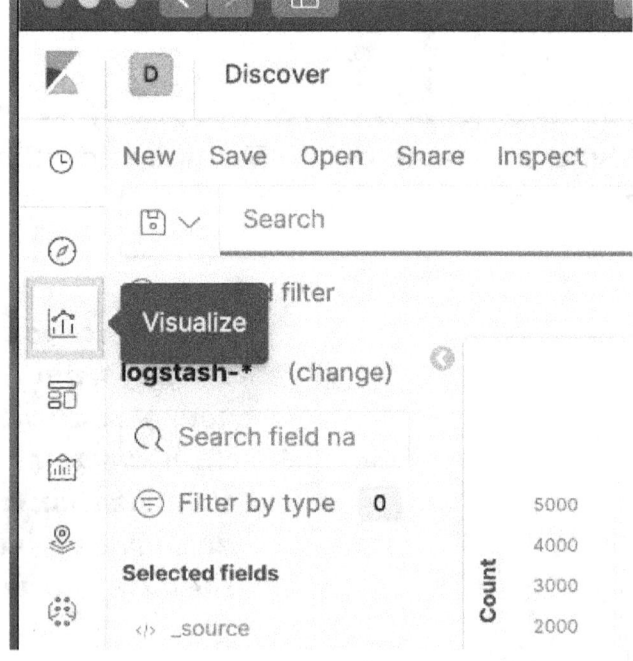

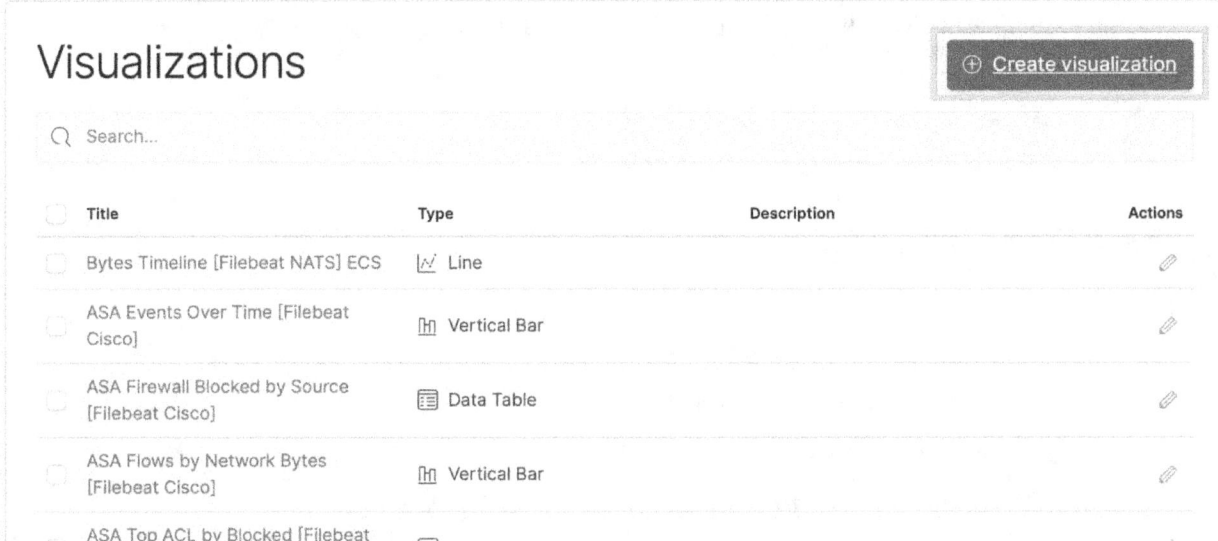

Left Click Coordinate Map:

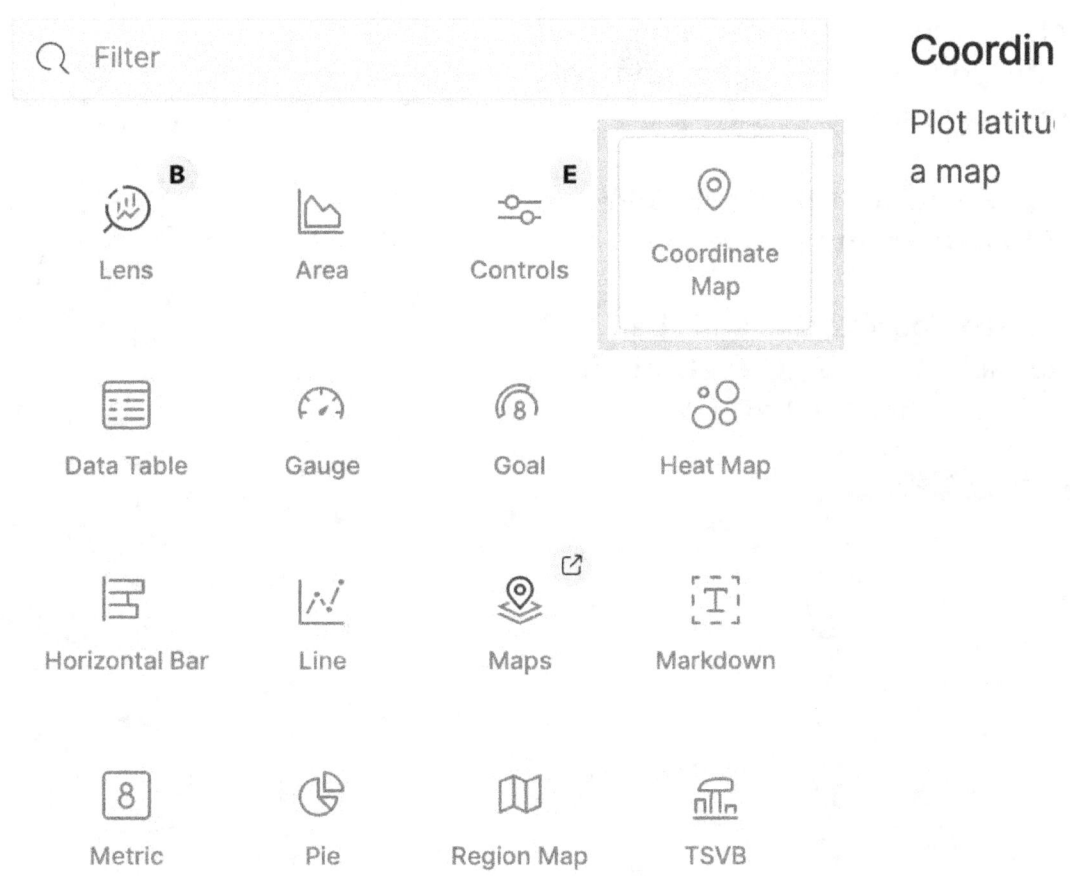

Type log — or logstash and Left Click logstash-*:

New Coordinate Map / Choose a source

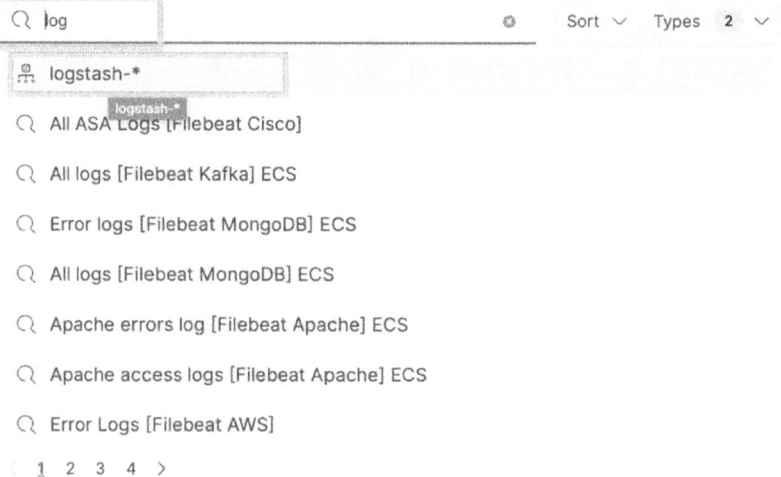

Left Click the Value drop down and **Left Click** the **Aggregation** text box, and scroll down and **Left Click Unique Count**:

Left Click the **Field** drop down, and scroll down until you see **geo_point**, and **Left Click geoip.location**:

In the Buckets pane, **Left Click Add** and the **Left Click Geo coordinates**:

Left Click Geo Coordinates and then **Left Click** the **Select an Aggregation drop down**, and **Left Click Geohash**:

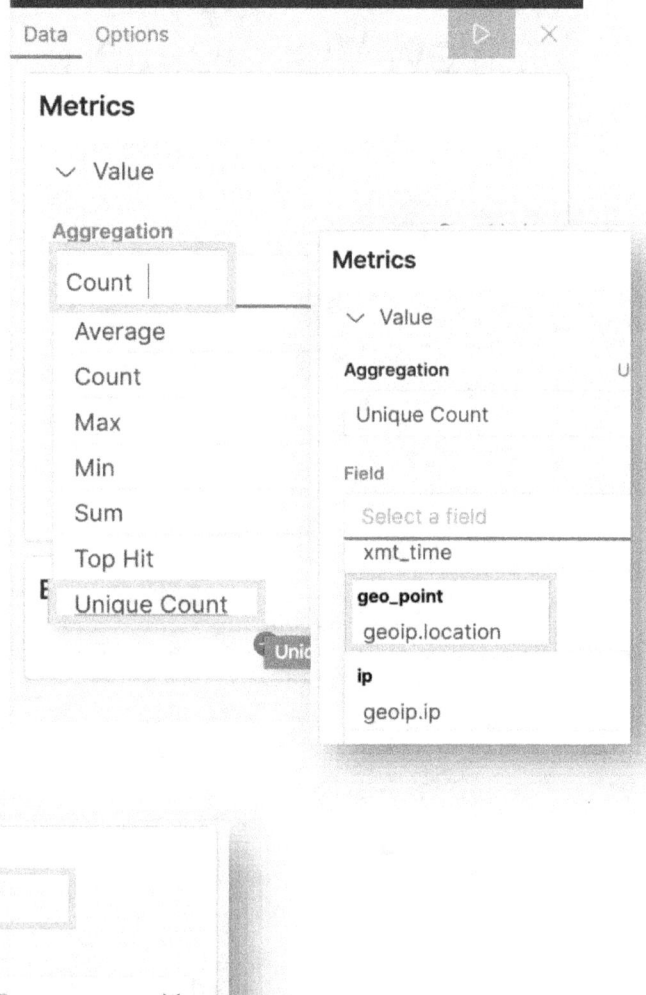

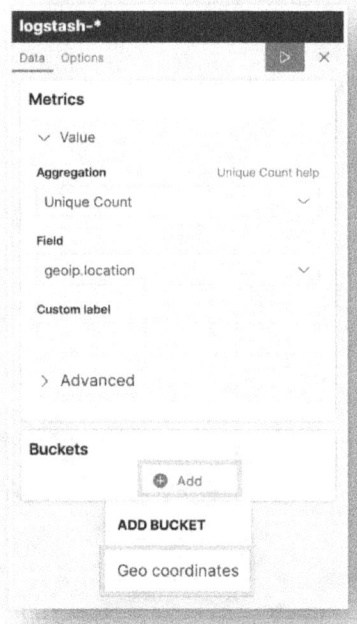

231

Left Click the **Save** radio button just like the last Visualization:

Note: Ensure that geoip.location is selected in the Field drop down just like the heat map we created earlier. Mine was auto populated, but if it isn't just select it.

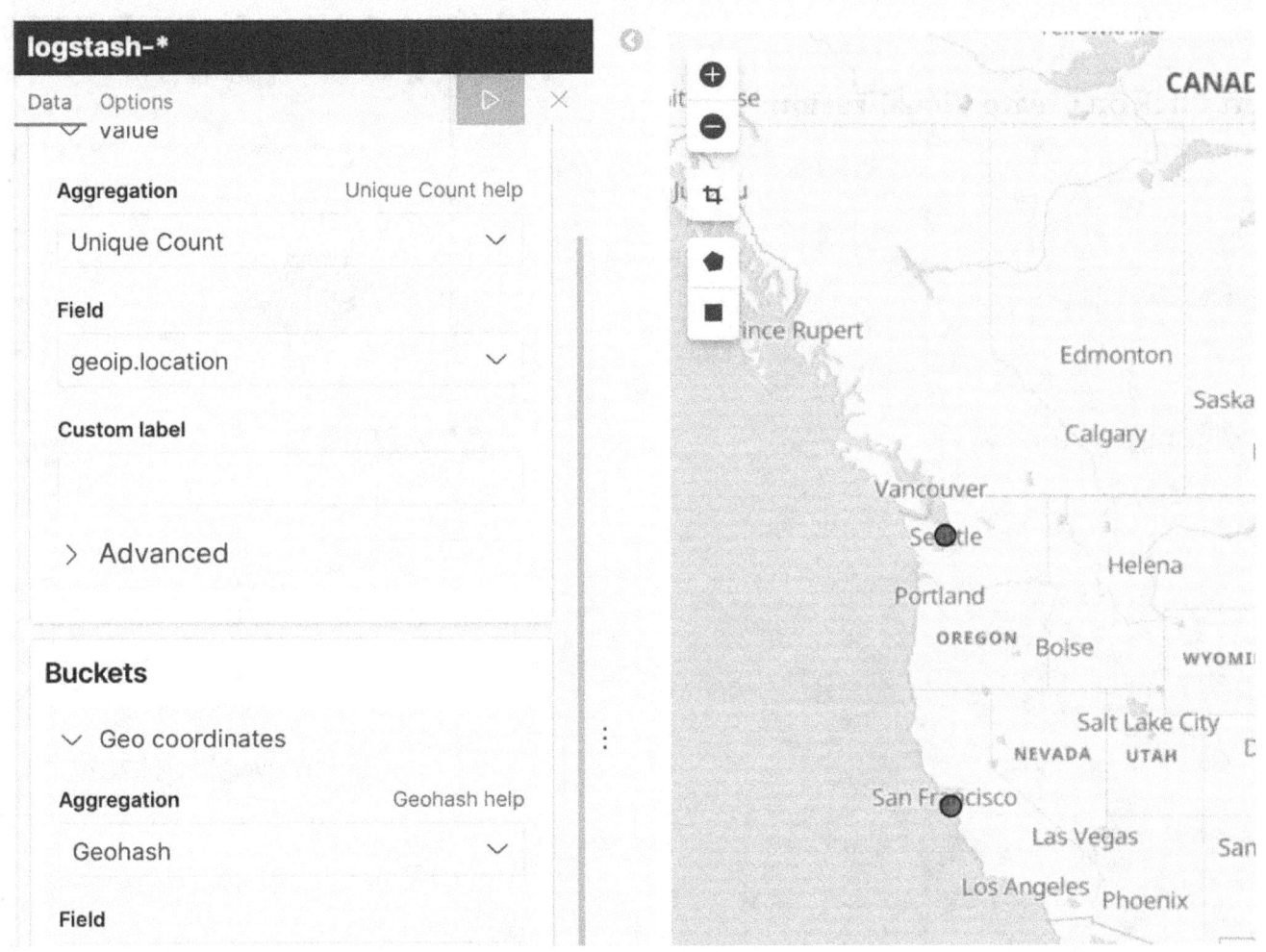

Note: Once you hit play you can see an output of dots similar to the picture above. You can go to options and change the colors if you want, but the default for mine is reds. Once you are finished save this Visualization — I named this Visualization SIEM GeoIP Unique Count — just like the last one and name it something you'll remember.

Top Network Traffic Generation

We are going to create a pie chart that can quickly show you which IP Addresses are generating the most network traffic on the network you are monitoring.

Left Click on **Visualize**:

Left Click on **Create Visualization**:

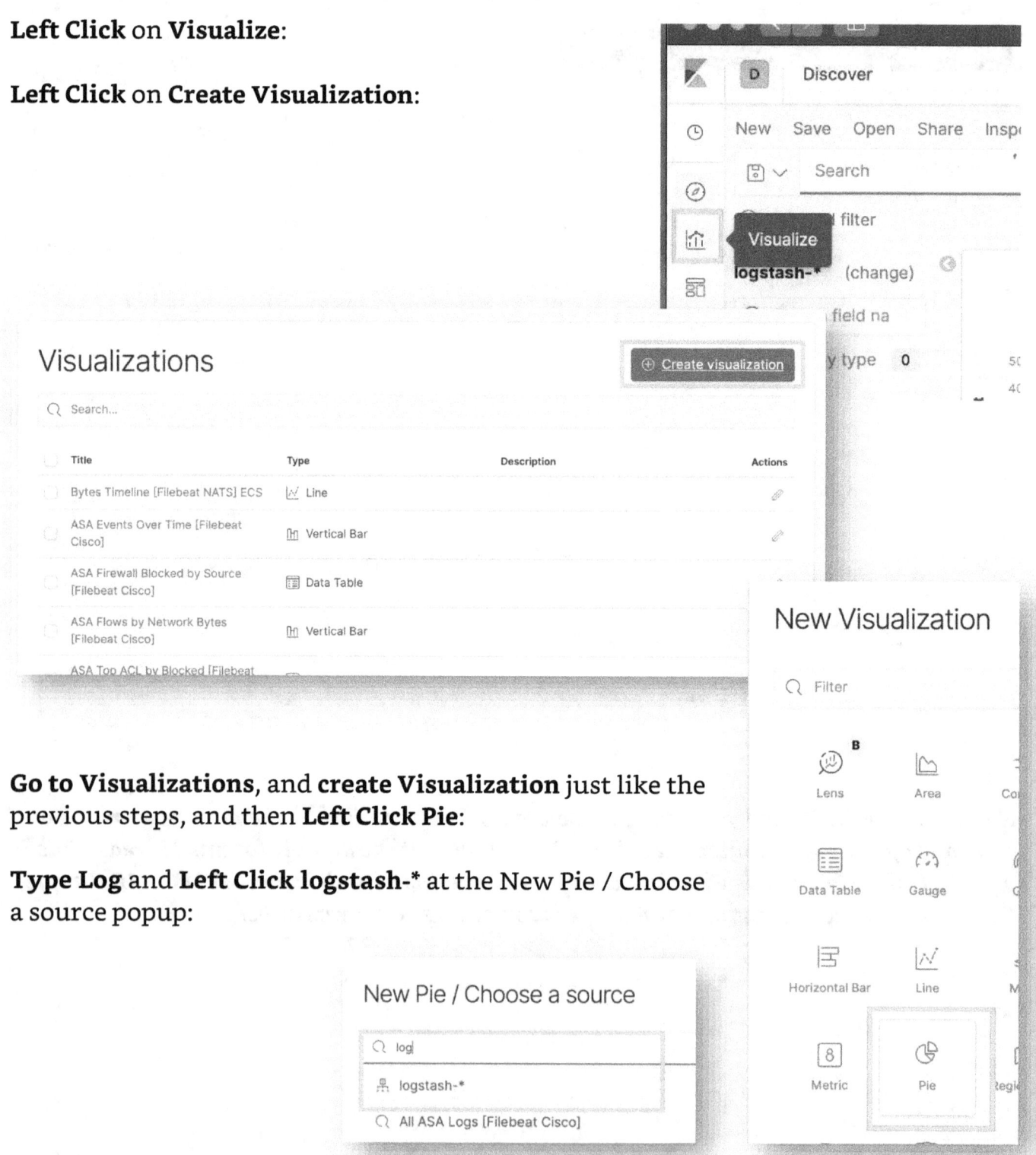

Go to Visualizations, and **create Visualization** just like the previous steps, and then **Left Click Pie**:

Type Log and **Left Click logstash-*** at the New Pie / Choose a source popup:

Left Click + Add — under the Buckets pane —

Left Click Split Slices:

Left click Aggregation

Left Click Significant Terms — once the Field menu pops up —

Left Click id_orig_host.keyword — you may have to scroll down to it — and the **type 10** in under size and press return, or hit the play button for it to update the pie chart with those settings:

Save the **Visualization** the way we saved it in the previous steps — I saved mine as SIEM Top Network Traffic Generation.

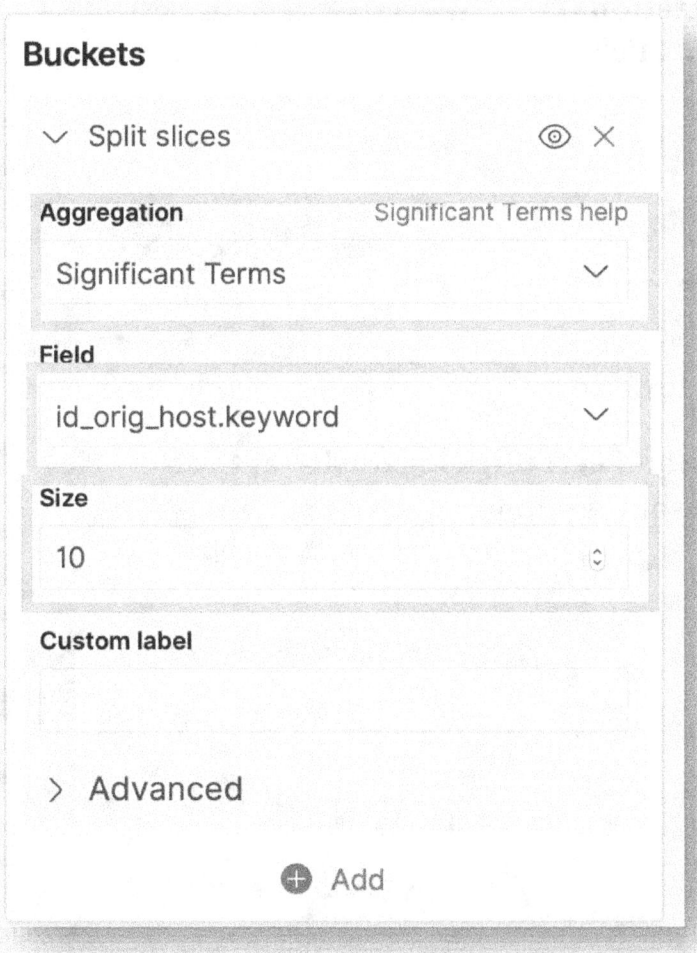

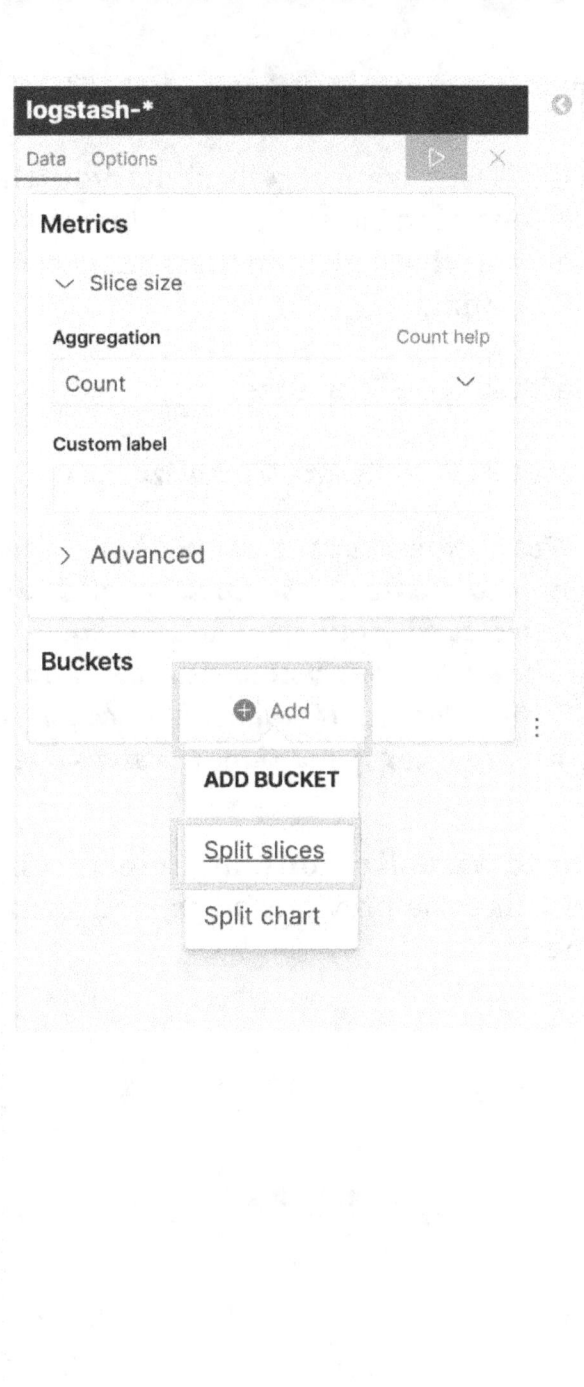

You should see a similar output to the following

Top Network Applications

This Visualization will show you the top network Applications based off the OSI Presentation Layer 6 data that is traversing your network. This Visualization will help you see what kind of data is being sent across the network, and what applications may be running.

Left Click on **Visualize**:

Left Click on **Create Visualization**:

> *Note: Now that you should have a good idea of how to create a Visualization and save it, I will start combining some of the steps, and show what selections you should make to create the Visualization. If you need to see anything new I will slow down and show the steps one at a time.*

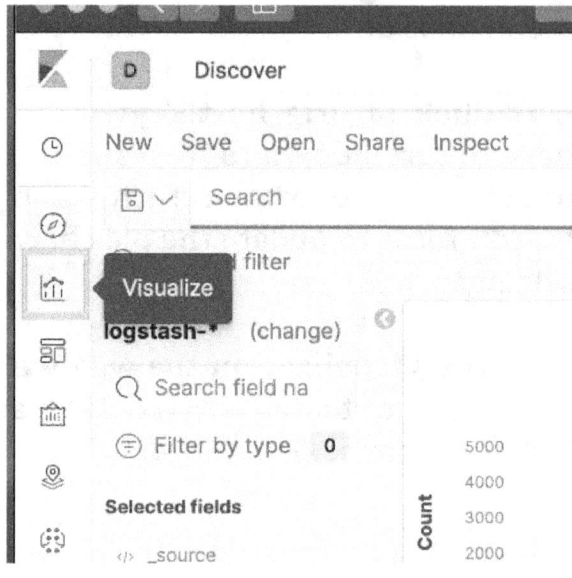

Go to Visualizations, and **create Visualization** just like the previous steps, and then **Left Click Pie**:

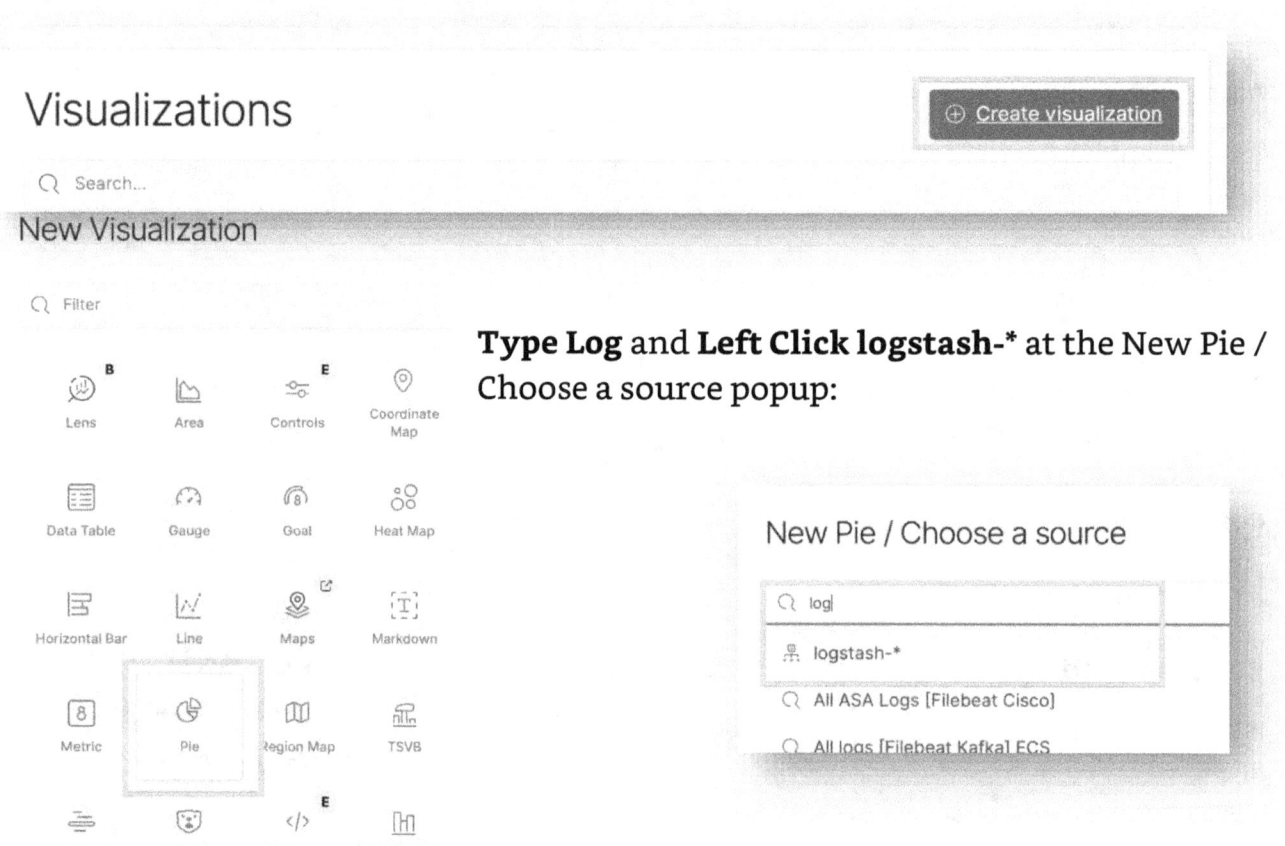

Type Log and **Left Click logstash-*** at the New Pie / Choose a source popup:

Left Click the **+ Add** selection under Buckets

Left Click Split Slices:

Left Click Significant Terms under Aggregation

Left Click service.keyword under **Field**

Type 10 under **Size**

Left Click play or press **Enter / Return**:

Note: At this point you should see something similar to the above picture. I didn't generate that many logs for this example, so I'm only showing http, https, and SSL. The Size of 10 means you will see up to the top 10 presentation or session layer types.

At this point you need to save the Visualization and name it — I named this Visualization as **SIEM Top Network Applications.**

Top Network Traffic Destination

This Visualization is going to show you the top Network Traffic Destinations. This is good for knowing what your big traffic producers are. When combined with the Zeek (Bro) Signature for detected exfiltration, this can come in handy. It's also good to know because you can also tweak some network settings — if needed — to accommodate the large producers on the network for load balancing and overall throughput. You always want to have a good idea of what is generating or receiving the most traffic on the network.

Left Click on **Visualize**:

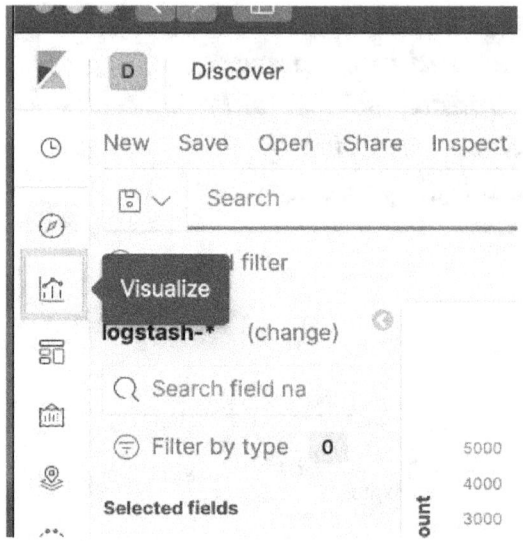

Left Click on **Create Visualization**:

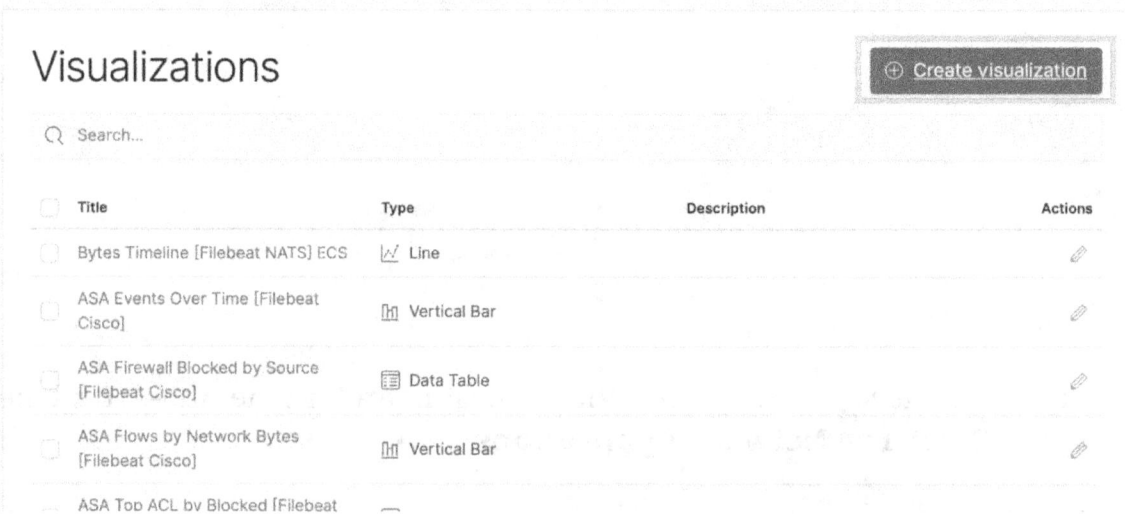

Go to Visualizations and **create Visualization** just like the previous steps.
Left Click Pie:

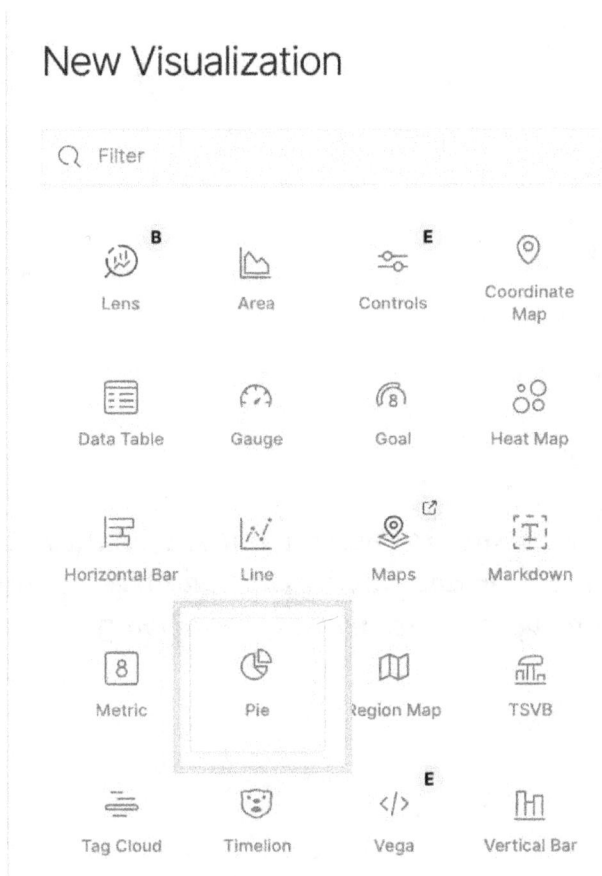
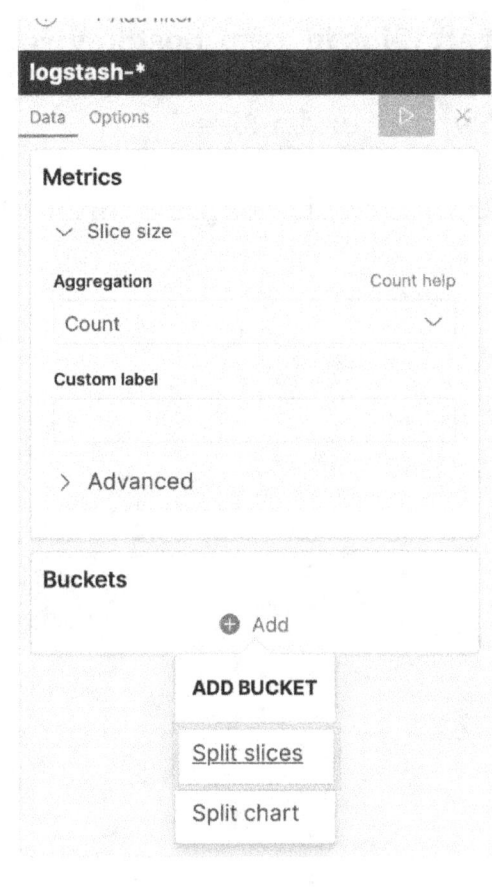

Type Log and **Left Click logstash-*** at the New Pie / Choose a source popup:

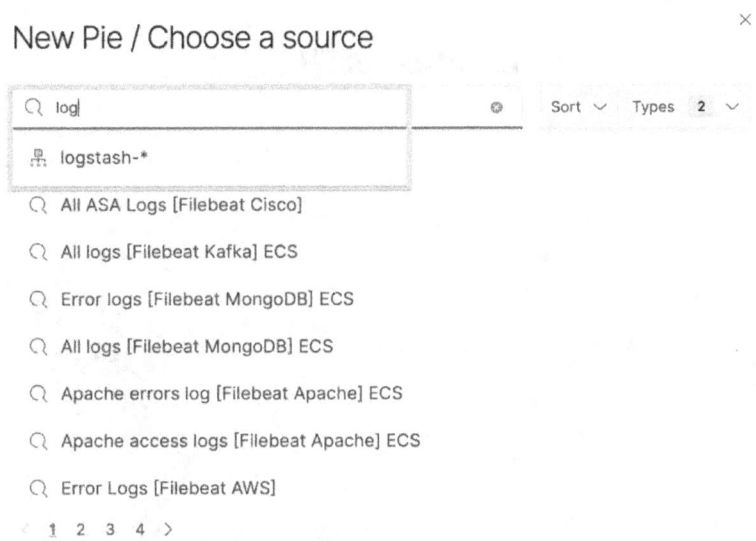

Left Click + Add — under the Buckets pane —

Left Click Split Slices:

Left Click Significant Terms under Aggregation,

Left Click id_resp_host.keyword under **Field**

Type 10 under **Size**

Left Click play or press **Enter / Return**:

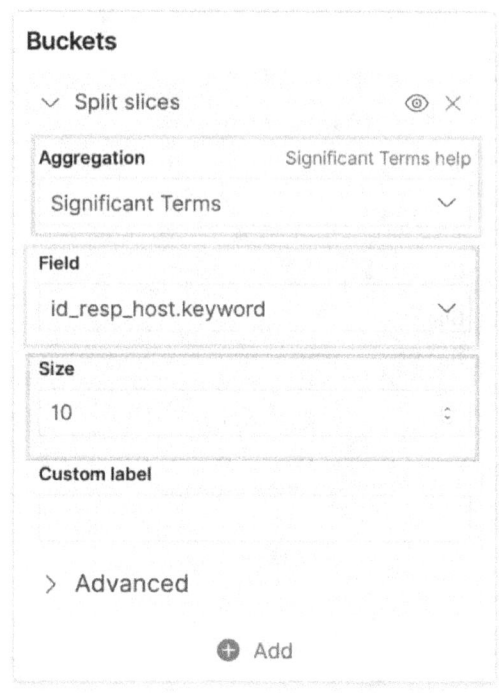

Note: You should see an output similar to the following. I am not placing the IP addresses from the top hand right corner legend, for privacy.

At this point you need to save the Visualization and name it — I named this Visualization as **SIEM Top Network Traffic Destinations.**

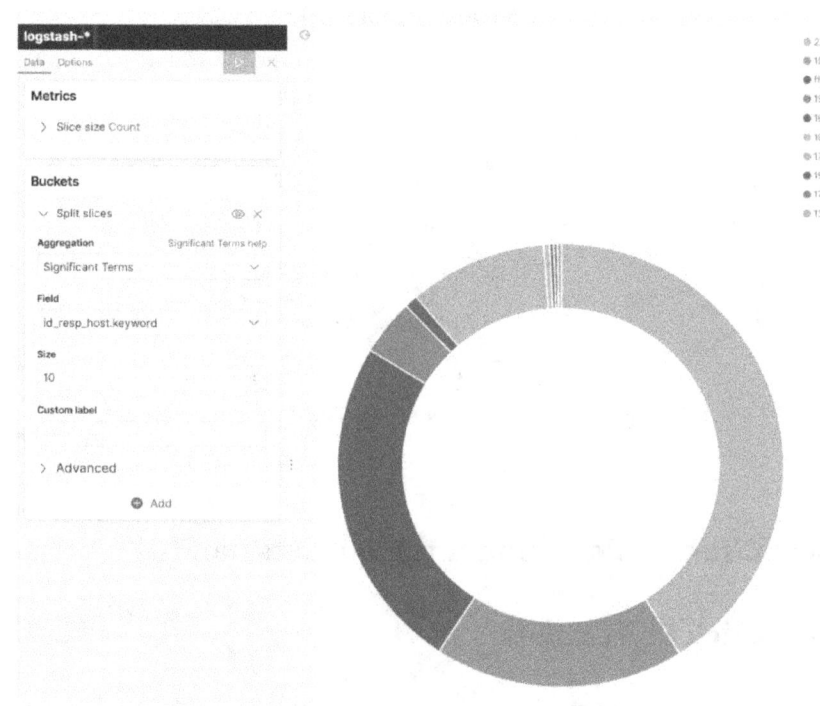

Average Missed Bytes

This Visualization will show you a gauge that uses metrics to determine if your SIEM / IDS is missing any network packets. You do not want there to be a high number here, because that means something is not working right. This will allow you to trouble shoot any issues that could arise and will quickly point out that something is wrong.

Left Click on **Visualize**:

Left Click on **Create Visualization**:

Go to Visualizations, and **create Visualization** just like the previous steps, and then **Left Click Metric**:

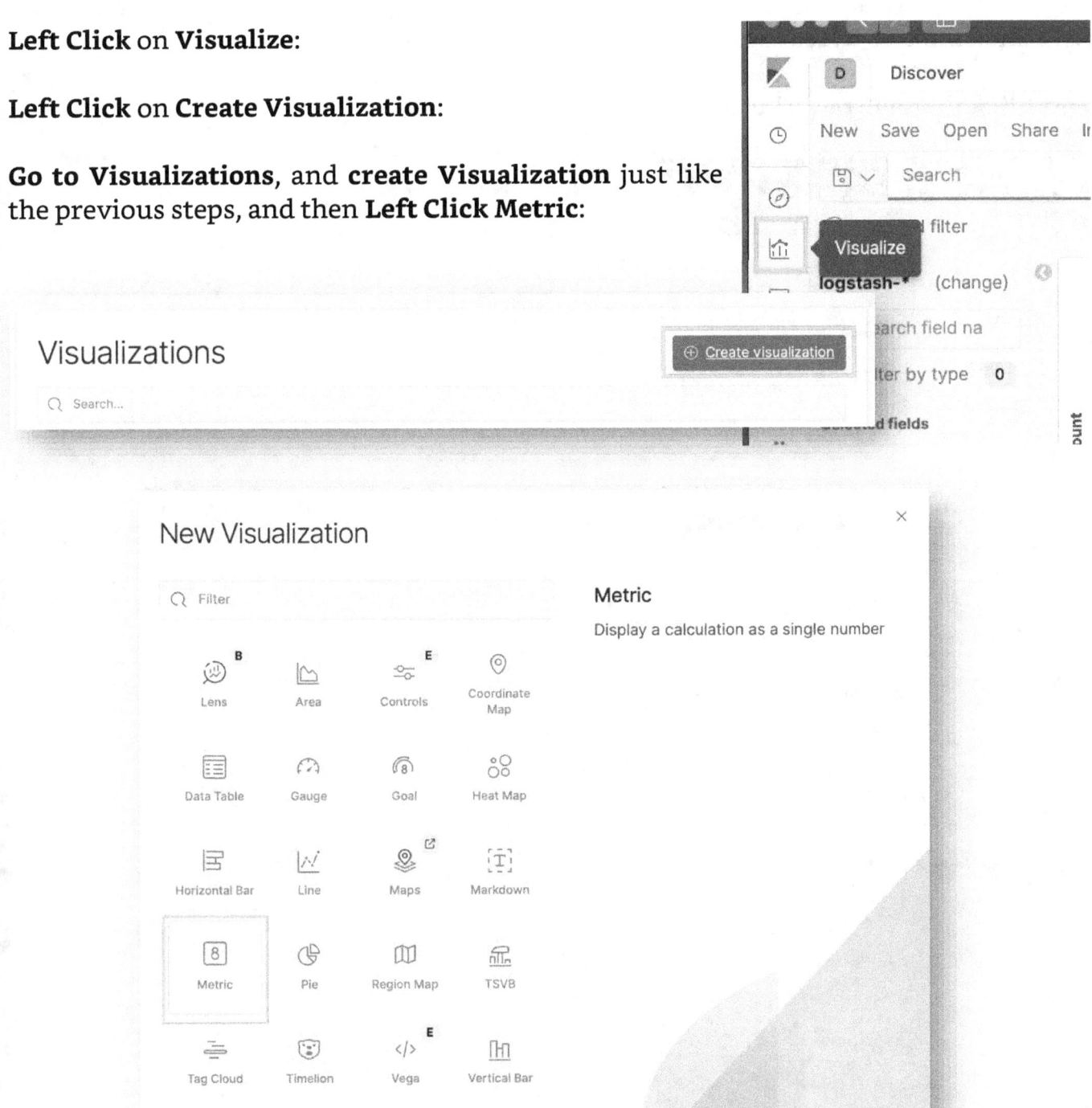

Type Log and **Left Click logstash-*** at the New Metric / Choose a source popup:

Left Click Aggregation drop down

Left Click Average

Left Click Field

Left Click missed_bytes

Left Click the **save** radio button:

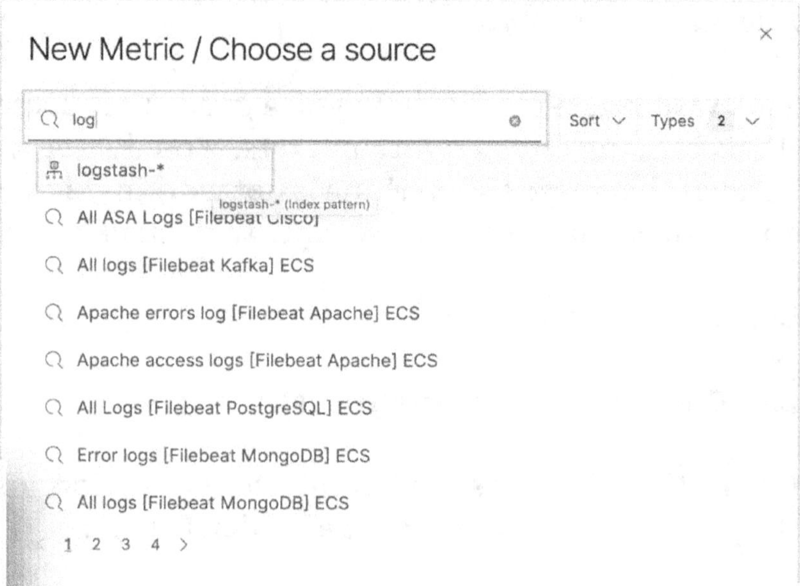

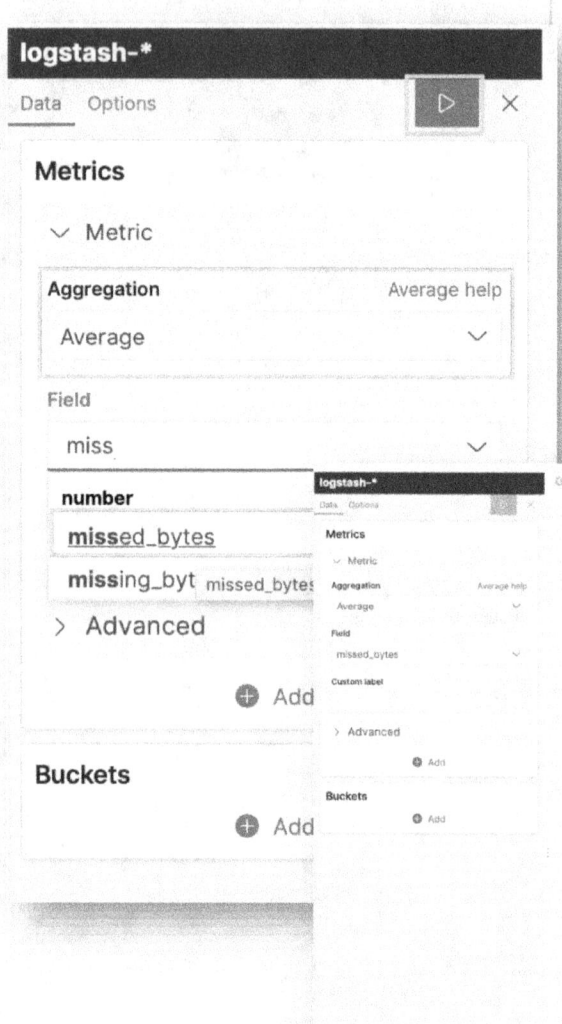

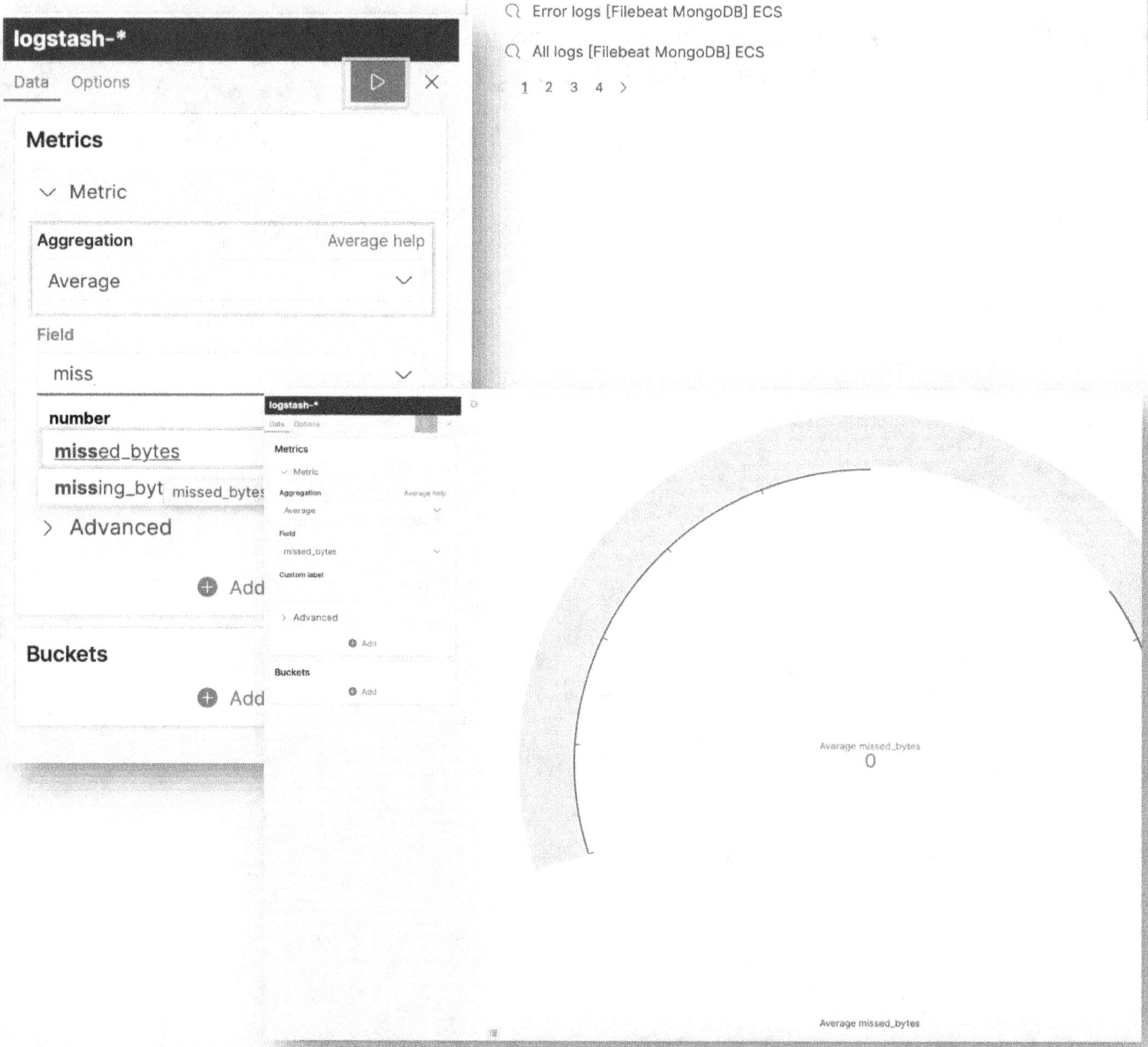

Note: You should see an output similar to the following. Zero missed bytes is a good thing, and I tested this out by making some tweaks with Zeek (Bro), and the SIEM will pick up if anything is missing.

241

Sum of Bytes

This Visualization will show you the total Sum of Bytes captured on the network. It's important to quickly see that your SIEM is working and capturing traffic, and this metric allows you to do just that.

Left Click on **Visualize**:

Left Click on **Create Visualization**:

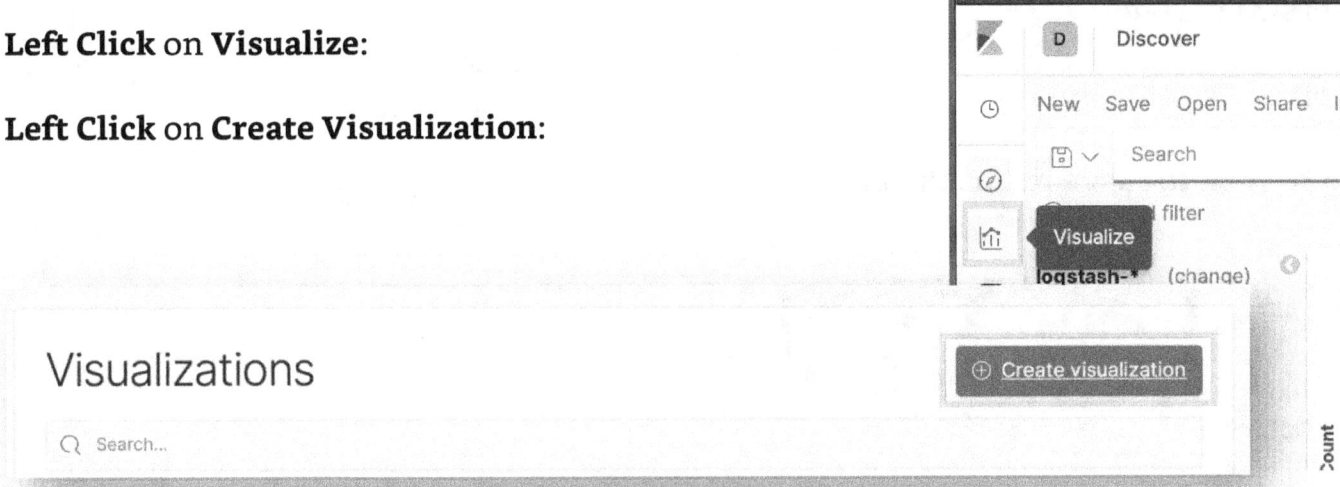

Go to Visualizations and **create Visualization** just like the previous steps.

Left Click Metric:

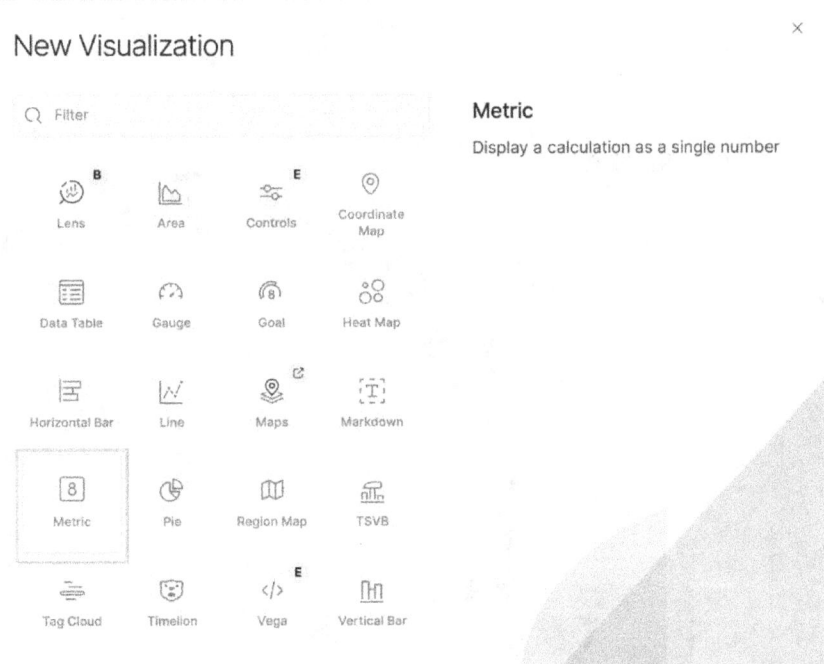

Type Log and **Left Click logstash-*** at the New Metric / Choose a source popup:

Left Click Aggregation drop down.

Left Click Sum

Left Click Field

Left Click total_bytes

Left Click the **save** radio button:

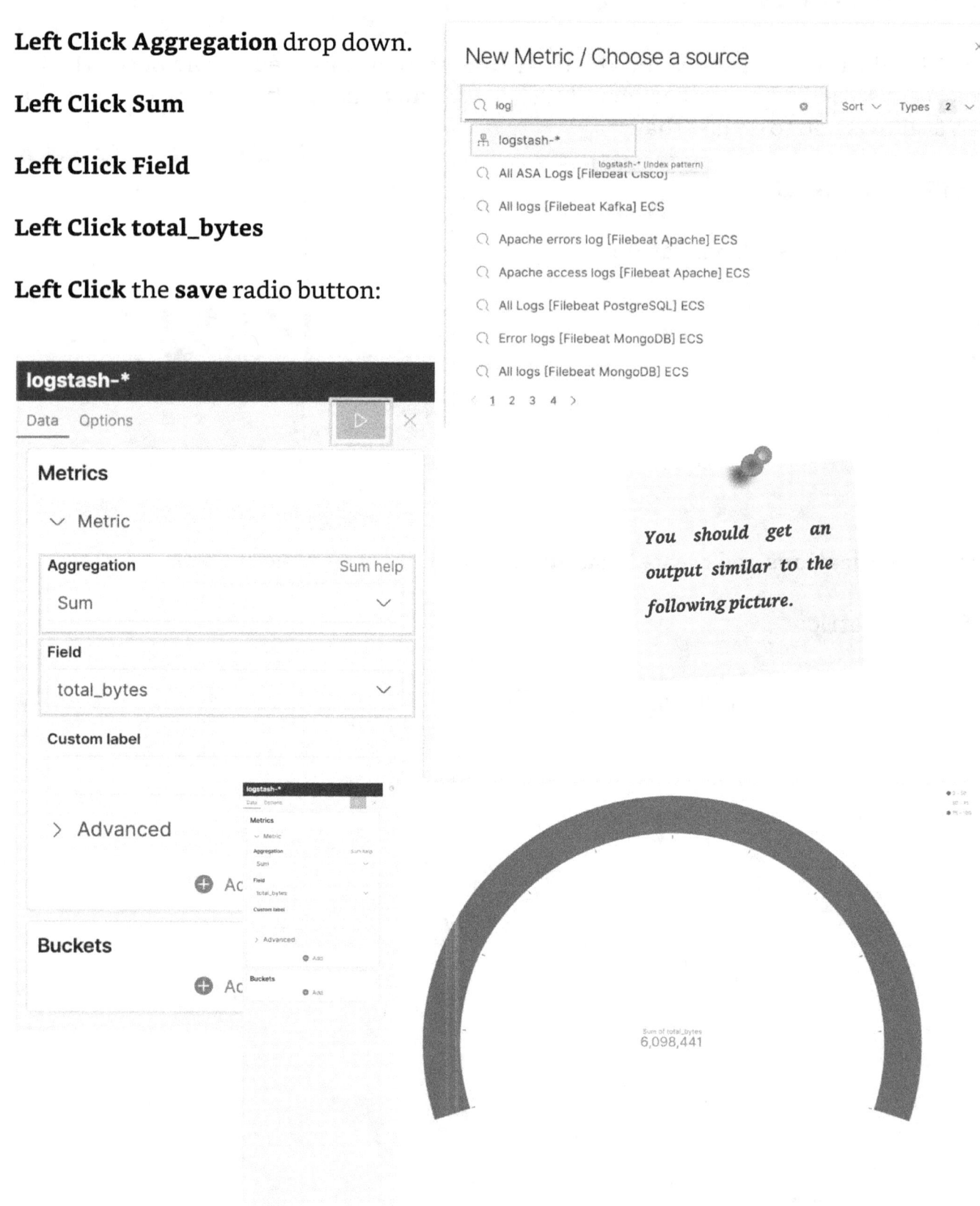

You should get an output similar to the following picture.

Notices Generated

This Visualization is one of the most important ones you will have — notices generated by Zeek(Bro). This is a quick way to show you how many notices have occurred. These notices are generated by Zeek (Bro) when it detects an anomaly on the network — signatures are used to generate the notices and you can use many different kinds of signatures for whatever reason you choose.

Left Click on **Visualize**:

Left Click on **Create Visualization**:

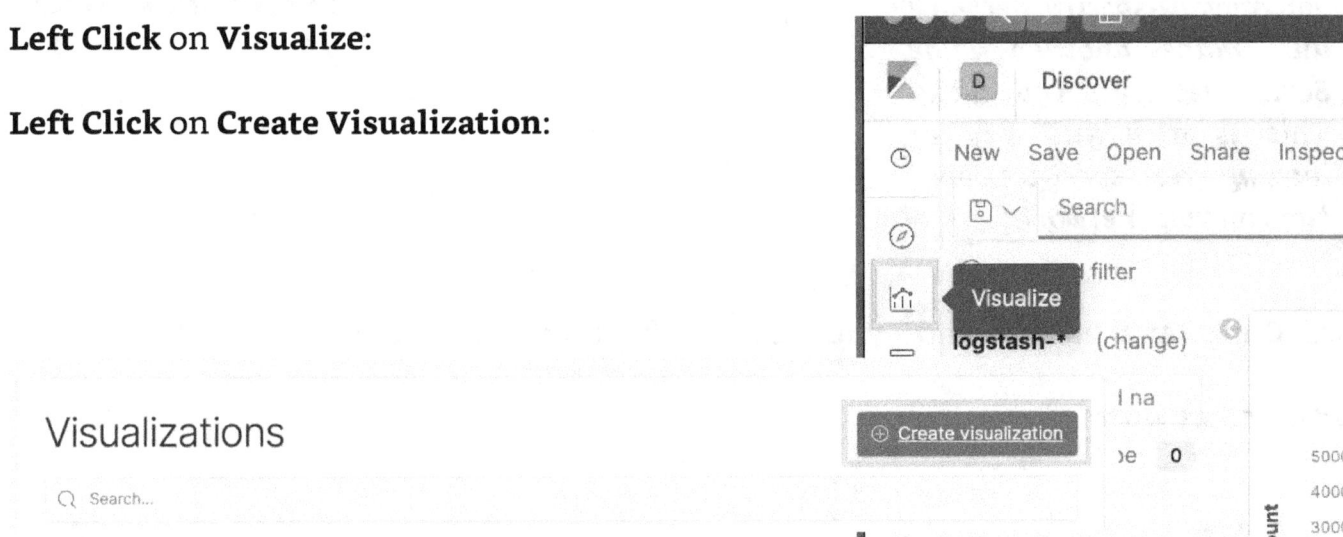

Go to Visualizations and **create Visualization** just like the previous steps.

Left Click TSVB:

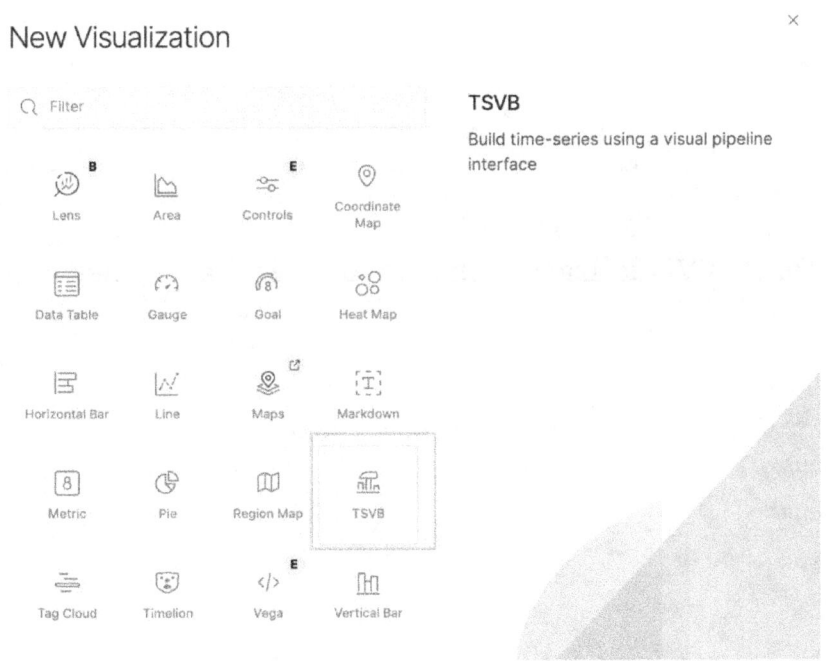

Left Click the Color Box that is green and make it a color you want to stand out - I chose red:

Left Click Label and type **Notices**:

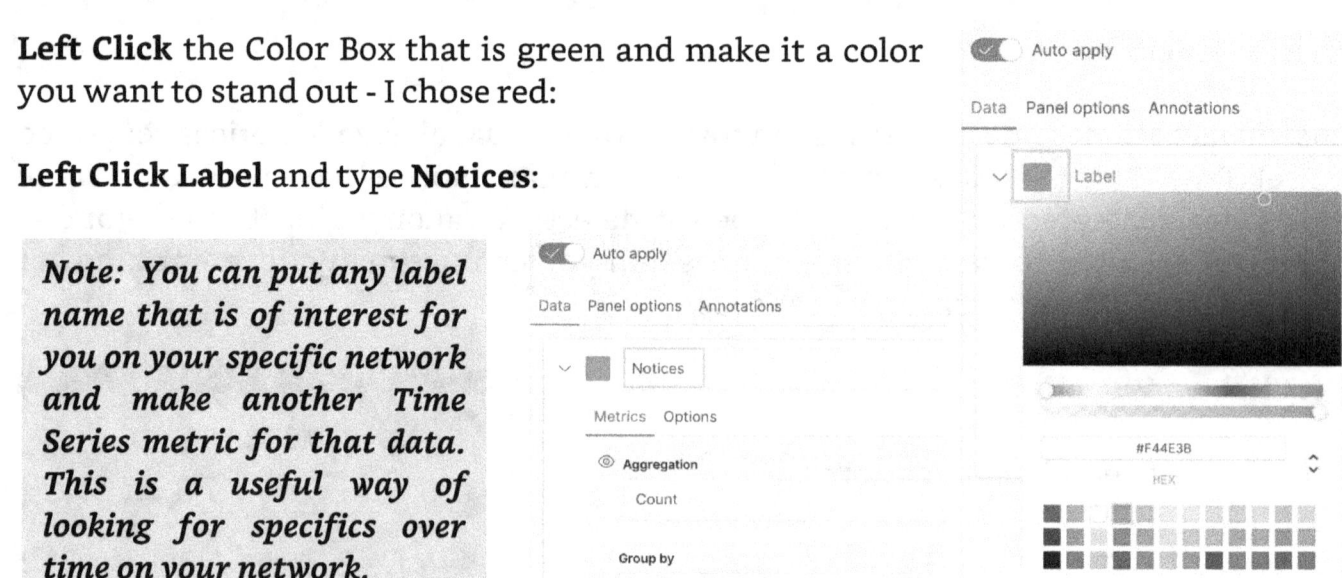

Note: You can put any label name that is of interest for you on your specific network and make another Time Series metric for that data. This is a useful way of looking for specifics over time on your network.

Left Click Panel options and **Type** the following under **Panel filter**:

actions.keyword :*

The final output for this Visualization should look similar to the following:

Mouse over on the data points to see the count of notices at any particular time you highlight.

245

Building the Dashboard

The Dashboard is an important tool for looking at information in your SIEM. It is essentially the view of your SIEM and built off of Visualizations. You can build this however you want, and you can use any visualization you choose. In the following steps I'm going to show you how to create your own dashboard. I had previously setup a dashboard for CSI Linux, so I will be using the Visualizations from that just to make it easy, and show what CSI Linux has available — it's a great digital forensic tool, and can be located at csilinux.com.

Left Click the **Dashboard** icon:

Left Click Create Dashboard:

Left Click Add:

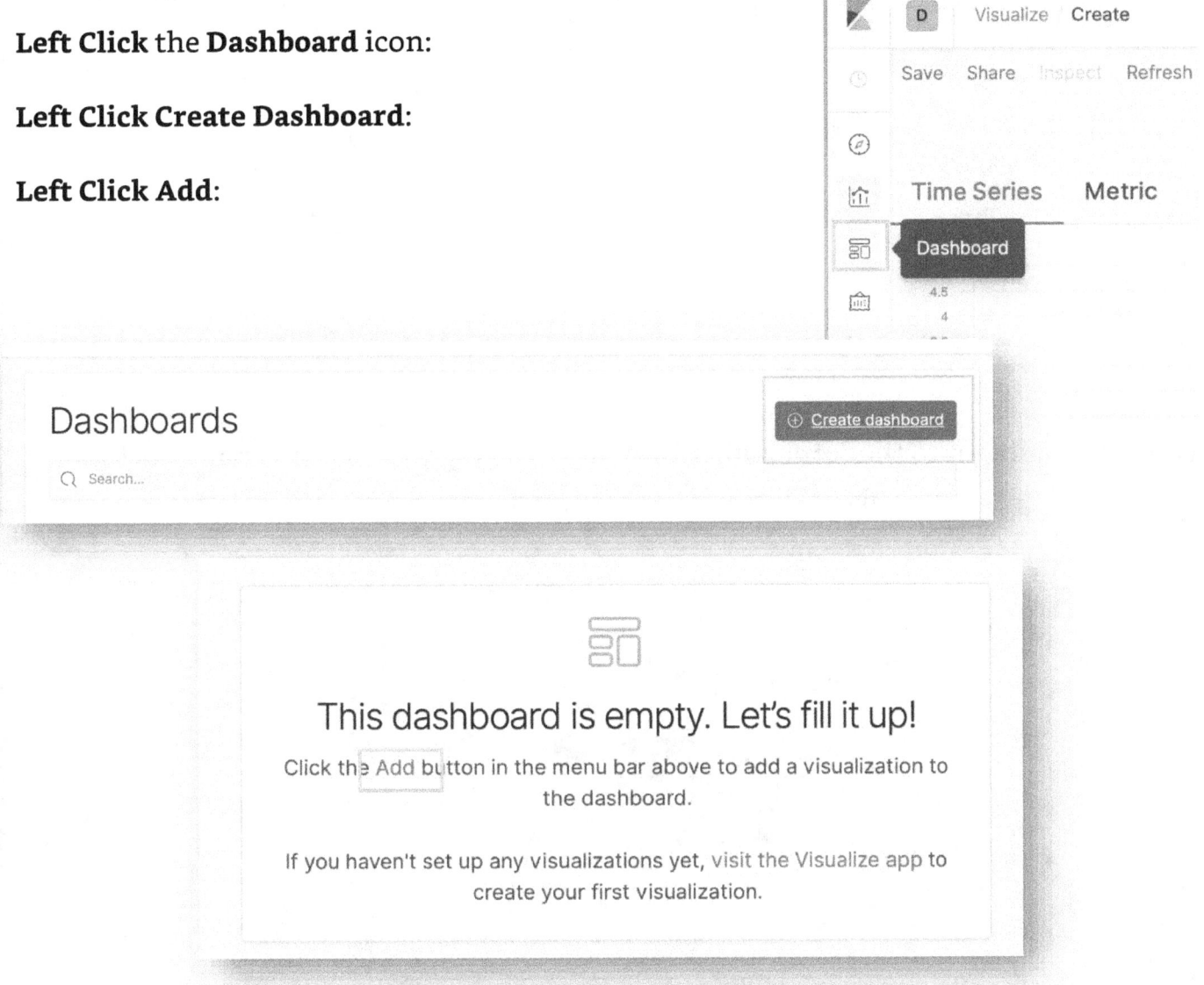

Note: You will get an output similar to the following. In order to move the panes around just click the top portion in the area where I highlighted, and you can also drag the dotted edges and re-size the panes. You can arrange this area any way you like, play around with it and see how you want it. You can click add up top and add more panes too.

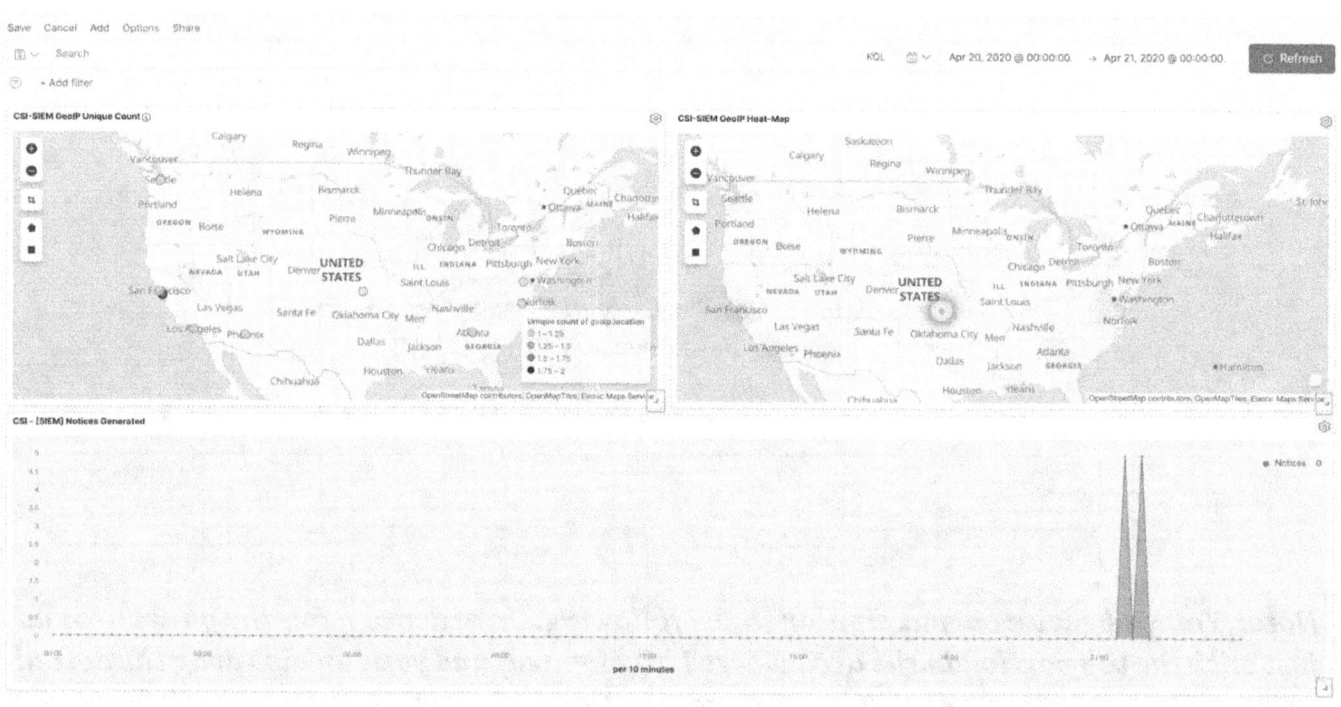

I added a highlight to the corner where you need to drag to re-size the panes as follows:

Now your dashboard is complete, we need to save the dashboard.

Saving the Dashboard

Left Click Save:

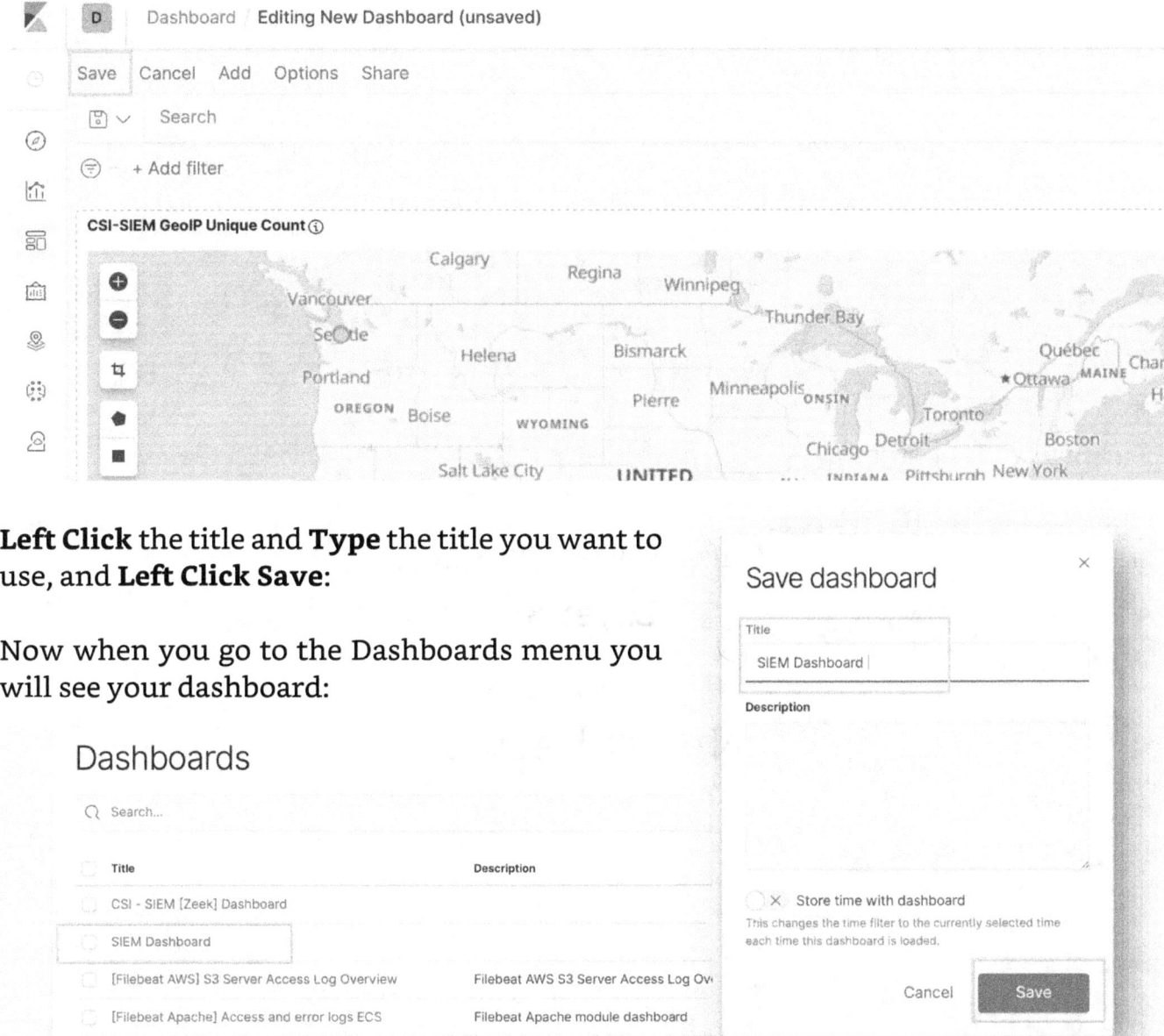

Left Click the title and **Type** the title you want to use, and **Left Click Save**:

Now when you go to the Dashboards menu you will see your dashboard:

That concludes the entire ELK Stack SIEM process. We learned how to set up Zeek (Bro), PF_Ring, ElasticSearch, Logstash, Filebeat, Kibana, and create a SIEM Dashboard. I challenge you to continue to create and modify your ELK Stack and use it to the best of your ability.

AWS Phishing
Layer 8

By
Nitin Sharma

Introduction

At the source of every error which is blamed on the computer, you will find at least two human errors, one of which is the error of blaming it on the computer.
- Tom Gilb

Cybersecurity is evolving at a rapid pace and so is the pace of Threat Landscape today. Sophisticated cyber-attacks are capable of bringing down enormous business empires. Staying resilient, responding intelligently and recovering quickly are the major aspects organizations are looking in cybersecurity enthusiasts. However, there is no change in human nature.

Photo by Chris Yang on Unsplash

All the technologies and inventions till date are considered as a boon for mankind. Instead of acting as enablers or force multipliers, these could go wrong with simple human error. Even the smartest ever solutions, need human intervention for successful operation thus becoming highly prone to human errors. Manipulation of human behavior creating new normal, to make them to believe in something, is psychologically possible too. One can say, people are an organization's most valuable asset, but they can also be its greatest vulnerability.

With all such scenarios keeping in mind, some additional layers to OSI model have been defined and adopted informally.

Extended OSI Model

Bruce Schneier and the company RSA Security LLC invented the concept of layers above the OSI layer. [1]

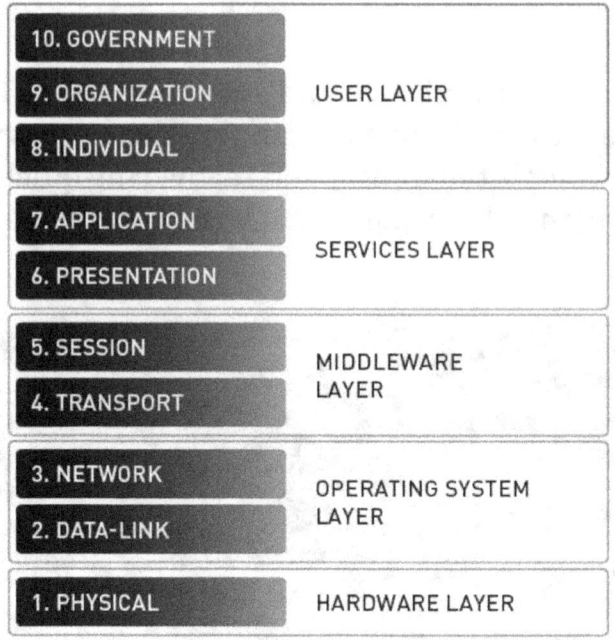

Extended OSI Model

As far as we have discussed about the 7-layer abstract model which describes an architecture of data communications for networked computers, the concern remains solely from technical perspective. To induce the feel of human intervention, these three layers were added [2],

1. **Layer 8 (Individual/Human Layer)** covers the realm for human interactions where people deal with technology interfaces. This is where we engineer solutions and architectures which allow for the human factors, psychology, and sociology. E.g. DLP (Data Loss Prevention Solution).
2. **Layer 9 (Organization Layer)** covers the modularity aspect of people involved in business who work in a collective fashion to deal with technical aspects. Organizations are complex entities, and few people indeed have a handle on just how complex they are. As they get larger, organizational complexity increases exponentially against linear organization growth, because the number of linkages, data flows and relationships exponentially multiply. Example includes eGRC (Governance, Risk and Compliance) solutions like RSA Archer.
3. **Layer 10 (Legal and Compliance Layer)** covers the legal aspect of human involvement which encompasses technology layers with a set of compliance rules to be met. This is where an organization – government or non-government – specifies requirements which the organization must comply with. Often there are penalties for non-compliance, and sometimes those penalties drive controls right down the stack.

The primary concern for adding these layers is to bring user-in-the-loop factor to the traditional OSI model. Considering from a security perspective, let's assume a bank is going to be robbed. To achieve this, hackers target banking servers to attack. While attacking, they will not be able to bypass the banking firewalls, IDSs, IPSs. Now, they want another way for information to get into the banking servers. The prime target for such kind of attacks are people who work in that bank. Hackers will observe, follow, and extract the information from the behavior of bank employees. These all aspects are covered in a single term called Social Engineering which is an art of manipulating people. The extended OSI model comes to rescue when considering social engineering and similar attempts.

Layer 8: Perspective and Use Cases

Layer 8 hypothesis include all user errors to be considered while managing troubleshooting efforts. When the users do not know about the solution to a problem, they try to judge and devise their own solutions and commit mistakes. This is one of the causes and use cases for Layer 8. However, it does not mean that everything is done unknowingly – "BY MISTAKE". When people go beyond authorized well defined rules trying to help someone or to achieve early completion of assigned tasks, they commit human errors knowingly.

In a web-application, when someone input a wrong field value in a form, he often sees it as, not found, or non-applicable upon submission of form. Even if he knows this, and he will submit a series of such values, once he will reach a point to be able to break into the application, irrespective of the time and process constraints. If you observe the minute details, this time constraint could be reduced, and process constraint could be improved. In Layer 8, the same applies to human behavior which acts as a web application form field, give the input, observe the output, and improvise upon this.

We have more often heard about the acronyms generally utilized to cite "USER ERROR" in a more anticipated and humorous fashion like,
- Fault Isolated in Layer 8
- Problem in Chair, Not in Computer (PICNIC)
- Problem Exists between Keyboard and Chair (PEBKAC)
- Code 18 Error which implies problem is sitting about 18" away from the screen.

Some more Layer 8 use cases include,
- Employees who find a prepared USB stick in the company car park and plug it into the USB slot of a company computer.
- Users who receive a telephone call where the other person pretends to be their boss and advises an urgent bank transfer.
- The careless handling of classic phishing emails containing malicious content.

Layer 8: The OSINT Connection

Open-Source intelligence (OSINT) are gathered from open sources, the publicly available information. OSINT can be further segmented by the source type: Internet/General, Scientific/Technical, and various HUMINT specialties, e.g. trade shows, association, meetings, and interviews.

Human beings are "social animal". Aspects, definable as social, such as self-representation, community and interaction are classical of real life, common to everyone, even though they also deeply define the online behavior of the same people whom equally feel the necessity to create a self-representation in the world they live in (real or virtual), to build up ties with who is around (real or virtual subjects) and to interact with the people sharing common experiences. [3]

In the online world, tools such as retweet, likes and shares have been adapted to facilitate a complex system of indirect methods to get in touch with the other. Obviously, there is nothing wrong in this. And this is great to amplify or diffuse the message to the public, to entertain or inform a specific audience, to comment a tweet, re-posting it and adding new contents, to demonstrate the presence as listener, etc. However, if you orient towards the perspective of an intelligence analyst, this could be really interesting. For example, a bank executive from ABC bank often tweets about his daily running status 9 am every morning and a running posture excerpt from a fitness running app.

Interesting things that one can observe from this daily activity includes,
- Estimate of his/her morning schedule.
- Estimate of track information for his running.

[Bit more information]
- Where he/she lives?
- Where he/she took a break on the way to his home?
- How many break intervals during long running schedules?
- How much time is he/she out of his house?
- At how much pace, he/she can run?

See the following sample tweet.

Utility of all such instances is vital when aggregated and correlated for predicting behaviors of concern. The inevitable surveillance of personal data might result in harmful or malicious circumstances with the technology combinations and OSINT and can make businesses to bear huge losses.

Analysis: AWS Phishing Campaign

Phishing is a classic example of the failure to engineer strong Layer 8 solutions. Most of the people receive emails from organizations which invite the receiver of email to log into portals using links embedded in the email, which don't go to the organization's main website. Those logins often aren't protected by SSL/TLS or use in-house CAs.

AWS Phishing Campaign is a very recent example where attackers tried to steal AWS accounts through phishing. [Detected by researchers from Cado Security [4] and Abnormal Security [5]]

1. The attack was seen in the mid of May, 2020 in which people received phishing emails from attackers disguised as AWS Support.

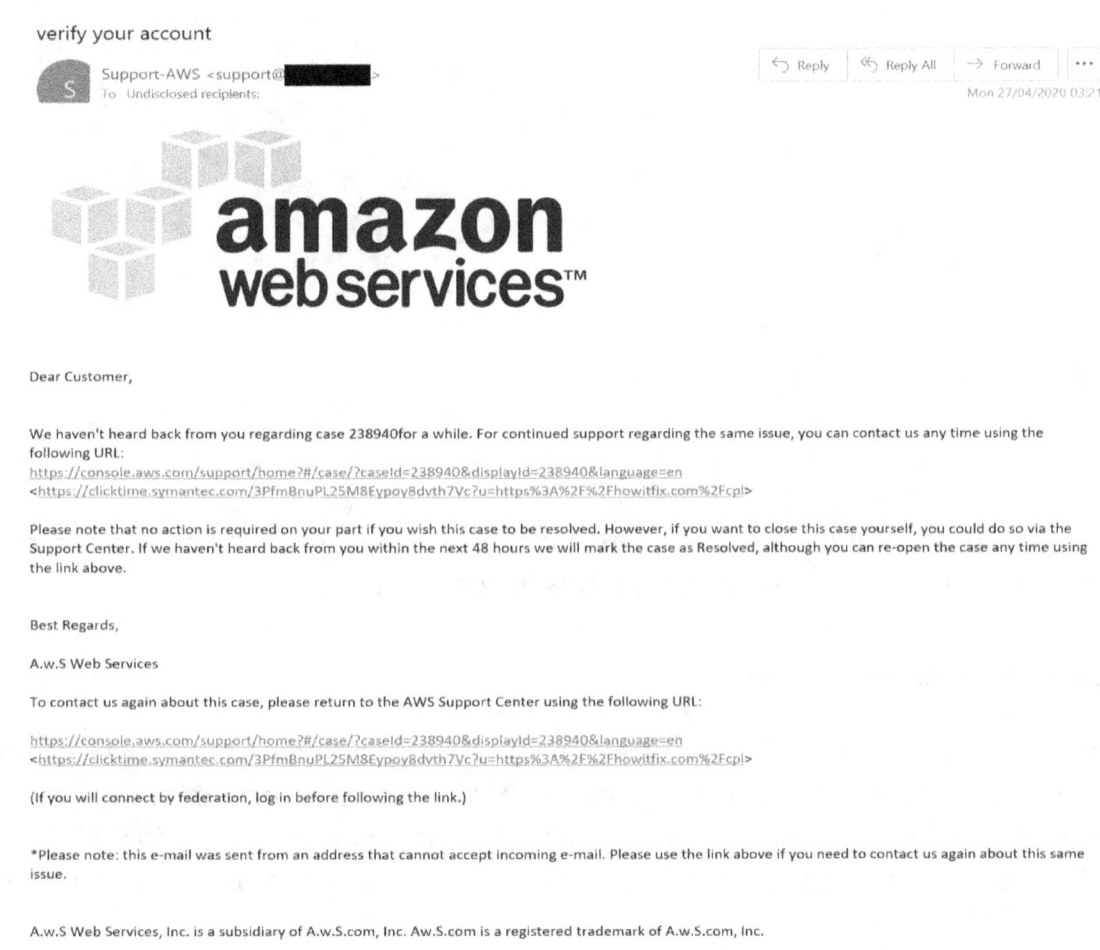

2. The links present in the email sends the user to "howitfix[.]com/app/aws - which is an AWS phishing page hosted on a compromised server.

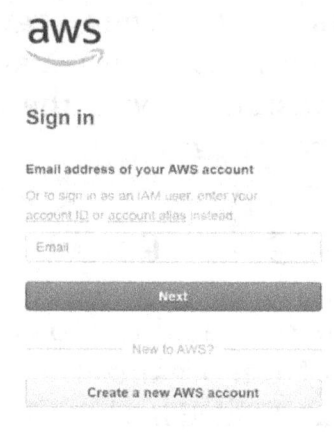

3. Researchers discovered that it was not an isolated attack. A network of AWS Phishing sites were using exactly the same AWS phishing template, served from compromised domains.

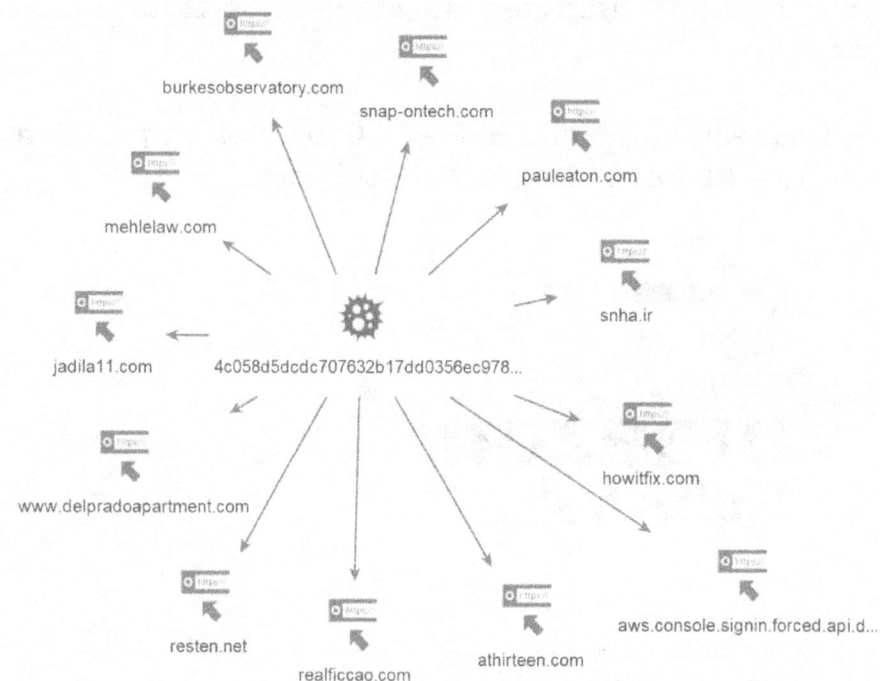

The investigation revealed that phishing emails are being sent from rented server, using an email address from an Irish web-hosting company.

Consequences and Compromise:

The victims when click the phishing email link will be redirected to an AWS Phishing page – a look alike with AWS login page. Submitting user credentials for an AWS account will result in a user compromise with all the resources an AWS IAM user has access to. However, submitting Root login credentials will compromise complete AWS account.

These compromised AWS accounts will be traded for as little as $4 (for free tier account) onwards. Also, these accounts could be utilized for phishing via Amazon Simple Email Service (SES).

Lessons Learnt

The Extended OSI Model has advantages when considering the other 3 layers while defining the IT security policies for an organization. Defining AUPs and restricting the control definitions appropriately provides an opportunity to monitor employees and their workflow.

OSINT philosophy and usage with Human Interaction Layer is a great way to find out and fulfilling the gaps in an IT security strategy. There is a need to think about business personnel as an integral part of organizational security aspect, such that both the personnel's as well as organizational security concerns will be considered. Security awareness trainings, phishing email exercises, etc. are some of the measures to follow and tighten the enterprise security posture.

We have seen the example for AWS Phishing Campaign which was carried recently. Now, that keeping in mind one can think of Google Cloud Platform Phishing Campaign or may be Azure next. There is no limit to social engineering as it always come up beyond one's expectation and imagination.

References

[1] Is it possible to Monitor OSI Model Layer 8, Sascha Neumeier, IT Insights, Paessler. Published on Sept. 9, 2019, Last Updated on June 15, 2020. Last Accessed on June 30, 2020. - blog.paessler.com/is-it-possible-to-monitor-osi-model-layer-8
[2] Engineering Security Solutions at Layer 8 and Above, Sam Curry. Published on Dec. 7, 2010. Last Accessed on June 30, 2020. - web.archive.org/web/20130524214239/blogs.rsa.com/engineering-security-solutions-at-layer-8-and-above/
[3] From SOCMINT to Digital Humint: re-frame the use of social media within the Intelligence Cycle, Marco Lombardi, Todd Rosenblum, Alessandro Burato. Last Accessed on June 30, 2020. - fondazionedegasperi.org/wp-content/uploads/2016/10/Paper-From-SOCMINT-to-Digital.pdf
[4] An ongoing AWS Phishing Campaign, Chris and James, cadosecurity.com. Published on Jun. 11, 2020. Last Accessed on June 30, 2020. - cadosecurity.com/2020/06/11/an-ongoing-aws-phishing-campaign/
[5] Abnormal Attack Stories: AWS Phishing, abnormalsecurity.com. Published on May 27, 2020. Last Accessed on June 30, 2020. - abnormalsecurity.com/blog/abnormal-attack-stories-aws-phishing/

CIR Contributors

Amy Martin, Editor
Carlyle Collins, Editor
Daniel Traci, Editor/Design
Jeremy Martin, Editor/Author
Richard K. Medlin, Editor/Author
Nitin Sharma, Editor/Author
Justin Casey, Author
LaShanda Edwards, Author
Mossaraf Zaman Khan, Author
Ambadi MP, Author

If you are interested in writing an article or walkthrough for the Cyber Intelligence Report, please send an email to cir@InformationWarfareCenter.com

If you are interested in contributing to the CSI Linux project, please send an email to: csilinx@informationwarfarecenter.com

I wanted to take a moment to discuss some of the projects we are working on here at the Information Warfare Center. They are a combination of commercial, community driven, & Open Source projects.

Cyber WAR (Weekly Awareness Report)

Everyone needs a good source for Threat Intelligence and the Cyber WAR is one resource that brings together over a dozen other data feeds into one place. It contains the latest news, tools, malware, and other security related information.

InformationWarfareCenter.com/CIR

CSI Linux (Community Linux Distro)

CSI Linux is a freely downloadable Linux distribution that focuses on Open Source Intelligence (OSINT) investigation, traditional Digital Forensics, and Incident Response (DFIR), and Cover Communications with suspects and informants. This distribution was designed to help Law Enforcement with Online Investigations but has evolved and has been released to help anyone investigate both online and on the dark webs with relative security and peace of mind.

At the time of this publication, CSI Linux 2020.3 was released.

CSILinux.com

Cyber "Live Fire" Range (Linux Distro)

This is a commercial environment designed for both Cyber Incident Response Teams (CIRT) and Penetration Testers alike. This product is a standalone bootable external drive that allows you to practice both DFIR and Pentesting on an isolated network, so you don't have to worry about organizational antivirus, IDP/IPS, and SIEMs lighting up like a Christmas tree, causing unneeded paperwork and investigations. This environment incorporates Kali and a list of vulnerable virtual machines to practice with. This is a great system for offline exercises to help prepare for Certifications like the Pentest+, Licensed Penetration Tester (LPT), and the OSCP.

Cyber Security TV

We are building a site that pulls together Cyber Security videos from various sources to make great content easier to find.

Cyber Secrets

Cyber Secrets originally aired in 2013 and covers issues ranging from Anonymity on the Internet to Mobile Device forensics using Open Source tools, to hacking. Most of the episodes are technical in nature. Technology is constantly changing, so some subjects may be revisited with new ways to do what needs to be done.

Just the Tip

Just the Tip is a video series that covers a specific challenge and solution within 2 minutes. These solutions range from tool usage to samples of code and contain everything you need to defeat the problems they cover.

Quick Tips

This is a small video series that discusses quick tips that covers syntax and other command line methods to make life easier

CyberSec.TV

 Active Facebook Community: Facebook.com/groups/cybersecrets

Information Warfare Center Publications

Threat Intelligence and Hacking training. The Cyber Intelligence Report series covers hacking, forensics, threat intelligence, and everything in between. This issue will focus on a little SCADA/ICS, Dark Web, and how to identify a vulnerability and write an exploit for it. Here is a list of some of the chapters: Triton... The Russia-Linked Cyber ICS WMD, Advanced Persistent Threats, The Cyber Kill Chain, Securing Data at Rest and Data in Transit Anonymity on the Internet, Zeek (Bro) IDS - Installation & Configuration, and VulnServer: TRUN Buffer Overflow walk through. amzn.to/2MI2xxI

Dive Into the 5th Domain: Threat Intelligence includes: Cyber Attacks Can Kill, Dark Web News and Dark Market Exit Scams, OSINT & Online Investigation Tips, Online and Dark Web Investigations: CSI Linux, CSI Linux Forensic Challenge, Chain of Custody Template, Data destruction & recoverability, Anonymity on the Web (Tor and Privoxy), OSINT Reconnaissance (Recon-ng walkthrough), Autopsy Installation in Linux, Elastic Stack with Zeek (Bro) IDS Integration, Configuring Zeek (Bro) IDS Signatures, and more... amzn.to/37gPfBE

Red Teaming Around Your Backyard While Drinking Our Juice in The Hood includes OIT, Cyber Scams and Attacks, Software Defined Radio (SDR fun), Dark Web Information, Tools and Tips, Iranian Backed Fox Kitten APT, Red Team War Story, Post Exploit: Island Hopping/Pivoting, Hacking Challenge, Reverse Engineering using Ghidra Challenge, Online Privacy/Anonymity, Offensive Tactics, Reconnaissance with SpiderFoot, CVE Vulnerability Scanning using NMAP, Using NMAP for Exploitation, Penetration Testing and Exploitation Using NMAP and tools, SEH Buffer Overflow Exploitation on Windows 10, and more... amzn.to/3f4HT6W

A network defender's GUIde to threat detection: Using Zeek, Elasticsearch, Logstash, Kibana, Tor, and more. This book covers the entire installation and setup of your own SOC in a Box with ZEEK IDS, Elasticstack, with visualizations in Kibana. amzn.to/2AZqBJW

Do you want to learn how to conduct vulnerability assessments or penetration tests but don't know where to start? Are you getting into computer forensics and want some more hands on practice with more tools and environments? Well, we have something that might just save you some time and money. amzn.to/30xOvGX

www.ingramcontent.com/pod-product-compliance
Lightning Source LLC
Chambersburg PA
CBHW080452220526
45465CB00006B/2246